The
Social
Construction
of Gender

For our sisters and brothers
in SWS

The Social Construction ᵒᶠ Gender

Edited by

Judith Lorber
Susan A. Farrell

Published in cooperation with
Sociologists for Women in Society

SAGE PUBLICATIONS
The International Professional Publishers
Newbury Park   London   New Delhi

For information address:

SAGE Publications, Inc.
2455 Teller Road
Newbury Park, California 91320

SAGE Publications Ltd.
6 Bonhill Street
London EC2A 4PU
United Kingdom

SAGE Publications India Pvt. Ltd.
M-32 Market
Greater Kailash I
New Delhi 110 048 India

Printed in the United States of America

Library of Congress Cataloging-in-Publication Data

The Social construction of gender / edited by Judith Lorber, Susan A.
   Farrell.
          p.   cm.
   "A Gender & society reader. published in cooperation with
Sociologists for Women in Society."
   "A collection of readings . . . primarily selected from the first
four years of Gender & society"—Pref.
   Includes bibliographical references.
   ISBN 0-8039-3956-6. — ISBN 0-8039-3957-4 (pbk.)
   1. Sex role—United States.   2. Feminism—United States.
3. Women—United States—Social conditions.   I. Lorber, Judith.
II. Farrell, Susan A.
HQ1075.5.U6S62   1991
305.3—dc20   90-19483
                                                                    CIP

FIRST PRINTING, 1991

Sage Production Editor: Astrid Virding

CONTENTS

PREFACE

The Social Construction of Gender is a collection of readings with a unified perspective, primarily selected from the first four years of *Gender & Society*, a new journal founded by Sociologists for Women in Society (SWS) to publish feminist research and theory in the social sciences. The theoretical perspective is that of the social construction of gender, which informs a feminist understanding of the systemic aspects of the position of women in society and also integrates empirical research to demonstrate this reality in women's and men's lives. The focus of this reader is social structural, in that gender is seen as one of the foundations of every existing social order. In this perspective, women and men are not automatically compared; rather, gender categories (female-male, feminine-masculine, girls-boys, women-men) are analyzed to see how different social groups define them, and how they construct and maintain them in everyday life and in major social institutions, such as the family and the economy.

In our view, it makes more sense to talk of genders, not simply gender, because being a woman and being a man change from one generation to the next and are different for different racial, ethnic, and religious groups, as well as for the members of different social classes. What stays constant is that women and men have to be *distinguishable*. Biology does not distinguish them—in the gender category "woman," you find male-to-female transsexuals, who have changed their genitals and hormonal output but not their chromosomes, and *berdaches*, who are biologically intact males living out their lives as social women. In the gender category "man," you find women successfully passing as men in order to fight in a war or work in a man's occupation. You also find women presidents and premiers who have to be considered "men" in order to be able to sit with and eat with politicians who keep their wives and daughters veiled or segregated behind locked doors. Such "gender bending" does not alter accepted gender categories, it maintains them. The "benders" do not create new categories (a third gender), but have to fit into the two socially accepted categories.

The reason for gender categories and the constant construction and reconstruction of differences between them is that gender is an integral part of any social group's structure of domination and subordination and division of labor in the family and the economy. As a major social status (if not *the* major social status), gender shapes the individual's opportunities for education, work, family, sexuality, reproduction, authority, and the chance to make an impact on the production of culture and knowledge. Societies vary in the extent to which women and men are unequal, but where there is inequality, women are invariably devalued and allocated work that is also devalued, whether it is in the family or in the paid work force. In that way, the necessary work women do—maintaining the household and caring for the family emotionally and physically, as well as such jobs as nursing, teaching, social work, office work, factory work, selling, producing, and so on—can be paid for at a low rate, or not at all.

Gender is also intertwined with other socially constructed categories of differential evaluation, such as race. Men and women members of the favored categories command more power, more prestige, and more property than the members of the disfavored categories, but within all social categories, men are advantaged over women. Ironically, in racial ethnic groups with few resources, women and men tend to be more equal than in racial ethnic groups that are prosperous. Where there is little access to education, health care, good jobs, and political power, there is nothing for men to monopolize. However, in groups that have no legal power at all—such as slaves—women are more exploited because they can be raped and used as breeders of children.

Gender is built into the social order in other crucial ways. The major social institutions of control—law, medicine, religion, politics—treat women and men differently, generally disempowering all women, as well as men of disadvantaged racial ethnic groups and working class men. Women in disadvantaged groups are subject to the most social control, including violence.

Finally, dominant men are most likely to prescribe the content of education and the priorities for scientific research. They also provide the money for sports, movies, television shows, books, museums, concerts, operas, music videos, recordings, and so on. Therefore, their views of what is intellectually uplifting and factually important, as well as what is entertaining and exciting, are likely to prevail. As a result, what men think and do predominates in required courses, prestigious awards, lists of the best, cherished masterpieces, and scientific breakthroughs. Women's contributions, virtually invisible in Western culture, are valued where women are strong and powerful, as in African and African-American societies.

Recent feminist research has been able to document these findings and challenge upper- and middle-class White men's monopoly over knowledge. Feminists have also charted women's resistance to men's domination, examined claims of gender equality, and tried to envision a social order without gender.

The three chapters in the first section, Principles of Gender Construction, examine the main processes of gender construction—for men as well as women—and also analyze the ways gender and race intermesh in this construction.

In the second section, Gender Construction in Family Life, the three chapters look at men's nineteenth-century family roles, how women bargain for power in different kinds of patriarchal families, and the structure of families and women's position in varying racial ethnic groups.

The third section, Gender Construction in the Workplace, covers several themes. The first two chapters show how deeply gendered work organizations are. The third chapter compares women's and men's status in minority groups with more and fewer economic resources. The fourth chapter criticizes solutions to the generally low pay for women's jobs and to the large numbers of women living in poverty within the United States.

The fourth section, Feminist Research Strategies, provides a brief introduction to some of the problems of feminist research and ways they have been solved. The first chapter reports on how one set of researchers was able to include a good sample of minority and working-class women. The second chapter shows that having a woman researcher does not overcome class and ethnic bias.

The fifth section, Racial Ethnic Identity and Feminist Politics, teases out the threads of women's social identity where ethnic group identity is a major factor. The three ethnic groups examined are Asian Americans, Hispanic Americans, and Portuguese Americans. In the last chapter, a gang rape within an ethnic community pits women against men, women against women, and the members of a racial ethnic working-class society against the media representatives of the dominant culture.

The last section, Deconstructing Gender, examines three different strategies of change. One strategy is reorganization of work and family life for a small group without major societal or ideological challenge of gender roles; the second strategy is organized feminist resistance with an established institution, the Catholic Church; and the third strategy is restructuring the major institutions of society so they do not depend on the social construction of gender for the allocation of work and family responsibilities.

Each of these sections is prefaced by a brief review of recent research, theory, and practice in the area, and a more detailed summary of the chapters.

The language in this book reflects the style developed in *Gender & Society*. Since our focus is gender as a social construction, rather than a biological manifestation, "gender," "gendered," and "gender roles" are used rather than "sex," "sex-typed," "sex roles." For the same reasons, we use "women" and "men," rather than "females" and "males." Where "sex" is used, it connotes a biological or physiological category, with the understanding that health, fertility, sexuality, and competence in sports and other physical activities are also socially constructed. All racial and ethnic groups are capitalized, including White, in order to show that they are all significant social locations in the stratification system of the United States. Authors who always use their birth name and their married name are cited by both last names in the text. In the lists of citations in parentheses only the final name is given, and in the references authors' names are alphabetized by the first letter of the final name, as this usage is the practice in the English language.

The chapters and introductory material reflect feminist social science theory in concrete ways that make the text accessible to students and readers at both sophisticated and introductory levels. For sophisticated readers, *The Social Construction of Gender* presents a collection completely based on an increasingly used social science theory. The combination of theory and empirical research unifies and expands feminist constructionism. However, the book does not analyze gender away, but rather shows the power of the concept in feminist research and politics. For graduate and undergraduate teachers, the text provides accessible material with which to teach feminist theory, feminist research, and feminist practice.

ACKNOWLEDGMENTS

The following chapters were originally published as articles in *Gender & Society* and are reprinted with the permission of the authors: Joan Acker, "Hierarchies, Jobs, Bodies: A Theory of Gendered Organizations," 4(1990):139-58; Judith Buber Agassi, "Theories of Gender Equality: Lessons from the Israeli Kibbutz," 3(1989):160-86; Elizabeth M. Almquist, "Labor Market Gender Inequality in Minority Groups" 1(1987):400-14; Johanna Brenner, "Feminization of Poverty and Comparable Worth: Radical Versus Liberal Approaches," 1(1987):447-65; Lynn Weber Cannon, Elizabeth Higginbotham, and Marianne L. A. Leung, "Race and Class Bias in Qualitative Research on Women,"

2(1988):449-61; Lynn S. Chancer, "New Bedford, Massachusetts, March 6, 1983-March 22, 1984: The 'Before and After' of a Group Rape," 1(1987):239-60; Esther Ngan-Ling Chow, "The Development of Feminist Consciousness Among Asian American Women," 1(1987): 284-99; Karen Dugger, "Social Location and Gender-Role Attitudes: A Comparison of Black and White Women," 2(1988):425-48; Alma M. Garcia, "The Development of Chicana Feminist Discourse, 1970-1980," 3(1989):217-38; Karen V. Hansen, " 'Helped Put in a Quilt': Men's Work and Male Intimacy in Nineteenth-Century New England" 3(1989): 334-54; Deniz Kandiyoti, "Bargaining with Patriarchy," 2(1988):274-89; Michael A. Messner, "Masculinities and Athletic Careers," 3(1989): 71-88; Barbara F. Reskin, "Bringing the Men Back In: Sex Differentiation and the Devaluation of Women's Work," 2(1988): 58-81; Catherine Kohler Riessman, "When Gender Is Not Enough: Women Interviewing Women," 1(1987):172-207; Candace West and Don H. Zimmerman, "Doing Gender," 1(1987):125-51; Maxine Baca Zinn, "Family, Feminism, and Race in America," 4(1990):68-82.

Permission to reprint the following was granted by the author and publisher: Judith Lorber, "Dismantling Noah's Ark," *Sex Roles* 14(1986):567-80.

For their efforts in getting the *Gender & Society* reader launched, we would like to thank Pat Martin, who was Chair of the SWS Journals Committee, and Mitch Allen, *Gender & Society*'s Editor at Sage Publications. We also thank the members of SWS for conceiving the idea of a feminist social science journal, and for gestating, birthing, and nurturing *Gender & Society*.

Judith Lorber
Susan A. Farrell
New York City

I.

Principles of Gender Construction

Sex . . . sex roles . . . gender . . . gender roles. In explaining the social construction of gender, these terms can become very confusing. We live in a society that for a long time left these categories unexamined. Many people, social scientists included, still gloss over them as if everyone "knows what they mean." The term *sex* is assumed to be a biological category that stands for an understanding of what is "natural," what cannot be changed. However, biologists, endocrinologists, and social scientists have started to examine the categories of "female" and "male" more closely, because they have found that not everyone fits into one or the other as neatly as had been previously assumed (Fausto-Sterling 1985; Money 1986; Money and Tucker 1975; Stoller 1985).

In the social construction perspective, both *sex* and *gender* are socially developed statuses. Biologists and endocrinologists who study hormones now have a much more complicated picture of "sex." Female and male sex are no longer seen as two opposite, mutually exclusive categories. *Sex* is understood more as a continuum made up of chromosomal sex, gonadal sex, and hormonal sex (Money 1986), all of which "work in the presence and under the influence of a set of environments" (Fausto-Sterling 1985, p. 71).

Gender identity is another major component of "femaleness" and "maleness." Gender identity includes psychosexual development, learning social roles, and shaping sexual preferences. Social rearing, or socialization, is a crucial element for gender identity (Gagnon and Henderson 1985). Sexual preference and choice of sexual object are tied to gender identity. Boys who consider themselves male and girls who consider themselves female are supposed to be sexually attracted to each other. This added social dimension constitutes "compulsory heterosexuality," according to Rich (1980). In the United States, the social construction of masculinity emphasizes heterosexuality to the point of homophobia (Herek 1987). Thus, the social construction of gender is also in part the social construction of sexuality, which includes sexual feelings, sexual preferences, and sexual practices (Greenberg 1988; Stein 1989).

7

In sum, the biological dimension of gender, which has been called sex, is only part of "an individual's capacities [which] emerge from a web of interactions between the biological being and the social environment" (Fausto-Sterling 1985, p. 8). In addition to the increased complexities that biologists and endocrinologists now see in sexual development, transsexuals—people whose sex organs are ambiguous or who believe their gender identity to be in contradiction to their genitalia—use surgery and hormonal treatments to change from one sex-gender status to the other. Transsexuals do not challenge the culturally prescribed rules for "doing gender." Because they believe that "nature" made a mistake, they want to bring their genital anatomy into agreement with what they feel is their true gender identity (Green and Money 1969). Similarly, the new procreative technologies, which have split up procreative collaborators into egg donor, sperm donor, embryo donor, gestator-birther, and parent (not to forget doctor, lawyer, banker, and later, professional caretaker and teacher), but have not altered the rules of kinship and family patterns. These two examples indicate that, although sex and gender are mutable for individuals, the social categories are far more intractable.

In reality, girls and boys, women and men are more alike than they are different, but as Rubin (1975) says, societies impose a "sameness taboo" on them. Together with race, ethnicity, and social class, *gender categories* are institutionalized cultural and social statuses. These statuses or social locations shape every individual's life from birth. Not only are sexual and procreative behaviors socially scripted, but other seemingly physiological outcomes, such as birth weight, musculature, time of menarche, and longevity are deeply influenced by the social locations of class and racial ethnic group as well as gender category. Although some societies are homogeneous with regard to race, ethnicity, and sometimes even economic status, no society ignores gender. The division of the social world into women and men is so deeply ingrained that from the moment of birth, when the sex assignment of a newborn is made, parents, doctors, midwives, and all those around the infant, "do gender"—starting with a name.

Tackling this problem of conceptualization and terminology of sex, gender, and sexuality, Candace West and Don H. Zimmerman, in Chapter 1, "Doing Gender," deconstruct the categories of sex and gender. Using an ethnomethodological approach based on Garfinkel's work, along with the latest insights from researchers in biology, sexology, and anthropology, they propose distinctions among *sex* (birth classification), *sex category* (social membership), and *gender* (processual validation of that membership). West and Zimmerman illustrate the pervasiveness of "doing gender" in social interaction. Even well into adult life, when gender status is supposed to be stabilized, we routinely fashion gender in every situation. Gender, in reality and in everyday practice, suffuses all aspects of our lives, from the micro- to the macro-levels. In West and Zimmerman's view, gender as a social status is fundamental, institutionalized, and enduring, yet, because members of social groups must constantly (whether they realize it or not) "do gender" to maintain their proper status, the seeds of change are ever present.

In Chapter 2, "Social Location and Gender-Role Attitudes: A Comparison of Black and White Women," Karen Dugger examines the intersections of race ethnicity and social class with the social status of gender. More and more scholars are insisting that racial ethnic stratification, social class position, and gender status cannot be treated as analytically distinct, but rather should be viewed as a tripartite system in which each component is intertwined with the others, and each of the systems depends on the others. For example, the class system needs the unpaid labor of all women and the low-paid labor of women and men of color. Gender and race are ascribed statuses onto which positions in a system of supposed achievement are grafted. Then gender ideology (women are family-oriented, not job-oriented) and race ideology (the low-ranked group is unreliable, present-oriented) justify a stratification system that benefits White, upper-class men.

In *Feminist Theory: From Margin to Center,* Bell Hooks (1984) says that in the United States, all men are oppressors and all Whites are oppressors—White men oppress White women and men and women of color; men of color oppress women of color; and White women oppress men and women of color. Thus, in daily actions and experiences, the systems of domination are constructed and reinforced. As Thornton Dill and Baca Zinn said in a paper given at the 1988 American Sociological Association meetings, "There are multiple hierarchies of resources and rewards, and . . . these hierarchies condition the material and subjective experiences of women and men in our society."

Race, class, and gender form *synergistic* (more than the sum of the parts, in medical parlance) systems of domination and oppression. They also reinforce the claim of many feminists of color that without knowing how those who live oppressed lives understand their lives, data will have little meaning. Dugger, enlarging our understanding of gender by highlighting the intersection of race and gender, says:

> In teaching my first course on the sociology of women some years ago, I constructed a syllabus that I considered inclusive. This assumption of

inclusiveness rested on my incorporation of Black women's critiques of the women's movement. Half way into the course, in entries to their journals, this assumption was challenged by three Black women students in the class. Each in different ways stated that the theories and descriptions of womanhood and the socialization of women presented in the readings did not reflect or affirm their experiences. These comments pointed out to me the universalistic assumptions underlying my conception of the social construction of womanhood and prompted me to broaden my understanding of inclusiveness. I trace the impetus for my research on social location and gender-role belief systems to these three students. (Dugger 1990)

In Chapter 2, Dugger talks about race-gender groups that could dispel the problematic universalizing of White women's experience as all women's experience, a notion that has plagued the feminist movement from its beginnings. Subjects' social locations make their attitudes explicable, and their attitudes in turn construct their social world for them. Without attention to individual histories, the specific perspectives of Black women and White women will not show up in research data, and global explanations of attitudes and behavior may be false (see Chapter 12).

Dugger clearly shows both the differences and commonalities in Black and White women's lives, thus supporting various studies that at first seem contradictory but, when brought together and put into the context of women's lives, illustrate the crucial importance of including all aspects of all women's lives. The intersection of the social locations of gender, race and ethnicity, and class in women's lives has contributed not only to commonalities and differences but also the very contradictions that so often seem to plague us, but which also make for good sociological and feminist theorizing.

In Chapter 3, "Masculinities and Athletic Careers," Michael A. Messner uses insights gained from feminist perspectives and critiques of false universalization to look at men's lives. In particular, he sees organized sports as a way to examine not only the social construction of masculinities, but also the intersection of racial ethnic identity and masculine gender identity. According to Messner, disproportionate numbers of young Black men are systematically channeled into sports. However, class and racial ethnic identity do not fully explain this phenomenon. Messner reinforces the critique that most sociologists "view masculinity as a biologically determined tendency to act as provider and protector." The problems that Black men face are assumed to be the result of blocked fulfillment of their masculinity by racism and classism. Messner argues that the socially constructed notion of masculinity also contributes to "destructive relationships and lifestyles."

Following Rubin and Levinson, whom he cites, and Chodorow (1978), Gilligan (1982), and Connell (1987), as well as West and Zimmerman, Messner sees masculine identity as a "processual" unfolding "through interaction between the internal (psychological ambivalences) and the external (social, historical, and institutional) contexts." Gender, for men as well as for women, is a social construction relationally created within specific social and historical locations that both constrain and yet paradoxically also contain the potential for radical change. We can "do" gender in ways that maintain existing gender relations, or we can challenge them.

REFERENCES

Chodorow, N. J. 1978. *The Reproduction of Mothering*. Berkeley: University of California Press.

Connell, R. W. 1987. *Gender and Power*. Stanford, CA: Stanford University Press.

Dill, B. Thornton, and M. Baca Zinn. 1988. "Race and Gender." Paper presented at American Sociological Association Annual Meetings, Atlanta, GA.

Dugger, K. 1990. Personal communication.

Fausto-Sterling, A. 1985. *Myths of Gender: Biological Theories About Women and Men*. New York: Basic Books.

Gagnon, J., and B. Henderson. 1985. "The Social Psychology of Sexual Development." Pp. 145-51 in *Marriage and Family in a Changing Society*, edited by J. M. Henslin. New York: Free Press.

Gilligan, C. 1982. *In a Different Voice*. Cambridge, MA: Harvard University Press.

Green, R., and J. Money, eds. 1969. *Transsexualism and Sex Reassignment*. Baltimore, MD: Johns Hopkins University Press.

Greenberg, D. F. 1988. *The Construction of Homosexuality*. Chicago: University of Chicago Press.

Herek, G. M. 1987. "On Heterosexual Masculinity." Pp. 68-82 in *Changing Men: New Directions in Research on Men and Masculinity*, edited by M. S. Kimmel. Newbury Park, CA: Sage.

Hooks, B. 1984. *Feminist Theory: From Margin to Center*. Boston: South End Press.

Money, J. 1986. *Venuses Penuses: Sexology, Sexosophy and Exigency Theory*. Buffalo, NY: Prometheus Press.

——— and P. Tucker. 1975. *Sexual Signatures: On Being a Man or a Woman*. Boston: Little, Brown.

Rich, A. 1980. "Compulsory Heterosexuality and Lesbian Existence." *Signs: Journal of Women in Culture and Society* 5:631-60.

Rubin, G. 1975. "The Traffic in Women: Notes on the 'Political Economy' of Sex." Pp. 157-210 in *Toward an Anthropology of Women*, edited by R. R. Reiter. New York: Monthly Review Press.

Stein, A. 1989. "Three Models of Sexuality." *Sociological Theory* 7:1-13.

Stoller, R. J. 1985. *Presentations of Gender*. New Haven, CT: Yale University.

1. DOING GENDER

CANDACE WEST
DON H. ZIMMERMAN

In the beginning, there was sex and there was gender. Those of us who taught courses in the area in the late 1960s and early 1970s were careful to distinguish one from the other. Sex, we told students, was what was ascribed by biology: anatomy, hormones, and physiology. Gender, we said, was an achieved status: that which is constructed through psychological, cultural, and social means. To introduce the difference between the two, we drew on singular case studies of hermaphrodites (Money 1968, 1974; Money and Ehrhardt 1972) and anthropological investigations of "strange and exotic tribes" (Mead 1963, 1968).

Inevitably (and understandably), in the ensuing weeks of each term, our students became confused. Sex hardly seemed a "given" in the context of research that illustrated the sometimes ambiguous and often conflicting criteria for its ascription. And gender seemed much less an "achievement" in the context of the anthropological, psychological, and social imperatives we studied—the division of labor, the formation of gender identities, and the social subordination of women by men. Moreover, the received doctrine of gender socialization theories conveyed the strong message that while gender may be "achieved," by about age five it was certainly fixed, unvarying, and static—much like sex.

Since about 1975, the confusion has intensified and spread far beyond our individual classrooms. For one thing, we learned that the relationship between biological and cultural processes was far more complex—and reflexive—than we previously had supposed (Rossi 1984, especially pp. 10-14). For another, we discovered that certain structural arrangements, for example, between work and family, actually produce or enable some capacities, such as to mother, that we formerly associated with biology (Chodorow 1978 versus Firestone 1970). In the midst of all this, the notion of gender as a recurring achievement somehow fell by the wayside.

Our purpose in this chapter is to propose an ethnomethodologically informed, and therefore distinctively sociological, understanding of gender as a routine, methodical, and recurring accomplishment. We contend that the "doing" of gender is undertaken by women and men whose competence as members of society is hostage to its production. Doing gender involves a complex of socially guided perceptual, inter-actional, and micropolitical activities that cast particular pursuits as expressions of masculine and feminine "natures."

When we view gender as an accomplishment, an achieved property of situated conduct, our attention shifts from matters internal to the individual and focuses on interactional and, ultimately, institutional arenas. In one sense, of course, it is individuals who "do" gender. But it is a situated doing, carried out in the virtual or real presence of others who are presumed to be oriented to its production. Rather than as a property of individuals, we conceive of gender as an emergent feature of social situations: as both an outcome of and a rationale for various social arrangements and as a means of legitimating one of the most fundamental divisions of society.

To advance our argument, we undertake a critical examination of what sociologists have meant by *gender,* including its treatment as a role enactment in the conventional sense and as a "display" in Goffman's (1976) terminology. Both *gender role* and *gender display* focus on behavioral aspects of being a woman or a man (as opposed, for example, to biological differences between the two). However, we contend that the notion of gender as a role obscures the work that is involved in producing gender in everyday activities, whereas the notion of gender as a display relegates it to the periphery of interaction. We argue instead that participants in interactions organize their various and manifold activities to reflect or express gender, and they are disposed to perceive the behavior of others in a similar light.

To elaborate our proposal, we suggest at the outset that important but often overlooked distinctions should be observed among *sex, sex category,* and *gender. Sex* is a determination made through the application of socially agreed upon biological criteria for classifying persons as females or males.[1] The criteria for classification can be genitalia at birth or chromosomal typing before birth, and they do not necessarily agree with one another. Placement in a *sex category* is achieved through application of the sex criteria, but in everyday life, categorization is established and sustained by the socially required identificatory displays that proclaim one's membership in one or the other category. In this sense, one's sex category presumes one's sex and stands as proxy for it in many situations, but sex and sex category can vary independently; that is, it is possible to claim membership in a sex category even when the sex criteria are lacking. *Gender,* in contrast, is the activity of managing situated conduct in light of normative conceptions of attitudes and activities appropriate for one's sex category. Gender activities emerge from and bolster claims to membership in a sex category.

We contend that recognition of the analytical independence of sex, sex category, and gender is essential for understanding the relationships among these elements and the interactional work involved in "being" a gendered person in society. While our primary aim is theoretical, there will be occasion to discuss fruitful directions for empirical research that follow from the formulation of gender we propose.

We begin with an assessment of the received meaning of gender, particularly in relation to the roots of this notion in presumed biological differences between women and men.

PERSPECTIVES ON SEX AND GENDER

In Western societies, the accepted cultural perspective on gender views women and men as naturally and unequivocally defined categories of being (Garfinkel 1967, pp. 116-8) with distinctive psychological and behavioral propensities that can be predicted from their reproductive functions. Competent adult members of these societies see differences between the two as fundamental and enduring, and these differences are seemingly supported by the division of labor into women's and men's work and an often elaborate differentiation of feminine and masculine attitudes and behaviors that are prominent features of social organization. Things are the way they are by virtue of the fact that men are men and women are women—a division perceived to be natural and rooted in biology, producing in turn profound psychological, behavioral, and social consequences. The structural arrangements of a society are presumed to be responsive to these differences.

Analyses of sex and gender in the social sciences, although less likely to accept uncritically the naive biological determinism of the view just presented, often retain a conception of sex-linked behaviors and traits as essential properties of individuals (for good reviews, see Hochschild 1973; Thorne 1980; Tresemer 1975; Henley 1985). The "sex differences approach" (Thorne 1980) is more commonly attributed to psychologists than to sociologists, but the survey researcher who determines the gender of respondents on the basis of the sound of their voices over the telephone is also making trait-oriented assumptions. Reducing gender to a fixed set of psychological traits or to a unitary "variable" precludes serious consideration of the ways it is used to structure distinct domains of social experience (Stacey and Thorne 1985, pp. 307-8).

Taking a different tack, role theory has attended to the social construction of gender categories, called "sex roles" or, more recently, "gender roles" and has analyzed how these are learned and enacted. Beginning with Linton (1936) and continuing through the works of Parsons (Parsons 1951; Parsons and Bales 1955) and Komarovsky (1946, 1950), role theory has emphasized the social and dynamic aspect of role construction and enactment (Connell 1983; Thorne 1980). But at the level of face-to-face interaction, the application of role theory to gender poses problems of its own (for good reviews and critiques, see Connell 1983, 1985; Kessler, Ashendon, Connell, and Dowsett 1985; Lopata and Thorne, 1978; Stacey and Thorne, 1985; Thorne 1980). Roles are *situated* identities—assumed and relinquished as the situation demands—rather than *master* identities (Hughes 1945), such as sex category, that cut across situations. Unlike most roles, such as "nurse," "doctor", and "patient" or "professor" and "student", gender has no specific site or organizational context. Moreover, many roles are already gender marked, so that special qualifiers—such as "female doctor" or "male nurse"—must be added to exceptions to the rule. Thorne (1980) observes that conceptualizing gender as a role makes it difficult to assess its influence on other roles and reduces its explanatory usefulness in discussions of power and inequality. Drawing on Rubin (1975), Thorne calls for a reconceptualization of women and men as distinct social groups, constituted in "concrete, historically changing—and generally unequal—social relationships" (Thorne 1980, p. 11).

We argue that gender is not a set of traits, nor a variable, nor a role, but the product of social doings of some sort. What then is the social doing of gender? It is more than the continuous creation of the meaning of gender through human actions (Gerson and Peiss 1985). We claim that gender itself is constituted through interaction.[2] To develop the implications of our claim, we turn to Goffman's (1976) account of "gender display." Our object here is to explore how gender might be exhibited or portrayed through interaction, and thus be seen as "natural," while it is being produced as a socially organized achievement.

GENDER DISPLAY

Goffman contends that when human beings interact with others in their environment, they assume that each possesses an "essential nature"—a nature that can be discerned through the "natural signs given off or expressed by them" (1976, p. 75). Femininity and masculinity are regarded as "prototypes of essential expression—something that can be conveyed fleetingly in any social situation and yet something that strikes at the most basic characterization of the individual" (1976, p. 75). The means through which we provide such expressions are "perfunctory, conventionalized acts" (1976, p. 69), which convey to others our regard for them, indicate our alignment in an encounter, and tentatively establish the terms of contact for that social situation. But they are also regarded as expressive behavior, testimony to our "essential natures."

Goffman (1976, pp. 69-70) sees *displays* as highly conventionalized behaviors structured as two-part exchanges of the statement-reply type, in which the presence or absence of symmetry can establish deference or dominance. These rituals are viewed as distinct from but articulated with more consequential activities, such as performing tasks or engaging in discourse. Hence, we have what he terms the "scheduling" of displays at junctures in activities, such as the beginning or end, to avoid interfering with the activities themselves. Goffman (1976, p. 69) formulates *gender display* as follows:

> If gender be defined as the culturally established correlates of sex (whether in consequence of biology or learning), then gender display refers to conventionalized portrayals of these correlates.

These gendered expressions might reveal clues to the underlying, fundamental dimensions of the female and male, but they are, in Goffman's view, optional performances. Masculine courtesies may or may not be offered and, if offered, may or may not be declined (1976, p. 71). Moreover, human beings "themselves employ the term 'expression', and conduct themselves to fit their own notions of expressivity" (1976, p. 75). Gender depictions are less a consequence of our "essential sexual natures" than interactional portrayals of what we would like to convey about sexual natures, using conventionalized gestures. Our *human* nature gives us the ability to learn to produce and recognize masculine and feminine gender displays, "a capacity [we] have by virtue of being persons, not males and females" (1976, p. 76).

Upon first inspection, it would appear that Goffman's formulation offers an engaging sociological corrective to existing formulations of gender. In his view, gender is a socially scripted dramatization of the culture's idealization of feminine and masculine natures, played for an audience that is well schooled in the presentational idiom. To continue the metaphor, there are scheduled performances presented in special locations, and like plays, they constitute introductions to or time out from more serious activities.

There are fundamental equivocations in this perspective. By segregating gender display from the serious business of interaction, Goffman obscures the effects of gender on a wide range of human activities.

Gender is not merely something that happens in the nooks and crannies of interaction, fitted in here and there and not interfering with the serious business of life. Although it is plausible to contend that gender displays—construed as conventionalized expressions—are optional, it does not seem plausible to say that we have the option of being seen by others as female or male.

It is necessary to move beyond the notion of gender display to consider what is involved in doing gender as an ongoing activity embedded in everyday interaction. Toward this end, we return to the distinctions among sex, sex category, and gender introduced earlier.

SEX, SEX CATEGORY, AND GENDER

Garfinkel's (1967, pp. 118-40) case study of Agnes, a transsexual raised as a boy who adopted a female identity at age 17 and underwent a sex reassignment operation several years later, demonstrates how gender is created through interaction and at the same time structures interaction. Agnes, whom Garfinkel characterized as a "practical methodologist," developed a number of procedures for passing as a "normal, natural female" both prior to and after her surgery. She had the practical task of managing the facts that she possessed male genitalia and that she lacked the social resources a girl's biography would presumably provide in everyday interaction. In short, she needed to display herself as a woman, simultaneously learning what it was to be a woman. Of necessity, this full-time pursuit took place at a time in her life when most people's gender would be well-accredited and routinized. Agnes had to consciously contrive what the vast majority of women do without thinking. She was not faking what real women do naturally. She was obliged to analyze and figure out how to act within socially structured circumstances and conceptions of femininity that women born with appropriate biological credentials take for granted early on. As in the case of others who must "pass," such as tranvestites, Kabuki actors, or Dustin Hoffman's "Tootsie," Agnes's case makes visible what culture has made invisible—the accomplishment of gender.

Garfinkel's (1967) discussion of Agnes does not explicitly separate three analytically distinct, although empirically overlapping, concepts—sex, sex category, and gender.

Sex

Agnes did not possess the socially agreed upon biological criteria for classification as a member of the female *sex*. Still, Agnes regarded herself as a female, albeit a female with a penis, which a woman ought not to possess. The penis, she insisted, was a "mistake" in need of remedy (Garfinkel 1967, pp. 126-7, 131-2). Like other competent members of our culture, Agnes honored the notion that there are essential biological criteria that unequivocally distinguish females from males. However, if we move away from the common-sense viewpoint, we discover that the reliability of these criteria is not beyond question (Money and Brennan 1968; Money and Ehrhardt 1972; Money and Ogunro 1974; Money and Tucker 1975). Moreover, other cultures have acknowledged the existence of "cross-genders" (Blackwood 1984; Williams 1986) and the possibility of more than two sexes (Hill 1935; Martin and Voorheis 1975, pp. 84-107; but see also Cucchiari 1981, pp. 32-5).

More central to our argument is Kessler and McKenna's (1978, pp. 1-6) point that genitalia are conventionally hidden from public inspection in everyday life; yet we continue through our social rounds to "observe" a world of two naturally, normally sexed persons. It is the *presumption* that essential criteria exist, and would or should be there if looked for, that provides the basis for sex categorization. Drawing on Garfinkel, Kessler and McKenna argued that "female" and "male" are cultural events—products of what they term the "gender attribution process"—rather than some collection of traits, behaviors, or even physical attributes. Illustratively, they cite the child who, viewing a picture of someone clad in a suit and a tie, contends, "It's a man, because he has a pee-pee" (Kessler and McKenna 1978, p. 154). Translation: "He must have a pee-pee [an essential characteristic] because I see the *insignia* of a suit and tie." Neither initial sex assignment (pronouncement at birth as a female or male) nor the actual existence of essential criteria for that assignment (possession of a clitoris and vagina or penis and testicles) has much—if anything—to do with the identification of sex category in everyday life. There, Kessler and McKenna note, we operate with a moral certainty of a world of two sexes. We do not think, "Most persons with penises are men, but some may not be" or "Most persons who dress as men have penises." Rather, we take it for granted that sex and sex category are congruent—that knowing the latter, we can deduce the rest.

Sex Categorization

Agnes's claim to the categorical status of female, which she sustained by appropriate identificatory displays and other characteristics, could be discredited before her transsexual operation if her possession of a penis became known and after by her surgically constructed genitalia (see Raymond 1979, pp. 37, 138). In this regard, Agnes had to be continually alert to actual or potential threats to the security of her sex category. Her problem was not so much living up to some prototype of essential femininity but preserving her categorization as female. This task was made easy for her by a very powerful resource, namely, the process of common-sense categorization in everyday life.

The categorization of members of society into indigenous categories, such as girl or boy, or woman or man, operates in a distinctively social way. The act of categorization does not involve a positive test, in the sense of a well-defined set of criteria that must be explicitly satisfied prior to making an identification. Rather, the application of membership categories relies on an "if-can" test in everyday interaction (Sacks 1972, pp. 332-35). This test stipulates that *if* people *can be seen* as members of relevant categories, *then categorize them that way.* That is, use the category that seems appropriate, except in the presence of discrepant information or obvious features that would rule out its use. This procedure is quite in keeping with the attitude of everyday life, in which we take appearances at face value unless we have special reason to doubt them (Bernstein 1986; Garfinkel 1967, pp. 272-7; Schutz 1943).[3] It should be added that it is precisely when we have special reason to doubt appearances that the issue of applying rigorous criteria arises, but it is rare, outside legal or bureaucratic contexts, to encounter insistence on positive tests (Garfinkel 1967, pp. 262-83; Wilson 1970).

Agnes's initial resource was the predisposition of those she encountered to take her appearance (her figure, clothing, hair style, and so on) as the undoubted appearance of a normal female. Her further resource was our cultural perspective on the properties of "natural, normally sexed persons." Garfinkel (1967, pp. 122-8) notes that in everyday life, we live in a world of two—and only two—sexes. This arrangement has a moral status in that we include ourselves and others in it as "essentially, originally, in the first place, always have been, always will be once and for all, in the final analysis, either 'male' or 'female' " (Garfinkel 1967, p. 122).

Consider the following case:

> This issue reminds me of a visit I made to a computer store a couple of years ago. The person who answered my questions was truly a *salesperson.* I could not categorize him/her as a woman or a man. What did I look for? (1) Facial hair: She/he was smooth skinned, but some men have little or no facial hair. (This varies by race, Native Americans and Blacks often have none.) (2) Breasts: She/he was wearing a loose shirt that hung from his/her

shoulders. And, as many women who suffered through a 1950s' adolescence know to their shame, women are often flat-chested. (3) Shoulders: His/hers were small and round for a man, broad for a woman. (4) Hands: Long and slender fingers, knuckles a bit large for a woman, small for a man. (5) Voice: Middle range, unexpressive for a woman, not at all the exaggerated tones some gay males affect. (6) His/her treatment of me: Gave off no signs that would let me know if I were of the same or different sex as this person. There were not even any signs that he/she knew his/her sex would be difficult to categorize and I wondered about that even as I did my best to hide these questions so I would not embarrass him/her while we talked of computer paper. I left still not knowing the sex of my salesperson, and was disturbed by that unanswered question (child of my culture that I am). (Margolis 1985)

What can this case tell us about situations such as Agnes's (cf. Morris 1974; Richards 1983) or the process of sex categorization in general? First, we infer from this description that the computer salesclerk's identificatory display was ambiguous, since she or he was not dressed or adorned in an unequivocally female or male fashion. It is when such a display *fails* to provide grounds for categorization that factors such as facial hair or tone of voice are assessed to determine membership in a sex category. Second, beyond the fact that this incident could be recalled after "a couple of years," the customer was not only "disturbed" by the ambiguity of the salesclerk's category but also assumed that to acknowledge this ambiguity would be embarrassing to the salesclerk. Not only do we want to know the sex category of those around us (to see it at a glance, perhaps), but we presume that others are displaying it for us in as decisive a fashion as they can.

Gender

Agnes attempted to be "120 percent female" (Garfinkel 1967, p. 129), that is, unquestionably in all ways and at all times feminine. She thought she could protect herself from disclosure before and after surgical intervention by comporting herself in a feminine manner, but she also could have given herself away by overdoing her performance. Sex categorization and the accomplishment of gender are not the same. Agnes's categorization could be secure or suspect, but did not depend on whether or not she lived up to some ideal conception of femininity. Women can be seen as unfeminine, but that does not make them "unfemale." Agnes faced an ongoing task of *being* a woman—something beyond style of dress (an identificatory display) or allowing men to light her cigarette (a gender display). Her problem was to produce configurations of behavior that would be seen by others as normative gender behavior.

Agnes's strategy of "secret apprenticeship," through which she learned expected feminine decorum by carefully attending to her fiancé's criticisms of other women, was one means of masking incompetencies and simultaneously acquiring the needed skills (Garfinkel 1967, pp. 146-7). It was through her fiancé that Agnes learned that sunbathing on the lawn in front of her apartment was "offensive" (because it put her on display to other men). She also learned from his critiques of other women that she should not insist on having things her way and that she should not offer her opinions or claim equality with men (Garfinkel 1967, pp. 147-8). (Like other women in our society Agnes learned something about power in the course of her "education.")

Popular culture abounds with books and magazines that compile idealized depictions of relations between women and men. Those focused on the etiquette of dating or prevailing standards of feminine comportment are meant to be of practical help in these matters. However, the use of any such source as a manual of procedure requires the assumption that doing gender merely involves making use of discrete, well-defined bundles of behavior that can simply be plugged into interactional situations to produce recognizable enactments of masculinity and femininity. The man "does" being masculine by, for example, taking the woman's arm to guide her across a street, and she "does" being feminine by consenting to be guided and not initiating such behavior with a man.

Agnes could perhaps have used such sources as manuals, but, we contend, doing gender is not so easily regimented (Mithers 1982; Morris 1974). Such sources may list and describe the sorts of behaviors that mark or display gender, but they are necessarily incomplete (Garfinkel 1967, pp. 66-75; Wieder 1974, pp. 183-214; Zimmerman and Wieder 1970, pp. 285-98). To be successful, marking or displaying gender must be finely fitted to situations and modified or transformed as the occasion demands. Doing gender consists of managing such occasions so that, whatever the particulars, the outcome is seen and seeable in context as gender-appropriate or purposefully gender-inappropriate, that is, *accountable*.

GENDER AND ACCOUNTABILITY

As Heritage (1984, pp. 136-7) notes, members of society regularly engage in "descriptive accountings of states of affairs to one another," and such accounts are both serious and consequential. These descriptions name, characterize, formulate, explain, excuse, excoriate, or merely take notice of some circumstance or activity and thus place it within some social framework (locating it relative to other activities, like and unlike).

Such descriptions are themselves accountable, and societal members orient to the fact that their activities are subject to comment. Actions are often designed with an eye to their accountability, that is, how they might look and how they might be characterized. The notion of accountability also encompasses those actions undertaken so that they are specifically unremarkable and thus not worthy of more than a passing remark, because they are seen to be in accord with culturally approved standards.

Heritage (1984, p. 179) observes that the process of rendering something accountable is interactional in character:

> [This] permits actors to design their actions in relation to their circumstances so as to permit others, by methodically taking account of circumstances, to recognize the action for what it is.

The key word here is *circumstances*. One circumstance that attends virtually all actions is the sex category of the actor. As Garfinkel (1967, p. 118) comments:

> [T]he work and socially structured occasions of sexual passing were obstinately unyielding to [Agnes's] attempts to routinize the grounds of daily activities. This obstinacy points to the *omnirelevance* of sexual status to affairs of daily life as an invariant but unnoticed background in the texture of relevances that compose the changing actual scenes of everyday life. (emphasis added)

If sex category is omnirelevant (or even approaches being so), then a person engaged in virtually any activity may be held accountable for performance of that activity *as a woman or a man,* and their incumbency in one or the other sex category can be used to legitimate or discredit their other activities (Berger, Cohen, and Zelditch 1972; Berger, Conner, and Fisek 1974; Berger, Fisek, Norman, and Zelditch 1977; Humphreys and Berger 1981). Accordingly, virtually any activity can be assessed as to its womanly or manly nature. And note, to "do" gender is not always to live up to normative conceptions of femininity or masculinity; it is to engage in behavior *at the risk of gender assessment.* Although it is individuals who do gender, the enterprise is fundamentally interactional and institutional in character, because accountability is a feature of social relationships and its idiom is drawn from the institutional arena in which those relationships are enacted. If this is the case, can we ever *not* do gender? Insofar as a society is partitioned by "essential" differences between women and men and placement in a sex category is both relevant and enforced, doing gender is unavoidable.

RESOURCES FOR DOING GENDER

Doing gender means creating differences between girls and boys and women and men, differences that are not natural, essential, or biological. Once the differences have been constructed, they are used to reinforce the "essentialness" of gender. In a delightful account of the "arrangement between the sexes," Goffman (1977) observes the creation of a variety of institutionalized frameworks through which our "natural, normal sexedness" can be enacted. The physical features of social settings provide one obvious resource for the expression of our "essential" differences. For example, the sex segregation of North American public bathrooms distinguishes "ladies" from "gentlemen" in matters held to be fundamentally biological, even though both "are somewhat similar in the question of waste products and their elimination" (Goffman 1977, p. 315). These settings are furnished with dimorphic equipment (such as urinals for men or elaborate grooming facilities for women), even though both sexes may achieve the same ends through the same means (and apparently do so in the privacy of their own homes). To be stressed here is the fact that:

> The *functioning* of sex-differentiated organs is involved, but there is nothing in this functioning that biologically recommends segregation; *that* arrangement is a totally cultural matter . . . toilet segregation is presented as a natural consequence of the difference between the sex-classes when in fact it is a means of honoring, if not producing, this difference. (Goffman 1977, p. 316)

Standardized social occasions also provide stages for evocations of the "essential female and male natures." Goffman cites organized sports as one such institutionalized framework for the expression of manliness. There, those qualities that ought "properly" to be associated with masculinity, such as endurance, strength, and competitive spirit, are celebrated by all parties concerned—participants, who may be seen to demonstrate such traits, and spectators, who applaud their demonstrations from the safety of the sidelines (1977, p. 322).

Assortative mating practices among heterosexual couples afford still further means to create and maintain differences between women and men. For example, even though size, strength, and age tend to be normally distributed among females and males (with considerable overlap between them), selective pairing ensures couples in which boys and men are visibly bigger, stronger, and older (if not "wiser") than the girls and women with whom they are paired. So, should situations emerge in which greater size, strength, or experience is called for, boys and men will be ever ready to display it and girls and women to appreciate its display (Goffman 1977, p. 321; West and Iritani 1985).

Gender may be routinely fashioned in a variety of situations that seem conventionally expressive to begin with, such as those that present "helpless" women next to heavy objects or flat tires. But, as Goffman notes, heavy, messy, and precarious concerns can be constructed from *any* social situation, "even though by standards set in other settings, this may involve something that is light, clean, and safe" (Goffman 1977, p. 324). Given these resources, it is clear that any interactional situation sets the stage for depictions of "essential" sexual natures. In sum, these situations "do not so much allow for the expression of natural differences as for the production of that difference itself" (Goffman 1977, p. 324).

Many situations are not clearly sex categorized, nor is what transpires in them obviously gender relevant. Yet any social encounter can be pressed into service in the interests of doing gender. Thus, Fishman's (1978) research on casual conversations found an asymmetrical "division of labor" in talk between heterosexual intimates. Women had to ask more questions, fill more silences, and use more attention-getting beginnings in order to be heard. Her conclusions are particularly pertinent here:

> Since interactional work is related to what constitutes being a woman, with what a woman *is,* the idea that it *is* work is obscured. The work is not seen as what women do, but as part of what they are. (Fishman 1978, p. 405)

We would argue that it is precisely such labor that helps to constitute the essential nature of women *as* women in interactional contexts (West and Zimmerman 1983, pp. 109-11; but see also Kollock, Blumstein, and Schwartz 1985).

Individuals have many social identities that may be donned or shed, muted, or made more salient, depending on the situation. One may be a friend, professional, citizen, and many other things to many different people or to the same person at different times. But we are always women or men—unless we shift into another sex category. What this means is that our identificatory displays will provide an ever-available resource for doing gender under an infinitely diverse set of circumstances.

Some occasions are organized to routinely display and celebrate behaviors that are conventionally linked to one or the other sex category. On such occasions, everyone knows his or her place in the interactional scheme of things. If an individual identified as a member of one sex category engages in behavior usually associated with the other category, this routinization is challenged. Hughes (1945, p. 356) provides an illustration of such a dilemma:

> [A] young woman . . . became part of that virile profession, engineering. The designer of an airplane is expected to go up on the maiden flight of the first plane built according to the design. He [sic] then gives a dinner to the engineers and workmen who worked on the new plane. The dinner is naturally a stag party. The young woman in question designed a plane. Her co-workers urged her not to take the risk—for which, presumably, men only are fit—of the maiden voyage. They were, in effect, asking her to be a lady instead of an engineer. She chose to be an engineer. She then gave the party and paid for it like a man. After food and the first round of toasts, she left like a lady.

On this occasion, the parties reached an accommodation that allowed a woman to engage in presumptively masculine behaviors. However, in the end, this compromise permitted demonstration of her "essential" femininity, through accountably "ladylike" behavior.

Hughes (1945, p. 357) suggests that such contradictions may be countered by managing interactions on a very narrow basis, for example, by "keeping the relationship formal and specific." But the heart of the matter is that even—perhaps, especially—if the relationship is a formal one, gender is still something one is accountable for. Thus, a woman physician (notice the special qualifier in her case) may be accorded respect for her skill and even addressed by an appropriate title. Nonetheless, she is subject to evaluation in terms of normative conceptions of appropriate attitudes and activities for her sex category and under pressure to prove that she is an "essentially" feminine being, despite appearances to the contrary (West 1984, pp. 97-101). Her sex category is used to discredit her participation in important clinical activities (Lorber 1984, pp. 52-4), while her involvement in medicine is used to discredit her commitment to her responsibilities as a wife and mother (Bourne and Wikler 1978, pp. 435-7). Simultaneously, her exclusion from the physician colleague community is maintained and her accountability *as a woman* is ensured.

In this context, "role conflict" can be viewed as a dynamic aspect of our current "arrangement between the sexes" (Goffman 1977), an arrangement that provides for occasions on which persons of a particular sex category can "see" quite clearly that they are out of place and that if they were not there, their current troubles would not exist. From the standpoint of interaction, what is at stake is the management of our "essential" natures and, from the standpoint of the individual, the continuing accomplishment of gender. If, as we have argued, sex category is omnirelevant, then any occasion, conflicted or not, offers the resources for doing gender.

We have sought to show that sex category and gender are managed properties of conduct that are contrived with respect to the fact that others will judge and respond to us in particular ways. We have claimed that a person's gender is not simply an aspect of what one is, but, more fundamentally, it is something that one *does,* and does recurrently, in interaction with others.

What are the consequences of this theoretical formulation? If, for example, individuals strive to achieve gender in encounters with others, how does a culture instill the need to achieve it? What is the relationship between the production of gender at the level of interaction and such institutional arrangements as the division of labor in society? And, perhaps most important, how does doing gender contribute to the subordination of women by men?

RESEARCH AGENDAS

To bring the social production of gender under empirical scrutiny, we might begin at the beginning, with a reconsideration of the process through which societal members acquire the requisite categorical apparatus and other skills to become gendered human beings.

Recruitment to Gender Identities

The conventional approach to the process of becoming girls and boys has been sex-role socialization. In recent years, recurring problems arising from this approach have been linked to inadequacies inherent in role theory per se: its emphasis on "consensus, stability and continuity" (Stacey and Thorne 1985, p. 307), its ahistorical and depoliticizing focus (Stacey and Thorne 1985, p. 307; Thorne 1980, p. 9), and the fact that its "social" dimension relies on "a general assumption that people choose to maintain existing customs" (Connell 1985, p. 263).

In contrast, Cahill (1982, 1986a, 1986b) analyzes the experiences of preschool children using a social model of recruitment into normally gendered identities. Cahill argues that categorization practices are fundamental to learning and displaying feminine and masculine behavior. Initially, he observes, children are primarily concerned with distinguishing between themselves and others on the basis of social competence. Categorically, their concern resolves itself into the opposition of "girl/boy" versus "baby" classification (the latter designating children whose social behavior is problematic and who must be closely supervised). It is children's concern with being seen as socially competent that evokes their initial claims to gender identities:

> During the exploratory stage of children's socialization . . . they learn that only two social identities are routinely available to them, the identity of "baby," or, depending on the configuration of their external genitalia, either "big boy" or "big girl." Moreover, others subtly inform them that the identity of "baby" is a discrediting one. When, for example, children engage in disapproved behavior, they are often told "You're a baby" or "Be a big boy." In effect, these typical verbal responses to young children's behavior convey to them that they must behaviorally choose between the discrediting identity of "baby" and their anatomically determined sex identity. (Cahill 1986a, p. 175)

Subsequently, little boys appropriate the gender ideal of "efficaciousness," that is, being able to affect the physical and social environment through the exercise of physical strength or appropriate skills. In contrast, little girls learn to value "appearance," that is, managing themselves as ornamental objects. Both classes of children learn that the recognition and use of sex categorization in interaction are not optional, but mandatory (see also Bem 1983).

Being a "girl" or a "boy," then, is not only being more competent than a "baby," but also being competently female or male, that is, learning to produce behavioral displays of one's "essential" female or male identity. In this respect, the task of four- to five-year-old children is very similar to Agnes's:

> For example, the following interaction occurred on a preschool playground. A 55-month-old boy (D) was attempting to unfasten the clasp of a necklace when a preschool aide walked over to him.
>
> A: Do you want to put that on?
> D: No. It's for girls.

A: You don't have to be a girl to wear things around your neck. Kings wear
   things around their necks. You could pretend you're a king.
D: I'm not a king. I'm a boy. (Cahill 1986a, p. 176)

As Cahill notes of this example, although D may have been unclear as
to the sex status of a king's identity, he was obviously aware that
necklaces are used to announce the identity "girl." Having claimed the
identity "boy" and having developed a behavioral commitment to it, he
was leery of any display that might furnish grounds for questioning his
claim.

In this way, new members of society come to be involved in a
self-regulating process as they begin to monitor their own and others'
conduct with regard to its gender implications. The recruitment process
involves not only the appropriation of gender ideals (by the valuation
of those ideals as proper ways of being and behaving) but also *gender
identities* that are important to individuals and that they strive to
maintain. Thus gender differences, or the sociocultural shaping of
"essential female and male natures," achieve the status of objective
facts. They are rendered normal, natural features of persons and provide
the tacit rationale for differing fates of women and men within the social
order.

Additional studies of children's play activities as routine occasions
for the expression of gender-appropriate behavior can yield new insights into how our "essential natures" are constructed. In particular,
the transition from what Cahill (1986a) terms "apprentice participation" in the sex-segregated world, which is common among elementary
school children, to "bona fide participation" in the heterosocial world,
which is so frightening to adolescents, is likely to be a keystone in our
understanding of the recruitment process (Thorne 1986; Thorne and
Luria 1986).

Gender and the Division of Labor

Whenever people face issues of *allocation*—who is to do what, get
what, plan or execute action, direct or be directed, incumbency in
significant social categories such as "female" and "male" seems to
become pointedly relevant. How such issues are resolved conditions the
exhibition, dramatization, or celebration of one's "essential nature" as
a woman or man.

Fenstermarker Berk (1985) offers an elegant demonstration of this
point in her investigation of the allocation of household labor and the
attitudes of married couples toward the division of household tasks.

Berk found little variation in either the actual distribution of tasks or perceptions of equity in regard to that distribution. Wives, even when employed outside the home, do the vast majority of household and child-care tasks. Moreover, both wives and husbands tend to perceive this as a "fair" arrangement. Noting the failure of conventional socio-logical and economic theories to explain this seeming contradiction, Berk contends that something more complex than rational arrangements for the production of household goods and services is involved:

> Hardly a question simply of who has more time, or whose time is worth more, who has more skill or more power, it is clear that a complicated relationship between the structure of work imperative and the structure of normative expectations attached to work as *gendered* determines the ultimate allocation of members' time to work and home. (Berk 1985, pp. 195-6)

She notes, for example, that the most important factor influencing wives' contribution of labor is the total amount of work demanded or expected by the household; such demands had no bearing on husbands' contributions. Wives reported various rationales (their own and their husbands') that justified their level of contribution and, as a general matter, underscored the presumption that wives are essentially respon-sible for household production.

Fenstermarker Berk (1985, p. 201) contends that it is difficult to see how people "could rationally establish the arrangements that they do solely for the production of household goods and services"—much less how people could consider them "fair." She argues that our current arrangements for the domestic division of labor support *two* production processes: household goods and services (meals, clean children, and so on) and, at the same time, gender. As she puts it:

> Simultaneously, members "do" gender, as they "do" housework and child care, and what [has] been called the division of labor provides for the joint production of household labor and gender; it is the mechanism by which both the material and symbolic products of the household are realized. (1985, p. 201)

It is not simply that household labor is designated as "women's work," but that for a woman to engage in it and a man not to engage in it is to draw on and exhibit the "essential nature" of each. What is produced and reproduced is not merely the activity and artifact of domestic life, but the material embodiment of wifely and husbandly roles and, deriv-atively, of womanly and manly conduct (see Beer 1983, pp. 70-89).

What are also frequently produced and reproduced are the dominant and subordinate statuses of the sex categories.

How does gender get done in work settings outside the home, where dominance and subordination are themes of overarching importance? Hochschild's (1983) analysis of the work of flight attendants offers some promising insights. She found that the occupation of flight attendant consisted of something altogether different for women than for men:

> As the company's main shock absorbers against "mishandled" passengers, their own feelings are more frequently subjected to rough treatment. In addition, a day's exposure to people who resist authority in a woman is a different experience than it is for a man. . . . In this respect, it is a disadvantage to be a woman. And in this case, they are not simply women in the biological sense. They are also a highly visible distillation of middle-class American notions of femininity. They symbolize Woman. Insofar as the category "female" is mentally associated with having less status and authority, female flight attendants are more readily classified as "really" females than other females are. (Hochschild 1983, p. 175)

In performing what Hochschild terms the "emotional labor" necessary to maintain airline profits, women flight attendants simultaneously produce enactments of their "essential" femininity.

Sex and Sexuality

What is the relationship between doing gender and a culture's prescription of "obligatory heterosexuality" (Rich 1980; Rubin 1975)? As Frye (1983, p. 22) observes, the monitoring of sexual feelings in relation to other appropriately sexed persons requires the ready recognition of such persons "before one can allow one's heart to beat or one's blood to flow in erotic enjoyment of that person." The appearance of heterosexuality is produced through emphatic and unambiguous indicators of one's sex, layered on in ever more conclusive fashion (Frye 1983, p. 24). Thus, lesbians and gay men concerned with passing as heterosexuals can rely on these indicators for camouflage; in contrast, those who would avoid the assumption of heterosexuality may foster ambiguous indicators of their categorical status through their dress, behaviors, and style. But "ambiguous" sex indicators are sex indicators nonetheless. If one wishes to be recognized as a lesbian (or heterosexual woman), one must first establish a categorical status as female. Even as popular images portray lesbians as "females who are not feminine"

(Frye 1983, p. 129), the accountability of persons for their "normal, natural sexedness" is preserved.

Nor is accountability threatened by the existence of sex-change operations—presumably, the most radical challenge to our cultural perspective on sex and gender. Although no one coerces transsexuals into hormone therapy, electrolysis, or surgery, the alternatives available to them are undeniably constrained:

> When the transsexual experts maintain that they use transsexual procedures only with people who ask for them, and who prove that they can "pass," they obscure the social reality. Given patriarchy's prescription that one must be *either* masculine or feminine, free choice is conditioned. (Raymond 1979, p. 135, italics added)

The physical reconstruction of sex criteria pays ultimate tribute to the "essentialness" of our sexual natures—as women *or* as men.

GENDER, POWER, AND SOCIAL CHANGE

Let us return to the question: Can we avoid doing gender? Earlier, we proposed that, insofar as sex category is used as a fundamental criterion for differentiation, doing gender is unavoidable. It is unavoidable because of the social consequences of sex-category membership: the allocation of power and resources not only in the domestic, economic, and political domains but also in the broad arena of interpersonal relations. In virtually any situation, one's sex category can be relevant, and one's performance as an incumbent of that category (i.e., gender) can be subjected to evaluation. Maintaining such pervasive and faithful assignment of lifetime status requires legitimation.

But doing gender also renders the social arrangements based on sex category accountable as normal and natural, that is, legitimate ways of organizing social life. Differences between women and men that are created by this process can then be portrayed as fundamental and enduring dispositions. In this light, the institutional arrangements of a society can be seen as responsive to the differences, the social order being merely an accommodation to the natural order. Thus if, in doing gender, men are also doing dominance and women are doing deference (cf. Goffman 1967, pp. 47-95), the resultant social order, which supposedly reflects "natural differences," is a powerful reinforcer and legitimator of hierarchical arrangements. Frye observes:

For efficient subordination, what's wanted is that the structure not appear to be a cultural artifact kept in place by human decision or custom, but that it appear *natural*—that it appear to be quite a direct consequence of facts about the beast which are beyond the scope of human manipulation. . . . That we are trained to behave so differently as women and men, and to behave so differently toward women and men, itself contributes mightily to the appearance of extreme dimorphism, but also, the *ways* we act as women and men, and the *ways* we act toward women and men, mold our bodies and our minds to the shape of subordination and dominance. We do become what we practice being. (Frye 1983, p. 34)

If we do gender appropriately, we simultaneously sustain, reproduce, and render legitimate the institutional arrangements that are based on sex category. If we fail to do gender appropriately, we as individuals—not the institutional arrangements—may be called to account (for our character, motives, and predispositions).

Social movements such as femininism can provide the ideology and impetus to question existing arrangements and the social support for individuals to explore alternatives to them. Legislative changes, such as those proposed by the Equal Rights Amendment, can also weaken the accountability of conduct to sex category, thereby affording the possibility of more widespread loosening of accountability in general. To be sure, equality under the law does not guarantee equality in other arenas. As Lorber points out, assurance of "scrupulous equality of categories of people considered essentially different needs constant monitoring." What such proposed changes *can* do is provide the warrant for asking why, if we wish to treat women and men as equals, there needs to be two sex categories at all (see Chapter 18).

The sex category/gender relationship links the institutional and interactional levels, a coupling that legitimates social arrangements based on sex category and reproduces their asymmetry in face-to-face interaction. Doing gender furnishes the interactional scaffolding of social structure, along with a built-in mechanism of social control. In appreciating the institutional forces that maintain distinctions between women and men, we must not lose sight of the interactional validation of those distinctions that confers upon them their sense of "naturalness" and "rightness."

Social change, then, must be pursued at the institutional and cultural levels of sex category and at the interactional level of gender. Such a conclusion is hardly novel. Nevertheless, we suggest that it is important to recognize that the analytical distinction between institutional and interactional sphere does not pose an either/or choice when it comes to the question of effecting social change. Reconceptualizing gender not as a simple property of individuals but as an integral dynamic of social orders implies a new perspective on the entire network of gender relations:

> the social subordination of women, and the cultural practices which help sustain it; the politics of sexual object-choice, and particularly the oppression of homosexual people; the sexual division of labor, the formation of character and motive, so far as they are organized as femininity and masculinity; the role of the body in social relations, especially the politics of childbirth; and the nature of strategies of sexual liberation movements. (Connell 1985, p. 261)

Gender is a powerful ideological device, which produces, reproduces, and legitimates the choices and limits that are predicated on sex category. An understanding of how gender is produced in social situations will afford clarification of the interactional scaffolding of social structure and the social control processes that sustain it.

NOTES

1. This definition understates many complexities involved in the relationship between biology and culture (Jaggar 1983, pp. 106-13). However, our point is that the determination of an individual's sex classification is a *social* process through and through.

2. This is not to say that gender is a singular "thing," omnipresent in the same form historically or in every situation. Because normative conceptions of appropriate attitudes and activities for sex categories can vary across cultures and historical moments, the management of situated conduct in light of those expectations can take many different forms.

3. Bernstein (1986) reports an unusual case of espionage in which a man passing as a woman convinced a lover that he/she had given birth to "their" child, who, the lover, thought, "looked like" him.

REFERENCES

Beer, W. R. 1983. *Househusbands: Men and Housework in American Families.* New York: Praeger.

Bem, S. L. 1983. "Gender Schema Theory and Its Implications for Child Development: Raising Gender-Aschematic Children in a Gender-Schematic Society." *Signs: Journal of Women in Culture and Society* 8:598-616.

Berger, J., B. P. Cohen, and M. Zelditch, Jr. 1972. "Status Characteristics and Social Interaction." *American Sociological Review* 37:241-55.

Berger, J., T. L. Conner, and M. Hamit Fisek, eds. 1974. *Expectation States Theory: A Theoretical Research Program.* Cambridge, MA: Winthrop.

Berger, J., M. Hamit Fisek, R. Z. Norman, and M. Zelditch, Jr. 1977. *Status Characteristics and Social Interaction: An Expectation States Approach.* New York: Elsevier.

Berk, S. Fenstermaker. 1985. *The Gender Factory: The Apportionment of Work in American Households.* New York: Plenum.

Bernstein, R. 1986. "France Jails 2 in Odd Case of Espionage." *New York Times* (May 11).

Blackwood, E. 1984. "Sexuality and Gender in Certain Native American Tribes: The Case of Cross-Gender Females." *Signs: Journal of Women in Culture and Society* 10:27-42.

Bourne, P. G., and N. J. Wikler. 1978. "Commitment and the Cultural Mandate: Women in Medicine." *Social Problems* 25:430-40.

Cahill, S. E. 1982. "Becoming Boys and Girls." Ph.D. dissertation, Department of Sociology, University of California, Santa Barbara.

———. 1986a. "Childhood Socialization as Recruitment Process: Some Lessons from the Study of Gender Development." Pp. 163-86 in *Sociological Studies of Child Development,* edited by P. Adler and P. Adler. Greenwich, CT: JAI Press.

———. 1986b. "Language Practices and Self-Definition: The Case of Gender Identity Acquisition." *Sociological Quarterly* 27:295-311.

Chodorow, N. 1978. *The Reproduction of Mothering: Psychoanalysis and the Sociology of Gender.* Los Angeles: University of California Press.

Connell, R. W. 1983. *Which Way Is Up?* Sydney, Australia: Allen and Unwin.

———. 1985. "Theorizing Gender." *Sociology* 19:260-72.

Cucchiari, S. 1981. "The Gender Revolution and the Transition from Bisexual Horde to Patrilocal Band: The Origins of Gender Hierarchy." Pp. 31-79 in *Sexual Meanings: The Cultural Construction of Gender and Sexuality,* edited by S. B. Ortner and H. Whitehead. New York: Cambridge.

Firestone, S. 1970. *The Dialectic of Sex: The Case for Feminist Revolution.* New York: William Morrow.

Fishman, P. 1978. "Interaction: The Work Women Do." *Social Problems* 25:397-406.

Frye, M. 1983. *The Politics of Reality: Essays in Feminist Theory.* Trumansburg, NY: The Crossing Press.

Garfinkel, H. 1967. *Studies in Ethnomethodology.* Englewood Cliffs, NJ: Prentice-Hall.

Gerson, J. M., and K. Peiss. 1985. "Boundaries, Negotiation, Consciousness: Reconceptualizing Gender Relations." *Social Problems* 32:317-31.

Goffman, E. 1967 (1956). "The Nature of Deference and Demeanor." Pp. 47-95 in *Interaction Ritual.* New York: Anchor/Doubleday.

———. 1976. "Gender Display." *Studies in the Anthropology of Visual Communication* 3:69-77.

———. 1977. "The Arrangement Between the Sexes." *Theory and Society* 4:301-31.

Henley, N. M. 1985. "Psychology and Gender." *Signs: Journal of Women in Culture and Society* 11:101-19.

Heritage, J. 1984. *Garfinkel and Ethnomethodology.* Cambridge, UK: Polity Press.

Hill, W. W. 1935. "The Status of the Hermaphrodite and Transvestite in Navaho Culture." *American Anthropologist* 37:273-9.

Hochschild, A. R. 1973. "A Review of Sex Roles Research." *American Journal of Sociology* 78:1011-29.

———. 1983. *The Managed Heart: Commercialization of Human Feeling.* Berkeley, CA: University of California Press.

Hughes, E. C. 1945. "Dilemmas and Contradictions of Status." *American Journal of Sociology* 50:353-9.

Humphreys, P., and J. Berger. 1981. "Theoretical Consequences of the Status Characteristics Formulation." *American Journal of Sociology* 86:953-83.

36   PRINCIPLES OF GENDER CONSTRUCTION

Jaggar, A. M. 1983. *Feminist Politics and Human Nature*. Totowa, NJ: Rowman & Allanheld.
Kessler, S., D. J. Ashendon, R. W. Connell, and G. W. Dowsett. 1985. "Gender Relations in Secondary Schooling." *Sociology of Education* 58:34-48.
Kessler, S. J., and W. McKenna. 1978. *Gender: An Ethnomethodological Approach*. New York: John Wiley.
Kollock, P., P. Blumstein, and P. Schwartz. 1985. "Sex and Power in Interaction." *American Sociological Review* 50:34-46.
Komarovsky, M. 1946. "Cultural Contradictions and Sex Roles." *American Journal of Sociology* 52:184-9.
———. 1950. "Functional Analysis of Sex Roles." *American Sociological Review* 15: 508-16.
Linton, R. 1936. *The Study of Man*. New York: Appleton-Century.
Lopata, H. Z., and B. Thorne. 1978. "On the Term 'Sex Roles.' " *Signs: Journal of Women in Culture and Society* 3:718-21.
Lorber, J. 1984. *Women Physicians: Careers, Status and Power*. New York: Tavistock.
Margolis, D. 1985. Personal communication.
Martin, M. K. and B. Voorheis. 1975. *Female of the Species*. New York: Columbia University Press.
Mead, M. 1963. *Sex and Temperament*. New York: Dell.
———. 1968. *Male and Female*. New York: Dell.
Mithers, C. L. 1982. "My Life as a Man." *Village Voice* 27 (October 5):1ff.
Money, J. 1968. *Sex Errors of the Body*. Baltimore: Johns Hopkins University Press.
———. 1974. "Prenatal Hormones and Postnatal Sexualization in Gender Identity Differentiation." Pp. 221-95 in *Nebraska Symposium on Motivation*, Vol. 21, edited by J. K. Cole and R. Dienstbier. Lincoln: University of Nebraska Press.
——— and J. G. Brennan. 1968. "Sexual Dimorphism in the Psychology of Female Transsexuals." *Journal of Nervous and Mental Disease* 147:487-99.
——— and A. A. Ehrhardt. 1972. *Man and Woman/Boy and Girl*. Baltimore: Johns Hopkins University Press.
——— and C. Ogunro. 1974. "Behavioral Sexology: Ten Cases of Genetic Male Intersexuality with Impaired Prenatal and Pubertal Androgenization," *Archives of Sexual Behavior* 3:181-206.
——— and P. Tucker. 1975. *Sexual Signatures*. Boston: Little, Brown.
Morris, J. 1974. *Conundrum*. New York: Harcourt Brace Jovanovich.
Parsons, T. 1951. *The Social System*. New York: Free Press.
——— and R. F. Bales. 1955. *Family, Socialization and Interaction Process*. New York: Free Press.
Raymond, J. G. 1979. *The Transsexual Empire*. Boston: Beacon.
Rich, A. 1980. "Compulsory Heterosexuality and Lesbian Existence." *Signs: Journal of Women in Culture and Society* 5:631-60.
Richards, R. (with J. Ames). 1983. *Second Serve: The Renée Richards Story*. Briarcliff Manor, NY: Stein & Day.
Rossi, A. 1984. "Gender and Parenthood." *American Sociological Review* 49:1-19.
Rubin, G. 1975. "The Traffic in Women: Notes on the 'Political Economy' of Sex." Pp. 157-210 in *Toward an Anthropology of Women*, edited by R. Reiter. New York: Monthly Review Press.
Sacks, H. 1972. "On the Analyzability of Stories by Children." Pp. 325-45 in *Directions in Sociolinguistics*, edited by J. J. Gumperz and D. Hymes. New York: Holt, Rinehart & Winston.

Schutz, A. 1943. "The Problem of Rationality in the Social World." *Economics* 10:130-49.

Stacey, J., and B. Thorne. 1985. "The Missing Feminist Revolution in Sociology." *Social Problems* 32:301-16.

Thorne, B. 1980. "Gender . . . How Is It Best Conceptualized?" Unpublished manuscript.

———. 1986. "Girls and Boys Together . . . But Mostly Apart: Gender Arrangements in Elementary Schools." Pp. 167-82 in *Relationships and Development,* edited by W. Hartup and Z. Rubin. Hillsdale, NJ: Lawrence Erlbaum.

——— and Z. Luria. 1986. "Sexuality and Gender in Children's Daily Worlds." *Social Problems* 33:176-90.

Tresemer, D. 1975. "Assumptions Made About Gender Roles." Pp. 308-39 in *Another Voice: Feminist Perspectives on Social Life and Social Science,* edited by M. Millman and R. Moss Kanter. New York: Anchor/Doubleday.

West, C. 1984. "When the Doctor is a 'Lady': Power, Status and Gender in Physician-Patient Encounters." *Symbolic Interaction* 7:87-106.

——— and B. Iritani. 1985. "Gender Politics in Mate Selection: The Male-Older Norm." Paper presented at the Annual Meeting of the American Sociological Association, August, Washington, DC.

——— and D. H. Zimmerman. 1983. "Small Insults: A Study of Interruptions in Conversations Between Unacquainted Persons." Pp. 102-17 in *Language, Gender and Society,* edited by B. Thorne, C. Kramarae, and N. Henley. Rowley, MA: Newbury House.

Wieder, D. L. 1974. *Language and Social Reality: The Case of Telling the Convict Code.* The Hague: Mouton.

Williams, W. L. 1986. *The Spirit and the Flesh: Sexual Diversity in American Indian Culture.* Boston: Beacon.

Wilson, T. P. 1970. "Conceptions of Interaction and Forms of Sociological Explanation." *American Sociological Review* 35:697-710.

Zimmerman, D. H. and D. L. Wieder. 1970. "Ethnomethodology and the Problem of Order: Comment on Denzin." Pp. 287-95 in *Understanding Everyday Life,* edited by N. J. Denzin. Hawthorne, NY: Aldine.

2. SOCIAL LOCATION AND GENDER-ROLE ATTITUDES: A COMPARISON OF BLACK AND WHITE WOMEN

KAREN DUGGER

An interactive analysis of the joint effects of racism and sexism sees them "as processes standing in dynamic relation to each other" and not as "independent parallel processes" that are cumulative in their effect (Smith and Stewart 1983, pp. 1, 6). For Black women, racism and sexism should be viewed as combining in such a way that they create a distinct social location rather than an additive form of "double disadvantage." The idea that the intersection of race and gender creates categories of people who occupy unique social spaces and whose collective historical experience powerfully shapes their gender identity and attitudes is articulated in Ransford and Miller's (1983) concept of "ethgender," which they derive from Gordon's (1964) concept of "ethclass." By conceptualizing race and gender interactively, researchers are forced to recognize that racism and sexism combine to produce race-specific gender effects that generate important experiential cleavages among women. These cleavages may in turn result in ideological differences, or differences in women's identity and gender-role attitudes (Dill 1983; Smith and Stewart 1983; White 1984).

If the forms and effects of sexism as well as responses to it vary according to race, more race-gender groups must be included in research designs (Smith and Stewart 1983). Identification of differences and commonalities among race-gender groups will dispel false universalization, which has portrayed the experience of White,[1] often middle-class, women as the experience of womankind and has distorted analyses of the operation and consequences of sexism. False universalization also sets up White women as the norm against which Black women may appear to be deviant cases (Gilkes 1979; Gump 1980). Realizing that generalizations about sexism are race-specific promotes a reevaluation of feminist theories by forcing us to ask to what gender-race group our knowledge applies and how current explanatory frameworks might be changed if the perspective and experiential base of Black women's lives were considered (Dill 1983; Hooks 1984; Smith and Stewart 1983).

Several theorists have maintained that women's position within two systems of social relations—production and reproduction—is primary in the formation of their gender-role attitudes and identity (Eisenstein 1981; Hartmann 1983; Petchesky 1983). At the crux of these theoretical formulations is the assertion that women's increased independence in both spheres makes them more likely to challenge the dominant culture's[2] views of gender. Concerning production, Eisenstein asserts that women's combined work as wage laborers and wives and mothers heightens the contradiction between the ideology of equal employment opportunity found in the marketplace and the patriarchal structuring of women's location in the marketplace and in the home. She further argues that women's labor-force participation encourages questioning the low valuation and justice of women's primary responsibility for domestic labor. In support of Eisenstein's thesis, research on White women has consistently demonstrated that employed women are more likely than women not in the labor force to hold nontraditional attitudes toward gender roles (Mason, Czajka, and Arber 1976; Spitze 1978; Thorton and Freedman 1979; Thorton, Alwin, and Camburn 1983). However, in the few studies that have included Black women, the results were mixed (Macke, Hudis, and Larrick 1977; Ransford and Miller 1983).

Concerning reproduction, Pollack Petchesky contends that women's reproductive relationships determine whether they will possess a "pro-life" or "pro-choice" orientation. For her, women highly invested in production, as evidenced by high labor-force participation and low fertility, are more likely to reject culturally dominant views of gender, whereas women highly invested in reproduction, as evidenced by low labor-force participation and high fertility, are likely to "adhere to traditional family forms and ideologies that certify women's primary function as a homemaker and childrearer" (1983, p. 236).

The interactive approach outlined above informs the aims and analytical strategy of this study. These aims are twofold: to explore the commonalities and differences in the gender-role attitudes of Black and White women and to assess the applicability to Black women of the hypothesis that investment in reproductive relations exerts a conservative influence on gender-role attitudes, whereas investment in productive relations has a radical impact.

SOURCES OF GENDER-ROLE ATTITUDES

The argument that the differential location of women in the systems of production and reproduction creates distinct life experiences and, hence, distinct attitudes toward gender roles suggests a wide gap between Black and White women. From slavery to the present, it is precisely with regard to productive and reproductive activities that racial oppression has most dramatically differentiated them. While nineteenth-century culture in the United States stereotyped White women as too frail and dainty to undertake physical labor, Black women were viewed as beasts of burden and subjected to the same demeaning labor and hardships as Black men (Hooks 1981; King 1975; Ladner 1971; Welter 1978). Davis asserts that slavery constructed for Black women an alternative definition of womanhood, which included a tradition of "hard work, perseverance and self-reliance, a legacy of tenacity, resistance and an insistence on sexual equality" (1981, p. 29).

The continued exploitation of Black labor into the twentieth century has meant the continued coercion of Black women into the paid labor force. Racial discrimination has produced high rates of unemployment among Black men and segregated them into low-paying jobs; thus the Black family has needed the labor of more than one wage earner. While Black women do not work only out of economic necessity (Gump 1980), the reality of racism continues to shape the context within which they develop and construct their definitions of womanhood. Thus, a primary cleavage in the life experiences of Black and White women is their past and present relationship to the labor process. In consequence, Black women's conceptions of womanhood emphasize self-reliance, strength, resourcefulness, autonomy, and the responsibility of providing for the material as well as emotional needs of family members (Ladner 1971). Black women do not see participation in the labor-force and being a wife and mother as mutually exclusive; rather, within Black culture, employment is an integral, normative, and traditional component of the roles of wife and mother (Gump 1980; Malson 1983).

Thus it could be hypothesized that Black women will be more likely than White women to challenge the dominant culture's definitions of women and their socially prescribed roles. However, recent demographic trends show a growing similarity in the productive and reproductive profiles of Black and White women. An increasing number of White women are having children outside marriage, living without husbands, and heading households, coming more to resemble Black women (Hartmann 1983). Almquist (1979) argues that the objective status of Black and White women is converging as their labor force participation rates, earnings, and occupational distribution have become virtually indistinguishable. On the basis of these trends, and the premise that productive and reproductive relationships are primary in constructing women's gender-role attitudes, we could expect White women also to reject a view of gender roles that makes market work and family work incompatible, and evidence exists that more and more they do (Cherlin and Walters 1981; Macke et al. 1977; Mason et al. 1976; Thorton et al. 1983; Thorton and Freedman 1979). But, in the few instances in which Black women formed a comparison group, they were *more* likely than White women to reject this view of appropriate roles for women (Cherlin and Walters 1981; Fulenwider 1980). Other confounding data showed Black women were at least as *accepting,* if not more accepting, than White women of views of women that emphasized femininity, self-sacrifice, and motherhood (Gump 1975; Hermons 1980; Hershey 1978).

In an attempt to reconcile these findings, Ransford and Miller (1983) took a multidimensional approach to measuring gender-role traditionalism and found no difference between Black and White women. They concluded that the Black female autonomy and independence described by Ladner does not appear to translate into a critique of women's traditional roles. Weitzman (1984) has argued that these inconsistencies may be due to social class differences in the populations studied. Although class variation in research samples may account to some degree for the discrepancies, nationally representative samples that controlled for class are also inconsistent (Cherlin and Walters 1981; Fulenwider 1980; Ransford and Miller 1983). Another source of the diverse results is the dimensions of gender roles used. Cherlin and Walters (1981) and Ransford and Miller (1983), for example, examined attitudes about the suitability and appropriateness of women's presence in the public worlds of work and politics, while Porter Gump (1975), Randon Hershey (1978), and Hermons (1980) measured women's identification with the values of "femininity" and the private roles of wife and mother.

Lastly, an important source of the diverse findings may simply be the contradictory nature of Black women's lives. Thornton Dill (1979) cautions that any analysis of Black women must consider the contradictions imposed on them by White norms and expectations. Black women have had to reconcile being strong, independent economic providers with simultaneously investing a substantial part of their identity in being wives and mothers and feminine women. The constant cultural assaults on their identity, being labeled "jezebels," "matriarchs," and "sapphires" (Gilkes 1979; White 1985), may have generated an idealization of certain components of the dominant culture's views of womanhood.

RESEARCH DESIGN

Hypotheses

This study investigates two competing hypotheses concerning the gender-role attitudes of Black and White women. The first is that Black women will be more rejecting of the dominant culture's views than White women because their productive and reproductive experiences have stood in greater contradiction to these views. Alternatively, it could be expected that there will be little difference in Black and White women's gender-role attitudes because White women's productive and reproductive profiles have increasingly come to resemble those of Black women, and because the dominant culture's assaults on Black women may lead them to embrace the views of gender embodied in these assaults.

The structures of racial privilege and racial oppression that have determined the historical experiences of Black and White women have created distinct cultural legacies. As discussed, the legacy available to Black women has been more at odds with culturally dominant definitions of gender than that of White women. The socialization of Black women into this cultural legacy, as well as the continued precarious condition of Black women collectively, may be more important in shaping their gender-role attitudes than their own individual productive and reproductive experiences. White women's history of race privilege, on the other hand, has served to affirm rather than undermine the dominant culture's definition of appropriate roles for women. Individual productive and reproductive experiences at variance with White women's cultural heritage may, therefore, play a more important part in shaping their gender-role attitudes. Given these considerations, it is expected that the hypothesis regarding investment in production and reproduction will be more applicable to White than Black women.

Sample

The data for this study come from the Roper Organization's 1980 Virginia Slims American Women's Opinion Poll. Roper employed a multistage stratified probability sample of the noninstitutionalized adult female population of the continental United States. There were 296 Black women and 2,607 White women in the sample.

Measures

Scales representing eight dimensions of gender-role attitudes were constructed from questionnaire items (see Appendix). The scales spanned a variety of gender-role attitudes. All were coded such that higher scores indicated greater rejection of culturally dominant views. Face validity of these scales implied congruence with challenges to culturally dominant definitions of gender roles found in recent feminist writings and articulated in a variety of women's movement activities. Perceptions of sex discrimination (*discrimination*), of women's ability to perform competently in public-sphere positions dominated by men (*public sphere*), admiration for women who are independent, intelligent, and outspoken (*female gender stereotyping*), and a rejection of stereotypical roles for boys and girls (*stereotyping of children's gender roles*) are core components of such challenges. Values concerning sexual freedom (*new morality*), the acceptance of nontraditional family structures (*traditional family*), rejection of marital roles that define the husband as provider and wife as nurturer (*traditional marriage*), and support for the efforts and goals of the women's movement (*women's movement*) are likewise integral components of contemporary challenges to culturally dominant views of appropriate gender roles.

Investment in production was measured by combining the scores on two variables: employment status (employed full- or part-time, not employed) and preference for working versus staying at home and taking care of a house and family. A 4-point continuum was constructed on which 1 = not working and prefer not to, 2 = working but prefer not to, 3 = not working but prefer to, and 4 = working and prefer to.

Marital status and having children were combined to create five dummy variables as indicators of *investment in reproduction:* married, no children; separated or divorced, no children; never married, no children; separated or divorced with children; and never-married with children. Married women with children served as the reference category.

Three other sociodemographic variables were included in the analysis: the respondent's education (measured on a 7-point scale ranging from 1 = no school to 7 = postgraduate), family income (measured on an 8-point scale ranging from 1 = under \$3,000 to 8 = over \$25,000), and age (measured on an 8-point scale ranging from 1 = 18-20 to 8 = 65 and over). Age was taken as an indicator of the cultural milieu in which the respondent was living and was socialized (Mason et al. 1976).

RESULTS

Effects of Race on Gender-Role Attitudes

The bivariate regressions showed Black women to be more rejecting of the dominant culture's views of gender than White women on all but two of the eight indices (see Table 2.1). The gender-role attitudes that evidenced the largest differences were *women's movement* ($b = .322$), *new morality* ($b = .234$), and *female gender stereotyping* ($b = .332$). Black women were also somewhat more likely than White women to reject the dominant culture's definitions of *traditional family* ($b = .155$) and *traditional marriage* ($b = .137$) and to believe that women are victims of *discrimination* ($b = .084$). No significant difference was found between Black and White women's attitudes toward women in the *public sphere* ($b = -.042$). In contrast to their greater rejection of *female gender stereotyping,* Black women were more likely than White women to support the *stereotyping of children's gender roles* ($b = -.089$). When other sociodemographic variables were controlled, the effects of *race* remained virtually unchanged or only slightly reduced on five of the six variables for which the bivariate regressions indicated significant racial differences (see Table 2.1). The original effect of *race* on *traditional marriage* ($b = .137$) was substantially reduced ($b = .034$).

Correlates of Gender-Role Attitudes
and Interaction Effects

The hypothesis that the impact of investment in production and reproduction on gender-role attitudes would be race-specific required a method for determining the presence of interaction effects. One such method would be to add product terms representing these interactions to the regression equations. However, to avoid problems of multicollinearity and to obtain more detailed data on the forms of the interactions, an alternative method was employed (Ransford and Miller 1983). Separate regressions for Black and White women were performed and differences in their slopes tested for significance.

The unstandardized regression coefficients for *investment in production* supported the hypothesis that its effects on gender-role attitudes would be race-specific and more radicalizing of White than Black women (see Tables 2.2 and 2.3). For White women, *investment in production* consistently predicted gender-role attitudes across all eight dimensions. For Black women, it significantly predicted only two dimensions: *women's movement* and *traditional marriage.* One-tail t-tests indicated that race interacted significantly with *new morality* ($p < .05$),

TABLE 2.1 Regression of Gender-Role Attitudes on Race Alone, and Controlling for Socioeconomic Status, Age, and Investment in Production and Reproduction

	Women's Movement		New Morality		Traditional Family		Traditional Marriage		Public Sphere		Discrimination		Stereotyping of Children's Gender Roles		Female Gender Stereotyping	
	b	β	b	β	b	β	b	β	b	β	b	β	b	β	b	β
Bivariate regression																
race	.322	.15**	.234	.11*	.155	.06**	.137	.07**	−.042	.04	.084	.05*	−.089	−.10**	.332	.11**
R^2		.021		.011		.004		.055		.001		.002		.010		.011
Multivariate regression																
race	.296	.14**	.187	.09**	.112	.05*	.034	.02	−.020	−.02	.079	.04*	−.058	−.06**	.331	.11**
education	.049	.09**	.012	.02	.040	.07**	.027	.06**	.041	.14**	.027	.06**	.034	.15**	.058	.07**
income	.015	.05*	.022	.07**	.019	.05*	−.002	−.01	.010	.06*	.019	.07**	.013	.10**	.003	.01
age	−.034	−.11**	−.068	−.23**	−.076	−.22	−.032	−.12**	−.042	−.25**	−.020	−.08**	−.004	−.03	−.046	−.10**
investment in production	.115	.22**	.061	.12**	.080	.13**	.174	.38**	.029	.10**	.044	.10**	.021	.10**	.037	.05*
never-married, with children	.149	.03	.401	.07**	.461	.07**	.10	.02	−.051	−.02	.228	.05*	.023	.01	.076	.01
never-married, no children	−.005	.00	.142	.06**	−.014	−.01	.020	.01	−.015	−.01	.012	.01	−.008	−.01	−.007	−.00
separated or divorced, with children	.124	.05**	.120	.05**	.207	.08**	.210	.10**	.057	.04*	.181	.09**	.064	.06**	.094	.03
separated or divorced, no children	.112	.02	.312	.06**	.185	.03	.249	.06**	.003	.00	.141	.03	.012	.01	.295	.04*
married, no children	.005	.00	.051	.03	−.022	−.01	.00	.00	−.011	−.01	−.023	−.01	−.056	−.07**	−.049	−.02
R^2		.13		.14		.13		.22		.14		.06		.08		.04
intercept		1.94		1.63		1.80		1.24		1.60		1.58		1.56		1.56

*p < .05; **p < .01.

traditional family (*p* < .05), and *traditional marriage* (*p* < .01). Thus, *investment in production* did predict White women's attitudes toward sexuality and family issues but failed to predict Black women's attitudes. While investment in production was an important predictor of both Black (*b* = .105, β = .19) and White (*b* = .180, β = .40) women's attitudes toward *traditional marriage,* its effect for Whites was significantly and substantially stronger.

Analysis of the unstandardized regression coefficients for *investment in reproduction* also demonstrated race-specific effects. According to Pollack Petchesky's hypothesis, we would expect never-married women and divorced or separated women without children to be the most rejecting of culturally dominant views. The results for White women (see Table 2.2) showed, however, that except on the issue of *new morality* (*b* = .127), never-married women without children did not differ significantly from married women with children in their gender-role attitudes. Rather, it was separated or divorced women *with* children who were most likely to challenge the dominant culture's views of gender roles, differing positively from married women with children on six of the eight dimensions. Children were also a radicalizing force for White never-married women who, compared to their married counterparts with children, were more rejecting of the dominant culture's views on four dimensions. Among White women, the most conservative reproductive category was married women without children. They were similar to married women with children except that they were more likely to hold gender-stereotyped views of children's roles (*b* = −.050). The only unequivocal support for the hypothesis that lack of investment in reproduction is radicalizing was the finding that on three of the dimensions of gender-role attitudes, separated or divorced women with no children were more liberal than married women with children.

Among Blacks, never-married women without children were most rejecting of the dominant culture's views of gender roles. They differed significantly from their married counterparts with children on four of the eight dimensions: *traditional family* (*b* = .477), *traditional marriage* (*b* = .427), *public sphere* (*b* = .276), and *discrimination* (*b* = .346). One-tail t-tests comparing these coefficients with those for White women of the same reproductive category showed all four were significantly different (*p* < .001). Thus the data demonstrated a significant gap in the gender-role attitudes of Black never-married women without children and Black married women with children. However, there was no such gap between the same categories of White women. This finding is contrary to the prediction that investment in reproduction would have

TABLE 2.2 Regression of Gender-Role Attitudes on Socioeconomic Status, Age, and Investment in Production and Reproduction for White Women

	Women's Movement		New Morality		Traditional Family		Traditional Marriage		Public Sphere		Discrimination		Stereotyping of Children's Gender Roles		Female Gender Stereotyping	
	b	β	b	β	b	β	b	β	b	β	b	β	b	β	b	β
Socioeconomic status																
education	.051	.09**	.008	.02	.041	.07**	.029	.06**	.047	.16**	.028	.06**	.037	.16**	.061	.08**
family income	.020	.06**	.016	.05*	.015	.04	-.002	-.01	.009	.05*	.018	.07**	.014	.10**	.00	.00
Age	-.035	-.11**	-.068	-.23**	-.079	-.23**	-.035	-.13**	-.046	-.28**	-.021	-.09**	-.005	-.04	-.047	-.11**
Social location																
investment in production	.113	.21**	.063	.12**	.087	.15**	.180	.40**	.031	.11**	.044	.11**	.022	.10**	.034	.05*
never-married, with children	.319	.04	.418	.05**	.588	.06**	.303	.05*	-.061	-.01	.287	.04*	-.015	-.00	.064	.01
never-married, no children	.020	.01	.127	.06**	-.080	-.03	-.032	-.02	-.047	-.04	-.030	-.02	-.012	-.01	.025	-.01
separated or divorced, with children	.155	.06**	.158	.07**	.235	.08**	.200	.09**	.027	.02	.186	.10**	.077	.08**	.106	.03
separated or divorced, no children	.169	.03	.332	.06**	.205	.03	.216	.05*	-.024	-.01	.108	.02	.015	.01	.332	.04*
married, no children	.007	.00	.049	.02	-.049	-.02	-.014	-.01	-.026	-.02	-.015	-.01	-.050	-.06**	-.052	-.02
R^2		.12		.12		.12		.24		.16		.05		.08		.03
intercept		1.90		1.67		1.82		1.24		1.60		1.59		1.54		1.58

*$p < .05$; **$p < .01$.

TABLE 2.3 Regression of Gender-Role Attitudes on Socioeconomic Status, Age, and Investment in Production and Reproduction for Black Women

	Women's Movement		New Morality		Traditional Family		Traditional Marriage		Public Sphere		Discrimination		Stereotyping of Children's Gender Roles		Female Gender Stereotyping	
	b	β	b	β	b	β	b	β	b	β	b	β	b	β	b	β
Socioeconomic status																
education	.029	.07	.023	.04	.025	.04	.029	.06	.000	.00	.016	.03	.008	.03	.014	.02
family income	-.013	-.06	.061	.21**	.059	.18*	.006	.02	.019	.12	.023	.08	.008	.06	.029	.07
Age	-.024	-.11	-.069	-.24**	-.055	-.16*	-.006	-.02	-.003	-.02	.007	.03	.007	.05	-.031	-.07
Social location																
investment in production	.134	.31**	.011	.02	.017	.03	.105	.19**	.017	.05	.051	.09	.023	.08	.085	.10
never-married, with children	-.043	-.02	.391	.16**	.526	.18**	.096	.04	.151	.11	.255	.11	.067	.06	.159	.04
never-married, no children	-.200	-.12	.224	.11	.477	.20**	.427	.20**	.276	.23**	.346	.17*	.031	.03	.150	.05
separated or divorced, with children	-.078	-.05	-.068	-.04	.149	.07	.355	.19**	.257	.24**	.181	.10	-.006	-.01	.015	.01
separated or divorced, no children	-.143	-.06	.239	.07	.167	.04	.410	.12*	.107	.06	.250	.08	-.021	-.01	.179	.04
married, no children	-.082	-.06	.062	.04	.131	.06	.065	.04	.053	.05	-.075	-.04	-.13	-.15*	-.029	-.01
R^2		.13		.24		.18		.15		.11		.10		.05		.05
intercept		2.40		1.71		1.81		1.23		1.43		1.56		1.57		1.73

*$p < .05$; **$p < .01$.

a more conservative influence on the gender-role attitudes of White than Black women.

Similar to the results for Whites, children were also a radicalizing force for Black never-married and separated or divorced women. Never-married mothers were more likely than married mothers to reject the belief that sexual freedom ($b = .391$) causes the disintegration of family and society and to view family forms other than the nuclear one as legitimate ($b = .526$). While not significant, most probably due to the small sample size for Black women, never-married mothers were also more likely to believe women to be competent in the *public sphere* ($b = .151$) and to be discriminated against in this sphere ($b = .255$). One-tail t-tests found no significant differences in the slopes of Black and White women in this reproductive category. Hence, having children without being married appears to affect the gender-role attitudes of Black and White women in similar ways.

The results for separated and divorced Black women with children showed that on two dimensions, *public sphere* ($b = .257$) and *traditional marriage* ($b = .355$), they were more likely than their married counterparts to reject the dominant culture's views of gender roles. The gap in gender-role attitudes between separated and divorced mothers and married mothers was, however, greater for White than for Black women. One-tail t-tests showed that on two variables, *women's movement* ($p < .05$) and *new morality* ($p < .05$), the unstandardized regression coefficients of Black separated and divorced women with children and those of White women in the same reproductive category were significantly different. Hence, being separated or divorced and having children appears to be more radicalizing for White than for Black women.

Other sociodemographic variables also evidenced race-specific effects. In general, among both Blacks and Whites, older women were more accepting of culturally dominant views of gender-roles. However, for White women, *age* predicted acceptance of *traditional marriage* ($b = -.035$) and rejection of women in the *public sphere* ($b = -.046$), whereas for Black women, it did not ($b = -.006$ and $b = -.003$, respectively). The differences in these coefficients were significant at $p < .01$ and $p < .001$, respectively.

On indicators of SES, *education* and *income* were important predictors of White women's gender-role attitudes, while for Black women, *income* exerted a stronger influence. That is, White women with more education and higher income rejected culturally dominant views of women; Black women with greater income also did so. On the variables *public sphere* ($b = .047$) and *stereotyping of children's gender roles* ($b = .037$), *education* substantially influenced the attitudes of White women and had virtually no effect on those of Black women ($b = .000$ and $b = .008$, respectively). Differences in the unstandardized regression coefficients of Black and White women on these variables were significant at $p < .01$ and $p < .05$, respectively. On the other hand, one-tail t-tests showed that *income* had a more liberalizing impact on Black women's attitudes toward *new morality* ($p < .01$) and *traditional family* ($p < .05$) than it did on White women's.

SUMMARY AND DISCUSSION

This chapter has examined the commonalities and differences in the gender-role attitudes of Black and White women. It has done so from a perspective that views the intersection of race and gender as creating distinct collective historical experiences for Black and White women that have differentially shaped their definitions of womanhood and gender-role expectations. The pattern of similarities and differences found in the data are consistent with, and offer some insights into, the contradictory results of past research.

To summarize, when sociodemographic variables other than race were controlled, on five of the eight dimensions of gender-role attitudes, Black women were more rejecting of culturally dominant views than White women. This set of findings supports the contention of Ladner (1971), Thornton Dill (1979), Davis (1981), and others that Black women's long history of economic participation has given rise to definitions of womanhood at odds with those of the dominant culture. On the other hand, the findings of no difference between Black and White women on the variables *traditional marriage* and *public sphere* are consistent with the research of Ransford and Miller (1983) and suggest that as the objective statuses of Black and White women become similar, we can expect greater similarity in their gender-role attitudes. The fact that *age* was more strongly correlated with these gender-role attitudes for White than for Black women strengthens this interpretation. Thus, Black and White women's views of gender roles appear to be most similar on issues related to preference for wage labor and the ability and right of women to achieve in the public-sphere worlds of work and politics, which makes sense given that the greatest demographic shift for White women has been the dramatic increase in their labor-force participation (Hartmann 1983; Smith 1979).

The finding that Black women were more likely than White women to hold stereotypical views of girls' and boys' domestic roles accords with the results of Porter Gump (1975), Hermons (1980), and Randon

Hershey (1978), and indicates that on issues of "femininity" and "masculinity," Black women's longer history of economic activity does not translate into a greater propensity to challenge the dominant culture's views. Their attitudes may be due to the labeling of Black women as "matriarchs" and "sapphires" who rob their sons and men in general of their manhood. This accusation, thrown at Black women by both the White and Black community (Bond and Peery 1970; Moynihan 1965; Staples 1971), may generate a defensive acceptance of the normative structure that produced the cultural assault in the first place (Terrelonge 1984).

Taken as a whole, the above data are compatible with the conclusion that the commonalities and differences in Black and White women's gender-role attitudes are partly explicable in terms of the extent of historical overlap and divergence in their collective productive and reproductive experiences. However, the finding that Black women are more accepting than White women of stereotypical gender roles for children suggests the importance of the dominant culture in creating different experiences for Black and White women and, therefore, different responses to gender-role prescriptions.

In addition to examining the gender-role attitudes of Black and White women, this study also assessed the applicability to Black women of the hypothesis that investment in reproduction exerts a conservative influence on women's gender-role attitudes whereas investment in production has a radical impact. This hypothesis was expected to be less valid for Black than for White women, and in part the data supported this contention. While investment in market work did influence the gender-role attitudes of both racial groups, it had a more extensive and pronounced effect on those of White women. Particularly important in this regard was the lack of correlation between Black women's commitment to labor-force participation and their attitudes toward family structure and sexual freedom. These issues are hallmarks of the "pro-life" platform and the dimensions of gender-role attitudes that, according to Pollack Petchesky (1983), investment in production should best predict.

The cultural legacies bequeathed to Black and White women by virtue of their distinct productive and reproductive histories may account for these results. Since the majority of White women have only recently entered the paid labor force, the experience has meant a greater break with the dominant culture's views of gender roles, which may, therefore, have provoked a wider and stronger questioning of these views. Conversely, within Black culture, wage labor has been a normative and integral component of womanhood. Moreover, Black women's experience of family has been fundamentally structured by racial oppression. The investment-in-production hypothesis ignores this reality. Yet it is reasonable to posit that the dynamics of racial subordination are as important, if not more so, in shaping Black women's gender-role attitudes, particularly those concerning issues of family, as the dynamics of gender subordination. Several writers have contended that White feminist analyses have portrayed the family as the major site of women's oppression, ignoring the reality of Black women, who view the family as a refuge from the racism of the larger society and who find family work, in contrast to market work, affirming of their humanity (Davis 1981; Dill 1983; Hooks 1984; White 1984). Moreover, racial discrimination in the labor market has produced low-wage jobs and high levels of unemployment among Black men, creating a higher incidence of woman-headed families in the Black than in the White community. Black women's long experience with family forms at odds with those of the dominant culture may partially explain the failure of investment in production to predict their attitudes toward family structure. The finding that investment in production did not predict Black women's attitudes toward sexual freedom may have similar roots. Because racial subordination has made Black family life highly problematic, Black women are likely to view the disintegration of their family and community life more as a product of racism than of sexual freedom for women.

The thesis that investment in reproduction commits women to conservative views of gender roles received limited support. On the contrary, both Black and White married women without children were no more rejecting of culturally dominant views of gender roles than married women with children. The finding that White never-married women without children were basically as accepting of the dominant culture's definition of gender roles as married women with children also contradicts the investment-in-reproduction argument. Finally, the data clearly demonstrated that single parenting could be a radicalizing experience. Among both Blacks and Whites, separated, divorced, and never-married women with children were more likely to challenge culturally dominant views of women's roles than were married women without children.

The contention that investment in reproduction would have a more conservative impact on the gender-role attitudes of White than Black women received mixed support. It was contradicted by the finding that, among Blacks, never-married women without children were most likely to challenge culturally dominant views, whereas among Whites, never-married women without children were as accepting of these views as married women with children. It was supported, however, by the results that showed that the gender-role attitudes of White separated or divorced mothers diverged more dramatically from those of White married mothers than was the case for Blacks.

The cultural traditions into which Black and White women are socialized may account for these race-specific effects. Joseph (1981) found that the messages White daughters received from their mothers conveyed a more positive view of men and a more romanticized notion of marriage than those received by Black women. Other researchers have pointed out that Black women hold negative attitudes toward the reliability of men and are skeptical of the desirability and security of marriage (Hershey 1978; Ladner 1971). Thus, being a separated or divorced woman with children is more likely to contradict the cultural expectations of White than Black women and consequently can be expected to have a greater impact on their gender-role attitudes. Conversely, White never-married women without children and White married women with and without children are less likely to have experienced circumstances dramatically at odds with their cultural heritage, and this may explain the similarity in their gender-role attitudes. Finally, the results also suggest that Black women's greater rejection of the dominant culture's views of gender roles is weakened by being married and, to a lesser extent, by having been married.

Implications for Feminist Theory

The results summarized above have several implications for constructing feminist theory. The data showing that single parenting could have a radicalizing impact on the gender-role attitudes of both Black and White women underscore the theoretical insights to be gained by theorizing from the perspective of women of color. For example, underlying the contention that high fertility makes women more likely to adopt conservative views of gender is the assumption that having children creates dependency on a male breadwinner and, therefore, commits women to a system of values that protects and promotes this dependency. Had the reality of Black women's lives informed this analysis, a more nuanced understanding of the role of reproduction in structuring women's views of gender would have emerged. To begin with, both Ladner (1971) and Stack (1974) have documented that, to ensure the survival of themselves and their children, Black women have developed kin networks centered on the close domestic cooperation of adult women, leaving them less reliant on husband, father, or the traditional family structure. Further, several writers have pointed out that it is often Black women's high investment in reproduction, that is, their commitment to family and children, that has been the force behind their political activism (Gilkes 1979, 1986; Jones 1982; White 1985).

The results of this study also illuminate the fallacy of treating race and gender as separable or discrete phenomena structured by dynamics unique to each. The race-specific effects found in the data become comprehensible only by considering how the dynamics of race have differentially structured Black and White women's experience of gender. Moreover, by recognizing that gender is constitutively related to race, we are forced to consider the historical and sociocultural context of women's lives when theorizing about the forces that shape their gender identity and attitudes. In so doing, we avoid the tendency to treat gender in abstract and universalistic ways. We also avoid treating such phenomena as production and reproduction as though the meaning and impact they have on women's lives is independent of their race (and class) location. In conclusion, the findings of this study make clear that as long as women of color are excluded from our analyses, the result will be a partial and distorted understanding of the forces structuring women's experience of and attitudes toward gender.

Appendix

(1) *New morality* was a five-item scale that measured beliefs about the effects of sexual freedom and the extent of disagreement with the premise that women's sexual liberation is responsible for weakening the family and the moral breakdown of society. Respondents were asked whether they agreed or disagreed with the following statements concerning the effects of the new morality:

(1) It will make for better, more successful marriages.
(2) People will make better choices of marriage partners.
(3) Couples will have more honest relationships with each other.
(4) The institution of marriage will be weakened.
(5) The country's morals will break down.

Questions 1, 2, and 3 were coded: agree = 3; don't know = 2; and disagree = 1. Questions 4 and 5 were coded: disagree = 3; don't know = 2; and agree = 1. The *alpha* reliability coefficient for this scale was .78 for White women and .75 for Black women.

(2) *Traditional family* was a variable that consisted of three items indicating approval of unmarried adults having or adopting children. The questions were:

(1) There is no reason why single women shouldn't have children and raise them if they want to.
(2) There is no reason why single men or women shouldn't adopt children and raise them alone if they want to.
(3) It should be legal for adults to have children without getting married.

Agreement with these statements was coded 3, don't know 2, and disagreement 1. *Alpha* = .71 for Whites and .70 for Blacks.

(3) *Women's movement* was a three-item scale indicating support for the ERA, efforts to change the status of women, and the belief that women's roles should continue to change in the future. The questions were:

(1) The various state legislatures are now voting on an amendment to the United States Constitution that would assure women equal rights under the law. As I'm sure you know, there is a lot of controversy for and against this amendment. How do you personally feel about it—are you in favor (coded 3) of the Equal Rights Amendment or opposed to it (coded 1). (Have mixed feelings or don't know were coded 2.)

(2) There has been much talk recently about changing women's status in society today. On the whole, do you favor (coded 3) or oppose (coded 1) most of the efforts to strengthen and change women's status in society today. (Don't know was coded 2.)

(3) Do you think women's roles should continue to change in the years to come (coded 3), or that the change in women's roles has gone about as far as it should (coded 2), or that the change has already gone too far (coded 1). *Alpha* = .76 for Whites and .65 for Blacks.

(4) *Discrimination* was a variable composed of eight items that measured the belief that women are discriminated against in such areas as education, employment, obtaining credit, and obtaining positions of leadership. The questions were

Do you feel women are discriminated against or not in

(1) getting skilled-labor jobs
(2) obtaining top jobs in the professions
(3) obtaining top jobs in government
(4) obtaining executive positions in business
(5) getting a college education
(6) getting into graduate professional schools (medical schools, law schools, etc.)
(7) being given leadership responsibility in groups with both men and women
(8) obtaining loans, mortgages, charge accounts, in their own names

Discriminated against was coded 3, don't know 2, and not discriminated against 1. *Alpha* = .80 for Whites and .88 for Blacks.

(5) *Public sphere* was a five-item scale tapping the perception that women are as competent as men to perform the duties associated with such occupations as doctor, lawyer, mayor, pilot, or police officer. The question was

Women are entering all kinds of different fields of work these days. I'm going to name some different occupations. In each case, and assuming that you didn't know the person, would you tell me if you would have more confidence in a man in that situation (coded 1), or more confidence in a woman, or wouldn't it have any effect on your confidence whether it was a man or a woman (the latter two response categories were both coded 2). Would you have more confidence in a man or a woman as—

(1) mayor of your community
(2) a police officer
(3) a lawyer defending you in a suit someone brought against you
(4) a doctor treating you for a serious injury in a hospital emergency room
(5) a pilot on a commercial jet plane

Alpha = .80 for both Black and White women.

(6) *Traditional marriage* consisted of one variable coded such that 1 = a preference for a marital arrangement where the wife takes care of home and family and the husband is the provider, 2 = a preference for husband and wife sharing economic and familial responsibilities, and 3 = all other forms of living arrangements. The question was

> In today's society there are many different life-styles, and some that are acceptable today that weren't in the past. Regardless of what you may have done or plan to do with your life, and thinking just of what would give you personally the most satisfying and interesting life, which one of these different ways of life do you think would the best way of life?

(1) a traditional marriage with the husband assuming the responsibility for providing for the family and the wife running the house and taking care of the children
(2) a marriage where the husband and wife share responsibilities more—both work, both share homemaking and child responsibilities
(3) living with someone of the opposite sex, but not marrying
(4) remaining single and living alone
(5) remaining single and living with others of the same sex
(6) living in a big family of people with similar interests, in which some of the people are married and others are not

(7) *Stereotyping of children's gender-roles* consisted of nine items and measured the degree to which respondents rejected the notion that certain household chores are appropriate only for girls and others only for boys. The question was

> Now I'm going to name some household chores that children might be expected to do, and for each one would you tell me whether it is something only boys should be asked to do, or something only girls should be asked to do, or something either boys or girls should be asked to do?

(1) wash or dry dishes
(2) do their own laundry
(3) help clean the house
(4) mend their clothes
(5) help with cooking
(6) help with grocery shopping
(7) mow the lawn
(8) carry out the garbage
(9) help with small repairs

Items 1 through 6 were regarded as stereotypically girls' chores and coded 1 = something only girls should be asked to do and 2 = something only boys should be asked to do or something either boys or girls should be asked to do. Items 7, 8, and 9 were considered stereotypically boys' chores and coded 1 = only boys should be asked to do and 2 = something only girls should be asked to do or something either boys or girls should be asked to do. Alpha = .83 for White women and .87 for Black women.

(8) *Female gender stereotyping* indicated the extent to which traits such as independence and competitiveness as compared to traits such as gentleness or expressing emotions are the ones most admired in women. This variable was measured by counting the number of nonstereotypical adjectives (i.e., those coded stereotypically male) selected from a list in response to the question "Which 3 or 4 [of the following] qualities do you admire most in a woman?" The adjectives were

coded stereotypically Male	*coded stereotypically Female*	*coded neutral*
intelligence	gentleness	a sense of humor
self-control	being sensitive to others' feelings	sex appeal
frankness	being able to express emotions	[none]
independence	willingness to compromise	
being competitive		
leadership ability		
competence		

The reliability of the scale is undetermined.

NOTES

1. We capitalize *White* and *Black* to emphasize the point that race structures the experiences of both groups, albeit in different ways. Both racial privilege and racial oppression create categories of people with unique historical experiences that significantly shape their gender identity and attitudes.

2. I use the concept *dominant culture,* instead of *traditional,* with regard to views of gender for two reasons. First, several authors have pointed out that the traditional role of women in the dominant White culture has differed from the traditional role of women in Black culture (Dill 1979; Gump 1980; Hooks 1984). Thus, using the term dominant culture, as opposed to traditional, avoids false universalization. Second, the term dominant culture acknowledges the cultural hegemony of Whites in defining the traditional role of womankind.

REFERENCES

Almquist, E. 1979. "Black Women and the Pursuit of Equality." Pp. 430-50 in *Women: A Feminist Perspective,* edited by J. Freeman. Palo Alto, CA: Mayfield.

Bond, J. Carey, and P. Peery. 1970. "Is the Black Male Castrated?" Pp. 113-8 in *The Black Woman: An Anthology,* edited by T. Cade. New York: New American Library.

Cherlin, A., and P. Walters. 1981. "Trends in United States Men's and Women's Sex-Role Attitudes: 1972-1978." *American Sociological Review* 46:453-60.

Davis, A. 1981. *Women, Race and Class.* New York: Random House.

Dill, B. Thornton. 1979. "The Dialectics of Black Womanhood." *Signs: Journal of Women in Culture and Society* 4:535-55.

———. 1983. "Race, Class, and Gender: Prospects for an All-Inclusive Sisterhood." *Feminist Studies* 9:131-49.

Eisenstein, Z. R. 1981. *The Radical Future of Liberal Feminism.* New York: Longman.

Fulenwider, C. Knoche. 1980. *Feminism in American Politics.* New York: Praeger.

Gilkes, C. Townsend. 1979. "Black Women's Work as Deviance: Social Sources of Racial Antagonism Within Contemporary Feminism." Working Paper No. 66. Center for Research on Women, Wellesley College, Wellesley, MA.

———. 1986. "Approaches to Social Change: Racial-Ethnic Women's Community Work." Paper presented at the Summer Research Institute on Race and Gender, Memphis State University, Memphis, TN.

Gordon, M. 1964. *Assimilation in American Life.* New York: Oxford University Press.

Gump, J. Porter. 1975. "Comparative Analysis of Black Women's and White Women's Sex-Role Attitudes." *Journal of Consulting and Clinical Psychology* 43:858-63.

———. 1980. "Reality and Myth: Employment and Sex-Role Ideology in Black Women." Pp. 349-80 in *The Psychology of Women: Directions in Research,* edited by J. Sherman and F. L. Denmark. New York: Psychological Dimensions.

Hartmann, H. 1983. "Changes in Women's Economic and Family Roles in Post World War II United States." Paper presented at the Conference on Women and Structural Trans-formation: The Crises of Work and Family Life, Rutgers University, New Brunswick, NJ.

Hermons, W. M. 1980. "The Women's Liberation Movement: Understanding Black Women's Attitudes." Pp. 285-99 in *The Black Woman,* edited by L. Rogers-Rose. Beverly Hills, CA: Sage.

Hershey, M. Randon. 1978. "Racial Differences in Sex-Role Identities and Sex Stereo-typing: Evidence Against a Common Assumption." *Social Science Quarterly* 58:583-96.

Hooks, B. 1981. *Ain't I a Woman?* Boston: South End Press.

———. 1984. *Feminist Theory: From Margin to Center.* Boston: South End Press.

Jones, J. 1982. "My Mother Was Much of a Woman: Black Women, Work, and the Family Under Slavery." *Feminist Studies* 8:235-69.

Joseph, G. 1981. "Black Mothers and Daughters: Their Roles and Functions in American Society." Pp. 75-126 in *Common Differences,* by G. Joseph and J. Lewis. Garden City, NY: Doubleday Anchor.

King, M. C. 1975. "Oppression and Power: The Unique Status of the Black Woman in the American Political System." *Social Science Quarterly* 56:116-28.

Ladner, J. 1971. *Tomorrow's Tomorrow.* Garden City, NY: Doubleday.

Macke, A. Statham, P. Hudis, and D. Larrick. 1977. "Sex-Role Attitudes and Employment Among Women: A Dynamic Model of Change and Continuity." Paper prepared for the Secretary of Labor's Invitational Conference on the National Longitudinal Surveys of Mature Women, Washington, DC.

Malson, M. Ridley. 1983. "Black Women's Sex Roles: The Social Context for a New Ideology." *Journal of Social Issues* 39:101-13.

Mason, K. Oppenheim, J. L. Czajka, and S. Arber. 1976. "Change in U.S. Women's Sex-Role Attitudes, 1964-1974." *American Sociological Review* 81:573-96.

Moynihan, D. 1965. *The Negro Family: The Case for National Action.* Office of Policy Planning and Research, Department of Labor, Washington, DC: Government Printing Office.

Petchesky, R. Pollack. 1983. "Reproduction and Class Divisions Among Women." Pp. 221-41 in *Class, Race, and Sex: The Dynamics of Control,* edited by A. Swerdlow and H. Lessinger. Boston: G. K. Hall.

Ransford, E. H. and J. Miller. 1983. "Race, Sex and Feminist Outlooks." *American Journal of Sociology* 48:46-59.

Smith, A. and A. J. Stewart. 1983. "Approaches to Studying Racism and Sexism in Black Women's Lives." *Journal of Social Issues* 39:1-15.

Smith, R. E. 1979. "The Movement of Women into the Labor Force." Pp. 1-29 in *The Subtle Revolution,* edited by R. E. Smith. Washington, DC: Urban Institute.

Spitze, G. D. 1978. "Labor Force and Work Attitudes: A Longitudinal Test of the Role Hiatus Hypothesis. *Journal of Marriage and the Family* 40:471-9.

Stack, C. B. 1974. *All Our Kin.* New York: Harper & Row.

Staples, R. 1971. "The Myth of Black Matriarchy." Pp. 149-59 in *The Black Family: Essays and Studies,* edited by R. Staples. Belmont, CA: Wadsworth.

Terrelonge, P. 1984. "Feminist Consciousness and Black Women." Pp. 557-67 in *Women: A Feminist Perspective,* edited by J. Freeman. Palo Alto, CA: Mayfield.

Thorton, A., D. F. Alwin, and D. Camburn. 1983. "Causes and Consequences of Sex-Role Attitudes and Attitude Change." *American Sociological Review* 48:211-27.

────── and D. Freedman. 1979. "Changes in the Sex-Role Attitudes of Women, 1962-1977: Evidence from a Panel Study." *American Sociological Review* 44:831-42.

Weitzman, L. J. 1984. "Sex-Role Socialization: A Focus on Women." Pp. 157-237 in *Women: A Feminist Perspective,* edited by J. Freeman, Palo Alto, CA: Mayfield.

Welter, B. 1978. "The Cult of True Womanhood: 1820-1860." Pp. 313-33 in *The American Family in Social-Historical Perspective,* edited by M. Gordon. New York: St. Martin's.

White, D. Gray. 1985. *Ain't I a Woman?* New York: Norton.

White, E. F. 1984. "Listening to the Voices of Black Feminism." *Radical America* 18:7-25.

3. MASCULINITIES AND ATHLETIC CAREERS

MICHAEL A. MESSNER

The growth of women's studies and feminist gender studies has in recent years led to the emergence of a new men's studies (Brod 1987; Kimmel 1987). But just as feminist perspectives on women have been justifiably criticized for falsely universalizing the lives and issues of White, middle-class, U.S. women (Hooks 1984; Zinn, Cannon, Higginbotham, and Dill 1986), so, too, men's studies has tended to focus on the lives of relatively privileged men. As Brod (1983-84) points out in an insightful critique of the middle-class basis and bias of the men's movement, if men's studies is to be relevant to minority and working-class men, less emphasis must be placed on personal life-style transformations, and more emphasis must be placed on developing a structural critique of social institutions. Although some institutional analysis has begun in men's studies, very little critical scrutiny has been focused on that very masculine institution, organized sports (Messner 1985; Sabo 1985; Sabo and Runfola 1980). Not only is the institution of sports an ideal place to study men and masculinity, but careful analysis would make it impossible to ignore the realities of race and class differences.

In the early 1970s, Edwards (1971, 1973) debunked the myth that the predominance of Blacks in sports to which they have access signaled an end to institutionalized racism. It is now widely accepted in sports sociology that social institutions such as the media, education, the economy, and (a more recent and controversial addition to the list) the Black family itself all serve to systematically channel disproportionately large numbers of young Black men into football, basketball, boxing, and baseball, where they are subsequently "stacked" into low-prestige and high-risk positions, exploited for their skills, and, finally, when their bodies are used up, excreted from organized athletics at a young age with no transferable skills with which to compete in the labor market (Edwards 1984; Eitzen and Purdy 1986; Eitzen and Yetman 1977).

While there are racial differences in involvement in sports, class, age, and educational differences seem more significant. Rudman's (1986) initial analysis revealed profound differences between Whites' and

Blacks' orientations to sports. Blacks were found to be more likely than Whites to view sports favorably, to incorporate sports into their daily lives, and to be affected by the outcome of sporting events. However, when age, education, and social class were factored into the analysis, Rudman found that race did not explain Whites' and Blacks' different orientations. Blacks' affinity to sports is best explained by their tendency to be clustered disproportionately in lower-income groups.

The 1980s has ushered in what Wellman (1986, p. 43) calls a "new political linguistics of race," which emphasize cultural rather than structural causes (and solutions) to the problems faced by Black communities. The advocates of the cultural perspective believe that the high value placed on sports by black communities has led to the development of unrealistic hopes in millions of Black youths. They appeal to family and community to bolster other choices based upon a more rational assessment of "reality." Visible Black role models in many other professions now exist, they say, and there is ample evidence to prove that sports careers are, at best, a bad gamble.

Critics of the cultural perspective have condemned it as conservative and victim blaming. But it can also be seen as a response to the view of Black athletes as little more than unreflexive dupes of an all-powerful system, which ignores the importance of agency. Gruneau (1983) has argued that sports must be examined within a theory that views human beings as active subjects who are operating within historically constituted structural constraints. Gruneau's reflexive theory rejects the simplistic views of sports as either a realm of absolute oppression or an arena of absolute freedom and spontaneity. Instead, he argues, it is necessary to construct an understanding of how and why participants themselves actively make choices and construct and define meaning and a sense of identity within the institutions in which they find themselves.

None of these perspectives consider the ways that gender shapes men's definitions of meaning and choices. Within the sociology of sports, gender as a process that interacts with race and class is usually ignored or taken for granted—except when *women* athletes are being studied. Attempting to come to grips with the experiences of Black men in general, and in organized sports in particular, sociologists have almost exclusively focused their analytic attention on the variable "Black," while uncritically taking "men" as a given. Hare and Hare (1984), for example, view masculinity as a biologically determined tendency to act as a provider and protector that for Black men is thwarted by socioeconomic and racist obstacles. Staples (1982) does view masculinity largely as a socially produced script, but he accepts this script as a given, preferring to focus on Black men's blocked access to masculine role fulfillment. These perspectives on masculinity fail to show how the male role itself, as it interacts with a constricted structure of opportunity, can contribute to locking Black men into destructive relationships and lifestyles (Franklin 1984; Majors 1986).

This chapter will examine the relationships among masculine identity, race, and social class by listening to the voices of former athletes. Then the similarities and differences in the choices and experiences of men from different racial and social class backgrounds will be discussed. Together, these choices and experiences help to construct what Connell (1987) calls "the gender order." Organized sports, it will be suggested, is a practice through which men's separation from and power over women is embodied and naturalized at the same time that hegemonic (White, heterosexual, professional-class) masculinity is clearly differentiated from marginalized and subordinated masculinities.

DESCRIPTION OF RESEARCH

Between 1983 and 1985, 30 open-ended, in-depth interviews were conducted with male former athletes. The purpose was to add a critical understanding of male gender identity to Levinson's (1978) conception of the "individual lifecourse"—specifically, to discover how masculinity develops and changes as a man interacts with the socially constructed world of organized sports. Most of the men interviewed had played the U.S. "major sports"—football, basketball, baseball, track. At the time of the interview, each had been retired from playing organized sports for at least 5 years. Their ages ranged from 21 to 48, with a median age of 33. Fourteen were Black, 14 were White, and 2 were Hispanic. Fifteen of the 16 Black and Hispanic men had come from poor or working-class families, whereas the majority (9 of 14) of the White men had come from middle-class or professional families. Twelve had played organized sports through high school, 11 through college, and 7 had been professional athletes. All had at some time in their lives based their identities largely on their roles as athletes and could therefore be said to have had athletic careers.

MALE IDENTITY AND ORGANIZED SPORTS

Early studies of masculinity and sports argued that sports socializes boys to be men (Lever 1976; Schafer 1975). Here, boys learn cultural values and behaviors, such as competition, toughness, and winning at all costs, which are culturally valued aspects of masculinity. While offering important insights, these early studies of masculinity and sports suffered from the limiting assumptions of a gender-role theory that seems to assume that boys come to their first athletic experience as blank slates onto which the values of masculinity are imprinted. This perspective oversimplifies a complex reality. In fact, young boys bring an already gendered identity to their first sports experiences, an identity that is struggling to work through the developmental task of individuation (Chodorow 1978; Gilligan 1982). Yet, as Benjamin (1988) has argued, individuation is accomplished, paradoxically, only through relationships with other people in the social world. So, although the major task of masculinity is the development of a "positional identity" that clarifies the boundaries between self and other, this separation must be accomplished through some form of connection with others. For the men in this study, the rule-bound structure of organized sports became a context in which they struggled to construct a masculine positional identity.

All of the men in this study described the emotional salience of their earliest experiences in sports in terms of relationships with other males. It was not winning and victories that seemed important at first; it was something "fun" to do with fathers, older brothers, or uncles, and eventually with same-aged peers. As a man from a White, middle-class family said, "The most important thing was just being out there with the rest of the guys—being friends." A 32-year-old man from a poor Chicano family, whose mother had died when he was 9 years old, put it more succinctly:

> What I think sports did for me is it brought me into kind of an instant family. By being on a Little League team, or even just playing with kids in the neighborhood, it brought what I really wanted, which was some kind of closeness.

Although sports participation may have initially promised "some kind of closeness," by the ages of 9 or 10, the less skilled boys were already becoming alienated from—or weeded out of—the highly competitive and hierarchical system of organized sports. Those who did experience some early successes received recognition from adult males (especially fathers and older brothers) and held higher status among peers. As a result, they began to pour more and more of their energies into athletic participation. It was only after they learned that they would get recognition from other people for being a good athlete—indeed, that this attention was contingent upon *being a winner*—that performance and winning (the dominant values of organized sports) became extremely important. For some, this created pressures that served to lessen or eliminated the fun of athletic participation (Messner 1987a, 1987b).

Although feminist psychoanalytic and developmental theories of masculinity are helpful in explaining boys' early attraction to and motivations in organized sports, the imperatives of core gender identity do not fully determine the contours and directions of the life course. As Rubin (1985) and Levinson (1978) have pointed out, an understanding of the lives of men must take into account the processual nature of masculine identity as it unfolds through interaction between the internal (psychological ambivalence) and the external (social, historical, and institutional) contexts.

To examine the impact of the social contexts, the sample was divided into two comparison groups. In the first group were 10 men from higher-status backgrounds, primarily White, middle-class, and professional families. In the second group were 20 men from lower-status backgrounds, primarily minority, poor, and working-class families. Although the data offered evidence for the similarity of experiences and motivations of men from poor backgrounds, independent of race, anecdotal evidence was also found of a racial dynamic that operates independently of social class. However, the sample was not large enough to separate race and class, and so they were combined to make two status groups.

In discussing these two groups, I will focus mainly on the high school years. During this crucial period, the athletic role may become a master status for a young man, and he is beginning to make assessments and choices about his future. It is here that many young men make a major commitment to—or begin to back away from—athletic careers.

Men from Higher-Status Backgrounds

The boyhood dream of one day becoming a professional athlete—a dream shared by nearly all the men interviewed in this study—is rarely realized. The sports world is extremely hierarchical. The pyramid of sports careers narrows very rapidly as one climbs from high school, to college, to professional levels of competition (Edwards 1984; Harris and Eitzen 1978; Hill and Lowe 1978). In fact, the chances of attaining professional status in sports are approximately 4/100,000 for a White man, 2/100,000 for a Black man, and 3/1,000,000 for a Hispanic man in the United States (Leonard and Reyman 1988). For many young athletes, their dream ends early when coaches inform them that they are not big enough, strong enough, fast enough, or skilled enough to

compete at the higher levels. But six of the higher-status men interviewed for this study did not wait for coaches to weed them out.
They made conscious decisions in high school or in college to shift
their attentions elsewhere, usually toward educational and career goals.
Their decision not to pursue an athletic career appeared to them in
retrospect to be a rational decision based on the growing knowledge of
how very slim their chances were to be successful in the sports world.
For instance, a 28-year-old White graduate student said:

> By junior high I started to realize that I was a good player—maybe even
> one of the best in my community—but I realized that there were all these
> people all over the country and how few will get to play pro sports. By high
> school, I still dreamed of being a pro—I was a serious athlete, I played
> hard—but I knew it wasn't heading anywhere. I wasn't going to play pro
> ball.

A 32-year old White athletic director at a small private college had
been a successful college baseball player. Despite considerable attention from professional scouts, he had decided to forego a shot at a
baseball career and to enter graduate school to pursue a teaching
credential. As he explained this decision:

> At the time I think I saw baseball as pissing in the wind, really. I was
> married, I was 22 years old with a kid. I didn't want to spend 4 or 5 years in
> the minors with a family. And I could see I wasn't a superstar; so it wasn't
> really worth it. So I went to grad school. I thought that would be better
> for me.

Perhaps most striking was the story of a high school student body
president and top-notch student who was also "Mr. Everything" in
sports. He was named captain of his basketball, baseball, and football
teams and achieved All-League honors in each sport. This young White
man from a middle-class family received attention from the press and
praise from his community and peers for his athletic accomplishments,
as well as several offers of athletic scholarships from universities. But
by the time he completed high school, he had already decided to quit
playing organized sports. As he said:

> I think in my own mind I kind of downgraded the stardom thing. I thought
> that was small potatoes. And sure, that's nice in high school and all that,
> but on a broad scale, I didn't think it amounted to all that much. So I decided
> that my goal's to be a dentist, as soon as I can.

In his sophomore year of college, the basketball coach nearly persuaded him to go out for the team, but eventually he decided against it:

> I thought, so what if I can spend two years playing basketball? I'm not going to be a basketball player forever and I might jeopardize my chances of getting into dental school if I play.

He finished college in three years, completed dental school and now, in his mid-30s, is again the epitome of the successful American man: a professional with a family, a home, and a membership in the local country club.

How and why do so many successful male athletes from higher-status backgrounds come to view sports careers as "pissing in the wind," or as "small potatoes"? How and why do they make this early assessment and choice to shift from sports toward educational and professional goals? The White, middle-class institutional context, with its emphasis on education and income, makes it clear to them that choices exist and that the pursuit of an athletic career is not a particularly good choice to make. Where young men once found sports to be a convenient institution within which to construct masculine status, the post-adolescent and young adult man from a higher-status background simply *transfers* these same strivings to other institutional contexts: education and careers.

For the higher-status men who had chosen to shift from athletic careers, sports remained important on two levels. First, having been a successful high school or college athlete enhances one's adult status among other men in the community—but only as a badge of masculinity that is *added* to his professional status. In fact, several men in professions chose to be interviewed in their offices, where they publicly displayed the trophies and plaques that attested to their earlier athletic accomplishments. Their high school and college athletic careers may have appeared to them as "small potatoes," but many successful men speak of their earlier status as athletes as having "opened doors" for them in their present professions and in community affairs. Similarly, Farr's (1988) research on "Good Old Boys Sociability Groups" shows how sports, as part of the glue of masculine culture, continues to facilitate "dominance bonding" among privileged men long after active sports careers end. The college-educated, career-successful men in Farr's study rarely express overtly sexist, racist, or classist attitudes; in fact, in their relationships with women, they "often engage in expressive intimacies" and "make fun of exaggerated 'machismo' " (p. 276). But although they outwardly conform more to what Pleck (1982) calls "the modern male role," their informal relationships within their sociability groups, in effect, affirm their own gender and class status by constructing and clarifying the boundaries between themselves and women and lower-status men. This dominance bonding is based largely on ritual forms of sociability (camaraderie, competition), "the superiority of which was first affirmed in the exclusionary play activities of young boys in groups" (Farr 1988, p. 265).

In addition to contributing to dominance bonding among higher-status adult men, sports remains salient in terms of the ideology of gender relations. Most men continued to watch, talk about, and identify with sports long after their own disengagement from athletic careers. Sports as a mediated spectacle provides an important context in which traditional conceptions of masculine superiority—conceptions recently contested by women—are shored up. As a 32-year-old White professional-class man said of one of the most feared professional football players today:

> A woman can do the same job as I can do—maybe even be my boss. But I'll be *damned* if she can go out on the football field and take a hit from Ronnie Lott.

Violent sports as spectacle provide linkages among men in the project of the domination of women, while at the same time helping to construct and clarify differences among various masculinities. The statement above is a clear identification with Ronnie Lott *as a man,* and the basis of the identification is the violent male body. As Connell (1987, p. 85) argues, sports is an important organizing institution for the embodiment of masculinity. Here, men's power over women becomes naturalized and linked to the social distribution of violence. Sports, as a practice, suppresses natural (sex) similarities, constructs differences, and then, largely through the media, weaves a structure of symbol and interpretation around these differences that naturalizes them (Hargreaves 1986, p. 112). It is also significant that the man who made the above statement about Ronnie Lott was quite aware that he (and perhaps 99 percent of the rest of the U.S. male population) was probably as incapable as most women of taking a "hit" from someone like Lott and living to tell of it. For middle-class men, the "tough guys" of the culture industry—the Rambos, the Ronnie Lotts who are fearsome "hitters," who "play hurt"—are the heroes who "prove" that "we men" are superior to women. At the same time, they play the role of the "primitive other," against whom higher-status men define themselves as "modern" and "civilized."

Sports, then, is important from boyhood through adulthood for men from higher-status backgrounds. But it is significant that by adolescence and early adulthood most of these young men have concluded that sports *careers* are not for them. Their middle-class cultural environment encourages them to decide to shift their masculine strivings in more "rational" directions: education and nonsports careers. Yet their previous sports participation continues to be very important to them in terms of constructing and validating their status within privileged male peer groups and within their chosen professional careers. And organized sports, as a public spectacle, is a crucial locus around which ideologies of male superiority over women, as well as higher-status men's superiority over lower-status men, are constructed and naturalized.

Men from Lower-Status Backgrounds

For the lower-status young men in this study, success in sports was not an added proof of masculinity; it was often their only hope of achieving public masculine status. A 34-year-old Black bus driver who had been a star athlete in three sports in high school had neither the grades nor the money to attend college, so he accepted an offer from the U.S. Marine Corps to play on their baseball team. He ended up in Vietnam, where a grenade blew four fingers off his pitching hand. In retrospect, he believed that his youthful focus on sports stardom and his concomitant lack of effort in academics made sense:

> You can go anywhere with athletics—you don't have to have brains. I mean, I didn't feel like I was gonna go out there and be a computer expert, or something that was gonna make a lot of money. The only thing I could do and live comfortably would be to play sports—just to get a contract—doesn't matter if you play second or third team in the pros, you're gonna make big bucks. That's all I wanted, a confirmed livelihood at the end of my ventures, and the only way I could do it would be through sports. So I tried. It failed, but that's what I tried.

Similar, and even more tragic, is the story of a 34-year-old Black man who is now serving a life term in prison. After a career-ending knee injury at the age of 20 abruptly ended what had appeared to be a certain road to professional football fame and fortune, he decided that he "could still be rich and famous" by robbing a bank. During his high school and college years, he said, he was nearly illiterate:

> I'd hardly ever go to classes and they'd give me Cs. My coaches taught some of the classes. And I felt, "So what? They *owe* me that! I'm an

athlete!" I thought that was what I was born to do—to play sports—and everybody understood that.

Are lower-status boys and young men simply duped into putting all their eggs into one basket? This study suggested that there was more than "hope for the future" operating here. There were also immediate psychological reasons that they chose to pursue athletic careers. By the high school years, class and ethnic inequalities had become glaringly obvious, especially for those who attended socioeconomically hetero-geneous schools. Cars, nice clothes, and other signs of status were often unavailable to these young men, and this contributed to a situation in which sports took on an expanded importance for them in terms of con-structing masculine identities and status. A White, 36-year-old man from a poor, single-parent family who later played professional baseball had been acutely aware of his low-class status in his high school:

> I had one pair of jeans, and I wore them every day. I was always afraid of what people thought of me—that this guy doesn't have anything, that he's wearing the same Levi's all the time, he's having to work in the cafeteria for his lunch. What's going on? I think that's what made me so shy. . . . But boy, when I got into sports, I let it all hang out—[laughs]—and maybe that's why I became so good, because I was frustrated, and when I got into that element, they gave me my uniform in football, basketball, and baseball, and I didn't have to worry about how I looked, because then it was *me* who was coming out, and not my clothes or whatever. And I think that was the drive.

Similarly, a 41-year-old Black man who had a 10-year professional football career described his insecurities as one of the few poor Blacks in a mostly White, middle-class school and his belief that sports was the one arena in which he could be judged solely on his merit:

> I came from a very poor family, and I was very sensitive about that in those days. When people would say things like "Look at him—he has dirty pants on," I'd think about it for a week. [But] I'd put my pants on and I'd go out on the football field with the intention that I'm gonna do a job. And if that calls on me to hurt you, I'm gonna do it. It's as simple as that. I demand respect just like everybody else.

"Respect" was what I heard over and over when talking with the men from lower-status backgrounds, especially Black men. I interpret this type of respect to be a crystallization of the masculine quest for recognition through public achievement, unfolding within a system of structured constraints due to class and race inequities. The institutional context of education (sometimes with the collusion of teachers and coaches) and the constricted structure of opportunity in the economy made the pursuit of athletic careers appear to be the most rational choices to these young men.

The same is not true of young lower-status women. Dunkle (1985) points out that from junior high school through adulthood, young Black men are far more likely to place high value on sports than are young Black women, who are more likely to value academic achievement. There appears to be a gender dynamic operating in adolescent male peer groups that contributes toward their valuing sports more highly than education. Franklin (1986, p. 161) has argued that many of the normative values of the Black male peer group (little respect for nonaggressive solutions to disputes, contempt for nonmaterial culture) contribute to the construction of Black men's views of desirable social positions, especially through education. In this study, a 42-year-old Black man who did succeed in beating the odds by using his athletic scholarship to get a college degree and eventually becoming a successful professional said:

> By junior high, you either got identified as an athlete, a thug, or a bookworm. It's very important to be seen as somebody who's capable in some area. And you *don't* want to be identified as a bookworm. I was very good with books, but I was kind of covert about it. I was a closet bookworm. But with sports, I was *somebody;* so I worked very hard at it.

For most young men from lower-status backgrounds, the poor quality of their schools, the attitudes of teachers and coaches, as well as the antieducation environment within their own male peer groups, made it extremely unlikely that they would be able to succeed as students. Sports, therefore, became *the* arena in which they attempted to "show their stuff." For these lower-status men, as Baca Zinn (1982) and Majors (1986) argued in their respective studies of Chicano men and Black men, when institutional resources that signify masculine status and control are absent, physical presence, personal style, and expressiveness take on increased importance. What Majors (1986, p. 6) calls "cool pose" is Black men's expressive, often aggressive, assertion of masculinity. This self-assertion often takes place within a social context in which the young man is quite aware of existing social inequities. As the Black bus driver, referred to above, said of his high school years:

See, the rich people use their money to do what they want to do. I use my ability. If you wanted to be around me, if you wanted to learn something about sports, I'd teach you. But you're gonna take me to lunch. You're gonna let me use your car. See what I'm saying? In high school I'd go where I wanted to go. I didn't have to be educated. I was well-respected. I'd go somewhere, and they'd say, "Hey, that's Mitch Harris,[1] yeah, that's a bad son of a bitch!"

Majors (1986) argues that although "cool pose" represents a creative survival technique within a hostile environment, the most likely long-term effect of this masculine posturing is educational and occupational dead ends. As a result, we can conclude, lower-status men's personal and peer-group responses to a constricted structure of opportunity—responses that are rooted, in part, in the developmental insecurities and ambivalences of masculinity—serve to lock many of these young men into limiting activities such as sports.

SUMMARY AND CONCLUSIONS

This research has suggested that, within a social context that is stratified by social class and by race, the choice to pursue—or not to pursue—an athletic career is explicable as an individual's rational assessment of the available means to achieve a respected masculine identity. For nearly all of the men from lower-status backgrounds, the status and respect that they received through sports was temporary; it did not translate into upward mobility. Nonetheless, a strategy of discouraging young Black boys and men from involvement in sports is probably doomed to fail, because it ignores the continued existence of structural constraints. Despite the increased number of Black role models in nonsports professions, employment opportunities for young Black men have actually deteriorated in the 1980s (Wilson and Neckerman 1986), and nonathletic opportunities in higher education have also declined. While Blacks constitute 14 percent of the college-aged (18-24 years) U.S. population, as a proportion of students in four-year colleges and universities, they have dropped to 8 percent. In contrast, by 1985, Black men constituted 49 percent of all college basketball players and 61 percent of basketball players in institutions that grant athletic scholarships (Berghorn, Yetman, and Hanna 1988). For young Black men, then, participation in organized sports appears to be more likely than their own efforts in nonathletic activities to get them to college.

But it would be a mistake to conclude that we simply need to breed socioeconomic conditions that make it possible for poor and minority men to mimic the "rational choices" of White, middle-class men. If we are to build an appropriate understanding of the lives of all men, we must critically analyze White middle-class masculinity, rather than uncritically taking it as a normative standard. To fail to do this would be to ignore the ways in which organized sports serves to construct and legitimate gender differences and inequalities among men and women.

Feminist scholars have demonstrated that organized sports gives men from all backgrounds a means of status enhancement that is not available to young women. Sports thus serves the interests of all men in helping to construct and legitimize their control of public life and their domination of women (Bryson 1987; Hall 1987; Theberge 1987). Yet recent empirical studies suggest that men's experiences within sports are not all of a piece. Brian Pronger's (1990) research suggests that gay men approach sports differently—with a sense of "irony"—than straight men do. And the interviews in this chapter suggest that, although sports are important for men from both higher- and lower-status backgrounds, there are crucial differences. In fact, it appears that the meaning that most men give to their athletic strivings has more to do with competing for status among men than with proving superiority over women. How can we explain this seeming contradiction between the feminist claim that sports links all men in the domination of women and the research findings that different groups of men relate to sports in very different ways?

The answer to this question lies in developing a means of conceptualizing the interrelationships between varying forms of domination and subordination. Marxist scholars of sports often falsely collapse everything into a class analysis; radical feminists often see gender domination as universally fundamental. Empirical examinations of sports, however, reveal complex and multilayered systems of inequality: Racial, class, gender, sexual preference, and age dynamics are all salient features of the athletic context. In examining this reality, Connell's (1987) concept of the "gender order" is useful. The gender order is a dynamic process that is constantly in a state of play. Moving beyond static gender-role theory and reductionist concepts of patriarchy that view men as an undifferentiated group that oppresses women, Connell argues that at any given historical moment, there are competing masculinities—some hegemonic, some marginalized, some stigmatized. Hegemonic masculinity (that definition of masculinity which is culturally ascendant) is constructed in relation to various subordinated masculinities as well as in relation to femininities. The project of men's domination of women may tie all men together, but men share very unequally in the fruits of this domination.

These are key insights in examining the contemporary meaning of sports. Utilizing the concept of the gender order, we can begin to conceptualize how hierarchies of race, class, age, and sexual preference among men help to construct and legitimize men's overall power and privilege over women. And how, for some Black, working-class men, or gay men, the false promise of sharing in the fruits of hegemonic masculinity often ties them into their marginalized and subordinate statuses within hierarchies of intermale dominance. For instance, Black men's development of what Majors (1986) calls "cool pose" within sports can be interpreted as an example of creative resistance to one form of social domination (racism); yet it also demonstrates the limits of an agency that adopts other forms of social domination (masculinity) as its vehicle. As Majors (1990) points out:

> Cool Pose demonstrates black males' potential to transcend oppressive conditions in order to express themselves *as men.* [Yet] it ultimately does not put black males in a position to live and work in more egalitarian ways with women, nor does it directly challenge male hierarchies. (p. 114)

Indeed, as Connell's (1990) analysis of an Australian "Iron Man" shows, the commercially successful, publicly acclaimed athlete may embody all that is valued in present cultural conceptions of hegemonic masculinity—physical strength, commercial success, supposed heterosexual virility. Yet higher-status men, although they admire the public image of the successful athlete, may also look down on him as a narrow, even atavistic, example of masculinity. For these higher-status men, their earlier sports successes are often status-enhancing and serve to link them with other men in ways that continue to exclude women. Their decisions not to pursue athletic careers are equally important signs of their status vis-à-vis other men. Future examinations of the contemporary meaning and importance of sports to men might take as a fruitful point of departure that athletic participation and sports as public spectacle serve to provide linkages among men in the project of the domination of women, while at the same time helping to construct and clarify differences and hierarchies among various masculinities.

NOTE

1. "Mitch Harris" is a pseudonym.

74   PRINCIPLES OF GENDER CONSTRUCTION

REFERENCES

Benjamin, J. 1988. *The Bonds of Love: Psychoanalysis, Feminism, and the Problem of Domination.* New York: Pantheon.

Berghorn, F. J., N. R. Yetman, and W. E. Hanna. 1988. "Racial Participation in Men's and Women's Intercollegiate Basketball: Continuity and Change, 1958-1985." *Sociology of Sport Journal* 5:107-24.

Brod, H. 1983-84. "Work Clothes and Leisure Suits: The Class Basis and Bias of the Men's Movement." *M: Gentle Men for Gender Justice* 11:10-12, 38-40.

Brod, H. (ed.). 1987. *The Making of Masculinities: The New Men's Studies.* Winchester, MA: Allen & Unwin.

Bryson, L. 1987. "Sport and the Maintenance of Masculine Hegemony." *Women's Studies International Forum* 10:349-60.

Chodorow, N. 1978. *The Reproduction of Mothering.* Berkeley: University of California Press.

Connell, R. W. 1987. *Gender and Power.* Stanford, CA: Stanford University Press.

———. 1990. "An Iron Man: The Body and Some Contradictions of Hegemonic Masculinity." Pp. 83-96 in *Sport, Men, and the Gender Order: Critical Feminist Perspectives,* edited by M. A. Messner and D. S. Sabo. Champaign, IL: Human Kinetics.

Dunkle, M. 1985. "Minority and Low-Income Girls and Young Women in Athletics." *Equal Play* 5(Spring-Summer):12-13.

Duquin, M. 1984. "Power and Authority: Moral Consensus and Conformity in Sport." *International Review for Sociology of Sport* 19:295-304.

Edwards, H. 1971. "The Myth of the Racially Superior Athlete." *The Black Scholar* 3(November).

———. 1973. *The Sociology of Sport.* Homewood, IL: Dorsey Press.

———. 1984. "The Collegiate Athletic Arms Race: Origins and Implications of the 'Rule 48' Controversy." *Journal of Sport and Social Issues* 8:4-22.

Eitzen, D. S., and D. A. Purdy. 1986. "The Academic Preparation and Achievement of Black and White College Athletes." *Journal of Sport and Social Issues* 10:15-29.

Eitzen, D. S., and N. B. Yetman. 1977. "Immune from Racism?" *Civil Rights Digest* 9:3-13.

Farr, K. A. 1988. "Dominance Bonding Through the Good Old Boys Sociability Group." *Sex Roles* 18:259-77.

Franklin, C. W. II. 1984. *The Changing Definition of Masculinity.* New York: Plenum.

———. 1986. "Surviving the Institutional Decimation of Black Males: Causes, Consequences, and Intervention." Pp. 155-70 in *The Making of Masculinities: The New Men's Studies,* edited by H. Brod. Winchester, MA: Allen & Unwin.

Gilligan, C. 1982. *In a Different Voice: Psychological Theory and Women's Development.* Cambridge, MA: Harvard University Press.

Gruneau, R. 1983. *Class, Sports, and Social Development.* Amherst: University of Massachusetts Press.

Hall, M. A. (ed.). 1987. "The Gendering of Sport, Leisure, and Physical Education." *Women's Studies International Forum* 10:361-474.

Hare, N., and J. Hare. 1984. *The Endangered Black Family: Coping with the Unisexualization and Coming Extinction of the Black Race.* San Francisco, CA: Black Think Tank.

Hargreaves, J. A. 1986. "Where's the Virtue? Where's the Grace? A Discussion of the Social Production of Gender Through Sport." *Theory, Culture and Society* 3:109-21.

Harris, D. S., and D. S. Eitzen. 1978. "The Consequences of Failure in Sport." *Urban Life* 7:177-88.

Hill, P., and B. Lowe. 1978. "The Inevitable Metathesis of the Retiring Athlete." *International Review of Sport Sociology* 9:5-29.

Hooks, B. 1984. *Feminist Theory: From Margin to Center.* Boston: South End Press.

Kimmel, M. S. (ed.). 1987. *Changing Men: New Directions in Research on Men and Masculinity.* Newbury Park, CA: Sage.

Leonard, W. M. II, and J. M. Reyman. 1988. "The Odds of Attaining Professional Athlete Status: Refining the Computations." *Sociology of Sport Journal* 5:162-69.

Lever, J. 1976. "Sex Differences in the Games Children Play." *Social Problems* 23: 478-87.

Levinson, D. J. 1978. *The Seasons of a Man's Life.* New York: Ballantine.

Majors, R. 1986. "Cool Pose: The Proud Signature of Black Survival." *Changing Men: Issues in Gender, Sex, and Politics* 17:5-6.

———. 1990. "Cool Pose: Black Masculinity in Sports." Pp. 109-114 in *Sport, Men, and the Gender Order: Critical Feminist Perspectives,* edited by M. A. Messner and D. S. Sabo. Champaign, IL: Human Kinetics.

Messner, M. A. 1985. "The Changing Meaning of Male Identity in the Lifecourse of the Athlete." *Arena Review* 9:31-60.

———. 1987a. "The Meaning of Success: The Athletic Experience and the Development of Male Identity." Pp. 193-209 in *The Making of Masculinities: The New Men's Studies,* edited by H. Brod. Winchester, MA: Allen & Unwin.

———. 1987b. "The Life of a Man's Seasons: Male Identity in the Lifecourse of the Athlete." Pp. 53-67 in *Changing Men: New Directions in Research on Men and Masculinity,* edited by M. S. Kimmel. Newbury Park, CA: Sage.

Pleck, J. H. 1982. *The Myth of Masculinity.* Cambridge: MIT Press.

Pronger, B. 1990. "Gay Jocks: A Phenomenology of Gay Men in Athletics." Pp. 141-52 in *Sport, Men, and the Gender Order: Critical Feminist Perspectives,* edited by M. A. Messner and D. S. Sabo. Champaign, IL: Human Kinetics.

Rubin, L. B. 1985. *Just Friends: The Role of Relationship in Our Lives.* New York: Harper & Row.

Rudman, W. J. 1986. "The Sport Mystique in Black Culture." *Sociology of Sport Journal* 3:305-19.

Sabo, D. 1985. "Sport, Patriarchy, and Male Identity: New Questions About Men and Sport." *Arena Review* 9:1-30.

——— and R. Runfola (eds.). 1980. *Jock: Sports and Male Identity.* Englewood Cliffs, NJ: Prentice-Hall.

Schafer, W. E. 1975. "Sport and Male Sex Role Socialization." *Sport Sociology Bulletin* 4:47-54.

Staples, R. 1982. *Black Masculinity.* San Francisco, CA: Black Scholar Press.

Theberge, N. 1987. "Sport and Women's Empowerment." *Women's Studies International Forum* 10:387-93.

Wellman, D. 1986. "The New Political Linguistics of Race." *Socialist Review* 87/88: 43-62.

Wilson, W. J., and K. M. Neckerman. 1986. "Poverty and Family Structure: The Widening Gap Between Evidence and Public Policy Issues." Pp. 232-59 in *Fighting Poverty,* edited by S. H. Danzinger and D. H. Weinberg. Cambridge, MA: Harvard University Press.

Zinn, M. Baca. 1982. "Chicano Men and Masculinity." *Journal of Ethnic Studies* 10: 29-44.

———, L. Weber Cannon, E. Higginbotham, and B. Thornton Dill. 1986. "The Costs of Exclusionary Practices in Women's Studies." *Signs: Journal of Women in Culture and Society* 11:290-303.

II.

Gender Construction in Family Life

The structure and functions of families and the roles of women and men in them are a perennial topic in feminist scholarship. By now, it is accepted knowledge that there is no such entity as "the family." As an institution, family and kinship have common features throughout the world, but in particular times and places, families are diverse.

A common principle of family and kinship is that they are a nexus of production and procreation. In prehistorical human development, Siskind (1978) argues, the gendered division of labor and kinship emerged together:

> The most obvious similarity among all groups that anthropologists have described as structured by kinship is a splitting of the labor process into two halves, male and female. . . . This common division of labor involves not only the actual labor but rights to resources, tools, and products. . . . [K]inship and marriage may be . . . understood as the necessary categories and essential relations involved in organizing production based on this division of labor between the sexes. (p. 861)

Once the mode of production divides the labor process between men and women, you need kinship to organize reciprocity and responsibility between women and men and between children and adults. Marriage then assigns which individual man and woman are in reciprocal productive relations, and also assigns which individual man and woman are responsible for raising which children (Lévi-Strauss 1971).

These relations may be reciprocal, but they are also characterized by degrees of inequality. Where women contribute heavily to the family economy, they have a higher status than they do in societies where men are the main breadwinners. According to Deniz Kandiyoti in Chapter 5, "Bargaining with Patriarchy," these differences in family patterns mean that women must engage in very different strategies to maintain their status in the family. This strategizing within a set of concrete restraints reveals and defines what she calls the patriarchal bargain. For women throughout the world, the concrete restraints are class, racial ethnic identities, historical and geographic locations. All of these structural variables shape "women's gendered subjectivity and determine the nature of gender ideology in different contexts," according to Kandiyoti.

Using women's experiences under two systems of domination by men, Kandiyoti illustrates how women can have more or less autonomy in the domestic sphere based on their position in the economy as well as on their husbands' class position. Any economic advantage strengthened their marital bargaining power both individually and as a communal group. This outcome is predicted by research on how women's contribution to family subsistence and control over resources affects their status in both non-industrial and industrialized societies (Blumberg 1978; Hendrix and Hossain 1988; Sacks 1979; Smith 1987; Tilly and Scott 1978). Similar reasoning has been used in trying to understand the choices of conservative women in the United States, particularly with regard to abortion (Luker 1984).

But what happens when the marital bargain isn't kept or fails? Weitzman (1985) and Gerstel (1988) have amply illustrated the consequences of divorce for women who seemed to have made good "bargains." In the United States, divorced middle-class wives do not have the resources to maintain a middle-class lifestyle because their own earning power is at the low working-class level. They experience a jarring sense of social dislocation because their attitudes and tastes have been shaped by life in the middle class (Grella 1990). Chesler (1986) has criticized the new, supposedly gender-neutral child custody decisions. Judges are beginning to favor men because of their higher earning capabilities. Chesler argues that once again men are asserting their rights of ownership of children as commodities and using them as weapons against women's attempts for independence.

Bernard (1972) first characterized the gender differences in marriage by talking of "his and her marriage"—women's and men's radically different expectations of and experiences with marriage and parenting. Women are largely responsible for child care and domestic labor, even though they may be working outside the home, whereas men do little within the home and are characterized as the "breadwinner" or "head of household." Hochschild calls women's work in the home "the second shift" (1989). However, with more and more dual-earning couples, due in large measure to shifts in the U.S. economy, Hochschild also sees a shift in the amount of domestic labor done by men. In fact, says Hochschild, "The happiest two-job marriages I saw were between men and women who did not load the former role of the housewife-mother onto the women and did not devalue it as one would a bygone 'peasant' way of life. They shared the role between them" (p. 270).

Brigham Nims, in Karen V. Hansen's chapter, " 'Helped Put in a Quilt': Men's Work and Male Intimacy in Nineteenth-Century New England," illustrates that even in mid-nineteenth century America, the dichotomy of separate spheres for men and women may not have been the only form for the familial division of labor. According to Nims's own diaries and letters, as well as evidence from family members and friends, Nims participated in and enjoyed what have been traditionally understood to be women's tasks, like quilting, cooking, ironing, and sewing. Nor was he stigmatized for doing so. In addition, contrary to some theories of gender differentiation in emotional relationships (Chodorow 1978), Nims maintained very close, intimate, and warm ties with his men friends. He did not seem fearful of connectedness or threatened by intimacy and displays of emotion.

Hansen demonstrates that we must be very careful not to character- ize the past by the present. Overlaying present social structures and assumptions about gender onto different historical periods can lead to misunderstandings and false universalizing, just as ethnocentrism can lead to false conclusions about the rightness or wrongness of present-day emotional, sexual, and family practices of women and men in cultures other than our own and even within our pluralistic society. Thus, Hansen points out, expressions of intimacy between men and between women in the previous century do not necessarily carry the same meanings as today. Homosexuality and heterosexuality as defini- tions of sexual identities did not exist until very recently (D'Emilio 1983; Foucault 1978). People did not think of their sexual practices as defining who they were, and they were not considered peculiar for the love and affection they exchanged with friends. In a still largely rural America, neighbors and friends were just as important as family.

In trying to account for the still strong expectations that women will do the mothering and the bulk of the child care in families as well as the housework, some feminists have drawn on the psychoanalytic tra- dition and object-relations theory (Benjamin 1988; Chodorow 1978; Dinnerstein 1976). They argue that as long as it is primarily women who mother, traditional gender roles and statuses will be internalized and reproduced through the psychological processes of the resolution of the oedipal crisis for boys and the continued attachment to and lack of differentiation from the mother for girls. However, they neglect signif- icant structural variables such as race, ethnicity, and class.

Middle- and upper-class lifestyles, as Maxine Baca Zinn shows in Chapter 6, "Family, Feminism, and Race in America," depend heavily on the productive labor of working-class women and men, especially those members of disadvantaged racial ethnic groups. In these communities, women's double day of work and men's meager earning power have necessitated a family structure where everyone who can work, does. Often, working-class racial ethnic men must leave their families to find work, and the women must pool resources to survive. As Baca Zinn argues, this matri-focal family structure and community sharing have been wrongly castigated as "deviant" or a "social problem" by researchers and policy-makers who have idealized the middle-class, male-earner, nuclear family household. What is more detrimental to family theory is that feminists have not broadened their view of "the family" to include historical and contemporary evidence of diversity in structure and roles.

Another aspect of family ignored in the ideal version is physical and sexual violence. Here, too, historical evidence shows that family violence can only be understood by examining the interplay of the economic situation and family structure of working-class families, the conflicting cultural attitudes and professional practices of middle-class social workers, and the survival techniques of beleaguered women (Gordon 1988). The continued increase in battered and abused women and children has forced feminists to examine and analyze the pervasive and systemic use of violence by men as endemic to this "society in which dominance and subordination are eroticized" (Bart, Miller, Moran, and Stanko 1989, p. 431). Family theorizing and analysis is incomplete if the fact of violence against women and children is not examined and accounted for.

Feminist theories of family and kinship need to weave together the common structural aspects that endure over time as well as transformations in their form and shape that create the possibilities for change in these social institutions. The persistence of seemingly oppressive aspects and forms of marriage, family, kinship networks, and sexual practices in the face of economic, technological, social, and political changes must be explained. At the same time, women's and men's expected and actual behavior and experiences of family and kinship, which may be very positive, may belie more negative critiques of institutional patterns. The next three chapters are part of the process of theorizing about the intersections of race, class, gender, and sexuality which go into the creation and maintenance of both the universal aspects as well as the historical particulars of what it is to be family.

REFERENCES

Bart, P. B., P. Y. Miller, E. Moran, and E. A. Stanko. 1989. "Guest Editors' Introduction," Special Issue on Violence. *Gender & Society* 3:431-6.

Benjamin, J. 1988. *The Bonds of Love.* New York: Pantheon.

Bernard, J. 1972. *The Future of Marriage.* New York: World.

Blumberg, R. Lesser. 1978. *Stratification: Socioeconomic and Sexual Inequality.* Dubuque, IA: William C. Brown.

Chesler, P. 1986. *Mothers on Trial: The Battle for Children and Custody.* New York: McGraw-Hill.

Chodorow, N. J. 1978. *The Reproduction of Mothering.* Berkeley, CA: University of California Press.

D'Emilio, J. 1983. "Capitalism and Gay Identity." Pp. 100-13 in *Powers of Desire,* edited by A. Snitow, C. Stansell and S. Thompson. New York: Monthly Review Press.

Dinnerstein, D. 1976. *The Mermaid and the Minotaur: Sexual Arrangements and Human Malaise.* New York: Harper & Row.

Foucault, M. 1978. *The History of Sexuality, Vol. 1: An Introduction.* New York: Vintage Books.

Gerstel, N. 1988. "Divorce, Gender, and Social Integration." *Gender & Society* 2:343-67.

Gordon, L. 1988. *Heroes of Their Own Lives: The Politics and History of Family Violence.* New York: Viking Penguin.

Grella, C. E. 1990. "Irreconcilable Differences: Women Defining Class After Divorce and Downward Mobility." *Gender & Society* 4:41-55.

Hendrix, L., and Z. Hossain. 1988. Women's Status and Mode of Production: A Cross-Cultural Test. *Signs: Journal of Women in Culture and Society* 13:437-53.

Hochschild, A. 1989. *The Second Shift: Working Parents and the Revolution at Home.* New York: Viking.

Lévi-Strauss, C. 1971. "The Family." Pp. 261-85 in *Man, Culture and Society,* edited by H. Shapiro. New York: Oxford University Press.

Luker, K. 1984. *Abortion and the Politics of Motherhood.* Berkeley, CA: University of California Press.

Sacks, K. 1979. *Sisters and Wives.* Urbana: University of Illinois Press.

Siskind, J. 1978. "Kinship and Mode of Production." *American Anthropologist* 80:860-71.

Smith, D. 1987. "Women's Inequality and the Family." Pp. 23-54 in *Families and Work,* edited by N. Gerstel and H. Engel Gross. Philadelphia: Temple University Press.

Tilly, L. A., and J. W. Scott. 1978. *Women, Work and Family.* New York: Holt, Rinehart, & Winston.

Weitzman, L. 1985. *The Divorce Revolution: The Unexpected Social and Economic Consequences for Women and Children in America.* New York: Free Press.

4. "HELPED PUT IN A QUILT": MEN'S WORK AND MALE INTIMACY IN NINETEENTH-CENTURY NEW ENGLAND

KAREN V. HANSEN

Since the mid-1970s, students of women's history and the sociology of gender have attempted to explain the status of women in society by using a theory, originating in the nineteenth century, that divides society into men's and women's realms of influence and power, generally known as "separate spheres." Smith-Rosenberg (1985) and Cott (1977), among others, have demonstrated that gender-segregated work lives provided the fertile conditions for a separate "female world" where support and intimacy were shared with other women. The corollary to these findings is that all-male environments laid the foundations for men's friendships. For example, D'Emilio and Freedman (1988) and Pleck and Pleck (1980) argue that, like their female counterparts, men had the opportunity to socialize free from distractions from women, which enabled them to develop intimate relationships with each other. In theory, gender segregation led to enormous emotional distances between men and women, dramatically inhibiting intimacy between them, and so for deep emotional relationships, they turned to a homosocial world. Although on the face of it, this perspective is compelling, one could reasonably argue the opposite: male culture, with its emphasis on competition, could reduce the possibility for intimate friendship of the female variety.

Embedded in this conceptualization of separate spheres are many assumptions about class status, appropriate behavior for women and men, the geographic boundaries of life, and the omnipotence of ideology. This chapter argues that overlapping and integrated work lives of women and men in a rural setting in nineteenth-century America provided a basis for intimacy between them, as well as allowing for intimacy between friends of the same gender. In particular, men were allowed to develop a full range of work skills and emotional expression and, as a result, were free to develop intimate caring relationships with other men. An all-male, antifemale environment was *not* a necessary precondition for male friendship, and same-gender friendships did not preclude between-gender emotional intimacy.

These new hypotheses prompt other questions: (1) Was there a gendered division of labor in most rural households in the nineteenth century, and if so, how did the separation of spheres affect men's personal lives? (2) In what ways did the ideology of domesticity influence men to observe gender boundaries and gendered social roles? (3) What was the nature of friendship for men who were artisans, day laborers, and farmers? Was there a men's "world of love and ritual" that paralleled that of women? How do we interpret sexual innuendoes between friends of the same sex, which today would be unhesitatingly labeled homosexual?

The data come from the diaries and letters of a man who lived in New Hampshire prior to the Civil War, and are part of a larger study of laboring men and women in antebellum New England.

THE CASE OF BRIGHAM NIMS

A somewhat cryptic diary entry, dated April 30, 1845, provides a few clues about the nature of everyday life in the mid-nineteenth century:

> Work about home helped put in a quilt and worked it. P.M.E. & F. Buckminster M. Stebbins A. & M. Davis E. & A. & L. Towns quilted. Filled the Leach with Ashes &e.[1]

The diarist did household chores, sewed, and quilted in the company of others. The eight fellow quilters were neighbors and friends. The leach was probably used for making lye and soap. Because the division of labor between men and women in the mid-nineteenth century is typically assumed to be circumscribed by household boundaries, the casual reader would attribute these activities—housework, sewing, a quilting bee—to a woman.

Yet the diarist is a man, Brigham Nims, a 34-year-old citizen of Roxbury, New Hampshire, who lived on his family's farm virtually all his life, taught school, served as a town selectman, and died a respected man in his community. He was born in 1811 to farmers Matthew and Lucy Nims; he lived and died on the family homestead. Nims was the fourth son in a family of six boys and two girls—the girls were both younger than he. He married in 1853 at age 42, a late marriage but not unusually so. Roxbury was incorporated in 1812, claimed 366 residents in 1820, and thereafter declined. Nearby Keene (population 3,392 in 1850), served as the more important marketing and cultural center (Griffin 1904).

Brigham Nims was typical of his era in many ways; he was "the common man," the good citizen of village life in New England. He worked seasonally as a teacher over a period of 19 years. As with most teachers in the 1830s and 1840s, he had other jobs as well because teaching kept him busy only 16 weeks of the year and paid low wages.[2] To supplement his income, he was intermittently employed as a clerk in his brother Reuel's store, as an itinerant tailor (living at people's homes while he sewed for them), as a blacksmith and carpenter, as a stone splitter in the farm's rock quarry, as a farm day laborer, and most important, as a farmer. Given his employment as both artisan and laborer, and the fluctuating social and economic status of each, Nims's class location is difficult to define. His situation was similar to many of those who fell in the broadly defined "middling class"—those who were above subsistence-level income, might own a house or farm, who before industrialization could not be accurately classified as working class, but who were much less privileged than middle-class professionals. After his father died, he held title to the family farm, which was valued at $1,800 in 1850, above the median property holdings of male household heads (Dublin 1979, p. 35).

Nims may have broken many stereotypes of nineteenth-century manhood in doing household work, but in spite of his apparent lack of conformity, he won the respect of his New Hampshire community. Very active in civic affairs, over the course of his life he was a town selectman, a representative to the general court, the town treasurer, a member of the school committee, and a school superintendent. His obituary referred to him as "a man of prominence":

> He was interested in every good work, was a man of integrity and industry, possessed a vigorous mind and body, and was strong in his convictions. In politics he was a staunch Republican. (Obituary, June 5, 1893)

As evidence of the admiration and fondness he engendered in the community, the obituary recounted his 75th birthday celebration, at which his neighbors and friends honored him with a black walnut writing desk and chair.

NIMS'S INTIMATE RELATIONSHIPS

In addition to the many volumes of diaries, Nims left a small collection of letters sent to him between 1832 and 1839, primarily from his friend, J. Foster Beal. The few clues to their relationship exist only in the letters. When Nims was 20, he made the acquaintance of Beal, who became a close confidant. The circumstances of their meeting in 1831 remain a mystery, but it was probably during the two years Nims worked in Boston in a box factory. Letters from Beal to Nims exist only for the years 1832-1834, and the last reference to Beal is in a letter from Nims to his sister Laura in 1839. Beal married in 1838 and had died by 1850. Nims began keeping a diary in 1840; in it he made no explicit mention of Beal, so it is not clear how long the friendship continued. However, the letters reveal a vital, loving friendship sustained in spite of physical distance (Nims was teaching in Roxbury and in Nelson, New Hampshire, and Beal was based in Boston).

The earliest letter reveals a rowdy joyfulness in their relationship, with a decidedly masculine physical component:

Dear friend Sir B Boston March 21st 1832

I received your letter by G Tuffs which I read with the greatest pleasure I rejoice to hear that you are in good health, and the rest of your friends I want to see you very much indeed to have a good box with you which you said you should like to have with me I think if you are as fat as I be we should puff and blow. (March 21, 1832, NHSA)

Beal's letter reflects a casual friendliness and conveys a sense of delight in the friendship. The physicality it refers to is jousting, organized play, and competitiveness—masculine expressions of affection (and sometimes attraction).

A letter two years later expresses a similar teasing camaraderie. Beal chides Nims for his successes and reminds him of his more humble origins. Although in jest, these comments have a hostile edge and reveal the importance of the shared class background and the potential threat to their relationship of the social and economic mobility of the early nineteenth century. At the same time, Beal reminds Nims of the affectionate time they spent together and his role in nursing Nims through an illness, and admonishes him for neglecting to write:

Well Brig:

I suppose you have got to be a school master, since you was in Boston, you need not be so stuck up (as jock Downing says) because you are tucked down in the least post of Nelson, I have been there myself, I guess you have forgot all about you being at Boston last Sept. when you was so sick, and I took care of you, doctored you up, even took you in the bed with myself; you will not do as much, as, to write me,—(December 17, 1834, NHSA)

To share a bed in nineteenth-century Boston was not uncommon; with the lack of space in most homes, visitors frequently shared beds with their hosts. What is striking, however, is the tender image of Beal nursing Nims, which challenges our conception of what men did.

The letters between Beal and Nims were not a literary exercise between elite men cleverly hinting at romance; they were written by a school teacher and box-factory hand, frequently punctuated with misspellings and grammatical errors, honestly discussing their friendship. In contrast, letters from Nims's brother Kendall were very matter-of-fact, without reference to times they spent together—good or bad—or to their relationship. While this coolness is not necessarily surprising, the two were close in age and theoretically could have been close friends.

Some passages in the Beal letters reflect the romantic tradition of the 1830s and are similar to the letters exchanged between women who were intimates:

> can not forget those happy hours [th]at we spent at G. Newcombs and the evening walks; but we are deprived of that privilege now we are separated for a time we cannot tell how long perhaps before our eyes behold each other in this world. (March 21, 1832, NHSA)

In fact, this passage, like Nims's diary entry, if not clearly attributed, could easily be read as written by a female hand.

In contrast, like Nims's letters to his brother, his prenuptial missives to Selina Susan Gould were starkly businesslike. Nims left behind a small collection of letters to and from her that includes several drafts of his proposal of marriage and the negotiations regarding wedding arrangements. They met for the first time less than a year before they married, and saw each other only a few times—once on a visit with Nims's brother Rufus and his wife, and once when she came to the Nims farm to work for a few days. Because their encounters had never remotely indicated romance, Selina was surprised to receive a letter broaching the subject of matrimony. In a courtship letter to Selina discussing the meaning of life-long commitments, Nims forewarned her that living with his mother was a condition of the marriage:

> You will excuse me if I should write more freely my mind, than the limited acquaintance would seem to justify, as was hinted in a line to you that my situation, being the house of the Family and care of my Mother is different

from most persons settling in life, and it is my wish that they should feel themselves at home when they are here and take all the comfort they can while I remain here, and should I ever be so fortunate as to have a companion to go through this life's thorny road with me, that she may be the one that will strive to make a pleasant & happy home to all. (August 1, 1853, NHHS)

Selina agreed to the terms of the marriage; they wed a month later, and she bore him three children. She died when the youngest was only four (in 1866), leaving Nims's mother to become, once again, the female head of the household.

Although it is difficult to reconstruct Nims's personality and character from the terse diary entries he left behind or from the local obituaries, he did leave an important clue in one prenuptial letter to Selina:

I know that my owne temper and disposition is not so easily governed as I would wish, and that has been one reason why I waited so long, is to have it grow [better] before I should attempt to live with another But as I grow no better there seems to be no other alternative than a *gentler hand* to smooth the path of life. (August 1, 1853, NHSA. Emphasis in the original)

His tone is very contractual and matter-of-fact, which may be attributable to a popular literary style for marriage proposals, as well as reflect attitudes toward marriage in general, which had not yet been affected by Victorian sentimentality. Despite their lack of familiarity and the absence of an intimate relationship, Nims appears to feel no compunction about his character failings, and forthrightly divulges them. He and his future wife shared no history of friendship, and the letters are formal and awkward. He wrote to Selina 20 years after he received letters from J. Foster Beal, and the "sentimental years" of the 1830s had passed. In the correspondence to Selina, Nims was writing to an acquaintance, a virtual stranger.

Beal was writing to an intimate friend. From limited evidence, it is difficult to sort out which is more important in coloring Nims's relationship to Selina—gender or lack of familiarity. The separate spheres argument would contend that men and women led emotionally separate lives and therefore we would expect them not to be intimate with one another—as peers or as marital partners.

Nims, however, had a relationship with another woman who figures prominently in his life: his sister Laura. There are a few letters to and from Laura in the 1830s, and numerous entries about her in Nims's diaries. The letters reveal a shared understanding, a knowledge of each other. In one letter in May of 1834 from school, Laura wrote: "Dear Brother I steal away a few moments to addss a friend" (NHSA). Other letters express joy in seeing him and hearing from him. As was not unusual for correspondents or brothers and sisters, Laura also was concerned, at least for a while, about Nims's eternal soul and his involvement with religion:

> Mr. Rawson sent me world by Mr. Newel that my Brother Brigham had obtained a hope in Christ. rejoiceing news indeed. I am verry glad to hear you have given your heart to Jesus. I hope you will persevere in duty, and not give away to the numerous temptations which surround us. It is school time, and I cannot write anymore now. Forget me not in your prayers that I may live more to the glory of God.
>
> From your unworthy
> Sister La M N. (May 21, 1834, NHSA)

Their correspondence suggests that, like other siblings in the nineteenth century (Atkins 1988), Nims did have an intimate relationship with a woman—his sister. Not surprisingly, the intimacy with Laura differs from that between Nims and Beal; however, Nims and Laura were constant companions and shared secrets. One letter in particular reveals Nims's trust in her; he closes with: "Foster stands laughing over my shoulder who can write. I am the same *do not expose this* B. Nims" (18 September 1839, NHSA, emphasis added). Before she married in 1845 at age 30, Laura and Nims were constant companions and at one point journeyed together to upstate New York to visit relatives. They shared the profession of school teaching and both made their base at the Nims homestead in Roxbury. When Laura married, Nims toured the countryside inviting guests to come to the wedding, as was a custom at the time (Rothman 1984). He even helped bake her wedding cake and afterward carefully recorded the recipe in his diary.[3]

NIMS AND THE GENDERED DIVISION OF LABOR

In her review of American household work practices over two centuries, Schwartz Cowan (1983) noted that men and women sewed, but different items. If the fabric was leather, for instance, it became the man's task. Although men were supposed to perform chores that required great strength, women did the wash and made soap, which required enormous physical stamina. In essence, there were traditions regarding the division of labor, but they lacked a consistent principle.

Faragher (1979) found that midwestern farms in the mid-nineteenth century had a fairly rigid division of labor, with little overlap between men's and women's work. The situation he researches is one of extreme hardship, and given the need for maximum adaptability on the frontier, the hard and fast rules he describes regarding the division of labor are not adequately explained. In contrast, Grey Osterud (1987) found that while men and women were responsible for specific tasks in Nanticoke Valley, New York, the division of labor was flexible, depending on a combination of choice and necessity.

Nims's work patterns were similar to those of Nanticoke Valley. However, over time, the types of chores he performed at home, or at least those he recorded in his diary, changed. As a young single man in the 1840s and early 1850s, he was responsible for many domestic chores. He routinely performed general household work, as well as farm chores:

> Fixt my cloths, Cleaned, Ironed, & mended, &c. (August 29, 1843, NHHS)
>
> Helped Mother Iron then mowed the oats. (August 12, 1853, NHHS)
>
> Washed and Ironed. (August 22, 1853, NHHS)

Nims had two younger sisters and an able-bodied mother. Despite the availability of female hands, Nims did household work by himself and with other women. The following example sounds very much like spring cleaning with hired help:

> Worked helping clean the square room Mrs. Towns & Aunt harriet helped scoured it pretty well went down and helped Kendall [raise] his big wheel about 2 o'clock staid about 2 hours. (May 25, 1850, NHHS)

Nims also cooked:

> stewed some Apple Sauce &e eve. pared apples &e. (November 15, 1850, NHHS)

Nims regularly engaged in sewing. It was temporarily his occupation:

> Staid at Barlets marking and cutting patterns till half past 3 then came home. (August 13, 1842, NHHS)
>
> Work on cloak till noon then went to Dakins to see about cutting pants came home cut out pants &e. (September 12, 1842, NHHS)

But it was also a pastime:

Staid about home till 11 oclock hemed handkerchiefs &e. (June 6, 1843, NHHS)

Staid about the home knit some. (November 27, 1843, NHHS)

Men have been tailors for centuries, but it is not clear how commonly they went to live with those they served, as Nims did. Also, we do not know how often men used their tailoring skills to mend, knit, and sew for their own households, as there were no other tailors in the larger study, only female tailors' assistants.

Other men in the larger study wrote about doing laundry, caring for children, and attending quilting parties, but Nims was the only one to record sewing activities. A primary indicator of typicality was the matter-of-fact way that Nims recorded these activities.

A change in Nims's household work participation occurred after his father died in 1849, when Brigham was 38 years old. At this point, he became responsible for the farm as a whole, and in the house, he became more of a manager of household tasks than a participant. As before, he hired a constant stream of local women (mostly friends and neighbors) to work—Mary Phillip, Lucy Towns, Mrs. Davis, Mrs. Newcomb—but he performed fewer household chores with them. His marriage to Selina two years later did not bring a change corresponding to his new status as husband in addition to head of household. He continued to help occasionally with the wash and large-scale cooking tasks, such as shucking corn at harvest and paring apples to make cider. He nursed Selina through her illness following the birth of their first daughter, and later occasionally cared for the baby on Sundays when Selina went to church.

It is difficult, if not impossible, to determine whether the change in Nims's household involvement can be attributed to more rigid social rules or to his new status as property-owning household head and husband. It is possible that the cultural transition, "boundlessness to consolidation" (Higham 1969), touched Nims, causing him to reconsider his household activities in a new light. Alternatively and more likely, Nims's status as property owner and head of household altered his financial status and elevated him from a youth to a patriarch.

A SEPARATION OF SPHERES?

Nims needs to be situated within the social and economic processes that altered the fabric of life in antebellum New England. Industrial development, urbanization, and western expansion fundamentally reordered American society in the pre-Civil War period. All three resulted in massive shifts in population as marginal farm workers sought jobs in newly established shoe or textile factories, moved to the city to learn a trade, or migrated west to the ever-expanding frontier to homestead cheap land. Industrialization in particular had a tremendous impact on the organization of life. It resulted in movement of production out of the household, supposedly creating a separation between "home life" and "work life." But as long as a majority of Americans lived in rural areas through the nineteenth century (Bureau of the Census 1975), it was not uncommon for men and women to go back and forth between factory and farm employment and city and country living arrangements. So, for example, even though Nims lived most of his life on the farm in rural New Hampshire, he spent a few years in Boston working at a factory and living in a boarding house, witnessing firsthand the developing capitalist economic system and the emerging urban culture. On the farm, the preindustrial economy organized a different division of labor and social life for him.

To what extent either the city or the farm produced a strict separation of work and home is debatable. One school of thought, dominant in the mid-1970s, claims that the division of labor into paid production and unpaid reproduction created physically, emotionally, and culturally separate spheres of influence and activity for men and women. Some historians retrospectively interpreted the divide as absolute: "By definition the domestic sphere was closed off, hermetically sealed from the poisonous air of the world outside" (Halttunen 1982, p. 59). But in actuality, although the spheres were not equal, they were complementary and interdependent, and in some instances, boundaries were blurred. In the cities, men left the home to work in factories, offices, and government, leaving some women to care for children and attend exclusively to family needs. For other women, urban life meant poverty and the need to work as domestics or in the garment industry. On farms, the gendered division of labor was less clear. Some women went to work in the developing network of textile factories in the New England hinterland, while others did piecework in the proto-industrial "outwork" system, binding shoes, sewing buttons on cards, or making straw hats. Still other women, who were bound to the home and responsible for household chores, made and sold dairy products. Although men had more employment options out of the home and greater geographical mobility, little is said about what work they did *in* the home. The assumption is that men did no work in the home.

The prescriptive cultural manifestation of the separation of home and paid work was the "cult of true womanhood," propagated by middle-class reformers such as Catherine Beecher (Welter 1966). The burgeoning domestic advice and religious literature of the 1830s and 1840s encouraged homemakers to be "true women." That is, women were supposed to guard their sphere and rightful place—the home— with all the virtues imbued in a proper wife-mother: "piety, purity, submissiveness and domesticity" (Welter 1966, p. 152). While the ideology had a solid audience within the urban middle class, the extent to which it resonated with working-class, poor, and rural women is unclear. Although it failed to influence some people for economic, cultural, and geographic reasons, the message capitalized on the widespread fear and insecurity that resulted from geographic mobility and the shifting modes of production that marginalized large numbers of women workers (Ryan 1983, p. 118).

Much feminist research of the 1970s rests on the assumption of the nineteenth-century emergence of separate spheres for men and women (Cott 1977; Sklar 1973; Smith-Rosenberg 1985). Smith-Rosenberg (1985), for example, claimed that this extreme geographic and cultural separation led middle-class women to develop emotional relationships with those with whom they shared their everyday lives and cares: other women. She argued that women shared a common experience based on gender roles and biological rites of passage, and their relationships functioned as mutual support systems providing security, companionship, and self-esteem in a self-contained world that was whole and integral without men.

What did this separate life mean for men? Men were to be "the movers, the doers, the actors," those who provided for and protected the family (Welter 1966, p. 159). One source of prescriptive literature— marriage manuals of the mid-nineteenth century—identified the ideal husband as a "religious man, of good character and in excellent health" (Gordon 1980, p. 154). However, the thousands of prescriptive exegeses imploring women to use their feminine wiles to guide their husbands' and sons' hands imply that the male impulse, unmonitored by women, was sinful and neglectful of God. Although many treatises on women spoke of the virtue of women's submissiveness, Gordon found that only a minority of marriage manuals recommended that the husband be dominant in the relationship. The male version of the "true woman," according to Ryan (1981), was the self-made man. Rotundo (1988) similarly points to the critical transition to middle-class manhood that involved a strong commitment to a career, marriage, and a house of one's own: "The identity of a middle-class man was founded in independent action, cool detachment and sober responsibility" (p. 43).

Recent scholarship, particularly that which investigates the working class, challenges the notion that divisions were absolute (Blewett 1987;

Nicholson 1986; Pateman 1983; Pleck 1976; Stansell 1986). Ryan (1981) argues that, even for middle-class women, the boundaries were more fluid than domestic ideology purported, at least until after the Civil War. For example, in contrast to the demands of the cult of true womanhood, women's labors in the home were often a part of the local economy, and significant numbers of women were gainfully employed outside of the home. In addition, women were actively involved in the church, and in voluntary associations and charitable organizations (p. 191).

In her study of nineteenth-century rural New York, Osterud (1987) directly challenges the notion of a separate female culture. She finds extensive commingling of men and women—economically, socially, and emotionally. In the upstate New York community she studied, men were routinely involved in household chores, and women labored in the fields: "The degree to which they shared farm and household labor was exceeded only by the commonality of their social activities" (p. 89). In social life, women were involved in female networks of support, but they did not necessarily prefer them to relationships with men. "Rather," Osterud says, "they strove to create mutuality in their marriages, reciprocity in their performance of labor, and integration in their patterns of sociability" (pp. 91-2).

GENDERED INTIMACY

Did separate spheres create separate emotional worlds for men and for women? Smith-Rosenberg (1985) asserts that middle-class women had homosocial work lives and emotional circles. Dublin's study (1979) of New England mill workers demonstrates that women who left the farm to work were also in largely female worlds, owing to the gendered segregation of factories and boarding houses. D'Emilio and Freedman (1988) point to the all-male worlds of battlefields, the wild western frontier, and, later on, prisons, as environments where men congregated together and shared intimacy.

Smith-Rosenberg (1985) argues that the close bonds between women often became passionate and sometimes erotic. In their homogeneous world, even at great distances and in the context of heterosexual marriage, women professed their great love to each other in letters. Smith-Rosenberg convincingly argues that explicitly loving relationships between women as expressed in a literary form were seen as normal, natural, and acceptable by their families, neighbors, and society. However, her research has sparked a debate about the degree to

which women's affection for one another expressed the cultural roman-
ticism dominant in the early nineteenth century, reflected a unique
women's culture, or revealed a subterranean homosexual practice.
Smith-Rosenberg suggests that rather than try to label the behavior
normal or deviant, we should consider it a part of a sexual continuum
ranging from homosexual to heterosexual.

Men's friendships with men are less well-documented, or at least
until recently they have not been investigated from a gender perspective. The evidence is conclusive that elite men had romantic correspondence with other men in the nineteenth century. In foraging archives
for evidence of gay relationships, Katz (1976) unearthed a variety of
romantic letters written by male political and literary figures to other
men. For example, he cites a letter from Alexander Hamilton to John
Laurens, a friend and fellow soldier in South Carolina during the
American Revolution, written in April, 1779:

> Cold in my professions, warm in [my] friendships, I wish, my Dear
> Laurens, it m[ight] be in my power, by action rather than words, [to]
> convince you that I love you. I shall only tell you that 'till you bade us
> Adieu, I hardly knew the value you had taught my heart to set upon you.
> (p. 453)

In another letter, dated September 11, 1779, Hamilton writes:

> I acknowledge but one letter from you, since you left us, of the 14th of
> July which just arrived in time to appease a violent conflict between my
> friendship and my pride. I have written you five or six letters since you
> left Philadelphia and I should have written you more had you made proper
> return. But like a jealous lover, when I thought you slighted my caresses,
> my affection was alarmed and my vanity piqued. I had almost resolved
> to lavish no more of them upon you and to reject you as an inconstant
> and an ungrateful _____. But you have now disarmed my resentment and
> by a single mark of attention made up the quarrel. You must at least allow
> me a large stock of good nature. (p. 455)

Although the title and content of his book frame the letters as homo-
erotic, like Smith-Rosenberg, Katz rejected the impulse to label the
relationships homosexual:

> The term *homosexual*, with its emphasis on same-sex genital contact
> directed toward orgasm, is particularly inadequate as a means of encom-
> passing and understanding the historical variety of same-sex relations.

> Categorizing human relations as homosexual or heterosexual should be replaced by research aimed at revealing the multiple aspects of the particular relations under study. (p. 446)

Katz (1976) was careful to situate the letters within their historical context:

> For example the loving letters of Alexander Hamilton to John Laurens present the dilemma of interpreting to what extent his epistolary language is a mere formal, literary convention and to what extent it is an honest expression of emotion, referring to some deep felt, perhaps physical relation. (p. 451)

He says that the mere existence of these letters, so casually kept, "suggests more lenient social attitudes toward male-male intimacy" than we would expect of Victorian society, and than we find today (p. 451). In their assessment of the material, other historians range from a conviction that the language reflects only a spiritual love (Richards 1987) to a skeptical ambivalence about the innocence of the erotic messages (D'Emilio and Freedman 1988).

Similar to D'Emilio and Freedman (1988), the Plecks (1980) argue that, parallel to the experience of women, men's distinct social world allowed them to develop their own culture and "encouraged manly intimacy and affection, a love between equals, which was often lacking in sentiments toward the other sex" (p. 13). They point to the men-only spaces that nurtured male culture in the colonial and antebellum periods—lodges, clubs, lyceums (also attended by women, however), militia, fire departments, taverns, and voluntary associations that would have encouraged verbal rather than written affection. In her investigation of fraternal organizations of the nineteenth century, such as the Masons and Odd Fellows, Clawson (1986) argues that their core identity rested on the exclusion of women and gave men an opportunity "to construct and sustain the fraternal bond" (p. 41). But rather than creating an environment rife with male intimacy, Clawson states that "their effect was to promote solidarity among men, to reinforce men's separation from women, and thus to validate and facilitate the exercise of masculine power" (p. 41).

Rotundo's (1988) research on male friendships independent of organizations shows that middle-class men in the nineteenth century formed friendships throughout their lives, but established *intimate* relationships with men virtually only in the period between boyhood and manhood. He defines intimacy as "a sharing of innermost thoughts and secret emotions" (p. 1). During their youth, he notes that men psychologically break from their families and seek to establish themselves in the world, "a time when a young male had reached physical maturity but had not yet established the two identifying marks of middle-class manhood—a career and marriage" (p. 31). This was a time, according to Rotundo, that a young man passed "from the security and moral rectitude of women's sphere to the freedom and competitive rigor of men's sphere" (p. 32).

The male-male relationships ranged from casual to intimate to romantic (sometimes incorporating all three dimensions), and men's letters spoke of a physical component that may or may not have been explicitly sexual, but at least included hugs, kisses, and sleeping together. The casual relationship provided companionship for socializing, working, drinking, playing sports, and going to events. The intimate one included a sharing of secrets and a serious attachment that may or may not have included physical intimacy. For example, Rotundo likens the relationship between Daniel Webster and Hervey Bingham to a comfortable but happy marriage:

> Seven years' intimacy has made him dear to me; he is like a good old pen knife, the longer you have it the better it proves, and wears brighter till it wears out. (pp. 8-9)

Like the Hamilton-Laurens correspondence, James Blake's friendship with Wyck Vanderhoef ventures into romance and speaks of love:

> After an acquaintance of nearly three years I have chosen [Wyck] as my friend, and he has reciprocated; May he live long and happy, and may the tie of pure friendship which has been formed between us, never be severed, but by the hand of death . . . ever keep us as we now are in oneness, one life, one interest, one heart, one love. (p. 10)

Major methodological questions emerge from this nascent literature on male intimacy. How do scholars properly interpret this intimacy without distorting its meaning? How are they to evaluate its prevalence as a mode of communication and self-expression? Rotundo claims that physical expressions of affection—embracing, sharing a bed—carried no real stigma for the men in the nineteenth century, and in fact were culturally supported. Rotundo gives an example from the diary of James Blake about Wyck Vanderhoef:

> We retired early, but long was the time before our eyes were closed in slumber, for this was the last night we shall be together for the present, and our hearts were full of that true friendship which we could not find utterance by words, we laid our heads upon each other's bosom and wept, it may be unmanly to weep, but I care not, the spirit was touched. (p. 13)

As Rotundo notes, it was not the physical closeness that Blake felt embarrassed about, but the fact that he wept. My own research also shows that emotional self-control indicated manhood. When Francis Bennett, Jr. left his Gloucester home to work as a clerk in Boston, he wrote:

> I found it pretty hard to keep from crying on leaving the home of my childhood. But I had resolved to be as manly as possible about it. Mother would not say goodbye. (August 28, 1854, AAS)

Rotundo argues that manhood was not threatened by physical intimacy because the word *homosexual* was not in the nineteenth-century vocabulary, and the culture as a whole did not stigmatize the behavior. "The modern terms *homosexuality* and *heterosexuality* do not apply to an era that had not yet articulated these distinctions" (D'Emilio and Freedman 1988, p. 121, emphasis in the original). The concept of a sexual continuum, ranging from verbal endearment to genital play or intercourse, better explains same-sex relationships than do discrete categories.

Rotundo finds middle-class men's friendships similar to Smith-Rosenberg's female relationships in their social acceptability, daily content, and physical dimension. The primary difference he observes is that the male relationships were bound by the life cycle; they did not continue into married life, as did their female equivalents. Rotundo claims that the reason is that men had to enter the competitive marketplace, which affected their values and attitudes, making them more calculating and instrumental in dealing with other men. Although this explanation is convincing, in part, if taken to its logical conclusion, it would indicate that anyone involved in economic activity under capitalism was incapable of intimate relations. Granted, men's primary competitors in the nineteenth-century work world were other men, but not necessarily their close friends. What would cause men to generalize their cold aggressiveness toward competitors to close friends and cut themselves off from a realm of feeling that had great depth and meaning? Furthermore, the vast majority of research has investigated the middle and upper classes—primarily professionals, politicians, and literary men (Katz 1976; Mangan and Walvin 1987; Rotundo 1987,

1988). Can we assume that what was true of the elite was also true for laboring people? Studies that investigate working-class culture and leisure activities typically do not discuss intimacy (e.g., Peiss 1986; Rosenzweig 1983), so that we do not know if they, too, divided their world into friends and competitors.

CONCLUSION

There is no denying that Nims was an unusual man—the mere fact that he kept a diary on a regular basis for over 40 years makes him atypical. However, even if he was different from many of his contemporaries in his extensive involvement in housework, he was not in his relationship with his friend, and the community accepted and admired him. The question remains as to what degree his experience was shared by his fellow male citizens. Rather than focus on what may have been Nims's deviance, I suggest that we rethink our gender-typing of home and work activities and intimacy, and question the rigidity of boundaries between women's and men's lives, particularly for rural people.

The division of labor in the Nims household was not absolute. Nims was easily able to cross work boundaries and do "women's work." He may not have been typical in the amount of household work he did, but he was not self-conscious about it, suggesting that negative personal and social sanctions were few. Why was he able to do this? One explanation relates to the mode of production, as evidenced in the Osterud (1987) research. Self-employment as an artisan or farmer enabled involvement in the various kinds of activities—productive and maintenance—that took place in the household. When production was in the home, boundaries between paid and use-value work and between men's and women's work were fluid, if indeed they existed at all. Osterud claims the solidification of separate spheres for men and women applied only to the urban middle class, where the distinction between work and home life was more pronounced, because capitalism and industrialism had taken greater hold over the organization of work.

A second possible explanation is that prescriptive literature did not capture the range of lived behavior. It might have set standards for debate, but it did not always have substantial influence on how people lived their lives. Our reliance on prescriptive literature for studying history, in the form of magazines, how-to books, and published sermons, has distorted our perceptions of lived behavior. Diaries such as Nims's indicate that prescriptions were not as hard and fast as contemporary historians have implied. The ideology of true womanhood and the separation of spheres may not have reached or affected the New

England hinterlands until much later than it did urban centers, and not in the same degree. An alternative method of evaluating the ideology in the prescriptive literature is to consider it as a way of trying to instill order in a chaotic world that was economically, socially, and politically in flux.

A third explanation returns us to the issue of need. The "need" argument is that poor people wanted to, indeed aspired to, observe the ideal of domesticity, but because of their economic circumstances, they were unable to do so. For example, Blewett's (1987) research on shoe binders in New England found that when married women had the option to stop working, they did so. She concludes, "In developing and living the dual model of working girl and homebound wife, working women actively helped to create a sense of proper gender relationships within the new economic system and redefined the ideology of early nineteenth-century domesticity in accordance with their own class experience" (p. 428). In contrast, Scott and Tilly argue that daughters in nineteenth-century France worked outside the home because they were more expendable to the household than their mothers were (1975, p. 52). Their argument challenges the notion that working-class women embraced domesticity. Neither explanation, however, directly illuminates the case of Brigham Nims, but both are relevant. Nims lived on a small farm; it was necessary for him to earn wages off the farm, as did at least one brother and one sister. Blewett would argue that the Nims family could not afford to practice the cult of domesticity and therefore shaped the ideology to fit their circumstances. The logic applied to housework is less compelling. Other female hands were available to do housework, and although it was labor-intensive and required the help of many, conceivably Nims would not have *had* to do it. His brothers did not do housework, as far as we can tell from Nims's diaries. Yet Nims's participation did not seem to threaten the domesticity of the household, his masculinity, or the femininity of the women, at least not from his perspective. Perhaps he molded the ideology to his circumstance. Equally likely is that his family lived unhindered by ideas of proper men's and women's work. The ideology of separate spheres may have penetrated their geographical remoteness and disinterest, but it was not automatically adopted by all those exposed to it.

Women's ability to cross boundaries in the opposite direction remains an area for further investigation. Ryan (1981) claims the social and political boundaries did not rigidify until the Civil War, and much research has documented the blurring of boundaries prior to that point. Work boundaries were regularly ignored, particularly for young, single women (Blewett 1987; Dublin 1979). Not all occupations were open to them, but they did work in mills and factories in large numbers, as well as in domestic service and teaching. However, further research is necessary to determine whether men or women faced greater social resistance to engaging in work that was perceived to be for the opposite gender.

The overarching problem regarding the role of separate spheres remains. Industrialization did bring a reorganization of economic forces and social life. Although we can test the limits of its power, we cannot deny the widespread consequences it had. Although their exclusivity has been overstated, female networks existed and were central to many women's material and emotional lives. However, as the Nims case demonstrates, men participated in the domestic work of the rural family household and hence in the female world of work and social relations. To what degree they shared a relationship beyond coexistence needs to be explored further. Nims was a companion and confidant to his sister. To what degree was this typical? Osterud (1987) found similar patterns in rural households.

What is the relationship between the division of labor and intimacy? To what extent was same-gender commingling and closeness responsible for laying the groundwork for male-male intimacy? If separate spheres created conditions for men's friendship, how did it simultaneously allow for a division of labor that was *not* determined by gender? Nims's involvement with Beal may have been launched because of an all-male phase in his life cycle. He could have pursued the relationship with the consent and endorsement of his social world, or he may have quietly defied acceptable interpersonal conventions. But then so did many other men in the nineteenth century, as other historians have found. If the separation was observed as rigidly as it was advocated in prescriptive literature, then it is unlikely that Nims, in his male world, would have been involved in household chores and quilting with womenfolk. All of the historical clues indicate that he was a respected and beloved member of his community, *not* in spite of his deviance, but because he was just like everyone else.

The evidence in this chapter suggests a dramatic difference between the social worlds of those who lived in rural versus urban areas. The predominance of the effects of industrialization in the urban environment created a separation between work and family life for both the middle and working class. Even when women were employed outside the home, they worked largely in female environments. In contrast, while it may have also been affected by industrialization, the rural household continued to be the locus of work for both men and women, requiring a less absolute and gender-determined division of labor and facilitating the intermingling of social lives, giving men the freedom to be intimate with other men.

NOTES

1. Brigham Nims Diary, April 30, 1845, NHHS. The spelling, punctuation, and capitalization appear as they did in the original.
2. Nims's wages were $15 a month in 1850—twice as much as women teachers were paid. (For a discussion of the teaching profession, see Mattingly 1975.)
3. The recipe begins, "6 lbs Butter, 6 lbs Flour, 6 lbs Sugar, 4½ lbs Currants, 3 lbs Raisins, 6 lbs or 4½ dozen eggs with the Spices" (August 22, 1845, NHHS).

REFERENCES

Atkins, A. 1988. "Brothers, Sisters, and Shared Spheres: An Introduction to a Work in Progress." Paper presented at the Pacific Coast Branch of the American Historical Association.
Blewett, M. 1987. "Women Shoeworkers and Domestic Ideology: Rural Outwork in Early Nineteenth-Century Essex County." *New England Quarterly* 60:403-28.
Bureau of the Census. 1975. *Historical Statistics of the United States, Colonial Times to 1970.* Washington, DC: Author.
Clawson, M. A. 1986. "Nineteenth-Century Women's Auxiliaries and Fraternal Orders." *Signs: A Journal of Women in Culture and Society* 12:40-61.
Cott, N. 1977. *Bonds of Womanhood.* New Haven, CT: Yale University Press.
Cowan, R. Schwartz. 1983. *More Work for Mother: The Ironies of Household Technology from the Open Hearth to the Microwave.* New York: Basic Books.
D'Emilio, J., and E. Freedman. 1988. *Intimate Matters: A History of Sexuality in America.* New York: Harper & Row.
Dublin, T. 1979. *Women at Work.* New York: Columbia University Press.
Faragher, J. M. 1979. *Women and Men on the Overland Trail.* New Haven, CT: Yale University Press.
Gordon, M. 1980. "The Ideal Husband as Depicted in the Nineteenth-Century Marriage Manual." Pp. 145-57 in *The American Man,* edited by E. Pleck and J. Pleck. Englewood Cliffs, NJ: Prentice-Hall.
Griffin, S. G. 1904. *History of the Town of Keene.* Keene, NH: Sentinel Printing Co.
Halttunen, K. 1982. *Confidence Men and Painted Women: A Study of Middle-Class Culture in America, 1830-1870.* New Haven, CT: Yale University Press.
Higham, J. 1969. *From Boundlessness to Consolidation: The Transformation of American Culture, 1848-1860.* Ann Arbor, MI: William L. Clements Library.
Katz, J. 1976. *Gay American History.* New York: Harper & Row.
Mangan, J. A., and J. Walvin (eds.). 1987. *Manliness and Morality.* New York: St. Martin's Press.
Mattingly, P. 1975. *The Classless Profession.* New York: New York University Press.
Nicholson, L. 1986. *Gender and History: The Limits of Social Theory in the Age of the Family.* New York: Columbia University Press.
Osterud, N. Grey. 1987. " 'She Helped Me Hay it as Good as a Man': Relations Among Women and Men in an Agricultural Community." Pp. 87-97 in *"To Toil the Livelong Day": America's Women at Work, 1780-1980,* edited by C. Groneman and M. B. Norton. Ithaca, NY: Cornell University Press.

Pateman, C. 1983. "Feminist Critiques of the Public/Private Dichotomy." Pp. 281-303 in *Public and Private in Social Life,* edited by S. Benn and G. Gaus. New York: St. Martin's Press.

Peiss, K. 1986. *Cheap Amusements: Working Women and Leisure in Turn-of-the-Century New York.* Philadelphia: Temple University Press.

Pleck, E. 1976. "Two Worlds in One: Work and Family." *Journal of Social History* 10:178-95.

———, and J. H. Pleck. 1980. *The American Man.* Englewood Cliffs, NJ: Prentice-Hall.

Richards, J. 1987. " 'Passing the Love of Women': Manly Love and Victorian Society." Pp. 92-122 in *Manliness and Morality: Middle-Class Masculinity in Britain and America, 1800-1940,* edited by J. A. Mangan and J. Walvin. New York: St. Martin's.

Rosenzweig, R. 1983. *Eight Hours for What We Will: Workers and Leisure in an Industrial City, 1870-1920.* New York: Cambridge University Press.

Rothman, E. K. 1984. *Hands and Hearts: A History of Courtship in America.* Cambridge, MA: Harvard University Press.

Rotundo, E. A. 1987. "Learning About Manhood: Gender Ideals and the Middle Class Family in Nineteenth-Century America." Pp. 35-51 in *Manliness and Morality: Middle-Class Masculinity in Britain and America, 1800-1940,* edited by J. A. Mangan and J. Walvin. New York: St. Martin's Press.

———. 1988. "Romantic Friendship: Male Intimacy and Middle-Class Youth in the Northern United States, 1800-1900." Unpublished manuscript, Andover, MA.

Ryan, M. 1981. *Cradle of the Middle Class: The Family in Oneida County, New York, 1790-1865.* New York: Cambridge University Press.

———. 1983. *Womanhood in America: From Colonial Times to the Present.* New York: Franklin Watts.

Scott, J. W., and L. A. Tilly. 1975. "Women's Work and the Family in Nineteenth-Century Europe." *Comparative Studies in Society and History* 17:36-64.

Sklar, K. K. 1973. *Catharine Beecher: A Study in American Domesticity.* New York: Norton.

Smith-Rosenberg, C. 1985. *Disorderly Conduct.* New York: Oxford University Press.

Stansell, C. 1986. *City of Women: Sex and Class in New York, 1789-1860.* New York: Knopf.

Welter, B. 1966. "The Cult of True Womanhood: 1820-1860." *American Quarterly* 18:159-74.

ARCHIVAL SOURCES

AAS American Antiquarian Society, Worcester, MA. Francis Bennett, Jr. Diary.
NHHS New Hampshire Historical Society, Concord, NH. Brigham Nims Diaries.
NHSA New Hampshire State Archives, Concord, NH: Roxbury Town Papers.

5. BARGAINING WITH PATRIARCHY

DENIZ KANDIYOTI

Of all the concepts generated by contemporary feminist theory, patriarchy is probably the most overused and, in some respects, the most undertheorized. This state of affairs is not due to neglect, since there is a substantial volume of writing on the question, but rather to the specific conditions of development of contemporary feminist usages of the term. While radical feminists encouraged a very liberal usage, to apply to virtually any form or instance of domination by men, socialist feminists have restricted themselves mainly to analyzing the relationships between patriarchy and class under capitalism. As a result, the term *patriarchy* often evokes an overly monolithic conception of domination by men, which is treated at a level of abstraction that obfuscates rather than reveals the intimate inner workings of culturally and historically distinct arrangements between the genders.

It is not my intention to provide a review of the theoretical debates around patriarchy (Barrett 1980; Beechey 1979; Delphy 1977; Eisenstein 1978; Hartmann 1981; McDonough and Harrison 1978; Mies 1986; Mitchell 1973; Young 1981). Instead, I would like to propose an important and relatively neglected point of entry for the identification of different forms of patriarchy through an analysis of women's strategies in dealing with them. I will argue that women strategize within a set of concrete constraints that reveal and define the blueprint of what I will term the *patriarchal bargain*[1] of any given society, which may exhibit variations according to class, caste, and ethnicity. These patriarchal bargains exert a powerful influence on the shaping of women's gendered subjectivity and determine the nature of gender ideology in different contexts. They also influence both the potential for and specific forms of women's active or passive resistance in the face of their oppression. Moreover, patriarchal bargains are not timeless or immutable entities, but are susceptible to historical transformations that open up new areas of struggle and renegotiation of the relations between women and men.

By way of illustration, I will contrast two systems of domination by men, rendered ideal-typical for the purposes of discussing their implications for women. I use these ideal types as heuristic devices that have the potential of being expanded and fleshed out with systematic, comparative, empirical content, although this chapter makes no pretense of providing anything beyond a mere sketch of possible variations. The two types are based on examples from sub-Saharan Africa, on the one hand, and the Middle East, South Asia, and East Asia on the other. My aim is to highlight a continuum ranging from less corporate forms of householding, involving the relative autonomy of mother-child units evidenced in sub-Saharan polygyny, to the more corporate male-headed entities prevalent in the regions identified by Caldwell (1978) as the "patriarchal belt." In the final section, I analyze the breakdown and transformation of patriarchal bargains and their relationship to women's consciousness and struggles.

AUTONOMY AND PROTEST:
SOME EXAMPLES FROM SUB-SAHARAN AFRICA

I had one of my purest experiences of culture shock in the process of reviewing the literature on women in agricultural development projects in sub-Saharan Africa (Kandiyoti 1985). Accustomed as I was to only one type of patriarchy (which I will describe in some detail later, under the rubric of classic patriarchy), I was ill prepared for what I found. The literature was rife with instances of women's resistance to attempts to lower the value of their labor and, more important, women's refusal to allow the total appropriation of their production by their husbands. Let me give some examples.

Wherever new agricultural schemes provided men with inputs and credit, and the assumption was made that as heads of household they would have access to their wives' unremunerated labor, problems seemed to develop. In the Mwea irrigated rice settlement in Kenya, where women were deprived of access to their own plots, their lack of alternatives and their total lack of control over men's earnings made life so intolerable to them that wives commonly deserted their husbands (Hanger and Moris 1973). In Gambia, in yet another rice-growing scheme, the irrigated land and credit were made available only to men, even though it was the women who traditionally grew rice in tidal swamps, and there was a long-standing practice of men and women cultivating their own crops and controlling the produce. Women's customary duties with respect to labor allocation to common and individual plots protected them from demands by their husbands that they provide free labor on men's irrigated rice fields. Men had to pay their wives wages or lend them an irrigated plot to have access to their labor. In the rainy season, when women had the alternative of growing their own swamp rice, they created a labor bottleneck for the men, who simply had to wait for the days women did not go to their own fields (Dey 1981).

In Conti's (1979) account of a supervised smallholder settlement project in Upper Volta, again, the men were provided with land and credit, leaving the women no independent resource base and a very inadequate infrastructure to carry out their daily household chores. The result was vocal protest and refusal to cooperate. Roberts (1989) similarly illustrates the strategies used by women to maximize their autonomy in the African context. Yoruba women in Nigeria, for instance, negotiate the terms of their farm-labor services to their husbands while they aim to devote more time and energy to the trading activities that will enable them to support themselves and ultimately give up such services. Hausa women, whose observance of Islamic seclusion reduces the demands husbands can make for their services, allocate their labor to trade, mainly the sale of ready-cooked foodstuffs.

In short, the insecurities of African polygyny for women are matched by areas of relative autonomy, which they clearly strive to maximize. Men's responsibility for their wives' support, although normative in some instances, is in actual fact relatively low. Typically, it is the woman who is primarily responsible for her own and her children's upkeep, including meeting the costs of their education, with variable degrees of assistance from her husband. Women have very little to gain and a lot to lose by becoming totally dependent on husbands; hence they quite rightly resist projects that tilt the delicate balance they strive to maintain. In their protests, wives are safeguarding already existing spheres of autonomy.

Documentation of a genuine trade-off between women's autonomy and men's responsibility for their wives can be found in some historical examples. Mann (1985) suggests that despite the wifely dependence entailed by Christian marriage, Yoruba women in Lagos accepted it with enthusiasm because of the greater protection they thought they would receive. Conversely, men in contemporary Zambia resist the more modern ordinance marriage, as opposed to customary marriage, because it burdens them with greater obligations for their wives and children (Munachonga 1982). A form of conjugal union in which the partners may openly negotiate the exchange of sexual and labor services seems to lay the groundwork for more explicit forms of bargaining. Commenting on Ashanti marriage, Abu (1983, p. 156) singles out as its most striking feature "the separateness of spouses' resources and activities and the overtness of the bargaining element in the relationship." Polygyny and, in this case, the continuing obligations of both men and women to their own kin do not foster a notion of the family or household as a corporate entity.

Clearly, there are important variations in African kinship systems with respect to marriage forms, residence, descent, and inheritance rules (Guyer and Peters 1987). These variations are grounded in complete cultural and historical processes, including different modes of incorporation of African societies into the world economy (Mbilinyi 1982; Murray 1987; S. Young 1977). Nonetheless, it is within a broadly defined Afro-Caribbean pattern that we find some of the clearest instances of noncorporateness of the conjugal family both in ideology and practice, a fact that informs marital and marketplace strategies for women. Works on historical transformations (for example, Etienne and Leacock 1980) suggests that colonization eroded the material basis for women's relative autonomy (such as usufructuary access to communal land or traditional craft production) without offering attenuating modifications in either marketplace or marital options. The more contemporary development projects discussed above also tend to assume or impose a male-headed corporate family model, which curtails women's options without opening up other avenues to security and well-being. The women perceive these changes, especially if they occur abruptly, as infractions that constitute a breach of their existing accommodations with the order dominated by men. Consequently, they openly resist them.

SUBSERVIENCE AND MANIPULATION:
WOMEN UNDER CLASSIC PATRIARCHY

These examples of women's open resistance stand in stark contrast to women's accommodations to the system I will call *classic patriarchy*. The clearest instance of classic patriarchy may be found in a geographical area that includes North Africa, the Muslim Middle East (including Turkey, Pakistan, and Iran), and South and East Asia (specifically, India and China).[2]

The key to the reproduction of classic patriarchy lies in the operations of the patrilocally extended household, which is also commonly associated with the reproduction of the peasantry in agrarian societies (E. Wolf 1966). Even though demographic and other constraints may have curtailed the numerical predominance of three-generational patrilocal households, there is little doubt that they represent a powerful cultural ideal. It is plausible that the emergence of the patriarchal extended family, which gives the senior man authority over everyone else, including younger men, is bound up in the incorporation and control of the family by the state (Ortner 1978), and in the transition from kin-based to tributary modes of surplus control (E. Wolf 1982). The implications of the patrilineal-patrilocal complex for women not only are remarkably uniform but also entail forms of control and subordination that cut across cultural and religious boundaries, such as those of Hinduism, Confucianism, and Islam.

Under classic patriarchy, girls are given away in marriage at a very young age into households headed by their husband's father. There, they are subordinate not only to all the men but also to the more senior women, especially their mother-in-law. The extent to which this represents a total break with their own kin group varies in relation to the degree of endogamy in marriage practices and different conceptions of honor. Among the Turks, there are lower rates of endogamy, and a husband is principally responsible for a woman's honor. Among the Arabs, there is much greater mutuality among affines, and a woman's natal family retains both an interest and a say in protecting their married daughter's honor (Meeker 1976). As a result, a Turkish woman's traditional position more closely resembles the status of the "stranger-bride" typical of prerevolutionary China than an Arab woman's position in the patriarchal household, which may be somewhat attenuated by endogamy and recourse to her natal kin.

Whether the prevalent marriage payment is dowry or bride-price, in classic patriarchy, women do not normally have any claim on their father's patrimony. Their dowries do not qualify as a form of premortem inheritance because they are transferred directly to the bridegroom's kin and do not take the form of productive property, such as land (Agarwal 1987; Sharma 1980). In Muslim communities, for a woman to press for her inheritance rights would be tantamount to losing her brothers' favor, her only recourse in case of severe ill-treatment by her husband or divorce. The young bride enters her husband's household as an effectively dispossessed individual who can establish her place in the patriliny only by producing male offspring.

Patrilineage totally appropriates both women's labor and progeny and renders their work and contribution to production invisible. Woman's life cycle in the patriarchally extended family is such that the deprivation and hardship she experiences as a young bride is eventually superseded by the control and authority she will have over her own subservient daughters-in-law. The cyclical nature of women's power in the household and their anticipation of inheriting the authority of senior women encourages a thorough internalization of this form of patriarchy by the women themselves. In classic patriarchy, subordination to men is offset by the control older women attain over younger women. However, women have access to the only type of labor power they can control, and to old-age security, through their married sons. Since sons are a woman's most critical resource, ensuring their life-long loyalty is an enduring preoccupation. Older women have a vested interest in the suppression of romantic love between youngsters to keep the conjugal bond secondary and to claim sons' primary allegiance. Young women have an interest in circumventing and possibly evading their mother-in-law's control. There are culturally specific examples of how this struggle works to the detriment of the heterosexual bond (Boudhiba 1985; Johnson 1983; Mernissi 1975; M. Wolf 1972), but the overall pattern is quite similar.

The class or caste impact on classic patriarchy creates additional complications. Among the wealthier strata, the withdrawal of women from nondomestic work is frequently a mark of status institutionalized in various seclusion and exclusion practices, such as the purdah system and veiling. The institution of purdah, and other similar status markers, further reinforces women's subordination and their economic dependence on men. However, the observance of restrictive practices is such a crucial element in the reproduction of family status that women will resist breaking the rules, even if observing them produces economic hardship. They forego economically advantageous options, such as the trading activities engaged in by women in parts of Africa, for alternatives that are perceived as in keeping with their respectable and protected domestic roles, and so they become more exploitable. In her study of Indian lacemakers in Narsapur, Mies (1982, p. 13) comments:

> Although domestication of women may be justified by the older forms of seclusion, it has definitely changed its character. The Kapu women are no longer *gosha*—women of a feudal warrior caste—but domesticated housewives and workers who produce for the world market. In the case of the lacemakers this ideology has become almost a material force. The whole system is built on the ideology that these women cannot work outside the house.

Thus, unlike women in sub-Saharan Africa who attempt to resist unfavorable labor relations in the household, women in areas of classic patriarchy often adhere as far and as long as they possibly can to rules that result in the unfailing devaluation of their labor. The cyclical fluctuations in their power position, combined with status considerations, result in their active collusion in the reproduction of their own subordination. They would rather adopt interpersonal strategies that maximize their security through manipulation of the affections of their sons and husbands. As M. Wolf's (1972) insightful discussion of the Chinese uterine family suggests, this strategy can even result in the aging male patriarch losing power to his wife. Even though these individual power tactics do little to alter the structurally unfavorable terms of the overall patriarchal script, women become experts in maximizing their own life chances.

Commenting on "female conservatism" in China, Johnson (1983, p. 21) remarks: "Ironically, women through their actions to resist passivity and total male control, became participants with vested interests in the system that oppressed them." M. Wolf (1974) comments similarly on Chinese women's resistance to the 1950 Marriage Law, of which they were supposed to be the primary beneficiaries. She concludes, however, that despite their reluctance to totally transform the old family system, Chinese women will no longer be content with the limited security their manipulation of family relationships can provide.

In other areas of classic patriarchy, changes in material conditions have seriously undermined the normative order. As expressed succinctly by Cain, Khanan, and Nahar (1979, p. 410), the key to and the irony of this system reside in the fact that "male authority has a material base, while male responsibility is normatively controlled." Their study of a village in Bangladesh offers an excellent example of the strains placed by poverty on bonds of obligation between kin and, more specifically, on men's fulfillment of their normative obligations toward women. Almost a third of the widows in the villages were the heads of their own households, struggling to make a living through waged work. However, the labor-market segmentation created and bolstered by patriarchy meant that their options for work were extremely restricted, and they had to accept very low and uncertain wages.

Paradoxically, the risks and uncertainties that women are exposed to in classic patriarchy create a powerful incentive for higher fertility, which under conditions of deepening poverty will almost certainly fail to provide them with an economic shelter. Greeley (1983) also documents the growing dependence of landless households in Bangladesh on women's wage labor, including that of married women, and discusses the ways in which the stability of the patriarchal family is thereby undermined. Stacey's (1983) discussion of the crisis in the Chinese family before the revolution constitutes a classic account of the erosion of the material and ideological foundations of the traditional system. She goes on to explore how Confucian patriarchy was superseded by and transformed into new democratic and socialist forms. In the next section, some of the implications of these processes of transformation will be analyzed.

THE DEMISE OF PATRIARCHAL BARGAINS:
RETREAT INTO CONSERVATISM OR RADICAL PROTEST?

The material bases of classic patriarchy crumble under the impact of new market forces, capital penetration in rural areas (Kandiyoti 1984), or processes of chronic immiseration. Although there is no single path leading to the breakdown of this system, its consequences are fairly uniform. The domination of younger men by older men and the shelter of women in the domestic sphere were the hallmarks of a system in which men controlled some form of viable joint patrimony in land, animals, or commercial capital. Among the propertyless and the dispossessed, the necessity of every household member's contribution to survival turns men's economic protection of women into a myth.

The breakdown of classic patriarchy results in the earlier emancipation of younger men from their fathers and their earlier separation from the paternal household. Although this process implies that women escape the control of mothers-in-law and head their own households at a much younger age, it also means that they themselves can no longer look forward to a future surrounded by subservient daughters-in-law. For the generation of women caught in between, this transformation may represent genuine personal tragedy, because they have paid the heavy price of an earlier patriarchal bargain, but are not able to cash in on its promised benefits. M. Wolf's (1975) statistics on suicide among women in China suggest a clear change in the trend since the 1930s, showing a sharp increase in the suicide rates of women over 45, whereas previously the rates were highest among young women, especially new brides. She relates this change explicitly to the emancipation of sons and their new possibility of escaping familial control in the choice of their spouse, which robs the older woman of her power and respectability as mother-in-law.

Despite the obstacles that classic patriarchy puts in women's way, which may far outweigh any actual economic and emotional security, women often resist the process of transition because they see the old normative order slipping away from them, leaving them without any empowering alternatives. In a broader discussion of women's interest, Molyneux (1985, p. 234) remarks:

This is not just because of "false consciousness" as is frequently supposed—although this can be a factor—but because such changes realized in a piecemeal fashion could threaten the short-term practical interests of some women, or entail a cost in the loss of forms of protection that are not then compensated for in some way.

Thus, when classic patriarchy enters a crisis, many women may continue to use all the pressure they can muster to make men live up to their obligations and will not, except under the most extreme pressure, compromise the basis for their claims by stepping out of line and losing their respectability. Their passive resistance takes the form of claiming their half of this particular patriarchal bargain—protection in exchange for submissiveness and propriety.

The response of many women who have to work for wages in this context may be an intensification of traditional modesty markers, such as veiling. Often, through no choice of their own, they are working outside their homes and are thus "exposed"; they must now use every symbolic means at their disposal to signify that they continue to be worthy of protection. It is significant that Khomeini's exhortations to keep women at home found enthusiastic support among many Iranian women despite the obvious elements of repression. The implicit promise of increased male responsibility restores the integrity of their original patriarchal bargain in an environment where the range of options available to women is extremely restricted. Younger women adopted the veil, Azari (1983, p. 68) suggests, because "the restriction imposed on them by an Islamic order was therefore a small price that had to be paid in exchange for the security, stability and presumed respect this order promised them."

This analysis of female conservatism as a reaction to the breakdown of classic patriarchy does not by any means exhaust the range of possible responses available to women. It is merely intended to demonstrate the place of a particular strategy within the internal logic of a given system, parallels to which may be found in very different contexts, such as the industrialized societies of Western Europe and the United States. Historical and contemporary analyses of the transformation of the facts and ideologies of Western domesticity imply changes in patriarchal bargains. Gordon's (1982) study of changing feminist attitudes to birth control in the nineteenth and twentieth centuries describes the strategy of voluntary motherhood as part of a broader calculus to improve women's situation. Cott's (1978) analysis of the ideology of passionlessness among Victorian women also indicates the strategic nature of women's choices.

For the modern era, Ehrenreich (1983) provides an analysis of the breakdown of the White middle-class patriarchal bargain in the United States. She traces the progressive opting out of men from the breadwinner role starting in the 1950s, and suggests that women's demands for greater autonomy came at a time when men's conjugal responsibility was already much diminished and alternatives for men outside the conjugal union had gained considerable cultural legitimacy. Despite intense ideological mobilization involving experts such as doctors, counselors, and psychologists who tried to reinforce the idea of the responsible male breadwinner and the domesticated housewife, alternative trends started to emerge and to challenge the dominant normative order. Against this background, Ehrenreich, evaluating the feminist and the antifeminist movements, says, "It is as if, facing the age-old insecurity of the family wage system, women chose opposite strategies: either to get out (figuratively speaking) and fight for equality of income and opportunity, or to stay home and attempt to bind men more tightly to them" (1983, p. 151). The familism of the antifeminist movement could therefore be interpreted as an attempt to reinstate an older patriarchal bargain, with feminists providing a convenient scapegoat on whom to blame current disaffection and alienation among men (Chafetz and Dworkin 1987). Indeed, Stacey (1987, p. 11) suggests that "feminism serves as a symbolic lightning rod for the widespread nostalgia and longing for lost intimacy and security that presently pervade social and political culture in the United States."

However, the forms of consciousness and struggle that emerge in times of rapid social change require sympathetic and open-minded examination, rather than hasty categorization. Thus Ginsburg (1984) evaluates antiabortion activism among women in the United States as strategic rather than necessarily reactionary. She points out that disengaging sexuality from reproduction and domesticity is perceived by many women as inimical to their best interests, because, among other things, it weakens the social pressure on men to take responsibility for the reproductive consequences of sexual activity. This concern and the general anxiety it expresses are by no means unfounded (English 1984) and speak to the current lack of viable alternatives for the emotional and material support of women with children. Similarly, Stacey (1987) identifies diverse forms of "postfeminist" consciousness of the postindustrial era. She suggests that a complex and often contradictory merging of depoliticized feminist attitudes toward work and family and of personal strategies to enhance stability and intimacy in marriage are currently taking place.

At the ideological level, broken bargains seem to instigate a search for culprits, a hankering for the certainties of a more traditional order, or a more diffuse feeling that change might have gone either too far or badly wrong. Rosenfelt and Stacey's (1987) reflections on postfeminism and Stacey's (1986) discussion of conservative profamily feminism, although they criticize the alarmist premises of neoconservative discourse, take some of the legitimate concerns it expresses seriously.

CONCLUSION

Systematic analyses of women's strategies and coping mechanisms can help to capture the nature of patriarchal systems in their cultural, class-specific, and temporal concreteness and reveal how men and women resist, accommodate, adapt, and conflict with each other over resources, rights, and responsibilities. Such analyses dissolve some of the artificial divisions apparent in theoretical discussions of the relationships among class, race, and gender, because participants' strategies are shaped by several levels of constraints. Women's strategies are always played out in the context of identifiable patriarchal bargains that act as implicit scripts that define, limit, and inflect their market and domestic options. The two ideal-typical systems of male dominance discussed in this article provide different baselines from which women negotiate and strategize, and each affects the forms and potentialities of their resistance and struggles. Patriarchal bargains do not merely inform women's rational choices but also shape the more unconscious aspects of their gendered subjectivity, because they permeate the context of their early socialization, as well as their adult cultural milieu (Kandiyoti 1987a, 1987b).

A focus on more narrowly defined patriarchal bargains, rather than on an unqualified notion of patriarchy, offers better prospects for the detailed analysis of processes of transformation. In her analysis of changes in sexual imagery and mores in Western societies, Janeway (1980) borrows Kuhn's (1970) terminology of scientific paradigms. She suggests, by analogy, that widely shared ideas and practices in the realm of sexuality may act as sexual paradigms, establishing the rules of normalcy at any given time, but are also vulnerable to change when "existing rules fail to operate, when anomalies can no longer be evaded, when the real world of everyday experience challenges accepted causality" (1980, p. 582). However, sexual paradigms cannot be fully comprehended unless they are inscribed in the rules of more specifically defined patriarchal bargains, as Janeway herself demonstrates in her discussion of the connection between the ideal of female chastity in Western societies and the transmission of property to legitimate heirs before the advent of a generalized cash economy.

To stretch the Kuhnian analogy even further, patriarchal bargains can be shown to have a normal phase and a crisis phase, a concept that modifies our very interpretation of what is going on in the world. Thus, during the normal phase of classic patriarchy, large numbers of women were in fact exposed to economic hardship and insecurity. They were infertile and had to be divorced, or orphaned and without recourse to their own natal family, or unprotected because they had no surviving sons or—even worse—had "ungrateful" sons. However, they were merely considered "unlucky" anomalies and accidental casualties of a system that otherwise made sense. It is only at the point of breakdown that every order reveals its systematic contradictions. The impact of contemporary socioeconomic transformations on marriage and divorce, on household formation, and on the gendered division of labor inevitably lead to a questioning of the fundamental, implicit assumptions behind arrangements between women and men.

However, new strategies and forms of consciousness do not simply emerge from the ruins of the old and smoothly produce a new consensus, but are created through personal and political struggles, which are often complex and contradictory (see Strathern 1987). The breakdown of a particular patriarchal system may, in the short run, generate instances of passive resistance among women that take the paradoxical form of bids for increased responsibility and control by men. A better understanding of the short- and medium-term strategies of women in different social locations could provide a corrective influence to ethnocentric or class-bound definitions of what constitutes a feminist consciousness.

NOTES

1. Like all terms coined to convey a complex concept, the term *patriarchal bargain* represents a difficult compromise. It is intended to indicate the existence of set rules and scripts regulating gender relations, to which both genders accommodate and acquiesce, yet which may nonetheless be contested, redefined, and renegotiated. Some suggested alternatives were the terms *contract, deal,* or *scenario*; however, none of these fully captured the fluidity and tension implied by *bargain*. I am grateful to Cynthia Cockburn and Nels Johnson for pointing out that the term *bargain* commonly denotes a deal between more or less equal participants, so it does not accurately apply to my usage, which clearly indicates an asymmetrical exchange. However, women as a rule bargain from a weaker position.

2. I am excluding not only Southeast Asia but also the Northern Mediterranean, despite important similarities in the latter regarding codes of honor and the overall importance attached to the sexual purity of women, because I want to restrict myself to areas where the patrilocal-patrilineal complex is dominant. Thus societies with bilateral kinship systems, such as Greece, in which women do inherit and control property and receive dowries that constitute productive property, do not qualify despite important similarities in other ideological respects. This is not, however, to suggest that an unqualified homogeneity of ideology and practice exists within the geographical boundaries indicated. For example, there are critical variations within the Indian subcontinent that have demonstrably different implications for women (Dyson and Moore 1983). Conversely, even in areas of bilateral kinship, there may be instances in which all the facets of classic patriarchy, namely, property, residence, and descent through the male line, may coalesce under specified circumstances (Denich 1974). What I am suggesting is that the most clear-cut

and easily identifiable examples of classic patriarchy may be found within the boundaries indicated in the text.

REFERENCES

Abu, K. 1983. "The Separateness of Spouses: Conjugal Resources in an Ashanti Town." Pp. 156-68 in *Female and Male in West Africa,* edited by C. Oppong. London: George Allen & Unwin.

Agarwal, B. 1987. "Women and Land Rights in India." Unpublished manuscript.

Azari, F. 1983. "Islam's Appeal to Women in Iran: Illusion and Reality." Pp. 1-71 in *Women of Iran: The Conflict with Fundamentalist Islam,* edited by F. Azari. London: Ithaca Press.

Barrett, M. 1980. *Woman's Oppression Today.* London: Verso.

Beechey, V. 1979. "On Patriarchy." *Feminist Review* 3:66-82.

Boudhiba, A. 1985. *Sexuality in Islam.* London: Routledge & Kegan Paul.

Cain, M., S. R. Khanan, and S. Nahar. 1979. "Class, Patriarchy, and Women's Work in Bangladesh." *Population and Development Review* 5:408-16.

Caldwell, J. C. 1978. "A Theory of Fertility: From High Plateau to Destabilization." *Population and Development Review* 4:553-77.

Chafetz, J. Saltzman, and A. G. Dworkin. 1987. "In Face of Threat: Organized Antifeminism in Comparative Perspective." *Gender & Society* 1:33-60.

Conti, A. 1979. "Capitalist Organization of Production Through Non-Capitalist Relations: Women's Role in a Pilot Resettlement Project in Upper Volta." *Review of African Political Economy* 15/16:75-91.

Cott, N. F. 1978. "Passionlessness: An Interpretation of Victorian Sexual Ideology, 1790-1850." *Signs: Journal of Women in Culture and Society* 4:219-36.

Delphy, C. 1977. *The Main Enemy.* London: Women's Research and Resource Centre.

Denich, B. S. 1974. "Sex and Power in the Balkans." Pp. 243-62 in *Women, Culture and Society,* edited by M. Z. Rosaldo and L. Lamphere. Palo Alto, CA: Stanford University Press.

Dey, J. 1981. "Gambian Women: Unequal Partners in Rice Development Projects." Pp. 109-22 in *African Women in the Development Process,* edited by N. Nelson. London: Frank Cass.

Dyson, T., and M. Moore. 1983. "On Kinship Structures, Female Autonomy and Demographic Behavior." *Population and Development Review* 9:35-60.

Ehrenreich, B. 1983. *The Hearts of Men.* London: Pluto Press.

Eisenstein, Z. 1978. "Developing a Theory of Capitalist Patriarchy and Socialist Feminism." Pp. 5-40 in *Capitalist Patriarchy and the Case for Socialist Feminism,* edited by Z. Eisenstein. New York: Monthly Review Press.

English, D. 1984. "The Fear That Feminism Will Free Men First." Pp. 97-102 in *Powers of Desire: The Politics of Sexuality,* edited by A. Snitow, C. Stansell, and S. Thompson. New York: Monthly Review Press.

Etienne, M., and E. Leacock (eds.). 1980. *Women and Colonization.* New York: Praeger.

Ginsburg, F. 1984. "The Body Politic: The Defense of Sexual Restriction by Anti-Abortion Activists." Pp. 173-88 in *Pleasure and Danger: Exploring Female Sexuality,* edited by C. S. Vance. London: Routledge & Kegan Paul.

Gordon, L. 1982. "Why Nineteenth-Century Feminists Did Not Support Birth Control and Twentieth-Century Feminists Do: Feminism, Reproduction and the Family." Pp. 40-53 in *Rethinking the Family: Some Feminist Questions,* edited by B. Thorne and M. Yalom. New York: Longman.

Greeley, M. 1983. "Patriarchy and Poverty: A Bangladesh Case Study." *South Asia Research* 3:35-55.

Guyer, J. I., and P. E. Peters. 1987. " 'Introduction' to Conceptualizing the Household: Issues of Theory and Policy in Africa." *Development and Change* 18:197-213.

Hanger, J., and J. Moris. 1973. "Women and the Household Economy." Pp. 209-44 in *Mwea: An Irrigated Rice Settlement in Kenya,* edited by R. Chambers and J. Moris. Munich: Weltforum Verlag.

Hartmann, H. 1981. "The Unhappy Marriage of Marxism and Feminism: Towards a More Progressive Union." Pp. 40-53 in *Women and Revolution,* edited by L. Sargent. London: Pluto Press.

Janeway, E. 1980. "Who Is Sylvia? On the Loss of Sexual Paradigms." *Signs: Journal of Women in Culture and Society* 5:573-89.

Johnson, K. A. 1983. *Women, the Family and Peasant Revolution in China.* Chicago: Chicago University Press.

Kandiyoti, D. 1984. "Rural Transformation in Turkey and Its Implications for Women's Studies." Pp. 17-29 in *Women on the Move: Contemporary Transformations in Family and Society.* Paris: UNESCO.

———. 1985. *Women in Rural Production Systems: Problems and Policies.* Paris: UNESCO.

———. 1987a. "Emancipated but Unliberated? Reflections on the Turkish Case." *Feminist Studies* 13:317-38.

———. 1987b. "The Problem of Subjectivity in Western Feminist Theory." Paper presented at the American Sociological Association Annual Meeting, Chicago.

Kuhn, T. 1970. *The Structure of Scientific Revolutions* (2nd ed.). Chicago: Chicago University Press.

Mann, K. 1985. *Marrying Well: Marriage, Status and Social Change Among the Educated Elite in Colonial Lagos.* Cambridge, UK: Cambridge University Press.

Mbilinyi, M. J. 1982. "Wife, Slave and Subject of the King: The Oppression of Women in the Shambala Kingdom." *Tanzania Notes and Records* 88/89:1-13.

McDonough, R., and R. Harrison. 1978. "Patriarchy and Relations of Production." Pp. 11-41 in *Feminism and Materialism,* edited by A. Kuhn and A. M. Wolpe. London: Routledge & Kegan Paul.

Meeker, M. 1976. "Meaning and Society in the Near East: Examples from the Black Sea Turks and the Levantine Arabs." *International Journal of Middle East Studies* 7: 383-422.

Mernissi, F. 1975. *Beyond the Veil: Male-Female Dynamics in a Muslim Society.* New York: John Wiley.

Mies, M. 1982. "The Dynamics of Sexual Division of Labor and the Integration of Women into the World Market." Pp. 1-28 in *Women and Development: The Sexual Division of Labor in Rural Societies,* edited by L. Benería. New York: Praeger.

———. 1986. *Patriarchy and Accumulation on a World Scale: Women in the International Division of Labour.* London: Zed.

Mitchell, J. 1973. *Women's Estate.* New York: Vintage.

———. 1986. "Reflections on Twenty Years of Feminism." Pp. 34-48 in *What Is Feminism?* edited by J. Mitchell and A. Oakley. Oxford: Basil Blackwell.

Molyneux, M. 1985. "Mobilization Without Emancipation? Women's Interests, the State and Revolution in Nicaragua." *Feminist Studies* 11:227-54.

Munachonga, M. L. 1982. "Income Allocation and Marriage Options in Urban Zambia: Wives Versus Extended Kin." Paper presented at the Conference on Women and Income Control in the Third World, New York.

Murray, C. 1987. "Class, Gender and the Household: The Developmental Cycle in Southern Africa." *Development and Change* 18:235-50.

Ortner, S. 1978. "The Virgin and the State." *Feminist Studies* 4:19-36.

Roberts, P. 1989. "Rural Women in Western Nigeria and Hausa Niger: A Comparative Analysis," Pp. 27-47 in *Serving Two Masters,* edited by K. Young. New Delhi: Allied Publishers.

Rosenfelt, D. and J. Stacey. 1987. "Second Thoughts on the Second Wave." *Feminist Studies* 13:341-61.

Sharma, U. 1980. *Women, Work and Property in North West India.* London: Tavistock.

Stacey, J. 1983. *Patriarchy and Socialist Revolution in China.* Berkeley: University of California Press.

———. 1986. "Are Feminists Afraid to Leave Home? The Challenge of Conservative Pro-Family Feminism." Pp. 219-48 in *What Is Feminism?* edited by J. Mitchell and A. Oakley. Oxford: Basil Blackwell.

———. 1987. "Sexism by a Subtler Name? Postindustrial Conditions and Postfeminist Consciousness in the Silicon Valley." *Socialist Review* (Nov.):7-28.

Strathern, M. 1987. "An Awkward Relationship: The Case of Feminism and Anthropology." *Signs: Journal of Women in Culture and Society* 12:276-92.

Wolf, E. 1966. *Peasants.* Englewood Cliffs, NJ: Prentice-Hall.

———. 1982. *Europe and the People Without History.* Berkeley: University of California Press.

Wolf, M. 1972. *Women and the Family in Rural Taiwan.* Palo Alto, CA: Stanford University Press.

———. 1974. "Chinese Women: Old Skills in a New Context." Pp. 157-72 in *Women, Culture and Society,* edited by M. Z. Rosaldo and L. Lamphere. Palo Alto, CA: Stanford University Press.

———. 1975. "Woman and Suicide in China." Pp. 111-41 in *Women in Chinese Society,* edited by M. Wolf and R. Witke. Palo Alto, CA: Stanford University Press.

Young, I. 1981. "Beyond the Unhappy Marriage: A Critique of the Dual Systems Theory." Pp. 43-69 in *Women and Revolution,* edited by L. Sargent. London: Pluto Press.

Young, S. 1977. "Fertility and Famine: Women's Agricultural History in Southern Mozambique." Pp. 66-81 in *The Roots of Rural Poverty in Central and Southern Africa,* edited by R. Palmer and N. Parsons. London: Heinemann.

6. FAMILY, FEMINISM, AND RACE IN AMERICA

MAXINE BACA ZINN

Rapid social changes have often besieged families. Much of the contemporary crisis in American family life is related to larger socioeconomic changes. Upheavals in the social organization of work have created a massive influx of women into the labor force. At the same time, the removal of certain kinds of work has left millions of workers without jobs. Both kinds of change have affected the well-being of American families.

As debates about the context and consequences of family change reach heightened proportions, the racial ethnic[1] composition of the United States is undergoing dramatic shifts. Massive waves of immigration from Latin America and Asia are posing difficult issues for a society that clings stubbornly to its self-image of the melting pot. Changes in fertility and immigration patterns are altering the distribution of Whites and people of color and, at the same time, creating a nation of varied racial ethnic groups. In many cities and communities, Blacks, Hispanics, Asians, and Native Americans outnumber the White population. Their families are distinctive not only because of their ethnic heritage but because they reside in a society where racial stratification continues to shape family resources and structures in important ways. The changing demography of race in the United States presents compelling challenges to family sociology.

Questions about what is happening to families in the United States and how this country's racial order is being reshaped are seldom joined. Yet they are more closely related than either popular or scholarly discourse on these topics would suggest. The national discussion about the erosion of inner-city Black and Latino families has not been applied to our understanding of the family in general. Although many sources of this crisis are rooted in new forms of race and class inequality in America, the empirical data can sharpen our theoretical understanding of "the family" and its relationship to wider social forces. Instead of marginalizing minority families as special cultural cases, it is time to bring race into the mainstream of our thinking about family life in America.

For the past two decades, family scholarship has been in the throes of revision. Both feminist revisions (for reviews see Andersen 1989; Gerstel and Gross 1987; Glenn 1987; Komorovsky 1988; Thorne 1982) and revisions of scholarship on families of racial ethnic groups (for reviews see Allen 1978b; Mirande 1977; Mullings 1986a; Ramirez and Arce 1981; Staples and Mirande 1980; Wilkinson 1987; Zinn 1982/83) have given us new perspectives, approaches, and explanations of American family life in this society. In contrast to discussions of the family two decades ago, issues of gender stratification are paramount today. Issues of racial stratification, however, have received little theoretical attention. While feminist scholarship has had a great impact on analysis of the family, revisionist research on minority families continues to be marginalized, absent even from much feminist scholarship. Without a framework for incorporating race and ethnicity into models of "the family," feminist reformulations cannot be inclusive.

In this chapter, I take a step toward incorporating race into the feminist revision of the concept of the family. One of its aims is to show that research on racially and ethnically diverse families can make an essential contribution to the study of the family. The intent is not to provide a theory of racial stratification and family life but to raise issues about the extent to which racial formation is a meaningful category for analyzing family experience.

THE FEMINIST REVISION

Feminist challenges to traditional family theory have been accomplished by decomposing the family, that is, by breaking the family into constituent elements so that the underlying structures are exposed. In doing so, feminists have brought into relief three aspects of that structure: ideologies that serve to mystify women's experiences as wives and mothers, hierarchical divisions that generate conflict and struggle within families, and the multiple and dynamic interconnections between households and the larger political economy (Glenn 1987, p. 358). An understanding of family dynamics has been transformed by exposing gender as a fundamental category of social relations both within and outside the family (Andersen 1989).

First evolved as a critique of functionalism and its emphasis on roles, the crucial impact of feminist scholarship on family research has been to recast the family as a system of gender stratification. Because roles neglect the political underpinnings of the family, feminists have directed attention outside the family "to the social structures that shape experience and meaning, that give people a location in the social world, and that define and allocate economic and social rewards" (Hess and Ferree 1987, p. 11). Once feminist scholars made it clear that gender roles are not neutral ways of maintaining order in family and society but benefit some at the expense of others, virtually everything about the family looked different. As Bridenthal (1982) said:

> Put another way, feminists have opened up a whole new vista by asking not what do women do for the family? (an older question) but what does the family do *for* women? What does it do *to* women? Whom does the family organization serve best and how? (pp. 231-2)

Rather than viewing the family as a unit shaped only by affection or kinship, we now know that families are settings in which people with different activities and interests often come into conflict with one another.

The last point has had important ramifications for thinking about diversity and family life. Feminists have challenged the monolithic ideology of the family that elevated the contemporary nuclear family with a breadwinner husband and a full-time homemaker wife as the only legitimate family form. We now give equal weight to the varied family structures and experiences that are produced by the organization of the economy, the state, and other institutions (Thorne 1982, p. 2). Some of these alternative family structures and living arrangements are nonmarital cohabitation, single-parent households, extended kinship units and expanded households, dual-worker families, commuter marriages, gay and lesbian households, and collectives.

REVISIONS IN RACE-RELATIONS SCHOLARSHIP

The revisioning of American scholarship on racial ethnic families different from those of the White middle class has run a similar but not intersecting course with feminist scholarship. Like feminist scholarship, this revisioning began with a critique of functionalist accounts of racially and ethnically diverse families as dysfunctional units that acted as barriers to their groups' mobility (Staples and Mirande 1980). The sociology of the family has been noted for its absence of a strong tradition of theory and for being heavily normative, moralistic, and mingled with social policy and the social objectives of various action groups (Morgan 1975, p. 3). Nowhere is this tendency more apparent than in its treatment of racial ethnic families in the United States.

The model of the backward and culturally deviant minority family originated within the sociology of race relations in the United States and its then guiding framework of assimilation and modernization. The preoccupation in race relations with "traditional" and "modern" social forms fit well with family sociology's preoccupation with the nuclear family, its wage-earner father, and domestic-caretaker mother. Minorities and others whose family patterns differed from the ideal were explained as cultural exceptions to the rule. Their slowness to acculturate and take on the normal patterns of family development left them behind as other families in American society modernized. They were peripheral to the standard family and viewed as problems because of their failure to adopt the family patterns of the mainstream.

The "social problems" origin of family studies in the nineteenth century also contributed to this perspective. Family study as a new field emerged out of a deep concern with the need to solve such problems as rising divorce rates and the effects of slavery and industrialization on the family (Thomas and Wilcox 1987, p. 82). Social reforms of the times favored the modern family as a way of combating social problems, a belief that remains widely held in American society, if not in American family sociology.

Mainstream American sociology thus supported popular ideology by legitimizing the marginalization of racial ethnic groups in the social hierarchy. As cultural holdovers in a modernizing world, minority families were relegated to the sidelines with no relevance to the core of family theory. Scholars of various disciplines have long refuted this culturally deviant model of family, arguing that alternative family patterns do not reflect deviance, deficiency, or disorganization and that alternative family patterns are related to but not responsible for the social location of minorities. Revisionist approaches have emphasized the structural conditions giving rise to varied family forms, rather than the other way around. Differences in family patterns have been reinterpreted as adaptations to the conditions of racial inequality and poverty, often as sources of survival and strength (see, for example, Billingsley 1968; Glenn 1983; Griswold del Castillo 1984; Gutman 1976; Hill 1972; Ladner 1971; Stack 1974; Wagner and Shaffer 1980).

ASSESSING THE REVISIONS

The feminist revisioning of the family and the revisioning of studies of families in race relations scholarship have common origins. Both gained momentum as critiques of functionalism by an emergent critical sociology. The family was an important starting point in the development of women's studies, Black studies, and Chicano studies. In each of these areas, study of the family represented a vital thread in the evolution of critical scholarship. Both bodies of scholarship locate family experience in societal arrangements that extend beyond the family and allocate social and economic rewards. Both begin with the assumption that families are social products and then proceed to study their interrelationships with other social structures. Just as feminist theories have reconceptualized the family along a gender axis of power and control, racial ethnic family scholarship has reconceptualized the family along the axis of race, also a system of power and control that shapes family life in crucial ways.

Because they both locate family experience in societal arrangements extending beyond the family, these two streams of revisionist scholarship fall within the "radical critical" tradition. Although they are not commonly identified with this framework (see Osmond 1987, p. 119), they do adopt basic assumptions, major premises, and general directions of this approach.

Despite such fundamental similarities in their intellectual roots, the feminist revision and the racial ethnic studies revision have not been combined, nor have they had the same impact on theories of the family. Feminist scholarship with its gender-as-power theme has had a far greater impact. Especially noteworthy in this regard has been the application of certain feminist insights to studies of minority families. In fact, gender-as-power and the racial division of labor have become key themes of recent studies of racial ethnic families. Nakano Glenn's study of Japanese families (1986) and Zavella's study of Chicano families (1987) are particularly meaningful because they explore the close connections between the internal dynamics of women's family lives and economic conditions as they are bound up in broader systems of class and race inequality.

Studying the intersection of gender, race, and class in minority families has enormously enhanced family scholarship. Now, in studying racial ethnic families, we routinely examine race and gender as interacting hierarchies of resources and rewards that condition material and subjective experiences within families (see, for example, Chapter 9).

Interacting race, class, and gender ideologies have shaped prevailing models of minority families, appearing even in the culturally deviant explanations of racial ethnic families. As Hill Collins (1989) explains, the new version of this argument is that because minority women and men do not follow dominant notions of masculinity and femininity, they are responsible for their subordinate class placement in society. As Bridenthal (1981) has put it:

> Black people have been called matriarchal (ruled by the mother) and Chicano families have been called patriarchal (ruled by the father). These supposedly opposite family structures and relationships have been blamed for the failure of many members of each group to rise to a higher socioeconomic level. In other words, black and Chicano families have been blamed for the effect of racial discrimination. (p. 85)

While revisionist research on racial ethnic families has incorporated many feminist insights, the reverse has not occurred. Knowledge about racial stratification has not been incorporated into much feminist research on the family, and race enters the discussion of family life only when minority families are concerned.

To be fair, feminist literature on the family does recognize the societal context of inequality that gives rise to distinctive family forms. Feminist rethinking of the family has dropped the cultural *deviant* perspective. But for the most part, it retains a *cultural* perspective. Most contemporary feminist thought takes great care to underscore class, race, and gender as fundamental categories of social organization, but when it comes to family patterns, race and ethnicity are used as elements of culture, not social structure. Descriptions of cultural diversity do not explain why families exhibit structural variations by race. While it is true that many family lifestyles are differentiated by ethnicity, structural patterns differ because social and economic conditions produce and may even require diverse family arrangements. Although the family nurtures ethnic culture, families are not the product of ethnic culture alone.

RACIAL INEQUALITY AND FAMILY LIFE

The feminist revision has been reluctant to grapple with race as a power system that affects families throughout society and to apply that understanding to "the family" writ large. As Nakano Glenn (1987) says, "Systematically incorporating hierarchies of race and class into feminist reconstruction of the family remains a challenge, a necessary next step in the development of theories of family that are inclusive" (1987, p. 368).

Social Location and Family Formation

In our quest to understand the structural sources of diversity in family life, we must examine all of the "socioeconomic and political arrangements and how they impinge on families" (Mullings 1986a, p. 13). Like class and gender hierarchies, racial stratification is a fundamental axis of American social structure. Racial stratification produces different opportunity structures that shape families in a variety of ways. Marriage patterns, gender relations, kinship networks, and other family characteristics result from the social location of families, that is, where they are situated in relation to societal institutions allocating resources.

Thinking about families in this way shifts the theoretical focus from cultural diversity or "ethnic lifestyles" of particular groups to race as a major element of hierarchical social relations that touches families throughout the social order (Omi and Winant 1986, p. 61). Racial stratification is a basic organizing principle in American society even though the forms of domination and discrimination have changed over time. Omi and Winant use the term "racial formation" to refer to the process by which social, economic, and political forces determine the content and import of racial categories and by which they are in turn shaped by racial meanings (1986, p. 61). As racial categories are formed and transformed over time, the meanings, practices, and institutions associated with race penetrate families throughout the society.

Social categories and groups subordinate in the racial hierarchy are often deprived of access to social institutions that offer supports for family life. Social categories and groups elevated in the racial hierarchy have different and better connections to institutions that can sustain families. Social location and its varied connection with social resources thus have profound consequences for family life.

If families are to be conceptualized in a way that relates them to social, historical, and material conditions, then racial stratification cannot be ignored. We are forced to abandon conventional notions that racial ethnic diversity is a cultural phenomenon best understood at the microstructural level. Instead of treating diversity as a given, or as a result of traditions alone, we must treat racial stratification as a macrostructural force situating families in ways requiring diverse arrangements. These macrostructural forces can be seen in two periods of economic upheaval in the United States—industrialization and the current shift from manufacture to information and services. In both of these transitions, the relationship between families and other institutions has been altered. Despite important differences, these economic transformations have produced new relations among individuals, families, and labor systems that have had profound effects on family development throughout American society. Industrialization and deindustrialization are not neutral transformations that touch families in uniform ways. Rather, they manifest themselves differently in their interaction with race and gender, and both periods of transition reveal racial patterning in family and household formation. The theme of historical variation has become increasingly accepted in family studies, but theories of the family have largely ignored the new knowledge about race, labor, and family formation.

INDUSTRIALIZATION AND FAMILY STRUCTURE

The past two decades of historical research on the family have revealed that industrialization has had momentous consequences for American families because of massive changes in the way people made a living. The industrial revolution changed the nature of work performed, the allocation of work responsibilities, and the kind of pay, prestige, and power that resulted from various positions in the economy. The effect of industrialization on American family life was uneven. Instead of a linear pattern of change in which families moved steadily to a more modern level, the pattern of change was checkered (Hareven 1987). Labor force exploitation produced various kinds of family and household adaptations on the part of slaves, agricultural workers, and industrial workers.

Both class and race were basic to the relations of production in the United States in this period. Race was intertwined with class; populations from various parts of the world were brought into the labor force at different levels, and racial differences were utilized to rationalize exploitation of women and men (Mullings 1986b, p. 56). European ethnics were incorporated into low-wage industrial economies of the North, while Blacks, Latinos, Chinese, and Japanese filled labor needs in colonial labor systems of the economically backward regions of the West, Southwest, and the South. These colonial labor systems, while different, created similar hardships for family life.

All these groups had to engage in a constant struggle for both immediate survival and long-term continuation of family and community, but women's and men's work and family patterns varied considerably within different racial labor structures, with fundamentally different social supports for family life. Thornton Dill (1988) has compared patterns of White families in nineteenth-century America with those of racial ethnics and identified important racial differences in the social supports for family life. She finds that greater importance was accorded Euro-American families by the wider society. As primary laborers in the reproduction and maintenance of family life, these women were acknowledged and accorded the privileges and protections deemed socially appropriate to their family roles. Although this emphasis on family roles denied these women many rights and privileges and seriously constrained their individual growth and development, it also revealed public support for White women's family roles. Women's reproductive labor was viewed as an essential building block of the family. Combined with a view of the family as the cornerstone of the nation, this ideology produced experiences within the White dominant culture very different from those of racial ethnics (Dill 1988, p. 418). Because racial ethnic men were usually unable to earn a "family wage," their women had to engage in subsistence and income-producing activities both in and out of the household. In addition, they had to struggle to keep their families together in the face of outside forces that threatened the integrity of their households (Glenn 1987, pp. 53-4).

During industrialization, class produced some similarities in the family experiences of racial ethnic women and those of White working-class immigrants. As Smith (1987) has argued, working-class women during this period were often far removed from the domestic ideal. The cults of domesticity and true womanhood that proliferated during this period were ideals attained more frequently by those Euro-American women whose husbands were able to earn enough to support their families (Mullings 1986b, p. 50).

This ideal was not attainable by Blacks, Latinos, and Asian Americans, who were excluded from jobs open to White immigrants. For example, in most cities, the constraints that prevented Black men from earning a family wage forced Black married women into the labor market in much greater proportions than White immigrant women. By 1880, about 50 percent of Black women were in the labor force, compared with 15 percent of White women (Degler 1980, p. 389). Furthermore, the family system of the White working class was not subject to institutional assaults, such as forced separation, directed against Black, Latino, and Chinese families (Glenn 1987, p. 73).

Racial ethnic women experienced the oppressions of a patriarchal society but were denied the protections and buffering of a patriarchal family. Their families suffered as a direct result of the labor systems in which they participated. Since they were a cheap and exploitable labor force, little attention was given to their family and community life except as it related to their economic productivity. Labor and not the existence or maintenance of families was the critical aspect of their role in building the nation. They were denied the social and structural supports necessary to make their families a vital element in the social order (Dill 1988, p. 418). Nevertheless, people take conditions that have been thrust upon them and out of them create a history and a future (Mullings 1986b, p. 46). Using cultural forms where possible and creating new forms where necessary, racial ethnics adapted their families to the larger social order. These adaptations were not exceptions to the rule; they were instead variations created by mainstream forces. One family type was not standard and the others peripheral. Different forms existed at the same time.

Once we recognize how racial stratification has affected family formation, we can understand why the idealized family was not a luxury shared by all. At the same time, we can see how some idealized family patterns were made possible because of the existence of alternative family forms and how all of these are products of the social and economic conditions of the times. Although Blacks, Mexicanos, and Asians were excluded from industrial work, all three groups helped build the agricultural and industrial base for subsequent industrial development. New ways of life and new family patterns sprang from industrialization. As Mullings (1986b) says, "It was the working class and enslaved men and women whose labor created the wealth that allowed the middle class and upper middle class domestic life styles to exist" (p. 50).

DE-INDUSTRIALIZATION AND FAMILIES

Vast changes in the social organization of work are currently transforming the American family across class and race groups. Not only are women and men affected differently by the transformation of the economy from its manufacturing base to service and high technology, but women and men in different racial categories are experiencing distinctive changes in their relationship to the economy. This transformation is profoundly affecting families as it works with and through race and gender hierarchies.

In the current American economy, industrial jobs traditionally filled by men are being replaced with service jobs that are increasingly filled by women. Married White women are now entering the labor force at a rate that, until recently, was seen exclusively among women of color (Smith 1987, p. 16). The most visible consequences of the increased labor force participation among White women include declining fertility and changes in marriage patterns. American White women are delaying marriage and childbearing and having fewer children over their lifetimes, living alone or as heads of their own households—living with neither parents nor husbands (Hartmann 1987, p. 36). The new economy is reshaping families as it propels these women into the labor force.

In minority communities across America, families and households are also being reshaped through new patterns of work and gender roles. The high level of female-headed families among Blacks and Hispanics (especially Puerto Ricans) is the outgrowth of changes in the larger economy. The long-term decline in employment opportunities for men is the force most responsible for the growth of racial ethnic families headed by women. Wilson's (1987) compelling work has shown that the shortage of Black men with the ability to support a family makes it necessary for many Black women to leave a marriage or forego marriage altogether. Adaptation to structural conditions leaves Black women disproportionately separated, divorced, and solely responsible for their children.

Families throughout American society are being reshaped by economic and industrial change: "The shifting economy produces and even demands diverse family forms—including for example, female headed households, extended kinship units, dual career couples, and lesbian collectives" (Gerstel and Gross 1987, p. 7). Families mainly headed by women have become permanent in all racial categories in America, with the disproportionate effects of change most visible among Blacks and Latinos. While the chief cause of the increase in female-headed households among Whites is the greater economic independence of White women, the longer delay of first marriage and the low rate of remarriage among Black women reflects the labor force problems of Black men (Wilson and Neckerman 1986, p. 256). Thus race creates different routes to female headship, but Whites, Blacks, and Latinos are all increasingly likely to end up in this family form.

CONCLUSION

Knowing that race creates certain patterns in the way families are located and embedded in different social environments, we should be able to theorize for all racial categories. Billingsley (1988) suggests that the study of Black families can generate important insights for White families: Families may respond in a like manner when impacted by larger social forces. To the extent that White families and Black families experience similar pressures, they may respond in similar ways, including the adaptation of their family structures and other behaviors. With respect to single-parent families, teenage childbirth, working mothers, and a host of other behaviors, Black families serve as barometers of social change and as forerunners of adaptive patterns that will be progressively experienced by the more privileged sectors of American society.

While such insights are pertinent, they should not eclipse the ways in which racial meanings inform our perceptions of family diversity. As social and economic changes produce new family arrangements, alternatives—what is sometimes called "family pluralism"—are granted greater legitimacy. Yet many alternatives that appear new to middle-class White Americans are actually variant family patterns that have been traditional within Black and other minority communities for many generations. Presented as the new lifestyles of the mainstream, they are, in fact, the same lifestyles that have in the past been deemed pathological, deviant, or unacceptable when observed in Black families (Peters and McAdoo 1983, p. 228).

In much popular and scholarly thinking, alternatives are seen as inevitable changes, new ways of living that are part of an advanced society. In other words, they are conceptualized as products of the mainstream. Yet such alternatives, when associated with racial ethnic groups, are judged against a standard model and found to be deviant. Therefore, the notion of family pluralism does not correctly describe the family diversity of the past or the present. Pluralism implies that alternative family forms *coexist* within a society. In reality, racial meanings create a hierarchy in which some family forms are privileged and others are subordinated, even though they are both products of larger social forces.

Treating race as a basic category of social organization can make the feminist reconstruction of the family more inclusive. The implications of this approach are also provocative and uncomfortable because they challenge some of our basic sociological and feminist assumptions about how families in different races (and classes) are related to the larger society, to each other, and how they are all changing as a result of ongoing social and economic changes. These are important issues for social scientists, policymakers, and others to ponder, understand, and solve.

NOTE

1. The term *racial ethnic* refers to groups labeled as races in the context of certain historical, social, and material conditions. Blacks, Latinos, and Asian Americans are racial groups that are formed, defined, and given meaning by a variety of social forces in

the wider society, most notably distinctive forms of labor exploitation. Each group is also bound together by ethnicity, that is, common ancestry and emergent cultural characteristics that are often used for coping with racial oppression. The concept racial ethnic underscores the social construction of race and ethnicity for people of color in the United States.

REFERENCES

Allen, W. P. 1978a. "Black Family Research in the United States: A Review, Assessment and Extension." *Journal of Comparative Family Studies* 9:167-89.

————. 1978b. "The Search for Applicable Theories of Black Family Life." *Journal of Marriage and the Family* 40:117-29.

Andersen, M. 1989. "Feminism and the American Family Ideal." Paper presented at the Eastern Sociological Society Annual Meeting, Baltimore.

Billingsley, A. 1968. *Black Families in White America.* Englewood Cliffs, NJ: Prentice-Hall.

————. 1988. "The Impact of Technology on Afro-American Families." *Family Relations* 7:420-5.

Bridenthal, R. 1981. "The Family Tree: Contemporary Patterns in the United States." Pp. 47-105 in *Household and Kin,* edited by A. Swerdlow, R. Bridenthal, J. Kelly, and P. Vine. Old Westbury, NY: Feminist Press.

————. 1982. "The Family: The View from a Room of Her Own." Pp. 225-39 in *Rethinking the Family,* edited by B. Thorne and M. Yalom. New York: Longman.

Collins, P. Hill. 1989. "A Comparison of Two Works on Black Family Life." *Signs: Journal of Women in Culture and Society* 14:875-84.

Degler, C. 1980. *At Odds: Women and the Family in America from the Revolution to the Present.* New York: Oxford University Press.

Dill, B. Thornton. 1988. "Our Mother's Grief: Racial Ethnic Women and the Maintenance of Families." *Journal of Family History* 13:415-31.

Gerstel, N., and H. E. Gross (eds.). 1987. *Families and Work.* Philadelphia: Temple University Press.

Glenn, E. Nakano. 1983. "Split Household, Small Producer, and Dual Wage Earner: An Analysis of Chinese-American Family Strategies." *Journal of Marriage and the Family* 45:35-46.

————. 1986. *Issei, Nisei, War Bride: Three Generations of Japanese American Women in Domestic Service.* Philadelphia: Temple University Press.

————. 1987. "Racial Ethnic Women's Labor: The Intersection of Race, Gender and Class Oppression." Pp. 46-73 in *Hidden Aspects of Women's Work,* edited by C. Bose, R. Feldberg, and N. Sokoloff. New York: Praeger.

Griswold del Castillo, R. 1984. *La Familia.* Notre Dame, IN: University of Notre Dame Press.

Gutman, H. 1976. *The Black Family in Slavery and Freedom, 1750-1925.* New York: Pantheon.

Hareven, T. 1987. "Historical Analysis of the Family." Pp. 37-57 in *Handbook of Marriage and the Family,* edited by M. B. Sussman and S. Steinmetz. New York: Plenum.

Hartmann, H. I. 1987. "Changes in Women's Economic and Family Roles in Post World War II United States." Pp. 33-64 in *Women, Households and the Economy,* edited by L. R. Benería and C. R. Stimpson. New Brunswick: Rutgers.

Hess, B., and M. Marx Ferree. 1987. "Introduction." Pp. 9-30 in *Analyzing Gender*, edited by B. Hess and M. Marx Ferree. Newbury Park, CA: Sage.

Hill, R. 1972. *The Strengths of Black Families*. New York: Emerson-Hall.

Komorovsky, M. 1988. "The New Feminist Scholarship: Some Precursors and Polemics." *Journal of Marriage and the Family* 50:585-93.

Ladner, J. 1971. *Tomorrow's Tomorrow: The Black Woman*. New York: Doubleday.

Mirande, A. 1977. "The Chicano Family: A Reanalysis of Conflicting views." *Journal of Marriage and the Family* 39:737-56.

Morgan, D. H. J. 1975. *Social Theory and the Family*. London: Routledge & Kegan Paul.

Mullings, L. 1986a. "Anthropological Perspectives on the Afro-American Family." *American Journal of Social Psychiatry* 6:11-6.

———. 1986b. "Uneven Development: Class, Race and Gender in the United States Before 1900." Pp. 41-51 in *Women's Work: Development and Division of Labor by Gender*, edited by E. Leacock, H. I. Safa, and contributors. South Hadley, MA: Bergin & Garvey.

Omi, M., and H. Winant. 1986. *Racial Formation in the United States*. London: Routledge & Kegan Paul.

Osmond, M. Withers. 1987. "Radical-Critical Theories." Pp. 103-24 in *Handbook of Marriage and the Family*, edited by M. B. Sussman and S. Steinmetz. New York: Plenum.

Peters, M., and H. P. McAdoo. 1983. "The Present and Future of Alternative Lifestyles in Ethnic American Cultures." Pp. 288-307 in *Contemporary Families and Alternative Lifestyles*, edited by E. D. Macklin and R. H. Rubin. Beverly Hills: Sage.

Ramirez, O., and C. H. Arce. 1981. "The Contemporary Chicano Family: An Empirically Based Review." Pp. 3-28 in *Explorations in Chicano Psychology*, edited by A. Baron, Jr. New York: Praeger.

Smith, D. E. 1987. "Women's Inequality and the Family." Pp. 23-54 in *Families and Work*, edited by N. Gerstel and H. Engel Gross. Philadelphia: Temple University Press.

Smith, J. 1987. "Transforming Households: Working-Class Women and Economic Crisis." *Social Problems* 34:416-36.

Stack, C. 1974. *All Our Kin*. New York: Harper & Row.

Staples, R., and A. Mirande. 1980. "Racial and Cultural Variations Among American Families: A Decennial Review of the Literature on Minority Families." *Journal of Marriage and the Family* 40:157-73.

Thomas, D. L., and J. E. Wilcox. 1987. "The Rise of Family Theory." Pp. 81-102 in *Handbook of Marriage and the Family*, edited by M. B. Sussman and S. Steinmetz. New York: Plenum.

Thorne, B. 1982. "Feminist Thinking on the Family: An Overview." Pp. 1-24 in *Rethinking the Family*, edited by B. Thorne and M. Yalom. New York: Longman.

Wagner, R. M., and D. M. Shaffer. 1980. "Social Networks and Survival Strategies: An Exploratory Study of Mexican-American, Black and Anglo Female Family Heads in San Jose, California." Pp. 173-90 in *Twice a Minority: Mexican American Women*, edited by M. Melville. St. Louis: C. V. Mosby.

Wilkinson, D. 1987. "Ethnicity." Pp. 183-210 in *Handbook of Marriage and the Family*, edited by M. B. Sussman and S. Steinmetz. New York: Plenum.

Wilson, W., and K. M. Neckerman. 1986. "Poverty and Family Structure: The Widening Gap Between Evidence and Public Policy Issues." Pp. 232-59 in *Fighting Poverty*, edited by S. H. Danziger and D. Weinberg. Cambridge: Harvard University Press.

Wilson, W. J. 1987. *The Truly Disadvantaged.* Chicago: University of Chicago Press.

Zavella, P. 1987. *Women's Work and Chicano Families.* Ithaca, NY: Cornell University Press.

Zinn, M. Baca. 1982/83. "Familism Among Chicanos: A Theoretical Review." *Humboldt Journal of Social Relations* 101:224-38.

—— and D. S. Eitzen. 1987. *Diversity in American Families.* New York: Harper & Row.

——. 1990. *Diversity in Families,* 2d ed. New York: Harper & Row.

III.

Gender Construction in the Workplace

In industrialized countries in the twentieth century, one of the most widespread and persistent features of work is that jobs are gender-typed as women's or men's work (Jacobs 1989; Reskin 1984, Reskin and Hartmann 1986). Although there are few occupations where all the workers are men or women, there are many where between 60 and 95 percent are of one gender (Bielby and Baron 1986). In most work places, from schools to supermarkets to factories to offices, men work with men and women work with women (Bielby and Baron 1984).

Every known society has women's work and men's work, but for different reasons. In subsistence-level economies, a division of labor expands food production (Marwell 1975). Where there are several ways of getting food—foraging for nuts, berries, edible roots; killing small animals; tracking and driving large animals into pits—tasks can be allocated to different groups, so more food can be obtained. Also, while hunting by tracking is difficult for child-minders and pregnant women, it can be done by adolescent girls, adolescent boys, and mature men (Brown 1970; Friedl 1975). Foraging, scavenging, and drive hunts are compatible with pregnancy, breast-feeding, and child-minding; this work would be the work of pregnant and lactating women and older men and women or of the whole band. In subsistence societies, all ways of getting food are important to survival; therefore, women's work is valued as highly as men's work.

Once plants and animals were domesticated and people lived in settled communities, women did the cultivating and harvesting and tended small animals; men cleared the fields and tended large animals, such as cattle and sheep, that had to roam to get enough grass to eat. Such societies still exist in Africa (Sudarkasa 1986). Again, women's work is compatible with child-minding. In these societies, because women's work produces most of the group's food, women have a high status (Blumberg 1978).

By the time human communities moved into less fertile territory, they had iron-tipped plows and used large animals for farming as well as for food. Plow agriculture, like shepherding, takes people into the fields or pastures for the whole day; it is incompatible with tending small children, and so it became the work of men (Ehrenberg 1989). Some men owned land and herds; other men worked for them. The wives of the owners, although they worked hard tending gardens, taking care of fowl and pigs, cooking, and supervising servants, were now economic dependents, valued more for their capacity to breed sons and heirs than for their production of food (Coontz and Henderson 1986). Women servants and wives of the hired workers had the lowest status of all.

At the beginning of the industrial revolution, whole families went to work in factories because the farmland they had rented was enclosed for sheep grazing or cotton growing. In other communities, contractors brought raw materials and machinery into farm cottages to be processed into yarn and cloth by women workers. The machines were owned by men, and the wages were paid to the male head of the household (Hartmann 1976). Gradually, all manufacturing took place in factories, and the work was segregated by gender.

The presence of machines does not distinguish men's and women's work; both women and men did manufacturing (so did young children) in the nineteenth century. Today, more women than men work with machines, but they work with word processors, data entry computers, fax and copy machines (Form and McMillen 1983). Once office machines like the typewriter were invented, office work became indispensable for the running of all kinds of businesses. Office work was designed to be done by cheaply paid workers who would not be promoted but encouraged to leave after several years—young women (Cohn 1985). In the global economy, women in Third World factories produce clothing and microchips—labor-intensive work that calls for a lot of workers who are paid low salaries (Nash and Fernández-Kelly 1983). Men design and service machines and work in capital-intensive industries, which need fewer workers; consequently, employers can pay them higher salaries. Even in worker-owned cooperatives, women workers are paid less because the men tend to obtain technological knowledge and skills (Hacker 1989).

Men's work has always paid more because, it was argued, they had to support families; they therefore deserved a "family wage" (Acker 1988). Women are considered secondary workers who need to support only themselves or to provide a supplement to the family income. All jobs in which most of the workers are women are paid significantly less than jobs in which most of the workers are men (Baron and Newman 1990). As a result, when women must support families, their low salaries mean that they barely eke out a living.

In sum, women's work is no longer shaped by the need for them to take care of small children (which has to fit into their need to contribute to their family's economic support), but rather by their usefulness as cheap labor. Women's jobs are structured so that the workers have less autonomy, less chance to move up the organizational hierarchy, and less pay. The jobs are made less desirable so there will be greater turnover and no pressure for raises and seniority benefits (Cohn 1985). If men do the work, they will be just as short-changed as the women doing the work; women (as a social category) will, however, be the organization's rationale for why the work is structured the way it is. In actuality, employers' profits and male workers' self-protection are at the heart of the modern gender-segregated work force (Cockburn 1983, 1985; Cohn 1985).

The chapters in this section examine the process of gender typing of occupations and its consequences. In Chapter 7, "Bringing the Men Back In: Sex Differentiation and the Devaluation of Women's Work," Barbara F. Reskin shows how the gendered division of work is maintained through the creation of artificial differences between women and men. These differences justify not only segregating women and men in a work organization, but also paying women lower wages by stereotyping them as primarily wives and mothers, whether they are or not. The result, gender-segregated work and lesser pay for women's work, is thus made so routine and expected that it seems almost immoral to suggest that women can do men's work and vice versa.

Continuing this theme of the social construction of gender-segregated work places, in Chapter 8, "Hierarchies, Jobs, Bodies: A Theory of Gendered Organizations," Joan Acker shows that there is no such thing as a gender-neutral job description because jobs have to be filled by real workers. For most jobs, these will be men, women behaving like men, or women behaving like women, who will be "wrong" for the job if it is highly paid and commands authority.

Racial ethnic status adds another dimension to job-market inequality. Elizabeth M. Almquist, in Chapter 9, "Labor Market Gender Inequality in Minority Groups," analyzes the differential distribution of scarce resources to women and men in minority groups of different socioeconomic status. Among the smaller and more affluent minorities, many of whom are recent immigrants to the United States, men tend to have significantly better jobs than women. The larger minority groups, such as Blacks, have less education and access to professional and managerial jobs, resources that are monopolized by the men in the more prosperous groups. As a result, Black women and men tend to have similar levels of jobs and income and to share resources.

The fourth chapter of this section, Johanna Brenner's "Feminization of Poverty and Comparable Worth: Radical Versus Liberal Approaches" shows how not only women's but minority men's disadvantages in the labor market produce the phenomenon known as the "feminization of poverty." However, as Brenner argues, women are not poor because they are women or because they have children and no husbands, but because the men of their social class cannot get jobs and help support the children, and because the jobs they themselves can get are poorly paid.

Comparable worth is a strategy that equates women's and men's work by allocating points for such components as education or training needed to get the job, skills needed to do the job, the extent of responsibility for others' work and for finances. One evaluation scheme assigned "worth points" for knowledge and skills, mental demands, accountability, and working conditions. (For evaluation methods, see Remick 1984 and Treiman and Hartmann 1981.) When women's jobs are compared to men's jobs with similar point values, there are glaring salary discrepancies. Comparable worth or pay equity lawsuits claim that workers in jobs with the same number of points should be paid the same. When these suits are successful, women's pay scales (and also those of some minority men's jobs) go up.

However, Brenner argues that in the evaluation scheme, components are weighed so that middle-class, White male workers are favored (see also Acker 1987, 1989; Blum 1987; Steinberg 1987). Management knowledge and skills always get a large number of points, but the invisible work done for managers by administrative support workers, such as editing, maintaining office machinery, keeping the boss' calendar, tactfully screening phone calls and visitors, and attending to myriad details does not (Amott and Matthaei 1988). In short, Brenner argues, comparable worth will not change the underlying social assumptions about the relative worth of women's and blue-collar men's work, nor will it give all people a decent standard of living regardless of the kind of work they do.

REFERENCES

Acker, J. 1987. "Sex Bias in Job Evaluation: A Comparable Worth Issue." Pp. 183-96 in *Ingredients of Women's Employment Policy,* edited by C. Bose and G. Spitze. Albany: SUNY Press.

———. 1988. "Class, Gender, and the Relations of Distribution." *Signs: Journal of Women in Culture and Society* 13:473-97.

———. 1989. *Doing Comparable Worth: Gender, Class, and Pay Equity.* Philadelphia: Temple University Press.

Amott, T., and J. Matthaei. 1988. "The Promise of Comparable Worth: A Socialist-Feminist Perspective." *Socialist Review* 88 (2):101-17.

Baron, J. N., and A. E. Newman. 1990. "For What It's Worth: Organizations, Occupations, and the Value of the Work Done by Women and Nonwhites." *American Sociological Review* 55:155-75.

Bielby, W., and J. Baron. 1984. "A Woman's Place Is With Other Women." In *Sex Segregation in the Workplace: Trends, Explanations, Remedies,* edited by B. F. Reskin. Washington, DC: National Academy Press.

———. 1986. "Men and Women at Work: Sex Segregation and Statistical Discrimination." *American Journal of Sociology* 91:759-99.

Blum, L. 1987. "Possibilities and Limits of the Comparable Worth Movement." *Gender & Society* 4:380-99.

Blumberg, R. Lesser. 1978. *Stratification: Socioeconomic and Sexual Inequality.* Dubuque, IA: William C. Brown.

Brown, J. K. 1970. "A Note on the Division of Labor by Sex." *American Anthropologist* 72:1074-8.

Cockburn, C. 1983. *Brothers: Male Dominance and Technological Change.* London: Pluto Press.

———. 1985. *Machinery of Dominance: Women, Men and Technical Know-How.* London: Pluto Press.

Cohn, S. 1985. *The Process of Occupational Sex-Typing.* Philadelphia: Temple University Press.

Coontz, S., and P. Henderson. 1986. *Women's Work, Men's Property: The Origins of Gender and Class.* London: Verso.

Ehrenberg, M. 1989. *Women in Prehistory.* Norman: University of Oklahoma Press.

Form, W., and D. B. McMillen. 1983. "Women, Men, and Machines." *Work and Occupations* 10:147-78.

Friedl, E. 1975. *Women and Men.* New York: Holt, Rinehart & Winston.

Hacker, S. L., with C. Elcorobairutia. 1978. "Women Workers in the Mondragon System of Industrial Cooperatives." *Gender & Society* 1:358-79.

Hartmann, H. I. 1976. "Capitalism, Patriarchy, and Job Segregation by Sex." *Signs: Journal of Women in Culture and Society* 1 (No. 3, Part 2):137-67.

Jacobs, J. A. 1989. "Long-Term Trends in Occupational Segregation by Sex." *American Journal of Sociology* 95:160-73.

Marwell, G. 1975. "Why Ascription? Parts of a More or Less Formal Theory of the Functions and Dysfunctions of Sex Roles." *American Sociological Review* 40:445-55.

Nash, J., and P. Fernández-Kelly (eds.). 1983. *Women, Men, and the International Division of Labor.* Albany: SUNY Press.

Remick, H. (ed.). 1984. *Comparable Worth and Wage Discrimination: Technical Possibilities and Political Realities.* Philadelphia: Temple University Press.

Reskin, B. F. (ed.). 1984. *Sex Segregation in the Workplace: Trends, Explanations, Remedies.* Washington, DC: National Academy Press.

——— and H. I. Hartmann (eds.). 1986. *Women's Work, Men's Work: Sex Segregation on the Job.* Washington, DC: National Academy Press.

Steinberg, R. 1987. "Radical Challenges in a Liberal World: The Mixed Success of Comparable Worth." *Gender & Society* 4:466-75.

Sudarkasa, N. 1986. " 'The Status of Women' in Indigenous African Societies." *Feminist Studies* 12:91-103.

Treiman, D. J., and H. I. Hartmann (eds.). 1981. *Women, Work and Wages.* Washington, DC: National Academy Press.

7. BRINGING THE MEN BACK IN: SEX DIFFERENTIATION AND THE DEVALUATION OF WOMEN'S WORK

BARBARA F. RESKIN

One of the most enduring manifestations of sex inequality in industrial and postindustrial societies is the wage gap.[1] In 1986, as in 1957, among full-time workers in the United States, men earned 50 percent more per hour than did women. This disparity translated to $8,000 a year in median earnings, an all-time high bonus for being male. Most sociologists agree that the major cause of the wage gap is the segregation of women and men into different kinds of work (Reskin and Hartmann 1986). Whether or not women freely choose the occupations in which they are concentrated, the outcome is the same: the more proportionately female an occupation, the lower its average wages (Treiman and Hartmann 1981). The high level of job segregation (Bielby and Baron 1984) means that the 1963 law stipulating equal pay for equal work did little to reduce the wage gap.[2]

This "causal model"—that the segregation of women and men into different occupations causes the wage gap—implies two possible remedies. One is to equalize men and women on the causal variable—occupation—by ensuring women's access to traditionally male occupations. The other is to replace occupation with a causal variable on which women and men differ less, by instituting comparable-worth pay policies that compensate workers for the "worth" of their job, regardless of its sex composition.

I contend, however, that the preceding explanation of the wage gap is incorrect because it omits variables responsible for the difference between women and men in their distribution across occupations. If a causal model is incorrect, the remedies it implies may be ineffective. Lieberson's (1985, p. 185) critique of causal analysis as it is commonly practiced explicates the problem by distinguishing between *superficial* (or surface) causes that *appear to* give rise to a particular outcome and *basic* causes that *actually* produce the outcome. For example, he cites the belief that the Black-White income gap is due to educational differences and thus can be reduced by reducing the educational disparity. As Lieberson pointed out, this analysis misses the fact that "the dominant group . . . uses its dominance to advance its own position" (p. 166), so that eliminating race differences in education is unlikely to reduce racial inequality in income because Whites will find another way to maintain their income advantage. In other words, what appear in this example to be both the outcome variable (the Black-White income gap) and the imputed causal variable (the Black-White educational disparity) may stem from the same basic cause (Whites' attempt to maintain their economic advantage). If so, then if the disparity in education were eliminated, some other factor would arise to produce the same economic consequence (Lieberson 1985, p. 164).

Dominant groups remain privileged because they write the rules, and the rules they write "enable them *to continue to write the rules*" (Lieberson 1985, p. 167; italics added). As a result, they can change the rules to thwart challenges to their position. Consider the following example. Because Asian American students tend to outscore Occidentals on standard/admissions tests, they are increasingly overrepresented in some university programs. Some universities have allegedly responded by imposing quotas for Asian students (Hechinger 1987, p. C1) or weighing more heavily admissions criteria on which they believe Asian Americans do less well.[3]

How can one tell whether a variable is a superficial or a basic cause of some outcome? Lieberson offered a straightforward test: Does a change in that variable lead to a change in the outcome? Applying this rule to the prevailing causal theory of the wage gap, we find that between 1970 and 1980 the index of occupational sex segregation declined by 10 percent (Beller 1984), but the wage gap for full-time workers declined by just under 2 percent (computed from data in Blau and Ferber 1986, p. 171). Although its meaning may be equivocal,[4] this finding is consistent with other evidence that attributing the wage gap to job segregation misses its basic cause: men's propensity to maintain their privileges. This claim is neither novel nor specific to men. Marxist and conflict theory have long recognized that dominant groups act to preserve their position (Collins 1975). Like other dominant groups, men are reluctant to give up their advantages (Goode 1982). To avoid having to do so, they construct "rules" for distributing rewards that guarantee them the lion's share (see also Epstein 1985, p. 30). In the past, men cited their need as household heads for a "family wage" (May 1982) and designated women as secondary earners. Today, when millions of women who head households would benefit from such a rule, occupation has supplanted it as the principle for assigning wages.

Neoclassical economic theory holds that the market is the mechanism through which wages are set, but markets are merely systems of rules

(Marshall and Paulin n.d., p. 15) that dominant groups establish for their own purposes. When other groups, such as labor unions, amassed enough power, they modified the "market" principle.[5] Steinberg (1987) observed that when consulted in making comparable-worth adjustments, male-dominated unions tended to support management over changes that would raise women's salaries (see also Simmons, Freedman, Dunkle, and Blau 1975, pp. 115-36; Hartmann 1976).

In sum, the basic cause of the income gap is not sex segregation but men's desire to preserve their advantaged position and their ability to do so by establishing rules to distribute valued resources in their favor.[6] Figure 7.1 represents this more complete causal model. Note that currently segregation is a superficial cause of the income gap, in part through "crowding" (Bergmann 1974), but that some other distributional system such as comparable-worth pay could replace it with the same effect.

With respect to income, this model implies that men will resist efforts to close the wage gap. Resistance will include opposing equalizing women's access to jobs because integration would equalize women and men on the current superficial cause of the wage gap—occupation. Men may also try to preserve job segregation because it is a central mechanism through which they retain their dominance in other spheres, and because many people learn to prefer the company of others like them. This theory also implies that men will resist efforts to replace occupation with alternative principles for assigning pay that would mitigate segregation's effect on women's wages (as pay equity purports to do).

Before I offer evidence for these claims, let us examine how dominant groups in general and men in particular maintain their privileged position. My analysis is formulated with reference to dominant groups to emphasize that the processes I discuss are not specific to sex classes. It also follows that, were women the dominant sex, the claims I make about men's behavior should hold for women.

DIFFERENTIATION, DEVALUATION, AND HIERARCHY

Differentiation—the practice of distinguishing categories based on some attribute—is the fundamental process in hierarchical systems, a logical necessity for differential evaluation and differential rewards. But differentiation involves much more than merely acting on a preexisting difference. In a hierarchical context, differentiation assumes, amplifies, and even creates psychological and behavioral differences in order to ensure that the subordinate group differs from the dominant

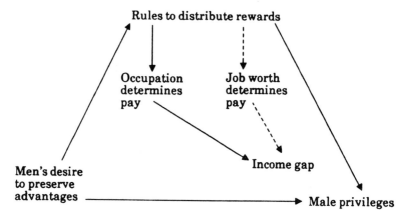

Figure 7.1 Heuristic Model of the Wage Gap

group (Epstein 1985, p. 36; Jaggar 1983, pp. 109-10; MacKinnon 1987, p. 38), "because the systematically differential delivery of benefits and deprivations require[s] making no mistake about who was who" (MacKinnon 1987, p. 40) and because "differences are inequality's post hoc excuse" (MacKinnon 1987, p. 8).

Differentiated status characteristics influence evaluations of people's behavior and their overall worth (Berger, Cohen, and Zelditch 1972; Pugh and Wahrman 1983). In hierarchical systems in which differentiation takes the form of an Aristotelian dichotomy, individuals are classified as either A ("the subject") or Not-A ("the other"). But these two classes are not construed as natural opposites that both have positive qualities; instead, A's characteristics are valued as normal or good and Not-A's as without value or negative (de Beauvoir 1953, p. xvi; Jay 1981).

The official response to the influx of south- and central-eastern European immigrants to the United States early in this century, when people assumed that each European country represented a distinct biological race (Lieberson 1980, p. 24), illustrates differentiation's central role in dominance systems. A congressionally mandated immigration commission concluded that "innate, ineradicable race distinctions separated groups of men from one another" and agreed on the

necessity of classifying these races to know which were most worthy of survival. The immediate problem was to ascertain "whether there may not be certain races that are inferior to other races . . . to discover some test to show whether some may be better fitted for American citizenship than others." (Lieberson 1980, pp. 2-26)

Thus differentiation in all its forms supports dominance systems by demonstrating that superordinate and subordinate groups differ in essential ways and that such differences are natural and even desirable.

"Sex Differentiation" Versus "Gender Differentiation"

Scholars speak of both "sex" and "gender" differentiation: the former when biological sex or the "sex category" into which people are placed at birth (see Chapter 1) is the *basis for* classification and differential treatment; the latter to refer to the *result of* that differential treatment. In order to emphasize that the initial biological difference (mediated through sex category) is the basis for differential treatment, I use the terms *sex differentiation* and *sex segregation*. This usage should not obscure the fact that the process of converting sex category into gender is a social one or that most differences that are assumed to distinguish the sexes are socially created. I agree with Kessler and McKenna (1978) that the "gender attribution process" assumes dimorphism and seeks evidence of it to justify classifying people as male and female and treating them unequally. This chapter examines how and why those differences are produced.

Sex Differentiation and Devaluation

Probably no system of social differentiation is as extensive as that based on sex category. Its prevalence led anthropologist Gayle Rubin to claim that there is "a taboo against the sameness of men and women, a taboo dividing the sexes into two mutually exclusive categories, a taboo that exacerbates the biological differences between the sexes and thereby *creates* gender" (1975, p. 178). Moreover, although femaleness is not always devalued, its deviation from maleness in a culture that reserves virtues for men has meant the devaluation of women (Jay 1981). Bleier's (1987) research on biological scientists' study of sex differences illustrates this point: the "search for the truth about differences, [implies] that difference means *different from the white male norm and, therefore, inferior*" (p. 2; italics added). In consequence, men's activities are typically valued above women's, regardless of their content or importance for group survival (Goode 1964; Mead 1949; Schur 1983, pp. 35-48), and both sexes come to devalue women's efforts (Major, McFarlin, and Gagnon 1984). Thus it should be no surprise that women's occupations pay less at least partly *because* women do them (Treiman and Hartmann 1981).

In short, differentiation is the sine qua non of dominance systems. Because of its importance, it is achieved through myriad ways:

> To go for a walk with one's eyes open is enough to demonstrate that humanity is divided into two classes of individuals whose clothes, faces, bodies, smiles, gaits, interests and occupations are manifestly different. (de Beauvoir 1953, p. xiv)

We differentiate groups in their location, appearance, and behavior, and in the tasks they do. Now let us turn to how these mechanisms operate to differentiate women and men.

PHYSICAL SEGREGATION

Dominant groups differentiate subordinate groups by physically isolating them—in ghettos, nurseries, segregated living quarters, and so on. Physical segregation fosters unequal treatment, because physically separate people can be treated differently and because it spares members of the dominant group the knowledge of the disparity and hides it from the subordinate group. Although women and men are integrated in some spheres, physical separation continues to differentiate them (Goffman 1977, p. 316).

Cohn's (1985) vivid account of women's physical segregation in the British Foreign Office in the nineteenth century illustrates the extent to which organizations have gone to separate the sexes. The Foreign Office hid its first female typists in an attic, but it failed to rescind the requirement that workers collect their pay on the ground floor. When payday came, managers evacuated the corridors, shut all the doors, and then sent the women running down the attic stairs to get their checks and go back up again. Only after they were out of sight were the corridors reopened to men.

This account raises the question of *why* managers segregate working men and women. What licentiousness did the Foreign Office fear would occur in integrated hallways? Contemporary answers are markedly similar to turn-of-the-century fears. Compare the scenario expressed in a 1923 editorial in the *Journal of Accountancy* ("any attempt at heterogeneous personnel [in after-hours auditing of banks] would hamper progress and lead to infinite embarrassment" [p. 151]) with recent reactions to the prospect of women integrating police patrol cars, coal mines, and merchant marine vessels (Martin 1980). At or just below the surface lies the specter of sexual liaisons. For years, McDonald's founder Ray Kroc forbade franchisees to hire women counter workers because they would attract "the wrong type" of customers (Luxenberg 1985). The U.S. Army ended sex-integrated basic training to "facilitate toughening goals" (National Organization for Women 1982), and the Air Force reevaluated whether women could serve on two-person Minuteman missile-silo teams because "it could lead to stress" (*New York Times* 1984).

My thesis offers a more parsimonious alternative to these ad hoc explanations—men resist allowing women and men to work together *as equals* because doing so undermines differentiation and hence male dominance.

BEHAVIORAL DIFFERENTIATION

People's behavior is differentiated on their status-group membership in far too many ways to adequately review the differences here. This section considers the differentiation of behaviors that occur in the workplace: task differentiation and social differentiation.

Task differentiation assigns work according to group membership. It was expressed in the extreme in traditional Hindu society in which caste virtually determined life work. Task assignment based on sex category—the sexual division of labor—both prescribes and proscribes assorted tasks to each sex, and modern societies still assign men and women different roles in domestic work (Pleck 1985), labor-market work (Reskin and Hartmann 1986), and emotional and interpersonal work (Fishman 1982; Hochschild 1983).[7] Task differentiation generally assigns to lower-status groups the least desirable, most poorly rewarded work: menial, tedious, and degraded tasks, such as cleaning, disposing of waste, and caring for the dying.[8] This practice symbolizes and legitimates the subordinate group's low status, while making it appear to have an affinity for these undesirable tasks. As an added benefit, members of the dominant group don't have to do them. Important to discussions of the male-female wage gap, because modern law and custom permit unequal pay for different work, task differentiation justifies paying the subordinate group lower wages, thereby ensuring their economic inferiority. Women's assignment to child care, viewed as unskilled work in our society, illustrates these patterns. Women are said to have a "natural talent" for it and similar work; men are relieved from doing it; society obtains free or cheap child care; and women are handicapped in competing with men. As researchers have shown, sex-based task differentiation of both non-market and market

work legitimates women's lower pay, hinders women's ability to succeed in traditionally male enterprises, and, in general, reinforces men's
hegemony (Coverman 1983).

Social differentiation is achieved through norms that set dominant
and subordinate groups apart in their appearance (sumptuary rules) or
behavior (etiquette rules [van den Berghe 1960]). When applied to
sex, Goffman's (1976) concept of "gender display" encompasses both.
Sumptuary rules require certain modes of dress, diet, or life-style of
members of subordinate groups as emblems of their inferior status, and
reserve other modes to distinguish the dominant group. For example,
Rollins (1985) discovered that White female employers preferred
Black domestic employees to dress shabbily to exaggerate their economic inferiority. Sex-specific sumptuary rules are epitomized in norms
that dictate divergent dress styles that often exaggerate physical sex
differences and sometimes even incapacitate women (Roberts 1977).[9]
An extreme example is the *burqua* fundamentalist Muslim women
wear as a symbol of their status and as a portable system of segregation
(Papanek 1973).

Etiquette rules support differentiation by requiring subordinate group
members to display ritualized deference toward dominants. Relations
between enlistees and officers (van den Berghe 1960) or female domestic workers and their employers (Rollins 1985) illustrate their role.
Although typically it is the subordinate group that must defer, gender
etiquette that requires middle- and upper-class men to display deference
to women of the same classes preserves differentiation by highlighting
women's differentness. Women who do not express gratitude or who
refuse to accept the deference are faced with hostility, shattering the
fiction that women hold the preferred position.

Physical segregation, behavioral differentiation, social separation,
and even hierarchy are functional alternatives for satisfying the need
for differentiation in domination systems. For example, when their
physical integration with the dominant group means that a subordinate
group's status differences might otherwise be invisible, special dress is
usually required of them, as servants are required to wear uniforms.
Physical separation can even compensate for the absence of hierarchy,
a point acknowledged in the Black folk saying that southern Whites
don't care how close Blacks get if they don't get too high, and northern
Whites don't care how high Blacks get if they don't get too close (Lukas
1985).

This substitutability explains why men will tolerate women in predominantly male work settings if they work in "women's" jobs and
accept women doing "men's" jobs in traditionally female settings, but

resist women doing traditionally male jobs in male work settings (Schroedel 1985). Physical proximity per se is not threatening as long as another form of differentiation sets women apart. But the absence of *any* form of differentiation precludes devaluation and unequal rewards and hence threatens the sex-gender hierarchy. Because of the centrality of differentiation in domination systems, dominant groups have a considerable stake in maintaining it.

DOMINANTS' RESPONSE TO CHALLENGES

Dominants respond to subordinates' challenges by citing the group differences that supposedly warrant differential treatment (Jackman and Muha 1984). Serious challenges often give rise to attempts to demonstrate biological differences scientifically.

The nineteenth-century antislavery and women's rights movements led reputable scientists to try to prove that women's and Blacks' brains were underdeveloped (Bleier 1987). The Great Migration to the United States in the first two decades of this century fueled a eugenics movement that purported to establish scientifically the inferiority of south- and central-eastern Europeans (Lieberson 1980, pp. 25-6). The civil rights movement of the 1960s stimulated renewed efforts to establish racial differences in intelligence. And we are once again witnessing a spate of allegedly scientific research seeking a biological basis for presumed sex differences in cognitive ability and, specifically, for boys' higher average scores on math questions in some standardized tests. As Bleier (1987) pointed out, "The implication if not purposes of [such] research is to demonstrate that the structure of society faithfully reflects the natural order of things" (1987, p. 11; see also Epstein 1985, pp. 32, 35, for a similar pattern in the social sciences). According to Bleier, reputable journals have published studies that violate accepted standards of proof, and the scientific press has given dubious findings considerable attention (as in the news story in *Science* that asked, "Is There a Male Math Gene?"). Although subsequently these studies have been discredited, the debate serves its purpose by focusing attention on how groups differ.[10]

MEN'S RESPONSE
TO OCCUPATIONAL INTEGRATION

An influx of women into male spheres threatens the differentiation of men and women, and men resist (Goode 1982). One response is to bar women's entry. Women have had to turn to the courts to win entry into Little League sports, college dining clubs, private professional clubs, and the Rotary (Anderson 1987; Association of American Colleges 1985, p. 11; Schafran 1981). Recently, University of North Carolina trustees decried the fact that women are now a majority of UNC students, and some proposed changing the weights for certain admission criteria to restore the male majority (Greene 1987).[11] Since a shortage of male recruits forced the army to lift its quota on women, it has twice reduced the number of jobs open to women (Becraft 1987, p. 3).

Numerous studies have documented men's resistance to women entering "their" jobs (Hartmann 1976; Schroedel 1985). Sometimes the resistance is simply exclusion; at other times it is subtle barriers that block women's advancement or open harassment (Reskin 1978). Now that more women hold managerial jobs, one hears of "a glass ceiling" that bars middle-management women from top-level positions (Hymowitz and Schellhardt 1986), and Moss Kanter (1987) claimed that organizations are changing the rules of what one must do to reach the top in order to make it more difficult for women to succeed.

My thesis implies that men will respond to women's challenge in the workplace by emphasizing how they differ from men. Especially common are reminders of women's "natural" roles as wife, mother, or sexual partner. Witness the recent—and subsequently disputed—claims that women who postponed marriage and childbearing to establish their careers had a negligible chance of finding husbands and were running the risk that their "biological clocks" would prevent pregnancy, and accounts of women dropping out of middle management to spend more time with their children.[12]

Men who cannot bar women from "male" jobs can still preserve differentiation in other spheres. Their attempts to do so may explain why so few husbands of wage-working women share housework (Pleck 1985, p. 146), as well as elucidate Wharton and Baron's (1987) finding that men working in sex-integrated jobs whose wives were employed were more dissatisfied than unmarried men or men married to homemakers.

Another response to women's challenge is to weaken the mechanisms that have helped women advance in the workplace. The Reagan administration sought to undermine equal-opportunity programs and affirmative-action regulations, and the campaign partly succeeded. Efforts to dilute or eliminate Equal Employment Opportunity (EEO) programs are advanced by claims that sex inequality has disappeared (or that men now experience "reverse discrimination"). For example, the *New York Times* (Greer 1987, pp. C1, 10) recently described the Department of Commerce announcement that women now compose the majority in professional occupations as a "historic milestone," adding that "the barriers have fallen."

THE ILLUSION OF OCCUPATIONAL INTEGRATION

If male resistance is so pervasive, how can we explain the drop in the index of occupational sex segregation in the 1970s and women's disproportionate gains in a modest number of male-dominated occupations (Rytina and Bianchi 1984)? In order to answer this question, Patricia Roos and I embarked on a study of the changing sex composition of occupations (Reskin and Roos 1990). The results of our case studies of a dozen traditionally male occupations in which women made disproportionate statistical gains during the 1970s cast doubt on whether many women can advance economically through job integration.

The case studies revealed two general patterns. First, within many occupations nominally being integrated, men and women remain highly segregated, with men concentrated in the highest-status and best-paying jobs. For example, although women's representation in baking grew from 25 percent in 1970 to 41 percent in 1980, men continue to dominate production baking. The increase in women bakers is due almost wholly to their concentration in proliferating "in-store" bakeries (Steiger 1987). Although women now make up the majority of residential real estate salespersons, men still monopolize commercial sales (Thomas and Reskin 1987).

The second pattern shows that women often gained access to these occupations after changes in work content and declines in autonomy or rewards made the work less attractive to men (Cockburn 1986, p. 76). In some occupations, the growth of functions already socially labeled as "women's work" (e.g., clerical, communications, or emotional work) spurred the change. For example, computerization and the ensuing clericalization prompted women's entry into typesetting and composing (Roos 1986) and insurance adjusting and examining (Phipps 1986). An increasing emphasis on communicating and interpersonal or emotional work contributed to women's gains in insurance sales (Thomas 1987), insurance adjusting, and examining (Phipps 1987), systems analysis (Donato 1986), public relations (Donato 1987), and bank and financial management (Bird 1987).

Brief summaries of our findings for two occupations illustrate these processes.[13] First, women's disproportionate gains in pharmacy have been largely confined to the retail sector (male pharmacists work disproportionately in research and management) and occurred after retail pharmacists lost professional status and entrepreneurial opportunities.

After drug manufacturers took over the compounding of drugs, pharmacists increasingly resembled retail sales clerks; their primary duties became dispensing and record keeping. As chain and discount-store pharmacies supplanted independently owned pharmacies, retail pharmacy no longer offered a chance to own one's own business, reducing another traditional attraction for men. The resulting shortages of male pharmacy graduates eased women's access to training programs and retail jobs (Phipps 1987).

Second, book editing illustrates how declining autonomy and occupational prestige contributed to feminization of an occupation. For most of this century, the cultural image of publishing attracted bright young men and women despite very low wages. But during the 1970s, multinational conglomerates entered book publishing, with profound results. Their emphasis on the bottom line robbed publishing of its cultural aura, and the search for blockbusters brought a greater role for marketing people in acquisition decisions, thereby eroding editorial autonomy. As a result, editing could no longer compete effectively for talented men who could choose from better opportunities. Because women's occupational choices are more limited than men's, editing still attracted them, and the occupation's sex composition shifted accordingly (Reskin 1987).

In summary, although sex integration appears to have occurred in the 1970s among census-designated detailed occupations (Beller 1984), our findings indicate that within these occupations women are segregated into certain specialties or work settings and that they gained entry because various changes made the occupations less attractive to men. The nominal integration that occurred in the 1970s often masks within-occupation segregation or presages resegregation of traditionally male occupations as women's work. In short, the workplace is still overwhelmingly differentiated by sex. Moreover, our preliminary results suggest that real incomes in the occupations we are studying declined during the 1970s; so reducing segregation at the occupational level appears to have been relatively ineffective in reducing the wage gap—and was certainly not the remedy many experts predicted. This brings us to the other possible remedy for the wage gap—comparable worth.

IMPLICATIONS FOR COMPARABLE WORTH

The comparable-worth movement calls for equal pay for work of equal worth. Worth is usually determined by job-evaluation studies that measure the skill, effort, and responsibility required, but in practice assessing worth often turns on how to conceptualize and measure skill.

Although some objective criteria exist for assessing skill (e.g., how long it takes a worker to learn the job [see Spenner 1985, pp. 132-6]), typically the designation of work as skilled is socially negotiated. Workers are most likely to win it when they control social resources that permit them to press their claims, such as a monopoly over a labor supply or authority based on their personal characteristics such as education, training, or sex (Phillips and Taylor 1980). As a result, the evaluation of "skill" is shaped by and confounded with workers' sex (Dex 1985, p. 100).

Groups use the same power that enabled them to define their work as skilled to restrict competition by excluding women (among others) from training for and practicing their trade or profession (Dex 1985, p. 103; see also Hartmann 1976), as Millicent Fawcett recognized almost a hundred years ago when she declared, "Equal pay for equal work is a fraud for women." Because men use their power to keep women "from obtaining equal skills, their work [cannot be] equal" (Hartmann 1976, p. 157). Roos's (1986) case history of the effect of technological change on women's employment in typesetting illustrates these points. When a Linotype machine was developed that "female typists could operate," the International Typographical Union (ITU) used its labor monopoly to force employers to agree to hire as operators only skilled printers who knew *all* aspects of the trade. By denying women access to apprenticeships or other channels to become fully skilled and limiting the job of operating the Linotype to highly skilled printers, the ITU effectively barred women from the new Linotype jobs. In short, the ITU used its monopoly power both to restrict women's access to skills and credentials and to define its members as "uniquely skilled" to operate the Linotype.

Excluded from occupations male workers define as skilled, women are often unable, for several reasons, to press the claim that work in traditionally female occupations is skilled. First, the devaluation of women's work leads whatever work women do to be seen as unskilled. Second, women's powerlessness prevents their successfully defining their work—caring for children, entering data, assembling microelectronic circuits—as skilled. Third, because many female-dominated occupations require workers to acquire skills before employment, skill acquisition is less visible and hence unlikely to be socially credited. Fourth, the scarcity of apprenticeship programs for women's jobs and women's exclusion from other programs denies women a credential society recognizes as denoting skill (Reskin and Hartmann 1986). Finally, "much of women's work involves recognizing and responding to subtle cues" (Feldberg 1984, p. 321), but the notion of "women's intuition" permits men to define such skills as inborn and hence not meriting compensation. Thus women are kept from both acquiring socially valued skills and being credited for those they do acquire (Steinberg 1984-85). As a result, the sex of the majority of workers in an occupation influences whether or not their work is classified as skilled (Feldberg 1984; Gregory 1987).

In view of these patterns, how effective can comparable worth be in reducing the wage gap? As with the Equal Pay Act, its implementation has symbolic value. Moreover, it would bar employers from underpaying women relative to their job-evaluation scores, the practice alleged in "AFSCME v. Washington State" (1985). But setting salaries according to an occupation's worth will reduce the wage gap only to the extent that (1) women have access to tasks that society values, (2) evaluators do not take workers' sex into account in determining a job's worth, and (3) implementers do not sacrifice equity to other political agendas.

Neither of the first two conditions holds. As I have shown, men already dominate jobs society deems skilled. Moreover, the tendency to devalue women's work is embedded in job-evaluation techniques that define job worth (Steinberg 1984-85); so such techniques may yield biased evaluations of traditionally female jobs and lower their job-evaluation scores (Treiman and Hartmann 1981; Marshall and Paulin n.d., p. 5). Beyond these difficulties is the problem of good-faith implementation. Acker (1987) and Steinberg (1987) have documented the problems in implementing comparable-worth pay adjustments. According to Steinberg (p. 8), New York State's proposed compensation model *negatively* values working with difficult clients, work performed in historically female and minority jobs (in other words, workers lose pay for doing it!), and Massachusetts plans to establish separate comparable-worth plans across sex-segregated bargaining units. For these reasons, the magnitude of comparable-worth adjustments have been about half of what experts expected—only 5 percent to 15 percent of salaries (Steinberg 1987; see also Chapter 10).

Moreover, to the extent that equity adjustments significantly raise salaries in women's jobs, men can use their power to monopolize them. It is no accident that the men who integrated the female semi-professions moved rapidly to the top (Grimm and Stern 1974). The recent experience of athletic directors provides an additional illustration. Title IX of the U.S. Civil Rights Act of 1964 required college athletic programs to eliminate disparities in resources between women's and men's programs, including salaries. Within ten years the proportion of coaches for women's programs who were male grew from 10 percent to 50 percent (Alfano 1985). Finally, men as the primary implementers of job evaluation have a second line of defense—they can and do subvert the process of job evaluation.

CONCLUSION

Integrating men's jobs and implementing comparable-worth programs have helped some women economically and, if more fully implemented, would help others. But neither strategy can be broadly effective because both are premised on a flawed causal model of the pay gap that assigns primary responsibility to job segregation. A theory that purports to explain unequal outcomes without examining the dominant group's stake in maintaining them is incomplete. Like other dominant groups, men make rules that preserve their privileges. With respect to earnings, the current rule—that one's job or occupation determines one's pay—has maintained White men's economic advantage because men and women and Whites and non-Whites are differently distributed across jobs.[14]

Changing the allocation principle from occupation to job worth would help non-Whites and women if occupation were the pay gap's *basic* cause. But it is not. As long as a dominant group wants to subordinate others' interests to its own and is able to do so, the outcome—distributing more income to men than women—is, in a sense, its own cause, and tinkering with superficial causes will not substantially alter it. The rule that one's occupation determines one's wages either exists *because* men and women hold different occupations, or men and women hold different occupations because we allocate wages according to one's occupation. Obviously the dominant group will resist attempts to change the rules. In "Lemons v. City and County of Denver" (1980), the court called comparable worth "pregnant with the possibility of disrupting the entire economic system" (Steinberg 1987). "Disrupting the entire White-male dominance system" would have been closer to the mark.

If men's desire to preserve their privileges is the basic cause of the wage gap, how can we bring about change? The beneficiaries of hierarchical reward systems yield their privileges only when failing to yield is more costly than yielding. Increasing the costs men pay to maintain the status quo or rewarding men for dividing resources more equitably may reduce their resistance.

As individuals, many men will gain economically if their partners earn higher wages. Of course, these men stand to lose whatever advantages come from out-earning one's partner (Hartmann 1976; Kollock, Blumstein, and Schwartz 1985). But more important than individual adjustments are those achieved through organizations that have the power to impose rewards and penalties. Firms that recognize their economic stake in treating women equitably (or can be pressed by women employees or EEO agencies to act as if they do) can be an important source of pressure on male employees. Employers have effectively used various incentives to overcome resistance to affirmative action (e.g., rewarding supervisors for treating women fairly [Shaeffer and Lynton 1975; Walshok 1981]). Employers are most likely to use such mechanisms if they believe that regulatory agencies are enforcing equal-opportunity rules (Reskin and Hartmann 1986). We can attack men's resistance through political pressure on employers, the regulatory agencies that monitor them, and branches of government that establish and fund such agencies.

Analyses of sex inequality in the 1980s implicitly advanced a no-fault concept of institutionalized discrimination rather than fixing any responsibility on men. But men *are* the dominant group, the makers and the beneficiaries of the rules. Of course, most men do not consciously oppose equality for women (Kluegel and Smith 1986) or try to thwart women's progress. When men and women work together, both can gain, as occurred when the largely male blue-collar union supported the striking Yale clerical and technical workers (Ladd-Taylor 1985; see also Glazer 1987). But, as a rule, this silent majority avoids the fray, leaving the field to those who do resist to act on behalf of all men (Bergmann and Darity 1981). It is time to bring men back into our theories of economic inequality. To do so does not imply that women are passive agents. The gains we have made in the last two decades in the struggle for economic equality—redefining the kinds of work women can do, reshaping young people's aspirations, and amassing popular support for pay equity despite opponents' attempt to write it off as a "loony tune" idea—stand as testimony to the contrary. Just as the causal model I have proposed views the dominant group's self-interest as the source of unequal outcomes, so too does it see subordinate groups as the agents of change.

NOTES

1. Women's incomes are not depressed uniformly. Women of color continue to earn less than White women, particularly when their hours of work are controlled. As I indicate below, the same general social processes that subordinate women as a group—differentiation and devaluation—operate to preserve the advantages of White men *and women.*

2. Workplace segregation occurs across occupations and, within occupations, across jobs. For convenience, I speak primarily of occupational segregation because most segregation and income data are for occupations, but my remarks apply as well to jobs.

3. My informant said that his campus now weighs the admissions essay more heavily for this reason.

4. For example, Smith and Ward (1984) attributed the wage gap's failure to narrow to the influx of less-experienced women into the labor force during the 1970s.

5. Some employers do reward productivity, as neoclassical economists predict, but for the most part wages are attached to occupations—the proximate cause of workers' wages.

6. Of course, only a subset of men—predominantly upper-class Whites—actually make rules, and the rules they make protect class- and race- as well as sex-based interests.

7. A full explanation of the specific forces that produce the sexual division of labor is beyond the scope of this chapter, but social-control systems, including gender ideology, "custom," socialization, and myriad institutionalized structures, shape the preferences of wives and husbands, workers and employers, women and men (Reskin and Hartmann 1986). These preferences in turn are played out in concert with institutional arrangements (training programs, personnel practices, child-care facilities, informal organization) to give rise to the task differentiation we observe in the home and workplace.

8. This is not to say that all tasks assigned to subordinate groups are unimportant or undesirable. Many, such as reproducing, socializing the young, and burying the dead, are essential. Others are more intrinsically pleasant (e.g., office work) than the work some dominant-group members do (which has led economists to argue that men's wages are higher than women's partly to compensate them for doing less desirable jobs [Filer 1985]).

9. This perspective elucidates the importance that the media attached to the wearing, spurning, and burning of bras in the early 1970s. Shedding or burning these symbols of women's sex (and hence their status) constituted insubordination.

10. For example, at the 1987 meetings of the American Educational Research Association, 25 sessions reported research on sex differences in interest or achievement in math and science (Holden 1987, p. 660).

11. Trustee John Pope remarked, "Any time you get over 50 percent, it's becoming more and more a girls' school . . . and I don't think favoritism should be given to the females" (Greene 1987). It apparently did not strike him as favoritism when the rules produced a male majority.

12. The return in the late 1970s of feminine dress styles following the entry of large numbers of women into professional and managerial jobs is probably not coincidental. Although caution is in order in drawing conclusions about changing dress styles, a quick trip through a department store should persuade readers that dresses and skirts have supplanted pants for women (see Reskin and Roos 1987). Although fashion is ostensibly a woman's choice, most women are aware of the sanctions that await those who fail to dress appropriately.

13. Limited space forces me to condense sharply the causes of women's disproportional gains in these occupations. For a full account, see the complete studies.

14. It also serves the interest of the economically dominant classes by legitimating a wide disparity in income. Comparable-worth pay would largely preserve that disparity, in keeping with the class interests of its middle-class proponents and its implementers (Brenner 1987).

REFERENCES

Acker, J. 1987. "Sex Bias in Job Evaluation: A Comparable-Worth Issue." Pp. 183-96 in *Ingredients for Women's Employment Policy,* edited by C. Bose and G. Spitze. Albany: SUNY Press.

AFSCME v. State of Washington. 1985. 770 F.2d 1401. 9th Circuit.

Alfano, P. 1985. "Signs of Problems Amid the Progress." *New York Times* (December 14):25, 28.

Anderson, S. Heller. 1987. "Men's Clubs Pressed to Open Doors for Women." *New York Times* (February 1).

Association of American Colleges. 1985. "Princeton's All-Male Eating Clubs Eat Crow." *Project on the Status and Education of Women* (Fall):11.

Becraft, C. 1987. "Women in the Military." Pp. 203-7 in *The American Woman: A Report in Depth,* edited by S. Rix. New York: Norton.

Beller, A. 1984. "Trends in Occupational Segregation by Sex and Race." Pp. 11-26 in *Sex Segregation in the Workplace: Trends, Explanations, Remedies,* edited by B. F. Reskin. Washington, DC: National Academy Press.

Berger, J., B. P. Cohen, and M. Zelditch. 1972. "Status Characteristics and Social Interaction." *American Sociological Review* 37:241-55.

Bergmann, B. R., 1974. "Occupational Segregation, Wages and Profits When Employers Discriminate by Race or Sex." *Eastern Economic Journal* 1:103-10.

—— and W. Darity. 1981. "Social Relations, Productivity, and Employer Discrimination." *Monthly Labor Review* 104:47-9.

Bielby, W. T., and J. N. Baron. 1984. "A Woman's Place Is with Other Women." Pp. 27-55 in *Sex Segregation in the Workplace: Trends, Explanations, Remedies,* edited by B. F. Reskin. Washington, DC: National Academy Press.

Bird, C. 1987. "Changing Sex Composition of Bank and Financial Managers." Unpublished manuscript. University of Illinois, Urbana.

Blau, F. D., and M. A. Ferber. 1986. *The Economics of Women, Men and Work.* Englewood Cliffs, NJ: Prentice-Hall.

Bleier, R. 1987. "Gender Ideology: The Medical and Scientific Construction of Women." Lecture presented at the University of Illinois, Urbana.

Cockburn, C. 1986. "The Relations of Technology: Implications for Theories of Sex and Class." Pp. 74-85 in *Gender and Stratification,* edited by R. Crompton and M. Mann. Cambridge, UK: Polity Press.

Cohn, S. 1985. *The Process of Occupational Sex Typing.* Philadelphia: Temple University Press.

Collins, R. 1975. *Conflict Sociology.* New York: Academic Press.

Coverman, S. 1983. "Gender, Domestic Labor Time, and Wage Inequality." *American Sociological Review* 48:623-37.

de Beauvoir, S. 1953. *The Second Sex.* New York: Knopf.

Dex, S. 1985. *The Sexual Division of Work.* New York: St. Martin's.

Donato, K. M. 1986. "Women in Systems Analysis." Paper presented at Annual Meetings, American Sociological Association. New York.

——. 1987. "Keepers of the Corporate Image: Women in Public Relations." Paper presented at Annual Meetings, American Sociological Association, Chicago.

Epstein, C. Fuchs. 1985. "Ideal Roles and Real Roles or the Fallacy of the Misplaced Dichotomy." *Research in Social Stratification and Mobility* 4:29-51.

Feldberg, R. L. 1984. "Comparable Worth: Toward Theory and Practice in the United States." *Signs: Journal of Women in Culture and Society* 10:311-28.

Filer, R. K. 1985. "Male-Female Wage Differences: The Importance of Compensating Differentials." *Industrial & Labor Relations Review* 38:426-37.

Fishman, P. 1982. "Interaction: The Work Women Do." Pp. 170-80 in *Women and Work,* edited by R. Kahn-Hut and A. Kaplan Daniels. New York: Oxford University Press.

Glazer, N. Y. 1987. "Where Are the Women? The Absence of Women as Social Agents in Theories of Occupational Sex Segregation." Paper presented at Annual Meetings, American Sociological Association, Chicago.

Goffman, E. 1976. "Gender Display." *Studies in the Anthropology of Visual Communication* 3:69-77.

———. 1977. "The Arrangement Between the Sexes." *Theory and Society* 4:301-31.

Goode, W. C. 1964. *The Family.* Englewood Cliffs, NJ: Prentice-Hall.

———. 1982. "Why Men Resist." Pp. 121-50 in *Rethinking the Family,* edited by B. Thorne with M. Yalom. New York: Longman.

Greene, E. 1987. "Too Many Women? That's the Problem at Chapel Hill, Say Some Trustees." *Chronicle of Higher Education* (January 28):27-8.

Greer, W. R. 1987. "In Professions, Women Now a Majority." *New York Times* (March 19):C1, 10.

Gregory, R. G. 1987. Lecture. Labor and Industrial Relations Institute, University of Illinois, Urbana.

Grimm, J. W., and R. N. Stern. 1974. "Sex Roles and Internal Labor Market Structures: The Female Semi-Professions." *Social Problems* 21:690-705.

Hartmann, H. 1976. "Capitalism, Patriarchy, and Job Segregation by Sex." *Signs: Journal of Women in Culture and Society* 1(Part 2):137-69.

Hechinger, F. M. 1987. "The Trouble with Quotas." *New York Times* (February 10):C1.

Hochschild, A. 1983. *The Managed Heart.* Berkeley: University of California Press.

Holden, C. 1987. "Female Math Anxiety on the Wane." *Science* 236:660-61.

Hymowitz, C., and T. D. Schellhardt. 1986. "The Glass Ceiling." *Wall Street Journal* (March 24):Section 4, 1.

Jackman, M., and M. Muha. 1984. "Education and Intergroup Attitudes." *American Sociological Review* 49:751-69.

Jaggar, A. M. 1983. *Feminist Politics and Human Nature.* Totowa, NJ: Rowman & Allanheld.

Jay, N. 1981. "Gender and Dichotomy." *Feminist Studies* 7:38-56.

Journal of Accountancy. 1984. "J of A Revisited: Women in Accountancy." 158:151-2.

Kanter, R. Moss. 1987. "Men and Women of the Change Master Corporation (1977-1987 and Beyond): Dilemmas and Consequences of Innovations of Organizational Structure." Paper presented at Annual Meetings, Academy of Management, New Orleans.

Kessler, S., and W. McKenna. 1978. *Gender: An Ethnomethodological Approach.* New York: John Wiley.

Kluegel, J. R., and E. R. Smith. 1986. *Beliefs about Inequality.* New York: Aldine de Gruyter.

Kollock, P., P. Blumstein, and P. Schwartz. 1985. "Sex and Power in Interaction." *American Sociological Review* 50:34-46.

Ladd-Taylor, M. 1985. "Women Workers and the Yale Strike." *Feminist Studies* 11:464-89.

Lemons v. City and County of Denver. 1980. 620 F.2d 228. 10th Circuit.

Lieberson. S. 1980. *A Piece of the Pie.* Berkeley: University of California Press.

———. 1985. *Making It Count.* Berkeley: University of California Press.

Lukas, J. Anthony. 1985. *Common Ground.* New York: Knopf.

Luxenberg, S. 1985. *Roadside Empires.* New York: Viking.

MacKinnon, C. 1987. *Feminism Unmodified.* Cambridge, MA: Harvard University Press.

Major, B., D. B. McFarlin, and D. Gagnon. 1984. "Overworked and Underpaid: On the Nature of Gender Differences in Personal Entitlement." *Journal of Personality and Social Psychology* 47:1399-412.

Marshall, R., and B. Paulin. N.D. "Some Practical Aspects of Comparable Worth." Unpublished manuscript.

Martin, S. E. 1980. *Breaking and Entering.* Berkeley: University of California Press.

May, M. 1982. "Historical Problems of the Family Wage: The Ford Motor Company and the Five Dollar Day." *Feminist Studies* 8:395-424.

Mead, M. 1949. *Male and Female.* New York: William Morrow.

National Organization for Women. 1982. *NOW Times* (July).

New York Times. 1984. "Air Force Studies Male-Female Missile Crews." (December 12).

———. 1987. "Dispute on Sex Ratio Troubles Women at North Carolina University." (March 22).

Papanek, H. 1973. "Purdah: Separate Worlds and Symbolic Shelter." *Comparative Studies in Society and History* 15:289-325.

Phillips, A., and B. Taylor. 1980. "Sex and Skill: Notes Towards a Feminist Economics" *Feminist Review* 6:79-88.

Phipps, P. 1986. "Occupational Resegregation: A Case Study of Insurance Adjusters, Examiners and Investigators." Paper presented at Annual Meetings, American Sociological Association, New York.

———. 1987. "Women in Pharmacy: Industrial and Occupational Change." Paper presented at Annual Meetings, American Sociological Association, Chicago.

Pleck, J. H. 1985. *Working Wives, Working Husbands.* Beverly Hills, CA: Sage.

Pugh, M. D., and R. Wahrman. 1983. "Neutralizing Sexism in Mixed-Sex Groups: Do Women Have to Be Better than Men?" *American Journal of Sociology* 88:746-62.

Reskin, B. F., 1978. "Sex Differentiation and the Social Organization of Science." *Sociological Inquiry* 48:6-36.

———. 1987. "Culture, Commerce and Gender: The Changing Sex Composition of Book Editors." Unpublished manuscript.

——— and H. I. Hartmann. 1986. *Women's Work, Men's Work, Sex Segregation on the Job.* Washington, DC: National Academy Press.

Reskin, B. F., and P. A. Roos. 1987. "Sex Segregation and Status Hierarchies." Pp. 1-21 in *Ingredients for Women's Employment Policy,* edited by C. Bose and G. Spitze. Albany: SUNY Press.

———. 1990. *Job Queues, Gender Queues: Explaining Women's Inroads into Male Occupations.* Philadelphia: Temple University Press.

Roberts, H. E. 1977. "The Exquisite Slave: The Role of Clothes in the Making of the Victorian Woman." *Signs: Journal of Women in Culture and Society* 2:554-69.

Rollins, J. 1985. *Between Women.* Philadelphia: Temple University Press.

Roos, P. A. 1986. "Women in the Composing Room: Technology and Organization as the Determinants of Social Change." Paper presented at Annual Meetings, American Sociological Association, New York.

Rubin, G. 1975. "The Traffic in Women: Notes on the 'Political Economy' of Sex." Pp. 157-210 in *Toward an Anthropology of Women,* edited by R. R. Reiter. New York: Monthly Review Press.

Rytina, N. F., and S. M. Bianchi. 1984. "Occupational Reclassification and Changes in Distribution by Gender." *Monthly Labor Review* 107:11-7.

Schafran, L. Hecht. 1981. *Removing Financial Support from Private Clubs That Discriminate Against Women.* New York: Women and Foundations Corporate Philanthropy.

Schroedel, J. Reith. 1985. *Alone in a Crowd.* Philadelphia: Temple University Press.

Schur, E. M. 1983. *Labeling Women Deviant.* New York: Random House.

Shaeffer, R. Gilbert, and E. F. Lynton. 1975. *Corporate Experience in Improving Women's Job Opportunities.* Report no. 755. New York: The Conference Board.

Simmons, A. A. Freedman, M. Dunkle, and F. Blau. 1975. *Exploitation from 9 to 5.* Lexington, MA: Lexington.

Smith, J. P., and M. Ward. 1984. *Women's Wages and Work in the Twentieth Century.* R-3119 NICHD. Santa Monica, CA: Rand Corporation.

Spenner, K. I. 1985. "The Upgrading and Downgrading of Occupations: Issues, Evidence, and Implications for Education." *Review of Educational Research* 55(Summer):125-54.

Steiger, T. 1987. "Female Employment Gains and Sex Segregation: The Case of Bakers." Paper presented at Annual Meetings, American Sociological Association, Chicago.

Steinberg, R. J. 1984-85. "Identifying Wage Discrimination and Implementing Pay Equity Adjustments." In *Comparable Worth: Issues for the 80s.* Vol. 1. Washington, DC: Commission on Civil Rights.

———. 1987. "Radical Challenges in a Liberal World: The Mixed Successes of Comparable Worth." *Gender & Society* 1:466-75.

Thomas, B. J. 1987. "Changing Sex Composition of Insurance Agents." Unpublished manuscript.

——— and B. F. Reskin. 1987. "Occupational Change and Sex Integration in Real Estate Sales." Paper presented at the Annual Meetings, American Sociological Association, Chicago.

Treiman, D. J., and H. Hartmann. 1981. *Women, Work and Wages: Equal Pay for Jobs of Equal Value.* Washington, DC: National Academy Press.

van den Berghe, P. 1960. "Distance Mechanisms of Stratification." *Sociology and Social Research* 44:155-64.

Walshok, M. Lindenstein. 1981. "Some Innovations in Industrial Apprenticeship at General Motors." Pp. 173-82 in *Apprenticeship Research: Emerging Findings and Future Trends*, edited by V. M. Briggs, Jr., and F. Foltman. Ithaca: New York State School of Industrial Relations.

Wharton, A., and J. Baron. 1987. "The Impact of Gender Segregation on Men at Work." *American Sociological Review* 52:574-87.

8. HIERARCHIES, JOBS, BODIES: A THEORY OF GENDERED ORGANIZATIONS

JOAN ACKER

Most of us spend most of our days in work organizations that are almost always dominated by men. The most powerful organizational positions are almost entirely occupied by men, with the exception of the occasional biological female who acts as a social man (Sorenson 1984). Power at the national and world level is located in all-male enclaves at the pinnacle of large state and economic organizations. These facts are not news, although sociologists paid no attention to them until feminism came along to point out the problematic nature of the obvious (Acker and Van Houten 1974; Kanter 1975, 1977). Writers on organizations and organizational theory now include some consideration of women and gender (Clegg and Dunkerley 1980; Mills 1988; Morgan 1986), but their treatment is usually cursory, and male domination is, on the whole, not analyzed and not explained (Hearn and Parkin 1983).

Among feminist social scientists there are some outstanding contributions on women and organizations, such as the work of Moss Kanter (1977), Feldberg and Nakano Glenn (1979), MacKinnon (1979), and Ferguson (1984). In addition, there have been theoretical and empirical investigations of particular aspects of organizational structure and process (Izraeli 1983; Martin 1985), and women's situations have been studied using traditional organizational ideas (Dexter 1985; Wallace 1982). Moreover, the very rich literature, popular and scholarly, on women and work contains much material on work organizations. However, most of this new knowledge has not been brought together in a systematic feminist theory of organizations.

A systematic theory of gender and organizations is needed for a number of reasons. First, the gender segregation of work, including divisions between paid and unpaid work, is partly created through organizational practices. Second, and related to gender segregation, income and status inequality between women and men is also partly

162

created in organizational processes; understanding these processes is necessary for understanding gender inequality. Third, organizations are one arena in which widely disseminated cultural images of gender are invented and reproduced. Knowledge of cultural production is important for understanding gender construction (Hearn and Parkin 1987). Fourth, some aspects of individual gender identity, perhaps particularly masculinity, are also products of organizational processes and pressures. Fifth, an important feminist project is to make large-scale organizations more democratic and more supportive of humane goals.

In this chapter, I examine organizations as gendered processes in which both gender and sexuality have been obscured through a gender-neutral, asexual discourse, and suggest some of the ways that gender, the body, and sexuality are part of the processes of control in work organizations. At the end, I point to some directions for feminist theory about this ubiquitous human invention.

INVISIBLE WOMEN

Both traditional and critical approaches to organizations originate in the male, abstract intellectual domain (Smith 1988) and take as reality the world as seen from that standpoint. As a relational phenomenon, gender is difficult to see when only the masculine is present. Since men in organizations take their behavior and perspectives to represent the human, organizational structures and processes are theorized as gender neutral. When it is acknowledged that women and men are affected differently by organizations, it is argued that gendered attitudes and behavior are brought into (and contaminate) essentially gender-neutral structures. This view of organizations separates structures from the people in them.

Current theories of organization also ignore sexuality. Certainly, a gender-neutral structure is also asexual. If sexuality is a core component of the production of gender identity, gender images, and gender inequality, organizational theory that is blind to sexuality does not immediately offer avenues into the comprehension of gender domination (Hearn and Parkin 1983, 1987). MacKinnon's (1982) compelling argument that sexual domination of women is embedded within legal organizations has not to date become part of mainstream discussions. Rather, behaviors such as sexual harassment are viewed as deviations of gendered actors, not, as MacKinnon (1979) might argue, as components of organizational structure.

FEMINIST ANALYSES OF ORGANIZATIONS

The treatment of women and gender most assimilated into the literature on organizations is Moss Kanter's *Men and Women of the Corporation* (1977). Moss Kanter sets out to show that gender differences in organizational behavior are due to structure rather than to characteristics of women and men as individuals (1977, pp. 291-2). She argues that the problems women have in large organizations are consequences of their structural placement, crowded in dead-end jobs at the bottom and exposed as tokens at the top. Gender enters the picture through organizational roles that "carry characteristic images of the kinds of people that should occupy them" (p. 250). Here, Moss Kanter recognizes the presence of gender in early models of organizations:

> A "masculine ethic" of rationality and reason can be identified in the early image of managers. This "masculine ethic" elevates the traits assumed to belong to men with educational advantages to necessities for effective organizations: a tough-minded approach to problems; analytic abilities to abstract and plan; a capacity to set aside personal, emotional considerations in the interests of task accomplishment; a cognitive superiority in problem-solving and decision making. (1974, p. 43)

Identifying the central problem of seeming gender neutrality, Moss Kanter observes: "While organizations were being defined as sex-neutral machines, masculine principles were dominating their authority structures" (1977, p. 46).

In spite of these insights, organizational structure, not gender, is the focus of Moss Kanter's analysis. In posing the argument as structure *or* gender, Moss Kanter also implicitly posits gender as standing outside of structure, and she fails to follow up her own observations about masculinity and organizations (1977, p. 22). Moss Kanter's analysis of the effects of organizational position applies as well to men in low-status positions. Her analysis of the effect of numbers, or the situation of the "token" worker, applies also to men as minorities in women-predominant organizations, but fails to account for gender differences in the situation of the token. In contrast to the token woman, White men in women-dominated workplaces are likely to be positively evaluated and to be rapidly promoted to positions of greater authority. The specificity of male dominance is absent in Moss Kanter's argument, even though she presents a great deal of material that illuminates gender and male dominance.

Another approach, using Moss Kanter's insights but building on the theoretical work of Hartmann (1976), is the argument that organizations have a dual structure, bureaucracy and patriarchy (Ressner 1986b). Ressner argues that bureaucracy has its own dynamic, and gender enters through patriarchy, a more or less autonomous structure, that exists alongside the bureaucratic structure. The analysis of two hierarchies facilitates and clarifies the discussion of women's experiences of discrimination, exclusion, segregation, and low wages. However, this approach has all the problems of two systems theories of women's oppression (Young 1981; see also Acker 1988): the central theory of bureaucratic or organizational structure is unexamined, and patriarchy is added to allow the theorist to deal with women. Like Moss Kanter, Ressner's approach implicitly accepts the assumption of mainstream organizational theory that organizations are gender-neutral social phenomena.

Ferguson, in *The Feminist Case Against Bureaucracy* (1984), develops a radical feminist critique of bureaucracy as an organization of oppressive male power, arguing that it is both mystified and constructed through an abstract discourse on rationality, rules, and procedures. Thus, in contrast to the implicit arguments of Moss Kanter and Ressner, Ferguson views bureaucracy itself as a construction of male domination. In response to this overwhelming organization of power, bureaucrats, workers, and clients are all "feminized," as they develop ways of managing their powerlessness that at the same time perpetuate their dependence. Ferguson argues further that feminist discourse, rooted in women's experiences of caring and nurturing outside bureaucracy's control, provides a ground for opposition to bureaucracy and for the development of alternative ways of organizing society.

However, there are problems with Ferguson's theoretical formulation. Her argument that feminization is a metaphor for bureaucratization not only uses a stereotype of femininity as oppressed, weak, and passive, but also, by equating the experience of men and women clients, women workers, and men bureaucrats, obscures the specificity of women's experiences and the connections between masculinity and power (Brown 1984; see also Martin 1987; Mitchell 1986; Ressner 1986a). Ferguson builds on Foucault's (1979) analysis of power as widely diffused and constituted through discourse, and the problems in her analysis have their origin in Foucault, who also fails to place gender in his analysis of power. What results is a disembodied, and consequently gender neutral, bureaucracy as the oppressor. That is, of course, not a new vision of bureaucracy, but it is one in which gender enters only as analogy, rather than as a complex component of processes of control and domination.

In sum, some of the best feminist attempts to theorize about gender and organizations have been trapped within the constraints of definitions of the theoretical domain that cast organizations as gender neutral and asexual. These theories take us only part of the way to understanding how deeply embedded gender is in organizations. There is ample empirical evidence: We know now that gender segregation is an amazingly persistent pattern and that the gender identity of jobs and occupations is repeatedly reproduced, often in new forms (Bielby and Baron 1987; Reskin and Roos 1987; Strober and Arnold 1987). The reconstruction of gender segregation is an integral part of the dynamic of technological and organizational change (Cockburn 1983, 1985; Hacker 1981). Individual men and particular groups of men do not always win in these processes, but masculinity always seems to symbolize self-respect for men at the bottom and power for men at the top, while confirming for both their gender's superiority. Theories that posit organization and bureaucracy as gender neutral cannot adequately account for this continual gendered structuring. We need different theoretical strategies that examine organizations as gendered processes in which sexuality also plays a part.

ORGANIZATIONS AS GENDERED PROCESSES

The idea that social structure and social processes are gendered has slowly emerged in diverse areas of feminist discourse. Feminists have elaborated gender as a concept to mean more than a socially constructed, binary identity and image. This turn to gender as an analytic category (Connell 1987; Harding 1986; Scott 1986) is an attempt to find new avenues into the dense and complicated problem of explaining the extraordinary persistence through history and across societies of the subordination of women. Scott, for example, defines gender as follows: "The core of the definition rests on an integral connection between two propositions; gender is a constitutive element of social relationships based on perceived differences between the sexes, and gender is a primary way of signifying relationships of power" (1986, p. 1067).

New approaches to the study of waged work, particularly studies of the labor process, see organizations as gendered, not as gender neutral (Cockburn 1985; Game and Pringle 1984; Knights and Willmott 1985; Phillips and Taylor 1980; Sorenson 1984) and conceptualize organizations as one of the locations of the inextricably intertwined production of both gender and class relations. Examining class and gender (Acker 1988), I have argued that class is constructed through gender and that class relations are always gendered. The structure of the labor market, relations in the workplace, the control of the work process, and the underlying wage relation are always affected by symbols of gender, processes of gender identity, and material inequalities between women and men. These processes are complexly related to, and powerfully support, the reproduction of the class structure. Here, I will focus on the interface of gender and organizations, assuming the simultaneous presence of class relations.

To say that an organization, or any other analytic unit, is gendered means that advantage and disadvantage, exploitation and control, action and emotion, meaning and identity, are patterned through and in terms of a distinction between male and female, masculine and feminine. Gender is not an addition to ongoing processes, conceived as gender neutral. Rather, it is an integral part of those processes, which cannot be properly understood without an analysis of gender (Connell 1987; see, also, Chapter 1). Gendering occurs in at least five interacting processes (cf. Scott 1986) that, although analytically distinct, are, in practice, parts of the same reality.

First is the construction of divisions along lines of gender—divisions of labor, of allowed behaviors, of locations in physical space, of power, including the institutionalized means of maintaining the divisions in the structures of labor markets, the family, the state. Such divisions in work organizations are well documented (e.g., Kanter 1977) as well as often obvious to casual observers. Although there are great variations in the patterns and extent of gender division, men are almost always in the highest positions of organizational power. Managers' decisions often initiate gender divisions (Cohn 1985), and organizational practices maintain them—although they also take on new forms with changes in technology and the labor process. For example, Cockburn (1983, 1985) has shown how the introduction of new technology in a number of industries was accompanied by a reorganization, but not abolition, of the gendered division of labor that left the technology in men's control and maintained the definition of skilled work as men's work and unskilled work as women's work.

Second is the construction of symbols and images that explain, express, reinforce, or sometimes oppose those divisions. These have many sources or forms in language, ideology, popular and high culture, dress, the press, and television. For example, as Moss Kanter (1975), among others, has noted, the image of the top manager or the business leader is an image of successful, forceful masculinity (see also Lipman-Blumen 1980). In Cockburn's studies, men workers' images of masculinity linked their gender with their technical skills; the possibility that women might also obtain such skills represented a threat to that masculinity.

The third set of processes that produce gendered social structures, including organizations, are interactions between women and men, women and women, men and men, including all the patterns that enact dominance and submission. For example, conversation analysis shows how gender differences in interruptions, turn taking, and setting the topic of discussion recreate gender inequality in the flow of ordinary talk (West and Zimmerman 1983). Although much of this research has used experimental groups, qualitative accounts of organizational life record the same phenomena: Men are the actors, women the emotional support (Hochschild 1983).

Fourth, these processes help to produce gendered components of individual identity, which may include consciousness of the existence of the other three aspects of gender, such as, in organizations, choice of appropriate work, language use, clothing, and presentation of self as a gendered member of an organization (Reskin and Roos 1987).

Finally, gender is implicated in the fundamental, ongoing processes of creating and conceptualizing social structures. Gender is obviously a basic constitutive element in family and kinship, but, less obviously, it helps to frame the underlying relations of other structures, including complex organizations. Gender is a constitutive element in organizational logic, or the underlying assumptions and practices that construct most contemporary work organizations (Clegg and Dunkerley 1980). Organizational logic appears to be gender neutral; gender-neutral theories of bureaucracy and organizations employ and give expression to this logic. However, underlying both academic theories and practical guides for managers is a gendered substructure that is reproduced daily in practical work activities and, somewhat less frequently, in the writings of organizational theorists (cf. Smith 1988).

Organizational logic has material forms in written work rules, labor contracts, managerial directives, and other documentary tools for running large organizations, including systems of job evaluation widely used in the comparable-worth strategy of feminists. Job evaluation is accomplished through the use and interpretation of documents that describe jobs and how they are to be evaluated. These documents contain symbolic indicators of structure; the ways that they are interpreted and talked about in the process of job evaluation reveal the underlying organizational logic. I base the following theoretical discussion on my observations of organizational logic in action in the job-evaluation component of a comparable-worth project (Acker 1987, 1989, 1990).

Job evaluation is a management tool used in every industrial country, capitalist and socialist, to rationalize the organizational hierarchy and to help in setting equitable wages (International Labour Office 1986). Although there are many different systems of job evaluation, the underlying rationales are similar enough so that the observation of one system can provide a window into a common organizational mode of thinking and practice.

In job evaluation, the content of jobs is described and jobs are compared on criteria of knowledge, skill, complexity, effort, and working conditions. The particular system I observed was built incrementally over many years to reflect the assessment of managers about the job components for which they were willing to pay. Thus today this system can be taken as composed of residues of these judgments, which are a set of decision rules that, when followed, reproduce managerial values. But these rules are also the imagery out of which managers construct and reconstruct their organizations. The rules of job evaluation, which help to determine pay differences between jobs, are not simply a compilation of managers' values or sets of beliefs, but are the underlying logic or organization that provides at least part of the blueprint for its structure. Every time that job evaluation is used, that structure is created or reinforced.

Job evaluation evaluates jobs, not their incumbents. The job is the basic unit in a work organization's hierarchy, a description of a set of tasks, competencies, and responsibilities represented as a position on an organizational chart. A job is separate from people. It is an empty slot, a reification that must continually be reconstructed, for positions exist only as scraps of paper until people fill them. The rationale for evaluating jobs devoid of actual workers further reveals the organizational logic: the intent is to assess the characteristics of the job, not of their incumbents who may vary in skill, industriousness, and commitment. Human beings are to be motivated, managed, and chosen to fit the job. The job exists as a thing apart.

Every job has a place in the hierarchy, another essential element in organizational logic. Hierarchies, like jobs, are devoid of actual workers and based on abstract differentiations. Hierarchy is taken for granted, only its particular form is at issue. Job evaluation is based on the assumption that workers in general see hierarchy as an acceptable principle, and the final test of the evaluation of any particular job is whether its place in the hierarchy looks reasonable. The ranking of jobs within an organization must make sense to managers, but, if the system of evaluation is to contribute to orderly working relationships, it is also important that most workers accept the ranking as just.

Organizational logic assumes a congruence between responsibility, job complexity, and hierarchical position. For example, a lower-level position, the level of most jobs, filled predominantly by women, must have equally low levels of complexity and responsibility. Complexity and responsibility are defined in terms of managerial and professional tasks. The child-care worker's responsibility for other human beings or the complexity facing the secretary who serves six different, temperamental bosses can be only minimally counted if the congruence between position level, responsibility, and complexity is to be preserved. In addition, the logic holds that two jobs at different hierarchical levels cannot be responsible for the same outcome; as a consequence, for example, tasks delegated to a secretary by a manager will not raise her hierarchical level because such tasks are still his responsibility, even though she has the practical responsibility to see that they are done. Levels of skill, complexity, and responsibility, all used in constructing hierarchy, are conceptualized as existing independently of any concrete worker.

In organizational logic, both jobs and hierarchies are abstract categories that have no occupants, no human bodies, no gender. However, an abstract job can exist, can be transformed into a concrete instance, only if there is a worker. In organizational logic, filling the abstract job is a disembodied worker who exists only for the work. Such a hypothetical worker cannot have other imperatives of existence that impinge upon the job. At the very least, outside imperatives cannot be included within the definition of the job. Too many obligations outside the boundaries of the job would make a worker unsuited for the position. The closest the disembodied worker doing the abstract job comes to a real worker is the male worker whose life centers on his full-time, lifelong job, while his wife or another woman takes care of his personal needs and his children. While the realities of life in industrial capitalism never allowed all men to live out this ideal, it was the goal for labor unions and the image of the worker in social and economic theory. The woman worker, assumed to have legitimate obligations other than those required by the job, did not fit with the abstract job.

The concept "a job" is thus implicitly a gendered concept, even though organizational logic presents it as gender neutral. A job already contains the gender-based division of labor and the separation between the public and the private sphere. The concept of a job assumes a particular gendered organization of domestic life and social production. It is an example of what Smith has called "the gender subtext of the rational and impersonal" (1988, p. 4).

Hierarchies are gendered because they also are constructed on these underlying assumptions. Those who are committed to paid employment are "naturally" more suited to responsibility and authority; those who must divide their commitments are in the lower ranks. In addition, principles of hierarchy, as exemplified in most existing job-evaluation systems, have been derived from already existing gendered structures. The best-known systems were developed by management consultants working with managers to build methods of consistently evaluating jobs and rationalizing pay and job classifications. For example, all managers with similar levels of responsibility in the firm should have similar pay. Job-evaluation systems were intended to reflect the values of managers and to produce a believable ranking of jobs based on those values. Such rankings would not deviate substantially from rankings already in place that contain gender typing and gender segregation of jobs and the clustering of women workers in the lowest and the worst-paid jobs. The concrete value judgments that constitute conventional job evaluation are designed to replicate such structures (Acker 1989). Replication is achieved in many ways; for example, skills in managing money, more often found in men's than in women's jobs, frequently receive more points than skills in dealing with clients or human relations skills, more often found in women's than in men's jobs (Steinberg and Haignere 1987).

The gender-neutral status of "a job" and of the organizational theories of which it is a part depend on the assumption that the worker is abstract, disembodied, although in actuality both the concept of "a job" and real workers are deeply gendered and "bodied." Pateman (1986), in a discussion of women and political theory, similarly points out that the most fundamental abstraction in the concept of liberal individualism is "the abstraction of the 'individual' from the body. In order for the individual to appear in liberal theory as a universal figure, who represents anyone and everyone, the individual must be disembodied" (p. 8). If the individual were not abstracted from bodily attributes, it would be clear that the individual represents one sex and one gender, not a universal being. The political fiction of the universal "individual" or "citizen," fundamental to ideas of democracy and contract, excluded women, judging them lacking in the capacities necessary for participation in civil society. Although women now have the rights of citizens in democratic states, they still stand in an ambiguous relationship to the universal individual who is "constructed from a male body so that his identity is always masculine" (Pateman 1988, p. 223). The worker with "a job" is the same universal individual who in social reality is a man. The concept of a universal worker excludes and marginalizes women who cannot, almost by definition, achieve the qualities of a real worker because to do so is to become like a man.

ORGANIZATIONAL CONTROL, GENDER, AND THE BODY

The abstract, bodiless worker, who occupies the abstract, gender-neutral job has no sexuality, no emotions, and does not procreate. The absence of sexuality, emotionality, and procreation in organizational logic and organizational theory is an additional element that both obscures and helps to reproduce the underlying gender relations.

New work on sexuality in organizations (Hearn and Parkin 1987), often indebted to Foucault (1979), suggests that this silence on sexuality may have historical roots in the development of large, all-male organizations that are the primary locations of societal power (Connell 1987). The history of modern organizations includes, among other processes, the suppression of sexuality in the interests of organization and the conceptual exclusion of the body as a concrete living whole (Burrell 1984, 1987; Hearn and Parkin 1987; Morgan 1986).

In a review of historical evidence on sexuality in early modern organizations, Burrell (1984, p. 98) suggests that "the suppression of sexuality is one of the first tasks the bureaucracy sets itself." Long before the emergence of the very large factory in the nineteenth century, other large organizations, such as armies and monasteries, which had allowed certain kinds of limited participation of women, were excluding women more and more and attempting to banish sexuality in the interests of control of members and the organization's activities (Burrell 1984, 1987; Hacker and Hacker 1987). Active sexuality was the enemy of orderly procedures, and excluding women from certain areas of activity may have been, at least in part, a way to control sexuality. As Burrell (1984) points out, the exclusion of women did not eliminate homosexuality, which has always been an element in the life of large all-male organizations, particularly if members spend all of their time in the organization. Insistence on heterosexuality or celibacy were ways to control homosexuality. But heterosexuality had to be practiced outside the organization, whether it was an army or a capitalist workplace. Thus the attempts to banish sexuality from the workplace were part of the wider process that differentiated the home, the location of legitimate sexual activity, from the place of capitalist production. The concept of the disembodied job symbolizes this separation of work and sexuality.

Similarly, there is no place within the disembodied job or the gender-neutral organization for other "bodied" processes, such as human reproduction (Rothman 1989) or the free expression of emotions (Hochschild 1983). Sexuality, procreation, and emotions all intrude upon and disrupt the ideal functioning of the organization, which tries to control such interferences. However, as argued above, the abstract worker is actually a man, and it is the man's body, its sexuality, minimal responsibility in procreation, and conventional control of emotions that pervades work and organizational processes. Women's bodies—female sexuality, their ability to procreate and their pregnancy, breast-feeding, and child care, menstruation, and mythic "emotionality"—are suspect, stigmatized, and used as grounds for control and exclusion.

The ranking of women's jobs is often justified on the basis of women's identification with childbearing and domestic life. Women are devalued because they are assumed to be unable to conform to the demands of the abstract job. Gender segregation at work is also sometimes openly justified by the necessity to control sexuality, and women may be barred from types of work, such as skilled blue-collar work or top management, where most workers are men, on the grounds that potentially disruptive sexual liaisons should be avoided (Lorber 1984). On the other hand, the gendered definition of some jobs "includes sexualization of the woman worker as a part of the job" (MacKinnon 1979, p. 18). These are often jobs that serve men, such as secretaries, or a largely male public (Hochschild 1983).

The maintenance of gendered hierarchy is achieved partly through such often-tacit controls based on arguments about women's reproduction, emotionality, and sexuality, helping to legitimate the organizational structures created through abstract, intellectualized techniques. More overt controls, such as sexual harassment, relegating childbearing women to lower-level mobility tracks, and penalizing (or rewarding) their emotion management, also conform to and reinforce hierarchy. MacKinnon (1979), on the basis of an extensive analysis of legal cases, argues that the willingness to tolerate sexual harassment is often a condition of the job, both a consequence and a cause of gender hierarchy.

While women's bodies are ruled out of order or sexualized and objectified, in work organizations, men's bodies are not. Indeed, male sexual imagery pervades organizational metaphors and language, helping to give form to work activities (see Hearn and Parkin 1987, for an extended discussion). For example, the military and the male world of sports are considered valuable training for organizational success and provide images for teamwork, campaigns, and tough competition. The symbolic expression of male sexuality may be used as a means of control over male workers, too, allowed or even encouraged within the bounds of the work situation to create cohesion or alleviate stress (Collinson 1988; Hearn and Parkin 1987). Management approval of pornographic pictures in the locker room or support for all-male work and play groups where casual talk is about sexual exploits or sports are examples. These symbolic expressions of male dominance also act as significant controls over women in work organizations because they are per se excluded from the informal bonding men produce with the "body talk" of sex and sports.

Symbolically, a certain kind of male heterosexual sexuality plays an important part in legitimating organizational power. Connell (1987) calls this hegemonic masculinity, emphasizing that it is formed around dominance over women and in opposition to other masculinities, although its exact content changes as historical conditions change. Currently, hegemonic masculinity is typified by the image of the strong, technically competent, authoritative leader who is sexually potent and attractive, has a family, and has his emotions under control. Images of male sexual function and patriarchal paternalism may also be embedded in notions of what the manager does when he leads his organization (Calas and Smircich 1989). Women's bodies cannot be adapted to hegemonic masculinity; to function at the top of male hierarchies requires women to render irrelevant everything that makes them women.

According to many management experts, the image of the masculine organizational leader could be expanded, without altering its basic elements, to include other qualities also needed in contemporary organizations, such as flexibility and sensitivity to the capacities and needs of subordinates. Such qualities are not necessarily the symbolic monopoly of women. For example, the wise and experienced coach is empathetic and supportive of his individual players and flexibly leads his team against devious opposition tactics to victory.

The connections between organizational power and men's sexuality may be even more deeply embedded in organizational processes. Hacker (1989) argues that eroticism and technology have common roots in human sensual pleasure and that for the engineer or the skilled worker, and probably for many other kinds of workers, there is a powerful erotic element in work processes. The pleasures of technology, Hacker continues, become harnessed to domination, and passion becomes directed toward power over nature, the machine, and other people, particularly women, in the work hierarchy. Hacker believes that men lose a great deal in this transformation of the erotic into domination, but they also win in other ways. For example, many men gain economically from the organizational gender hierarchy. As Crompton and Jones (1984) point out, men's career opportunities in white-collar work depend on the barriers that deny those opportunities to women. If the mass of female clerical workers were able to compete with men in such work, promotion probabilities for men would be drastically reduced.

Class relations as well as gender relations are reproduced in organizations. Critical, but nonfeminist, perspectives on work organizations argue that rational-technical systems for organizing work, such as job classification and evaluation systems and detailed specification of how work is to be done, are parts of pervasive systems of control that help to maintain class relations (Edwards 1979). The abstract job, devoid of a human body, is a basic unit in such systems of control. The positing of a job as an abstract category, separate from the worker, is an essential move in creating jobs as mechanisms of compulsion and control over work processes. Rational-technical (ostensibly gender-neutral) control systems are built upon and conceal a gendered substructure (Smith 1988) in which men's bodies fill the abstract jobs. Use of such abstract systems continually reproduces the underlying gender assumptions and the subordinated or excluded place of women. Gender processes, including the manipulation and management of women's and men's sexuality, procreation, and emotion, are part of the control processes of organizations, maintaining not only gender stratification but also contributing to maintaining class and, possibly, race and ethnic relations. Is the abstract worker White as well as male? Are White-male-dominated organizations also built on underlying assumptions about the proper place of people with different skin colors? Are racial differences produced by organizational practices as gender differences are?

CONCLUSION

Feminists who want to theorize about organizations face a difficult task because of the deeply embedded gendering of both organizational processes and theory. Commonsense notions, such as jobs and positions, which constitute the units managers use in making organizations and some theorists use in making theory, are posited on the prior exclusion of women. This underlying construction of a way of thinking is not simply an error, but rather a part of the processes of organization. This exclusion in turn creates fundamental inadequacies in theorizing about gender-neutral systems of positions to be filled. The creation of more adequate theory may come only as organizations are transformed in ways that dissolve the concept of the abstract job and restore the absent female body.

Such a transformation would be radical in practice because it would probably require the end of organizations as they exist today, along with a redefinition of work and work relations. The rhythm and timing of work would be adapted to the rhythms of life outside of work. Caring work would be just as important and well rewarded as other work: Having a baby or taking care of a sick mother would be as valued as making an automobile or designing computer software. Hierarchy would be abolished, and workers would run things themselves. Of course, women and men would share equally in different kinds of work. Perhaps there would be some communal or collective form of organization where work and intimate relations are closely related, children learn in places close to working adults, and workmates, lovers, and friends are all part of the same group. Utopian writers and experimenters have left us many possible models (Hacker 1989). But this brief listing begs many questions, perhaps the most important of which is how, given the present organization of economy and technology and the pervasive and powerful, impersonal, textually mediated relations of authority and hierarchy (Smith 1988), so radical a change could come about.

Feminist research and theorizing, by continuing to puzzle out how gender provides the subtext for arrangements of subordination, can make some contributions to a future in which collective action to do what needs doing—producing goods, caring for people, disposing of the garbage—is organized so that dominance, control, and subordination, particularly the subordination of women, are eradicated, or at least minimized, in our organizational life.

REFERENCES

Acker, J. 1987. "Sex Bias in Job Evaluation: A Comparable Worth Issue." Pp. 183-96 in *Ingredients for Women's Employment Policy,* edited by C. Bose and G. Spitze. Albany: SUNY Press.

―――. 1988. "Class, Gender and the Relations of Distribution." *Signs: Journal of Women in Culture and Society* 13:473-97.

―――. 1989. *Doing Comparable Worth: Gender, Class and Pay Equity.* Philadelphia: Temple University Press.

―――. 1990. "The Oregon Case." In *State Experience with Comparable Worth,* edited by R. Steinberg. Philadelphia: Temple University Press.

――― and D. Van Houten. 1974. "Differential Recruitment and Control: The Sex Structuring of Organizations." *Administrative Science Quarterly* 19:152-63.

Bielby, W. T., and J. N. Baron. 1987. "Undoing Discrimination: Job Integration and Comparable Worth." Pp. 211-9 in *Ingredients for Women's Employment Policy,* edited by C. Bose and G. Spitze. Albany: SUNY Press.

Brown, W. 1984. "Challenging Bureaucracy." *Women's Review of Books* 2(November): 14-7.

Burrell, G. 1984. "Sex and Organizational Analysis." *Organization Studies* 5:97-118.

———. 1987. "No Accounting for Sexuality." *Accounting Organizations and Society* 12:89-101.

Calas, M. B., and L. Smircich. 1989. "Voicing Seduction to Silence Leadership." Paper presented to the Fourth International Conference on Organizational Symbolism and Corporate Culture, Fontainebleau, France.

Clegg, S., and D. Dunkerley. 1980. *Organization, Class and Control.* London: Routledge & Kegan Paul.

Cockburn, C. 1983. *Brothers: Male Dominance and Technological Change.* London: Pluto Press.

———. 1985. *Machinery of Dominance: Women, Men and Technical Know-How.* London: Pluto Press.

Cohn, S. 1985. *The Process of Occupational Sex-Typing.* Philadelphia: Temple University Press.

Collinson, D. L. 1988. "Engineering Honour: Masculinity, Joking and Conflict in Shop-Floor Relations." *Organizational Studies* 9:181-9.

Connell, R. W. 1987. *Gender and Power.* Stanford, CA: Stanford University Press.

Crompton, R., and G. Jones. 1984. *White-Collar Proletariate: Deskilling and Gender in Clerical Work.* Philadelphia: Temple University Press.

Dexter, C. R. 1985. "Women and the Exercise of Power in Organizations: From Ascribed to Achieved Status." Pp. 239-58 in *Women and Work: Annual Review, Vol. I,* edited by L. Larwood, A. H. Stromberg, and B. A. Gutek. Beverly Hills, CA: Sage.

Edwards, R., 1979. *Contested Terrain.* New York: Basic Books.

Feldberg, R., and E. Nakano Glenn. 1979. "Male and Female: Job Versus Gender Models in the Sociology of Work." *Social Problems* 26:524-38.

Ferguson, K. E. 1984. *The Feminist Case Against Bureaucracy.* Philadelphia: Temple University Press.

Foucault, M. 1979. *The History of Sexuality, Vol. 1: An Introduction.* London: Allen Lane.

Game, A., and R. Pringle. 1984. *Gender at Work.* London: Pluto Press.

Hacker, S. 1981. "The Culture of Engineering: Women, Workplace, and Machine." *Women's Studies International Quarterly* 4:341-54.

———. 1989. *Pleasure, Power and Technology.* Boston: Unwin Heyman.

Hacker, B. C., and S. Hacker. 1987. "Military Institutions and the Labor Process: Noneconomic Sources of Technological Change, Women's Subordination, and the Organization of Work." *Technology and Culture* 28:743-75.

Harding, S. 1986. *The Science Question in Feminism.* Ithaca, NY: Cornell University Press.

Hartmann, H. 1976. "Capitalism, Patriarchy, and Job Segregation by Sex." *Signs: Journal of Women in Culture and Society* 1:137-70.

Hearn, J., and P. W. Parkin. 1983. "Gender and Organizations: A Selective Review and a Critique of a Neglected Area." *Organization Studies* 4:219-42.

———. 1987. *Sex at Work.* Brighton, UK: Wheatsheaf Books.

Hochschild, A. R. 1983. *The Managed Heart.* Berkeley, CA: University of California Press.

International Labour Office. 1986. *Job Evaluation.* Geneva: ILO.

Izraeli, D. N. 1983. "Sex Effects or Structural Effects? An Empirical Test of Kanter's Theory of Proportions." *Social Forces* 61:153-65.

Kanter, R. Moss. 1975. "Women and the Structure of Organizations: Explorations in Theory and Behavior." Pp. 34-74 in *Another Voice,* edited by R. Moss Kanter and M. Millman. Garden City, NY: Doubleday Anchor.

———. 1977. *Men and Women of the Corporation.* New York: Basic Books.

Knights, D., and H. Willmott. 1985. *Gender and the Labour Process.* Aldershot, UK: Gower.

Lipman-Blumen, J. 1980. "Female Leadership in Formal Organization: Must the Female Leader Go Formal?" Pp. 341-62 in *Readings in Managerial Psychology,* edited by H. J. Leavitt, L. R. Pondy, and D. M. Boje. Chicago: University of Chicago Press.

Lorber, J. 1984. "Trust, Loyalty, and the Place of Women in the Organization of Work." Pp. 371-81 in *Women: A Feminist Perspective, 3rd ed.,* edited by J. Freeman. Palo Alto, CA: Mayfield.

MacKinnon, C. A. 1979. *Sexual Harassment of Working Women.* New Haven, CT: Yale University Press.

———. 1982. "Feminism, Marxism, Method and the State: An Agenda for Theory." *Signs: Journal of Women in Culture and Society* 7:515-44.

Martin, P. Yancey. 1985. "Group Sex Composition in Work Organizations: A Structural-Normative View." Pp. 311-49 in *Research in the Sociology of Organizations,* edited by S. A. Bacharach and R. Mitchell. Greenwich, CT: JAI.

———. 1987. "A Commentary on *The Feminist Case Against Bureaucracy.*" *Women's Studies International Forum* 10:543-8.

Mills, A. J. 1988. "Organization, Gender and Culture." *Organization Studies* 9/3:351-69.

Mitchell, D. 1986. Review of Ferguson, *The Feminist Case Against Bureaucracy.* Unpublished manuscript.

Morgan, G. 1986. *Images of Organization.* Newbury Park: Sage.

Pateman, C. 1986. "Introduction: The Theoretical Subversiveness of Feminism." Pp. 1-12 in *Feminist Challenges,* edited by C. Pateman and E. Gross. Winchester, MA: Allen & Unwin.

———. 1988. *The Sexual Contract.* Cambridge, UK: Polity Press.

Phillips, A., and B. Taylor. 1980. "Sex and Skill: Notes Towards a Feminist Economics." *Feminist Review* 6:79-88.

Reskin, B. F., and P. A. Roos. 1987. "Status Hierarchies and Sex Segregation." Pp. 3-21 in *Ingredients for Women's Employment Policy,* edited by C. Bose and G. Spitze. Albany, NY: SUNY Press.

Ressner, U. 1986a. Review of K. Ferguson, *The Feminist Case Against Bureaucracy. Economic and Industrial Democracy* 7:130-43.

———. 1986b. *The Hidden Hierarchy.* Aldershot: Gower.

Rothman, B. Katz. 1989. *Recreating Motherhood: Ideology and Technology in a Patriarchal Society.* New York: Norton.

Scott, J. 1986. "Gender: A Useful Category of Historical Analysis." *American Historical Review* 91:1053-75.

Smith, D. E. 1988. *The Everyday World as Problematic.* Boston: Northeastern University Press.

Sorenson, B. A. 1984. "The Organizational Woman and the Trojan Horse Effect." Pp. 88-105 in *Patriarchy in a Welfare Society,* edited by H. Holter. Oslo: Universitetsforlaget.

Steinberg, R., and L. Haignere. 1987. "Equitable Compensation Methodological Criteria for Comparable Worth." Pp. 157-82 in *Ingredients for Women's Employment Policy,* edited by C. Bose and G. Spitze. Albany: SUNY Press.

Strober, M. H., and C. L. Arnold. 1987. "Integrated Circuits/Segregated Labor: Women in Computer-Related Occupations and High-Tech Industries." Pp. 136-82 in *Computer Chips and Paper Clips: Technology and Women's Employment,* edited by H. Hartmann. Washington, DC: National Academy Press.

West, C., and D. H. Zimmerman. 1983. "Small Insults: A Study of Interruptions in Conversations Between Unacquainted Persons." Pp. 102-17 in *Language, Gender and Society,* edited by B. Thorne, C. Kramarae, and N. Healy. Rowley, MA: Newbury House.

Wallace, P. A. (ed.). 1982. *Women in the Workplace.* Boston: Auburn House.

Young, I. 1981. "Beyond the Unhappy Marriage: A Critique of Dual Systems Theory." Pp. 43-69 in *Women and Revolution,* edited by L. Sargent. Boston: South End Press.

9. LABOR MARKET GENDER INEQUALITY IN MINORITY GROUPS

ELIZABETH M. ALMQUIST

The extent of gender inequality—differences between women and men in access to rewards, resources, positions, rights, and privileges—varies greatly from society to society, but in general men have greater access to the social perquisites than women. Theories of gender inequality (Blumberg 1984; Chafetz 1984) focus on societal structures and processes that affect all types of gender inequality among all men and women in a society. Recent research on the occupational attainments of women and men (Almquist forthcoming; Roos 1985) shows how gender inequality in jobs varies across societies as well. A logical extension of these efforts is to ask whether these theories can also explain labor-market gender inequality within groups that are smaller than whole societies.

Racial and ethnic minorities compose important and relatively distinct smaller groups within the United States. Much of the research on Blacks asks whether men or women suffer more in comparison with Whites in jobs and earnings (Almquist 1979). Because Black women are closer to White women in jobs and earnings than Black men are to White men, this research gives the misleading impression that Black women have higher labor-market status than Black men. Achievement relative to the majority group is quite a different matter than gender inequality within a specific group; no previous research has assessed gender inequality within groups.

The research presented here was designed to compare the level of gender inequality in professional and managerial positions across the 11 largest racial and ethnic minority groups in the United States, and to discover the correlates of this within-group inequality.

MINORITY GROUP STATUS AND GENDER STATUS

My central thesis is that minority groups with greater material resources exhibit higher levels of occupational gender inequality than groups with fewer resources. Material resources can be used to gain

180

education and training and equip people for higher-level jobs. Men have greater access to material resources in all groups, and their advantage is higher in groups with more resources. In addition, gender-related characteristics of minority groups affect the level of gender inequality in occupational attainment in diverse ways. The specific level of gender inequality within any group reflects both the amount of resources available and the way in which these resources are distributed between men and women within the group.

Some groups have acquired markedly fewer resources than others. In the United States, indigenous groups (Blacks, Native Americans, Mexican Americans) have experienced greater discrimination and exist at very low levels of socioeconomic status compared with several Asian groups that contain large numbers of recent immigrants with higher educational levels (U.S. Bureau of the Census 1984). While there are many reasons for the variations among minority groups in the level of resources and rewards attained, the task here is not to explain those variations but to indicate how differences in socioeconomic resources affect labor-market gender inequality within the specific groups.

Within all groups, men and women tend to share equally the goods and resources necessary to ensure basic survival, but men tend to control surplus goods and resources and use them to further enhance their advantaged position (Lenski 1966). Minority groups with the lowest levels of education, jobs, and income in American society have the fewest surplus resources. Their limited resources must be used for survival needs and will be shared rather equally between women and men. Thus the level of gender inequality will be low. By contrast, minority groups that have experienced the least discrimination and disadvantage in American society will have higher levels of education, jobs and income. Men will control a greater share of surplus resources, and the degree of gender inequality in the labor market will be high.

Men in the most disadvantaged groups should behave in a more egalitarian manner toward women than men in the most advantaged groups, at least in the distribution of scarce resources necessary for survival. Men who are unable to find work and who leave home so that their families can secure welfare payments are a possible example. Because of their greater income, men in the more advantaged groups can command more support, personal care-taking, and services from their wives than men in the less-advantaged groups. These men may be more consciously egalitarian in attitudes toward women than men in lower level jobs; nonetheless, they have the potential to exert more authority in household affairs (Steil 1984). The outcome is greater gender equality in groups with few resources and less gender equality in groups with more resources. This thesis contradicts the contention of many scholars that the most disadvantaged minority men will be the most dominating of women in their personal lives (Garcia-Bahne 1977).

DETERMINANTS OF GENDER INEQUALITY

Recent theoretical analyses by Chafetz (1984) and Lesser Blumberg (1984) identify characteristics that affect the unequal distribution of resources between men and women. Although their work is largely derived from pre-literate societies, their ideas explained significant proportions of the variation in gender inequality in jobs in 60 contemporary countries (Almquist 1985a) and in 312 metropolitan labor markets in the United States (Almquist 1985b). They may be useful in explaining occupational gender inequality within minority groups.

The greater the domestic burdens borne by women alone, the lower will be their occupational attainment relative to men's. Fertility levels and marital status provide measures of domestic burdens.

The proportion of women in a population has ambiguous effects on gender inequality. An oversupply of women may mean that they are devalued (Guttentag and Secord 1983), but an undersupply of men may create opportunities for women to assume positions of responsibility and leadership (Chafetz 1984; Sanday 1981).

Across societies, women's economic, political, and social status varies directly with the value and centrality of their work and inversely with the degree to which their labor is replaceable (Blumberg 1984; Chafetz 1984). Within a minority group, women's work may be highly valued if men are poorly paid or intermittently employed; in such groups, women should achieve higher education relative to men and hold a greater share of higher-status jobs than in groups in which men are regularly employed and highly paid. Labor force participation rates of both men and women reflect the values and attitudes held by each minority group, as well as employers' willingness to hire persons from each group. Therefore, labor force participation rates and unemployment rates can be seen as reflections of both gender-related characteristics and economic resources available to each group.

RESOURCES AVAILABLE TO MINORITY GROUPS

Several minority group characteristics affect the level of socioeconomic resources available to them; population size is the most noteworthy. Larger groups in the United States, such as Blacks and Native

Americans, have fewer resources than smaller groups, such as Chinese and Asian Indians. Among Blacks, Wilcox and Roof (1978) found that the larger the Black population in metropolitan areas, the greater the income and occupational inequality between Blacks and Whites. They suggest that the more visible the minority group, the greater the discrimination against it. In addition, the larger the minority group, the larger is the exploitable reserve supply of labor. Both men and women from large minority groups are likely to be employed in low-level production and service jobs; few group members of either gender will have the opportunity to attain high-status professional and managerial positions.

Two additional variables—proportion who are foreign-born and type of employment—can affect the level of resources. Immigrant groups (Chinese, Filipinos) typically are more affluent than refugee (Vietnamese) or indigenous groups. Government agencies and family-owned businesses may offer employment opportunities that private enterprise does not.

Variables that reflect (rather than create) the level of resources available to minority groups include median family income, proportion of families with incomes below poverty level, proportion of children living with both parents, and proportion who have completed high school and college.

METHODOLOGY

Aggregate-level 1980 census data (U.S. Bureau of the Census 1983, 1984) on the 11 largest racial and ethnic minorities in the United States were used for the analysis. In rough order of their time in the United States, the groups are Native Americans, Blacks, Mexican Americans, Puerto Ricans, Cubans, Chinese, Japanese, Filipinos, Koreans, Asian Indians, and Vietnamese. These 11 groups supply 17 percent of the women workers and 15 percent of the men workers in the United States.

Gender inequality in professional and in managerial occupations were the key dependent variables. Professional occupations included both professional specialty and technical and kindred occupations. Managerial occupations included executive, administrative, and managerial occupations. Gender inequality described the attainment of women compared with the attainment of men in such occupations.

In this research, gender inequality in the professions was measured by calculating the share of the total professional positions held by women in each group and then subtracting the women's share of the total labor force in each group. The result—women's adjusted share of the professional jobs—was a figure showing whether women are under-represented (negative value) or overrepresented (positive value) compared with men in their respective group. The groups were rank-ordered, so that the group in which women held the smallest adjusted share of professional positions received the highest rank (the greatest gender inequality) and the group in which women held the largest adjusted share received the lowest rank (the least gender inequality). The same procedures were applied to managerial jobs.

Using Spearman's *rho,* the rankings on gender inequality in professional and managerial jobs were correlated with each of the independent variables identified above. These methods limit the conclusions that can be drawn. Some of the independent variables were strongly correlated with each other. Rank-order correlation with data on groups rather than individuals made it impossible to distinguish the separate effects of each of the independent variables, to weight the variables for their relative importance in producing gender inequality in jobs, or to examine interactions among the variables. Still, these methods provided the first examination of gender inequality across the most important minority groups in the United States.

FINDINGS: GENDER INEQUALITY IN JOBS

Gender inequality was greater in managerial than in professional positions. Women were underrepresented in managerial positions in all 11 groups, and in professional positions in 6 groups (see Table 9.1). Averaging the rankings on both measures of gender inequality shows that Blacks (9.5), Mexican Americans (9.5), Native Americans (8.5), and Puerto Ricans (8.5) had the least gender inequality, while Koreans (1.5), Japanese (3.5), Chinese (4.5), and Cubans (5) had the most.

Do women in groups in which they have a larger share of the professions than of the total labor force have higher status than men? The answer is probably no. The professional category encompasses a very large number of occupations that vary widely in prestige, pay, and authority. Women are more heavily concentrated in the lower-status professional and technical jobs, whereas men are more concentrated in the higher-status professions. The census data provided detailed occupations for Native Americans, for Blacks, for all Hispanic groups together, and for all Asian groups together (U.S. Bureau of the Census 1984). When only the higher-status professional positions were considered, gender inequality existed in all four broad racial groupings. To examine all 11 groups separately, only the global category of professional and technical workers could be used, which greatly underestimated the extent of gender inequality in the professional sector.

TABLE 9.1 Gender Inequality in U.S. Minority Groups, 1980

Minority Group	Women's Share of		Gender Inequality	
	Professional Positions (%)	Labor Force (%)	Adjusted Share (%)	Rank
Native American	53.5	43.5	+10.0	(8)
Black	65.7	49.9	+15.8	(11)
Mexican American	47.8	37.5	+10.3	(9)
Puerto Rican	49.9	39.2	+10.7	(10)
Cuban	42.7	44.3	−1.6	(6)
Chinese	34.3	43.7	−9.4	(3)
Japanese	42.7	48.0	−5.3	(5)
Filipino	61.4	52.9	+8.5	(7)
Korean	39.6	52.3	−12.7	(2)
Asian Indian	26.9	34.9	−8.0	(8)
Vietnamese	28.6	41.6	−13.0	(1)
	Managerial Positions (%)	Labor Force (%)	Adjusted Share (%)	Rank
Native American	39.1	43.5	−4.4	(9)
Black	45.0	49.9	−4.9	(8)
Mexican American	33.3	37.5	−4.2	(10)
Puerto Rican	32.2	39.2	−7.0	(7)
Cuban	28.5	44.3	−15.8	(4)
Chinese	35.0	43.7	−8.7	(6)
Japanese	31.1	48.0	−16.9	(2)
Filipino	43.5	52.9	−9.4	(5)
Korean	30.0	52.3	−22.3	(1)
Asian Idnian	18.6	34.9	−16.3	(3)
Vietnamese	39.1	41.6	−2.5	(11)

SOURCE: U.S. Bureau of the Census (1983).

The same groups that exhibited a high level of gender inequality in managerial jobs also exhibited high gender inequality in professional positions, with the exception of the Vietnamese who were highest on gender inequality in the professions and lowest on gender inequality at the managerial level. When this group of very recent arrivals in American society was removed, the correlation between gender inequality in the two occupational categories rose from +.327 to +.870.

The relationships among women's relative status (gender inequality), women's absolute status (the proportion of women workers who are professionals or managers), and men's absolute status (the proportion of men workers who are professionals or managers) were all positive (see Table 9.2). The more men who were professionals or managers, the more women who also were professionals or managers. Yet in the groups in which more women were professionals or managers, the women's share of the total higher-status positions was smaller. In short, the groups in which a large proportion of women were able to attain professional and managerial jobs were also the groups that exhibited the highest levels of labor-market gender inequality. Studies that examine only women's and men's absolute status are likely to overlook these important variations in gender inequality.

DETERMINANTS OF GENDER INEQUALITY

Gender-Related Variables

Marital status was associated with labor-market gender inequality in the manner predicted by theories of gender inequality. Groups with large proportions of currently married women exhibited greater gender inequality in both professional and managerial jobs than groups with high proportions of either never-married or divorced women (see Table 9.3). Groups with high fertility rates exhibited low gender inequality, especially in managerial occupations. Inspecting the correlations among the independent variables (not shown) revealed that groups with low income and low educational attainment also have high fertility rates. In these groups, neither men nor women were able to acquire the credentials to enter higher-status occupations, and gender inequality was low.

An oversupply of women in the group increased labor market inequality, suggesting some devaluing of women in these minority groups. In education, the higher men's attainment compared with women's, the greater was their advantage in securing better jobs, especially professional positions.

The more women were in the labor force, the smaller was their share of the top jobs, especially in management. Although men's labor force participation rates were not related to occupational gender inequality, high unemployment among men markedly reduced gender inequality. These findings are consistent with the predictions that women's labor will be valued more in groups where men are intermittently employed, that higher rates of labor force participation will create a larger reserve supply of labor that employers exploit in lower-level service and production jobs, and that men will monopolize the surplus resources in the more advantaged groups.

TABLE 9.2 Correlations Among Measures of Women's and Men's Occupational Status in 11 U.S. Minority Groups

Variables	1	2	3	4	5	6
(1) Gender inequality in professional positions	—					
(2) Percentage of women workers who are professionals	.082	—				
(3) Percentage of men workers who are professionals	.827	.700	—			
(4) Gender inequality in managerial positions	.327	.436	.586	—		
(5) Percentage of women workers who are managers	.707	.586	.537	.527	—	
(6) Percentage of men workers who are managers	.301	.609	.727	.845	.854	—
Mean Score:	+0.5	16.9%	18.9%	−10.2	6.2%	10.3%

Economic Resources of Minority Groups

Three variables influenced the level of resources available to minority groups: population size, proportion of foreign born members, and class of worker. The larger the population of a group, the fewer resources are available and the smaller the gap between women and men in occupational attainment. Among groups with high proportions of immigrants, there was marked gender inequality in jobs, especially in the professions. Among immigrant groups, such as Koreans, Cubans, and Asian Indians, many men acquired professional training before or immediately after coming to this country. Their wives typically lack commensurate credentials, indicating again that in advantaged groups men, not women, benefit. Women may benefit indirectly, through marriage, but compared with men in their group their status will not be high (see Chapter 13).

Private wage and salary employment had negligible effects on labor-market gender inequality, but government employment (entered by very few immigrant groups) reduced gender inequality within the professions. Koreans, Chinese, and Japanese had higher proportions of self-employed and unpaid family workers than other groups. These two types of employment increase gender inequality in jobs. Men are the

TABLE 9.3 Determinants of Gender Inequality in Professional and Managerial Occupations in 11 U.S. Minority Groups

Independent Variables	Rank Order Correlation with Gender Inequality in	
	Professional Positions	Managerial Positions
Gender-Related Variables		
Marital status of women		
single, never married	−.409	−.809
currently married	+.709	+.627
divorced	−.725	−.116
Cumulative fertility	−.373	−.918
Percentage female population	+.154	+.545
Men's advantage in education	+.891	+.318
Percentage of women in labor force	+.209	+.418
Percentage of men in labor force	+.051	+.051
Percentage of men unemployed	−.673	−.727
Average absolute value of rho	.466	.503
Economic Resources		
Population size	−.891	−.436
Percentage of foreign born	+.773	+.327
Class of worker/type of employment		
private wage and salary workers	+.218	−.218
government employees	−.575	−.170
self-employed	+.500	+.709
unpaid family workers	+.784	+.543
Median family income	+.473	+.709
Percentage below poverty level	−.236	−.727
Children under 18 living with both parents	+.691	+.782
Percentage high school graduates	+.672	+.709
Average absolute value of rho	.581	.533

self-employed professionals in private practice or managers of the family enterprise. Women, on the other hand, become secretaries in their husband's offices or unpaid service workers in family businesses.

The remaining variables in the second panel of Table 9.3, which directly measured the level of resources available to the various groups, influenced gender inequality in jobs in precisely the manner predicted. Groups with more resources exhibited high levels of labor-market gender inequality; groups with few resources exhibited much lower levels of inequality.

Control of Surplus Resources

The view that men control surplus resources in advantaged minority groups and use those resources to support their own occupational achievement is admittedly speculative. Although this view could best be tested with longitudinal data tracing how men monopolize resources or with intensive cross-sectional data on the internal dynamics of minority groups revealing that families allocate more resources to husbands and sons than to wives and daughters, two pieces of evidence from this research fit the interpretation being advanced here.

First, in groups with high education and high incomes, men were very well represented in managerial and professional positions. In such groups, women exhibited high labor-force participation rates (correlations not shown), but the lower level of the jobs they held suggests that they are likely to be viewed as secondary earners. Their labor is not highly valued, and few efforts are expended to promote their occupational achievement. Second, men's advantage in educational attainment was correlated with median family income ($rho = .545$) and with the percentage who have completed high school ($rho = .673$). In short, the higher the resource level of the group, the greater men's advantage over women in acquiring education.

SUMMARY AND CONCLUSIONS

This study found lower levels of gender inequality in minority groups with large numbers of never-married or divorced women, with low family income and a high incidence of poverty, and with high fertility rates, so that neither boys nor girls have much opportunity for advanced education. These are groups in which women's labor-force participation rates are low, but women's work may be more valued because men are frequently unemployed. These groups find employment in private enterprise—frequently manufacturing—and government work, but rarely establish their own businesses. Neither men nor women have access to surplus resources, and so labor-market gender inequality is low. These are the large, mainly indigenous, groups in the United States: Native Americans, Blacks, Mexican Americans, and Puerto Ricans.

A composite portrait of minority groups with high levels of gender inequality in jobs includes these characteristics: more women than men in the population, large numbers of married women, low fertility rates, children typically living with both parents, high family income, and frequent self-employment in business or the professions. These groups

are characterized by high overall levels of educational attainment, bu
sharp disparities between men and women in schooling completed
These small, frequently foreign-born groups in the United States are the
Koreans, Japanese, Chinese, and Cubans. The Vietnamese, the newes
arrivals to date in the United States, have some of the characteristics
associated with low labor-market gender inequality: fewer women than
men in the group, high unemployment, frequent poverty, and little
employment in government work. The Vietnamese also have some
characteristics associated with high levels of labor-market gender in
equality: a small, foreign-born group with a distinct male advantage in
educational attainment. Removing the Vietnamese and recomputing
correlations among only 10 groups increased the size of nearly all of
the correlations in Table 9.3. However, none of the central patterns was
altered, and it would have been improper to omit one group simply
because it exhibited anomalous characteristics.

None of the variables employed in this research addressed the cultures of minority groups. Critics might suggest that traditional, conservative attitudes toward gender roles are more important in producing
gender inequality in jobs, especially among Asian immigrant groups
than the variables proposed in this study. In response, I would point out
that most Japanese Americans are second, third, or fourth generation
Americans but, as a group, exhibit a high level of gender inequality in
occupational attainment. Moreover, there are strong differences among
the Asian groups in the level of gender inequality; rankings on the two
occupational measures range from 1 to 11 among these groups. An
additional point that vitiates the traditional culture argument is that
Mexican American and Puerto Rican groups also have traditional,
patriarchal attitudes toward women, but low levels of gender inequality
While the proportion foreign-born is related to the variables of interest
here, gender and resource effects are much more pronounced.

Most of the gender-related characteristics of the minority groups included in this study were related to the economic resources they possess. For example, in high-income groups, more women were married
and fertility rates were lower. Groups in which large numbers of both
women and men were employed were more affluent than groups in
which fewer people work for pay. The higher the overall educational
attainment of the group, the more men's education exceeded wom-
en's. On average, economic-resource variables were only slightly more
strongly correlated with gender inequality in jobs than gender characteristics. But the data and statistics did not permit drawing a clear
distinction between the effects of gender characteristics and the effects

of economic resources on gender inequality. My best judgment is that the two sets of characteristics are intertwined; the economic-resource variables reflect what is available to minority groups, and the gender variables reflect how those resources are distributed between men and women.

The research reported here examined a previously unexamined issue (gender inequality) among the largest possible set of minority groups in this country. The single most important finding is that gender inequality is greatest among the most affluent groups and smallest among the most disadvantaged groups. This finding contradicts the view advanced by some minority scholars (e.g., Garcia-Bahne 1977) that the more discrimination minority men suffer from employers, the more they are inclined to discriminate against the women of their own group. Although this research did not measure attitudes, it did show that there is more equal sharing of resources between women and men in the more disadvantaged groups. Future research should be directed toward finding ways to improve the resources available to minority groups, without advancing men at the expense of women's achievement.

REFERENCES

Almquist, E. M. 1979. *Minorities, Gender and Work.* Lexington, MA: D. C. Heath.
———. 1985a. "Manufacturing and the Male Advantage: The Occupational Position of Women in Metropolitan Labor Markets." Paper presented at the Southwestern Social Science Association Meetings, Houston.
———. 1985b. "Inter- and Intra-Societal Variations in Women's Occupational Position: Three Studies Assessing Sources of Sexual Inequality in the Labor Market." Paper presented at the American Sociological Association Annual Meeting, Washington, DC.
———. Forthcoming. *Gender Inequality in the World of Work.* Albany: SUNY Press.
Blumberg, R. Lesser. 1984. "A General Theory of Gender Stratification." Pp. 252-70 in *Sociological Theory,* edited by R. Collins. San Francisco: Jossey-Bass.
Chafetz, J. Saltzman 1984. *Sex and Advantage: A Comparative, Macro-Structural Theory of Sex Stratification.* Totowa, NJ: Rowman and Allanheld.
Garcia-Bahne, B. 1977. "La Chicana and the Chicano Family." Pp. 152-61 in *Essays on la Mujer,* edited by R. Sanchez and R. M. Cruz. Los Angeles: University of California, Chicano Studies Center.
Guttentag, M. and P. Secord. 1983. *Too Many Women? The Sex Ratio Question.* Beverly Hills, CA: Sage.
Lenski, G. 1966. *Power and Privilege: A Theory of Social Stratification.* New York: McGraw-Hill.
Roos, P. 1985. *Gender and Work: A Comparative Analysis of Industrial Societies.* Albany: SUNY Press.
Sanday, P. Reeves. 1981. *Female Power and Male Dominance: On the Origins of Sexual Inequality.* Cambridge: Cambridge University Press.

Steil, J. M. 1984. "Marital Relationships and Mental Health: The Psychic Costs of Inequality." Pp. 113-23 in *Women: A Feminist Perspective,* edited by J. Freeman. Palo Alto, CA: Mayfield.

U.S. Bureau of the Census. 1983. *Characteristics of the Population, 1980.* Chapter C. General Social and Economic Characteristics, U.S. Summary. PC80-1-C1. Washington, DC: Government Printing Office.

———. 1984. *Characteristics of the Population, 1980.* Chapter D. Detailed Population Characteristics. U.S. Summary, PC80-1-D1-A. Washington, DC: Government Printing Office.

Wilcox, J., and W. C. Roof. 1978. "Percent Black and Black-White Status Inequality: Southern Versus Non-Southern Patterns." *Social Science Quarterly* 59:421-34.

10. FEMINIZATION OF POVERTY AND COMPARABLE WORTH: RADICAL VERSUS LIBERAL APPROACHES

JOHANNA BRENNER

$\mathbf{F}$eminization of poverty and comparable worth have become feminist issues in the United States in part to include in feminist politics the central concerns of working-class women and women of color. In both cases, women social scientists have played an important part as scholars producing data to attest to the social reality of gendered inequality and as technical advisers to organizations and governments concerned with remedying economic inequities (Cain 1985; Pearce and McAdoo 1981; Treiman and Hartmann 1981). Because of the role feminist social scientists play in both campaigns, we need to consider carefully the broader politics within which feminization of poverty and comparable worth are inserted.

Situated within a liberal political discourse, both the feminization of poverty and comparable worth campaigns, in practice, and often in rhetoric, fail to bridge class and race divisions among women and, instead, reinforce the separation of feminism from the movements of other subordinated groups. While appearing to speak to problems that women share, they have tended to unite only through a denial of race and class differences. My point is not that these campaigns and the issues they raise are mistaken. Rather, it is that the current organization of these campaigns, in particular the policy demands and their accompanying justifications, may not constructively address differences in the situations and needs of all classes of women. I will suggest an alternative framework that does not court the danger of strengthening the ideological and social underpinnings of women's subordination.

LIBERAL DISCOURSE ON EQUALITY

A liberal discourse on equality operates with two interrelated assumptions. The first assumption involves issues of organization and allocation: that is, how necessary social functions—governance, education, the production of goods, services, and knowledge—should be organized (hierarchy) and how resources and labor time should be allocated (differential rewards). The second assumption involves the issue of dependence and the related separation of the public and private spheres. Liberal thought assumes that social relationships of economy and polity are created by autonomous, independently contracting individuals. I will lay out each of these assumptions and then show how they are fundamental to feminist political discourse on women's poverty and gendered pay inequity.

A liberal discourse on equality centers on the ideal of meritocracy. Liberal political thought accepts the notion of inequality and hierarchy: some will have more, some less; some will command, others follow; some will create, others only implement. Equality is defined as equal opportunity, and thus, from a liberal perspective, fairness exists when the distribution of individuals within unequal positions reflects their individual qualities—their differential motivation, talent, intelligence, and effort—and not their gender, race, religion, or family background. Liberal demands have changed over time. In the eighteenth century, they were tied to the free market and unregulated competition; in the twentieth century, they are compatible with state intervention in the economy. But there is a continuity in liberal goals and argument. The free market was rejected when it became clear that the market alone would not distribute people in a meritocratic way. Inequalities in familial economic and social status and historic prejudices led to unfair outcomes for meritorious individuals. State intervention was required to ensure equality of opportunity. The goal of twentieth century policy is still a just distribution of individuals within a hierarchy of rewards and power.

The compelling character of this view is not surprising, since its crucial assumptions about social organization and human nature are widely accepted in advanced capitalist society. These assumptions are that there are large and significant differences among individuals in talent and potential, that a complex industrial society requires hierarchies, and that competition and differential rewards for various positions within the hierarchies will motivate the most talented people to fill the most central and important positions (Davis and Moore 1945). A radical critique challenges these assumptions, claiming that most individuals are capable of making valuable contributions to society and, collectively, of governing it.

In contrast to the assumptions underlying liberal political thought, socialists (and many radical and socialist feminists) have contended that hierarchy brings out the worst, not the best, in individuals, and that, although those at the bottom suffer particularly, everyone is distorted and narrowed by competitive striving. They also contend that collective decision-making and responsibility are workable alternative forms of social organization, even in an advanced industrial society, and that such forms promote the full development of individual talents and offer the greatest individual freedom (Ferguson 1984; Mason 1982; Rothschild-Whitt, 1979).

The second fundamental assumption of liberal political thought is that dependence belongs in the private sphere—there is no place for dependent individuals either in the notion of economic contact or in the concept of citizen. Indeed, political citizenship is defined by independence, by the capacity to make choices based on individual self-interest, free from control by others on whom one is dependent. Similarly, wage laborers own their own persons and can sell their labor power as independent contractors. As Bell so nicely puts it:

> The liberal theory of society was framed by the twin axes of individualism and rationality. The unencumbered individual would seek to realize his own satisfactions on the basis of his work—he was to be rewarded for effort, pluck, and risk—and the exchange of products with others was calculated by each so as to maximize his own satisfactions. Society was to make no judgments between men—only to set the procedural rules—and the most efficient distribution of resources was the one that produced the greatest net balance of satisfactions. (1972, p. 58)

The contribution of women within the family in reproducing the male breadwinner and replacing his labor over a generation is, of course, hidden in liberal economic theory. The dependence of the whole society, the economy, and political system, on the family and women's work within the family is ignored. As Gordon (1986, p. 81) argues, "Liberal political and economic theory rests on assumptions about the sexual division of labor and on notions of citizens as heads of families." A society of "freely contracting" male citizens relies on the prior existence of the noncontractual relationships of the family. Women and children (and other nonearners) are regarded as dependents of men. How they fare depends on the "effort" and "pluck" of their male protector. Barrett and McIntosh (1982, pp. 48-9) argue that "in order to elevate the morality of the market into an entire social ethic it is necessary to ignore all those members of society who do not themselves enter the market. . . . Those who cannot earn a living are subsumed under those who can." Women's dependence within the family makes them noncitizens (Okin 1979), and the family commitments make them politically suspect (Pateman 1980).

Welfare-state intervention is justified within a political framework that retains the notion of the independent citizen. Just as the society has an obligation to promote the conditions for a free and fair exchange between competing individuals but no obligation to secure their liveli-hood, the society has a collective obligation to care only for those in-dividuals who cannot legitimately be asked to care for themselves and who, through no fault of their own, cannot be cared for within the fam-ily system. Welfare policy has generally been constructed so as to re-store the male-breadwinner family, not to substitute for it (Lewis 1983; Zaretsky, 1982). Thus men and women have had a very different rela-tionship to the welfare state and different ways of legitimating their claims to state support. Women have had to prove that they are morally deserving (their dependence is assumed); whereas men have to prove they are legitimately dependent (their independence is assumed). For example, the rules and regulations of workman's compensation, disabil-ity programs, and unemployment insurance, developed primarily in re-sponse to the demands and needs of male workers, require that workers prove either that they are no longer "able-bodied" (in the first two instances) or that they are without work through no fault of their own (Nelson 1984).

ALTERNATIVE FRAMEWORKS

The radical alternative to the liberal framework has argued for inter-dependence and the legitimate claim of each individual on the commu-nity to meet his or her needs for good and productive work, physical sustenance, emotional support, and social recognition. Radical and so-cialist feminists have further argued that men are as dependent on women's unpaid labor (including women's emotional work) as women are on men's income and that parenthood is a social contribution and should be recognized as such. Socialist feminists have envisioned a society in which the right to contribute and the right to be cared for are shared equally by men and women. This depends on a reformulation of individual and collective responsibilities and the redistribution of ma-terial resources so that the care of dependent individuals is no longer primarily a private responsibility of the family (Barrett and McIntosh 1982).

Feminists have been divided on how to approach the state: whether to demand "a fair field and no favor" or "protection" (Kessler-Harris 1982; Lewis 1986). The comparable worth campaign is organized around the first approach—it is essentially a campaign to rectify distor-tions of the market, which has failed to reward women according to the value of their work. It therefore appeals directly to the liberal principle of meritocracy. The feminization-of-poverty campaign is organized around the second approach—it aims to rectify men's failure to provide for their wives through refusal of child and spousal support (in the case of divorced women) or through lack of life insurance (in the case of widows). Women's claims on the state for support are justified by their lack of a male breadwinner. In the rest of this chapter, I will discuss the ways in which the feminization of poverty and comparable worth campaigns reflect a liberal political discourse, outline the likely consequences, and suggest an alternative approach.

FEMINIZATION OF POVERTY

Two central assertions of the feminization of poverty campaign: "Divorce produces a single man and a single mother" and "40 percent of ex-husbands contribute nothing to their children's support" link women's poverty primarily to men's failure to support their families. They also picture women's poverty as something that happens even to good middle-class people. In this regard, the campaign shares with earlier feminist campaigns, such as the campaigns for women's legal right of separation and for mothers' pensions, an imagery of female victimization. While attempting to provide women an alternative to marriage, these campaigns operated within ideological terms and political limits that assumed, rather than undermined, the male-breadwinner family (Boris and Bardaglio 1983; Pleck 1983).

Like those campaigns, the feminization-of-poverty campaign responds to a real problem facing women and has a potentially radical side. On the other hand, also like those campaigns, in seeking to legitimize their demands and to be most effective in gathering political support, feminists have appealed to broadly held liberal political values and assumptions. As Folbre (1984) argues, the increasing pauperization of motherhood reflects a consensus that AFDC mothers are not among the "deserving" poor. The feminization-of-poverty campaign attempts to change this perception. Portraying poor women as innocent victims of men's irresponsibility may win sympathy for the plight of poor women but it does so at the cost of failing to challenge deeply held notions about feminine dependence on a male breadwinner and distinctions between the deserving and the nondeserving poor, in particular between the "good" woman who is poor because her husband refuses support and the "bad" woman who is poor because she has had a child outside of marriage or has married a poor man who cannot provide.

The feminization-of-poverty literature often assumes that women of all races and classes have a common destiny as poor single heads of families following divorce or widowhood. It is generally true that women's standard of living declines after divorce, while their ex-husbands' standard of living rises (Weitzman 1985). But relative deprivation is not impoverishment. Some women, for example, those with more affluent ex-husbands, those employed during marriage, and those with marketable job skills, are less likely to end up poor or near-poor (Weiss 1984; Weitzman 1985). Racial and ethnic differences are quite striking in this regard. The 1983 median income for Black and Hispanic women maintaining families was only 60 percent of the median income of White women maintaining families—$7,999 and $7,797 compared with $13,761. The unemployment rate for Black Hispanic women maintaining families is double that of White women—18.7 percent and 16.7 percent compared with 8.6 percent (Alliance Against Women's Oppression 1983). Although many White women are "only a husband away from poverty," many minority women *with* a husband are poor; 13.8 percent of all Black married-couple families were below the poverty level, compared with 6.3 percent of all White married-couple families (Bureau of the Census 1984a).

A study comparing separated and divorced women with children whose family income when married had been in the upper, middle, or lower thirds of the income distribution showed that although divorce and separation had a leveling effect, even after five years, significant differences in post-divorce or separation income remained among women. Women who when married had a family income in the top third lost the most (50 percent of family income); women in the poorest third experienced the least drop (22 percent of family income). But women from the highest third income bracket had post-divorce or separation incomes twice that of women from the lowest third, and 131 percent of the income of women from the middle third, because women from more affluent marriages were more likely to receive alimony and child support (Weiss 1984). Women from the lowest third income bracket were most likely to be eligible for welfare and food stamps (71 percent in the first year). In the first year, only one-fourth of the women from marriages in the middle third income bracket received welfare or food stamps, dropping to one-eighth by the fifth year.

In addition to ignoring class and race differences among women, the feminization-of-poverty campaign denies the poverty of men, especially minority men. Women make up an increasing proportion of the poor because more women are falling into poverty, not because more men are getting out. As Malvaux (1985) argues, the slogan that "by the year 2000 all the poor will be women and children," is true only if genocide (or full employment) is planned for minority men.

One reason poor women outnumber poor men is that men have a shorter life span: after age 65 there are 1.5 women for every one man. However, older Black men are twice as likely to be poor as older White women (and three times more likely to be in poverty than older White men). Hispanic men over 65 are also more impoverished than White women—20.7 percent compared with 7.2 percent (Bureau of the Census 1984a). In 1984, White widows had a mean family income of $23,469 and an average income per family member of $8,331, compared with a mean family income of $13,464 and $3,663 per family member for widowed Black women and $15,503 and $4,515 per family member for widowed Hispanic women (Bureau of the Census 1984b).

The astonishing growth in families headed by women between 1970 and 1984 (from 11.5 percent to 22.9 percent overall and from 33 percent to 56 percent among Blacks) and the consequent increasing poverty of women may be the result, at least in part, of the economic structure rather than men's neglect of their familial responsibilities. Many Black men do not have access to steady employment and higher-paid work. Stack (1974) describes the cross-household survival networks that organize family life among poor Blacks. Black fathers may contribute to their children's support while living in a different female-headed household. In 1979, 15 percent of Black men aged 25 to 60 were living in households in which they were not the head, compared with 6 percent of White men in the same age group (Bureau of the Census 1980). For the underclass, minority or White, poverty is not simply a problem of women without men, it includes their sons, husbands and ex-husbands, and fathers.

When the feminization-of-poverty campaign focuses on the increased standard of living of divorced men compared with that of their ex-wives and looks to child-support enforcement legislation as a solution to women's poverty, it fails to address this reality. By 1984, in the United States, never-married women constituted one-half of the household heads among Black women-headed families. Sixty percent of these women are under 30; Black men between the ages of 15 and 29 (who are most likely to be the fathers of these women's children) do not make enough money to support them. A substantial proportion have no income and a majority make less than $10,000 a year (Simms 1985-86). A California study found that half of the ex-husbands of women in the welfare system had incomes under $15,000 a year (Women's Economic Agenda Project n.d.).

There is surely a fine but very important line between the feminist demand that men take responsibility for their children and the anti-feminist demand that men have the obligation to be the family bread-winner. The new right recognized the poverty of abandoned women. Their solution is to force men to support women and children by making divorce more difficult (in order to tie men to their families), to force women on welfare to name the child's father and how to find him, and so forth (Ehrenreich and Stallard, 1982). The claim that women's poverty is caused by deadbeat fathers, similar to the claim that Black poverty is caused by teenage mothers, is not only factually incorrect but looks to the restoration of the nuclear family as the solution to the problem of dependent care (Darity and Myers 1980; Sarvasy and Van Allen 1984).

In the face of political opposition and constricted government budgets, expanded public services for single mothers—increased eligibility for means-tested benefits, inexpensive quality child care—will not be easy to win. The desperate need of poor women may seem to justify the use of whatever arguments appear politically effective. However, we ought to be alerted to the dangers of this temptation by the way that previous reform campaigns (for example, for protective legislation for women workers) appealed to prevailing gender ideals and thereby contributed to perpetuating a gender ideology that justified women's exclusion from public life (Brenner and Ramas 1984; Kessler-Harris 1982).

The alleviation of women's poverty ought to be incorporated in a broader program of social and economic change. The familistic ideology and state policy that denies collective responsibility for dependent individuals, forces women to take on the burdens of caring and assumes that only men have a claim to economic independence and citizenship, must be the transformed. For instance, a comprehensive system of supplements to low-income households, regardless of their composition, would benefit all the poor and near-poor, including women-headed families. Paid parental leave (for meeting the needs of older children as well as infants) would benefit single mothers as well as help men and married women to combine wage work and care-giving.

In the longer run, a living wage, quality child care, and good jobs are necessary for everyone, but especially for women who choose not to share child care with a man. A program that incorporates short-term reforms into the larger goal of expanded social responsibility for caring would counteract both the stereotypical dependence of women as care-givers and the stereotypical independence of men as citizenworkers. This approach would frame the feminization-of-poverty issue in a way that connects it to the movements of working-class people and people of color (Sarvasy and Van Allen 1984).

COMPARABLE WORTH

As its proponents have argued, comparable worth focuses attention on the systematic devaluation of women's work and the roots of that devaluation in a general cultural denigration of women and womanly activities. Unlike equal pay and affirmative action programs, comparable worth offers the possibility of raising the wages of the vast majority of women working in jobs that have traditionally been held mostly by women. Trade unions, especially in the public sector, have embraced comparable worth as a strategy for raising their members' wages, and many working women have been brought into union activities around this issue.

Because it has been taken up by trade unions and because it has met resistance from employers, employer organizations, and conservatives, comparable-worth advocates have tended to assume that the issue has radical or potentially radical force. Hartmann and Treiman (1983, p. 416) argue: "Claims of comparable worth force explicit discussion about relative pay rates. As such, they politicize wage setting in a new, possibly even revolutionary, way." Similarly, Feldberg (1984, p. 313) argues that comparable worth "has radical implications because it initiates an end to women's economic dependency and questions the market basis of wages."

Comparable worth is often referred to as the civil rights issue of the '80s. Yet the significance of comparable worth as a remedy to women's low pay and occupational segregation is limited. Its application has been most effective in public-worker settings because these workers are often unionized and because it is possible for these unions to bring pressure through legislatures or elected officials. The State of Washington finally bargained a comparable-worth settlement with the American Federation of State, County and Municipal Employees even though the union's comparable-worth lawsuit had lost on appeal. San Francisco was forced to give comparable-worth raises to women and members of minority groups, a step Mayor Dianne Feinstein resisted, after voters approved a ballot measure directing city officials to resolve the pay inequities (*New York Times* 1987). Without such political pressure, the chances for imposing comparable worth on the private sector through the courts are slim, at least in the near future, because such suits are rarely won (Hutner 1986), and because only a small proportion of women employees in the private sector are unionized (*Monthly Labor Review* 1986).

Although a demand for recognition of the value of their work and higher pay is a possible strategy for all women workers, raising wages by equating women's and men's wages in comparable jobs will not work in industries, such as insurance, in which men are employed mostly at the top and middle and women at the bottom (Remick 1984a). Affirmative action remains crucial to encouraging women's employment in nontraditional occupations and management. Furthermore, as even its supporters (Feldberg 1984; Malvaux 1985-86) point out, comparable worth will not improve the access of women of color to jobs and education.

As a political discourse, comparable worth's fundamental claim to legitimacy reinforces an existing ideology: the necessity and validity of meritocratic hierarchy. Rather than questioning the market as an arbiter of wages, comparable worth, as two of its most prominent advocates say, attempts to:

> pay a fair market wage to jobs historically done by women. This means that the wage rate should be based on the productivity-based job content characteristics of the jobs and not on the sex of the typical job incumbent. . . . Comparable worth advocates seek to disentangle and remove discrimination from the market. (Remick and Steinberg 1984, p. 289)

Job evaluations use wage surveys to fix a dollar value to the factor points for benchmark jobs, which are then used to establish a salary scale. Job evaluations measure only the traits of jobs; the money value of the traits is determined by the wages prevailing in the labor market (Aldrich and Buchele 1986). Thus comparable worth aims primarily to rationalize the existing sorting and selecting of individuals into unequal places and does *not* eliminate market criteria from job evaluation.

From this point of view, comparable worth is a relatively conservative approach to women's low pay in that it situates its rationale firmly within the hegemonic liberal political discourse. A radical approach to women's low pay would not only challenge the existing inequalities between women's and men's pay for comparable jobs, but also would contest the notion that people's income should be determined primarily by where they fit in an occupational hierarchy. If jobs are assessed in terms of their necessity to an integrated labor process, it is equally important that *all* jobs be done consistently and well. Anyone who contributes his or her best efforts in a particular job is as deserving as any other individual.

Western contemporary society will not accept "from each according to his or her ability, to each according to his or her need" as a standard of fairness. Nonetheless, the claim that everyone who labors deserves to live decently has been, particularly in periods of working-class mobilization, a central value. Of course, historically, the trade union movement appealed to the right of the working *man* to make a family wage. Perhaps because the strategy has served to institutionalize women's marginalization in wage labor, feminists have preferred to address the problem of women's low pay in terms other than women's life needs as individuals and as mothers. Perhaps also because it relies on broadly shared meritocratic values, comparable worth may appear to be a practical approach to raising women's pay. But so long as comparable worth efforts remain within that liberal discourse, they risk eventually increasing racial and occupational divisions among working women.

The heart of the comparable-worth strategy is the job evaluation. Certain dimensions of every job are measured and given a numerical rating; knowledge and skill, effort, responsibility, and working conditions are the major dimensions used. These dimensions are weighted. Typically, skill and responsibility are given higher weights than working conditions. In the Hay study on which an Idaho State employee's comparable-worth adjustment was based, the weight given the dimension of responsibility was 42 times the weight given to working conditions (Treiman 1984). Supervision of other people and responsibility for money or expensive equipment are measures that may not reflect responsibilities typical of women's jobs.

Zebrowitz McArthur (1985) argues that important dimensions of jobs are left out of most job evaluations. Opportunity for advancement, job security, and how boring a job is might also be considered as compensable factors; jobs might deserve higher compensation not only for poor physical working conditions but for poor psychological conditions. Of course, as she also reports, the more desirable a job is, the higher people judge its monetary worth, not the other way around. Therefore, the impact of a job evaluation scheme on a given work force will depend on how the evaluations are constructed. Treiman (1984) demonstrates that evaluation methods that put a low value on working conditions and physical strength will tend to assign higher scores to jobs typically done by Whites. He concludes:

> The choice of factors and factor weights in job evaluation schemes should not be regarded as a technical issue beyond the purview of affected parties

but rather as an expression of the values underlying notions of equity and hence as a matter to be negotiated as part of the wage-setting process. (p. 89)

To evaluate the probable impact of comparable worth, then, we need to consider who will participate in the negotiations over the factors and factor weights and with what sorts of assumptions. Since less than one-fifth of the U.S. work force and only 13 percent of all U.S. women workers are unionized (*Monthly Labor Review* 1986), we can expect that, in most cases, technical experts and management will formulate the evaluation policies. We can further expect that existing cultural biases in factors and factor weights will be replicated. Acker (1987) demonstrates how difficult it is to overcome experts' and managers' resistance to altering evaluation systems even in a unionized and public setting, especially when alterations might change the rank order of jobs or undermine pay differentials between management and non-management employees.

Malvaux (1985-86) contends that Black men and women will benefit from comparable-worth adjustments, because the jobs held by Black women and men tend to be even more underpaid relative to comparable White men's jobs than are White women's jobs. However, the implementation of a job evaluation scheme that all parties agree is equitable may legitimize large differences in pay among employees by race and occupation. Even after the implementation of comparable worth among Washington State employees, one of the highest non-management women's jobs will pay 149 percent of one of the lowest women's jobs (calculated from Remick 1984a). Estimating the impact of comparable-worth adjustments under different conditions, Aldrich and Buchele (1986) found the earnings gap between women workers by quintiles would be reduced by at most 6.5 percent. Since women are not distributed proportionately by race within job categories, large inequalities by race will remain, but appear to be reflections of differential merit and thus ultimately difficult to challenge.

Comparable worth may also exacerbate hierarchies in women's jobs. For example, hospital administrations do not currently award differential salaries among nursing specialties, although there is a clear hierarchy of rewards to medical specialties. Remick (1984b, p. 97) predicts that job evaluation systems may expose "internal squabbles that will have to be dealt with by the nursing profession." At hearings conducted by the U.S. Equal Employment Opportunities Commission in 1980, the American Nurses Association testified to the similarities between intensive care unit nurses and doctors (Eyde 1983). Comparable-worth adjustments may encourage nurses with such specialties to claim higher pay.

Comparable worth may very well open up discussion of how society values work, but that discussion must be framed by a broader challenge to the prevailing culture. The superior value of mental over manual skills and the greater importance of supervisory over other kinds of responsibility should not be assumed but questioned. Otherwise, we can expect comparable worth to readjust women's and men's pay but to change very little, perhaps even to solidify, the existing divisions in the work force: divisions between Whites and minority workers, between designated professionals and non-professionals, between white-collar and blue-collar workers. These divisions cut across gender and have been an important source of trade-union disunity. Yet any radical potential for "politicizing the wage-setting process" depends on the strength of worker organization.

Gender divisions within the work force have played an important part in perpetuating women's low pay. Male-dominated trade unions have been willing to take up the issue only as women workers have become organized. The kind of strategies used for raising the pay of women workers can undermine or aggravate men's resistance, increase or decrease the possibilities for overcoming employer opposition, and create a more unified—or more divided—work force.

Job evaluation studies often find men's job classes "overpaid" for the content of their jobs, especially craft jobs, which tend to be held by White men (Farnquist et al. 1983). Since market realities may be felt to require relatively higher wages in order to recruit and hold those workers, and it may be illegal to equalize pay scales by lowering men's wages, most plans attempt to achieve equity over a long run by gradually increasing women's wages. Some plans freeze men's wages; others simply raise men's wages more slowly, for example, giving all workers a cost-of-living raise and women workers an equity bonus. The plan selected influences the impact of a comparable-worth settlement on relationships between the men's and women's sections of a work force. Freezing men's wages is divisive, but because it is cheaper, comparable-worth adjustments will probably take that route, except when worker organization and union leadership mount effective opposition.

A less divisive strategy is to adjust women's wages to a level commensurate with the intrinsic value of their work. In the strike by women clerical workers at Yale, the union demanded higher pay on the ground that the women made an important contribution to the university, a contribution that has historically been undervalued because they were women. The union did not center its strategy on a direct comparison with men's wages or claims about the comparative value of men's and women's work. The women were well-organized; the unionized, predominantly blue-collar men had nothing to lose and much to gain from a united work force, so the men were willing to honor the women's picket line for the entire ten weeks of the strike. The women reciprocated and supported the men when their contract came up, which allowed the men to make gains that they had unsuccessfully struck for in the past (Ladd-Taylor 1985). In short, although the women's and men's pay scales were adjusted separately, not in relation to each other, the gender gap was narrowed.

In sum, comparable worth seems to offer an immediate remedy to a pressing problem, but it may institutionalize divisions among women and between women and men that will make future collective campaigns difficult. Although some supporters of comparable worth themselves signal potential dangers, such as the dominance of technocrats and managers in wage setting or divisions among women workers (Feldberg 1984; Remick 1984b), they tend to minimize the risks and overestimate its radical potential. It seems to me that unless a very different kind of organizing is done concerning the issue, this potential is not likely to be realized.

Comparable worth has been presented as a demand for removing discrimination and improving women's position within an existing system. The demand for equity could, however, be put forward as part of a broader set of longer-range goals that challenge the terms of the system itself. A radical strategy would argue for raising the pay of the lowest-paid workers, most of whom are women and minorities, on the grounds that everyone who contributes his or her labor deserves a comfortable and secure existence. This strategy would not only protest the under-valuation of women's work but also argue that existing salary differentials among jobs, especially between management and non-management jobs, are unnecessarily large. And it would argue that if we are looking at the work people do, then we should ask whether that work is productive, safe, and interesting, and whether it allows people to use their talents and skills and to develop new ones.

CONCLUSION

Feminist historians have written at length about the ways that the dual-spheres ideology of the nineteenth and early twentieth centuries shaped feminist politics and blunted the radical potential of the women's movement (e.g., Gordon and Dubois 1983). Liberal political discourse similarly has shaped contemporary feminist thinking. The feminization-of-poverty and comparable-worth campaigns argue their case in terms of claims that reflect and in turn reinforce the assumptions of a liberal political framework.

A radical framework contests these assumptions, challenges the hierarchical organization of work and the privatization of care giving, and generates a more inclusive set of claims. A language of rights does not have to be limited to a narrowly defined meritocratic standard but can be expanded to include the rights to contribute one's best efforts, to do work that enriches, and to receive in return a decent standard of living. It also can include the right of children to care from their community and the right of parents to economic and social support in carrying out their responsibilities to their children.

Neither the feminization of poverty nor comparable worth are inherently radical concepts. Their impact will depend on how solutions are conceptualized, how they are implemented, and how they are used politically.

REFERENCES

Acker, J. 1987. "Sex Bias in Job Evaluation: A Comparable Worth Issue." Pp. 183-96 in *Ingredients for Women's Employment Policy,* edited by C. Bose and G. Spitze. Albany: SUNY Press.

Aldrich, M., and R. Buchele. 1986. *Economics of Comparable Worth.* Cambridge, MA: Ballinger.

Alliance Against Women's Oppression. 1983. *Poverty: Not for Women Only.* San Francisco: Author.

Barrett, M., and M. McIntosh. 1982. *The Anti-Social Family.* London: Verso.

Bell, D. 1972. "On Meritocracy and Equality." *Public Interest* 29:29-68.

Boris, E., and P. Bardaglio. 1983. "The Transformation of Patriarchy: The Historic Role of the State." Pp. 70-93 in *Families, Politics, and Public Policy,* edited by I. Diamond. New York: Longman.

Brenner, J., and M. Ramas. 1984. "Rethinking Women's Oppression." *New Left Review* 144:33-71.

Bureau of the Census. 1980. *Detailed Population Characteristics: U.S. Summary.* Washington, DC: Government Printing Office.

————. 1984a. *Characteristics of the Population Below the Poverty Level: 1984.* Current Population Reports, Consumer Income, Series P-60, no. 152. Washington, DC: Government Printing Office.

————. 1984b. *Money Income of Households, Families, and Persons in The U.S.: 1984.* Current Population Reports, Consumer Income, Series P-60, no. 151. Washington, DC: Government Printing Office.

Cain, P. S. 1985. "The Role of the Sciences in the Comparable Worth Movement." Pp. 156-70 in *Social Science and Social Policy,* edited by R. L. Shotland and M. M. Mark. Beverly Hills, CA: Sage.

Darity, Jr., W. A., and S. L. Myers, Jr. 1980. "Changes in Black-White Income Inequality, 1968-1978: A Decade of Progress." *Review of Black Political Economy* 10:167-77.

Davis, K., and W. E. Moore. 1945. "Some Principles of Stratification." *American Sociological Review* 10:242-9.

Ehrenreich, B., and K. Stallard. 1982. "The Nouveau Poor." *MS* (July/August):217-24.

Eyde, L. D. 1983. "Evaluating Job Evaluation: Emerging Research Issues for Comparable Worth Analysis." *Public Personnel Management* 10:425-44.

Farnquist, R. L., et al. 1983. "Pandora's Worth: The San Jose Experience." *Public Personnel Management* 12:358-68.

Feldberg, R. L. 1984. "Comparable Worth: Toward Theory and Practice in the United States." *Signs: Journal of Women in Culture and Society* 10:311-28.

Ferguson, K. E. 1984. *The Feminist Case Against Bureaucracy.* Philadelphia: Temple University Press.

Folbre, N. 1984. "The Pauperization of Motherhood: Patriarchy and Public Policy in the United States." *Review of Radical Political Economics* 16:72-88.

Gordon, L., 1986. "Feminism and Social Control: The Case of Child Abuse and Neglect." Pp. 63-84 in *What Is Feminism? A Re-Examination,* edited by J. Mitchell and A. Oakley. New York: Pantheon.

—— and E. Dubois. 1983. "Seeking Ecstasy on the Battlefield: Danger and Pleasure in 19th Century Feminist Sexual Thought." *Feminist Studies* 8:451-70.

Hartmann, H. I., and D. J. Treiman. 1983. "Notes on the NAS Study of Equal Pay for Jobs of Equal Value." *Public Personnel Management* 12:404-17.

Hutner, F. C. 1986. *Equal Pay for Comparable Worth: The Working Woman's Issue of the Eighties.* New York: Praeger.

Kessler-Harris, A. 1982. *Out to Work: A History of Wage-Earning Women in the United States.* New York: Oxford University Press.

Ladd-Taylor, M. 1985. "Women Workers and the Yale Strike." *Feminist Studies* 11: 465-91.

Lewis, J. (ed.). 1983. *Women's Welfare/Women's Rights.* London: Croom Helm.

——. 1986. "Feminism and Welfare." Pp. 85-100 in *What Is Feminism? A Re-Examination,* edited by J. Mitchell and A. Oakley. New York: Pantheon.

Malvaux, J. 1985. "The Economic Interests of Black and White Women: Are They Similar?" *Review of Black Political Economy* 14(6):4-27.

——. 1985-86. "Comparable Worth and Its Impact on Black Women." *Review of Black Political Economy* 14:47-62.

Mason, R. M. 1982. *Participatory and Workplace Democracy: A Theoretical Development in Critique of Liberalism.* New York: Basic Books.

McArthur, L. Zebrowitz. 1985. "Social Judgment Biases in Comparable Worth Analysis." Pp. 53-70 in *Comparable Worth: New Directions for Research,* edited by H. I. Hartmann. Washington, DC: National Academy Press.

Monthly Labor Review. 1986. "Union Membership for Employed Wage and Salary Workers, 1985." 109:44-6.

Nelson, B. J. 1984. "Women's Poverty and Women's Citizenship: Some Political Consequences of Economic Marginality." *Signs: Journal of Women in Culture and Society* 10:209-31.

New York Times. 1987. "San Francisco Agrees to Pay Raise for Women." (March 20):11.

Okin, S. 1979. *Women in Western Political Thought.* Princeton, NJ: Princeton University Press.

Pateman, C. 1980. " 'The Disorder of Women': Women, Love, and the Sense of Justice." *Ethics* 91:20-34.

Pearce, D. M., and H. McAdoo. 1981. *Women and Children: Alone and in Poverty.* Washington, DC: National Advisory Council on Economic Opportunity.

Pleck, E. 1983. "Feminist Responses to 'Crimes Against Women,' 1868-1896." *Signs: Journal of Women in Culture and Society* 8:451-70.

Remick, H. 1984a. "Major Issues in *a priori* Applications." Pp. 99-117 in *Comparable Worth and Wage Discrimination,* edited by H. Remick. Philadelphia: Temple University Press.

———. 1984b. "Dilemmas of Implementation: The Case of Nursing." Pp. 90-8 in *Comparable Worth and Wage Discrimination,* edited by H. Remick. Philadelphia: Temple University Press.

——— and Ronnie J. Steinberg. 1984. "Technical Possibilities and Political Realities: Concluding Remarks." Pp. 285-302 in *Comparable Worth and Wage Discrimination,* edited by H. Remick. Philadelphia: Temple University Press.

Rothschild-Whitt, J. 1979. "The Collectivist Organization: An Alternative to Rational Bureaucratic Models." *American Sociological Review* 44:509-27.

Sarvasy, W., and J. Van Allen. 1984. "Fighting the Feminization of Poverty: Socialist-Feminist Analysis and Strategy." *Review of Radical Political Economics* 16:89-110.

Simms, M. C. 1985/6. "Black Women Who Head Families: An Economic Struggle." *Review of Black Political Economy* 14:140-51.

Stack, C. B. 1974. *All Our Kin: Strategies for Survival in a Black Community.* New York: Harper & Row.

Treiman, D. J. 1984. "Effect of Choice of Factor and Factor Weights in Job Evaluation." Pp. 79-89 in *Comparable Worth and Wage Discrimination: Technical Possibilities and Political Realities.* Philadelphia: Temple University Press.

——— and H. I. Hartmann (eds.). 1981. *Women, Work, and Wages: Equal Pay for Jobs of Equal Value.* Washington, DC: National Academy Press.

Weiss, R. S. 1984. "The Impact of Marital Dissolution on Income and Consumption in Single-Parent Households." *Journal of Marriage and the Family* 24:115-27.

Weitzman, L. J. 1985. *The Divorce Revolution: The Unexpected Social and Economic Consequences for Women and Children in America.* New York: Free Press.

Women's Economic Agenda Project. N.D. *Women's Economic Agenda.* Oakland, CA: Author.

Zaretsky, E. 1982. "The Place of the Family in the Origins of the Welfare State." Pp. 188-220 in *Rethinking the Family: Some Feminist Questions,* edited by B. Thorne with M. Yalom. New York: Longman.

IV.

Feminist Research Strategies

Feminist methods of doing research attempt to probe social realities that are layered, symbolic, and embedded in the concrete, the particular, everyday life. But are feminist methods different from masculinist methods?

Men's ways of knowing and thinking often claim to be universalistic, abstract, linear, and logically rule-bound (Harding 1986). These are rhetorical claims. In actuality, in their knowing and thinking activities, men ignore the rhetoric that touts such epistemology as superior. Science is supposed to be particularly universalistic and objective, but both men and women scientists on the cutting edge use insight and intuitive leaps of knowledge. For example, in a *New York Times* article, "In the Trenches of Science," Gleick (1987), in describing the race of all-male research teams for superconductive material, reported that one scientist said his best ideas came from dreams. Fox Keller's (1983) biography of Barbara McClintock, a Nobel Prize winner, is tellingly titled *A Feeling for the Organism*. According to Fox Keller, "scientists combine the rules of scientific methodology with a generous admixture of intuition, aesthetics, and philosophical commitment" (p. 145). Sayre (1975) described Rosalind Franklin, who contributed enormously to the discovery of DNA, as having

> a kind of determined rationality, an unconquerable conviction that reason dominated, that sane and sensible people . . . preferred to act in accordance with logic. . . . Like many other scientists, she had a natural affinity for objective evidence and objective proof, and no natural ease with wholly subjective reasoning or purely approximate thinking. This is not to suggest that the scientific mind is rigid or narrow, for Rosalind, like other good scientists, possessed a knack for the less-advertised side of science in which hunches and guesses and an instinctive feel for the problem play more of a role than is generally acknowledged. (pp. 47-8)

The point is that some men and some women scientists have more intuitive styles of working; other men and women scientists are more often methodical, objective, and distant from their materials; and many researchers use both styles. The contrast is not between male and female ways of thinking, but, as we say in sociology, between *verstehen* and objective understanding, induction and deduction. As good researchers know, each has its strengths and weaknesses.

In sociology, although most seemingly objective research has tended to be quantitative—to use large samples, randomly chosen and assumed to be representative of a whole population, to use preset questionnaire schedules or already collected data, to turn variables into numbers that can be manipulated statistically, to be replicable (that is, to be doable by anyone)—the results are never truly objective, but always biased by the theoretical assumptions, by the framing of the research question, and by the interpretation of the findings. Nonetheless, the methods themselves are not unusable by feminist researchers (Sprague and Zimmerman 1989).

The main problem with quantitative research is the way gender is categorized. First, it is usually assumed to be *sex,* not gender—that is, a biological given and not a social construction. Second, that there are two genders is taken as a given, and furthermore, it is assumed that any interviewer can recognize which of the two the respondent is. If the respondent is asked or fills in the little box, there is no question that perhaps you don't have a "normal, natural" woman or man—but perhaps a transvestite, a transsexual, or someone in transition. It is assumed that no one ever lies about it, too.

So gender is a two-fold variable in most quantitative research, and it is assumed to be the cause, a prior condition, not an effect of something else. Also assumed is that men and women are so different that they can be put into discrete categories. The researcher then usually goes on to see what difference sex, or gender, makes to the variation in the topic under study (attitudes, or voting behavior, or capacity for various kinds of work, for nurturance, etc.) If differences are found, they are assumed to be the result of whatever is in the category, male or female, or man or woman, which is a kind of tautology, because that is what you started out with. If differences are not found, then it is assumed that sex or gender is not salient to this particular variable, but again, there is no exploration of why that should be so.

Usually not examined, but frequently discussed at length, is what it is about the sex category or gender status that could be producing the differences. Here, theoretical assumptions are invoked—the underlying cause is assumed to be biological, in the way girls and boys are brought up, or in women's or men's status in society. These theories still assume a dichotomy—two sexes, two types of upbringing, or two social locations. Ignored are problematic gender identities, racial ethnic or religious or class differences in gender socialization, and the variety of social locations of women and men in any one particular society. In short, when sex or gender are used as global dichotomies, they are used in an *essentialist* way (as if they occurred naturally and always the same way).

A feminist would not necessarily reject quantitative research, but would design the research differently. First of all, a feminist would not assume only two categories—men and women—nor would a feminist assume that men and women would be either different or show no different effects. A feminist would look at the attitudes or behavior in question (let's say ambition to get ahead in work) and see how many patterns there were in terms of several variables—getting additional training, traveling for the job, working overtime, taking days off, and so on. Then she would see what causes there could be—educational level, social class of family of origin, marital status, number of children, ages of children, occupation of spouse, *and* gender.

What she might find is that at higher levels of education and middle-class family of origin, men and women are equally ambitious, but their career outcomes may be different because of organizational discrimination against women in general and women with children in particular. At lower levels of education and working-class family of origin, single men and women might be very similar in that they are not heavily invested in their not-very-interesting jobs, but that married men with children work hard to make more money and are rewarded by promotion, and married women with children use their jobs for extra income but put their families first and so do not get promoted (but do not resent it), while women who are single parents or married to men not making very much money do resent it and want day care.

The way that Lynn Weber Cannon, Elizabeth Higginbotham, and Marianne L. A. Leung assembled their respondents in Chapter 12, "Race and Class Bias in Qualitative Research on Women," was similar in that they looked beyond simple dichotomies. By getting data from Black and White women, and within each group, women raised working-class and raised middle-class, they were able to assess the effects of race and class on women's careers. Given a larger pool of subjects (and greater financial resources), this study could have used quantitative methods as well.

Qualitative research is often conducted by participant observation, where the researcher becomes a member of the group being researched, or by in-depth interviewing, which sometimes involves a sharing of experiences. Qualitative research engages the researcher in social interaction with the subject, and the research process has an effect on both—the researcher through putting herself in her subjects' shoes and the subject through greater consciousness and self-awareness. Thus, both teach and learn in the course of the study. The advantages are well-known—insightful understanding of the perspectives of others and of the meanings of others' experiences. The data have richness, complexity, and symbolic referents.

The problems of this type of research are perhaps less well-known. First, there is the problem of the insider and the outsider (Merton 1972). If you are a member of the group, you don't have to study it—just relate your own experiences. In Merton's words: "Insider as Insighter, one endowed with special insight into matters necessarily obscure to others, thus possessed of penetrating discernment" (p. 19). Despite the criticism of mainstream social scientists, making women's experiences visible and women's standpoint part of scientific discourse is one of the main strengths of feminist methodology (Cook and Fonow 1986; Hartsock 1983; Hawkesworth 1989).

But what group are you a member of? Everyone knows that women (and men) vary by social class (past and present), by where they live, where they were born, what language they speak, what culture they are comfortable with, what religion and politics they practice, what their sexual preferences and sexual experiences have been—so what is your group identity (Haraway 1988)? Reliance on insider knowledge can be severely shaken if it is assumed that women understand women because they are women, as Catherine Kohler Riessman describes in Chapter 11, "When Gender Is Not Enough: Women Interviewing Women." Her middle-class White interviewer could identify with the middle-class White subject, but she found it very difficult to follow the narrative of the working-class Hispanic woman.

The second problem is one of trust and betrayal. To do research, you must collect data, and your data are people's confidences to you once they trust you. Even if you are honest and aboveboard about your role as a researcher, and you are careful to preserve anonymity, people may be hurt when you publish your findings (Acker, Barry, and Esseveld 1983). In asking whether one can be a reflexive participant observer and a true feminist, Stacey (1988) honestly appraised the advantages and disadvantages of ethnography and her own use of and response to intensive interviewing and involvement with her respondents' lives. She concluded that researchers can be fooled by both the "delusion of alliance" and the "delusion of separateness."

It would be an unfortunate irony if feminists, in an attempt to shrug off the role of the male-oriented Other, felt comfortable only researching women like themselves, and only with methods that put them in their subject's shoes. Smith (1987) says that the feminist researcher must see "the everyday world as problematic, where the everyday world is taken to be various and differentiated matrices of experience—the place from which the consciousness of the knower begins" (p. 173). But she cautions that feminist social scientists have to go beyond the everyday world, which needs to be framed by a knowledge of larger structures and relationships. That is why, according to Smith, the everyday world is problematic. When the sociologist constructs the patterns of social reality from everyday experiences of subjects, she does so from the standpoint of her own social reality, and, as we have seen, even if the researcher and the subject are both women, they are not likely to come from the same social location. And even if they did, the social researcher still needs a bifurcated consciousness that can bring to bear a somewhat abstracted larger social reality (the social relations of capitalism, for instance) on the patterns and experience of the everyday world (Hartsock 1983).

If feminists do not have a unique methodology, totally different from non-feminist's or from men's, do they have a different perspective that frames research questions differently? Hill Collins (1986), in discussing the "insider-outsider" position of the Black feminist researcher, argued that she could uniquely contribute to social science by seeing patterns and interrelationships, causes and effects, and implications of questions that those who have never stood outside the dominant culture have not seen and still do not see. That is, the value of social science research is that it looks at the routine patterns of everyday life and accepted, institutional ways of doing things as if they were new and strange. Feminists, and even more so, feminists who are women of color, start with the advantage of a somewhat distanced stance. They are more likely to see the crucially informative contradictions in data. In short, they are able to look at the familiar world with the gaze of the unfamiliar because they are, still, outsiders.

REFERENCES

Acker, J., K. Barry, and J. Esseveld. 1983. "Objectivity and Truth: Problems in Doing Feminist Research." *Women's Studies International Forum* 6:423-35.

Cook, J. A., and M. M. Fonow. 1986. "Knowledge and Women's Interests: Issues of Epistemology and Methodology in Feminist Sociological Research." *Sociological Inquiry* 56:2-29.

Collins, P. Hill. 1986. "Learning from the Outsider Within: The Sociological Significance of Black Feminist Thought." *Social Problems* 33:S14-S32.

Gleick, J. 1987. "In the Trenches of Science." *New York Times Magazine* (August 16):29.

Haraway, D. 1988. "Situated Knowledges: The Science Question in Feminism and the Privilege of Partial Perspective." *Feminist Studies* 14:575-99.

Harding, S. 1986. *The Science Question in Feminism.* Ithaca, NY: Cornell University Press.

Hartsock, N.C.M. 1983. *Money, Sex and Power: Toward a Feminist Historical Materialism.* New York: Longman.

Hawkesworth, M. 1989. "Knowers, Knowing, Known: Feminist Theory and Claims of Truth." *Signs: Journal of Women in Culture and Society* 14:533-57.

Keller, E. Fox. 1983. *A Feeling for the Organism: The Life and Work of Barbara McClintock.* New York: W. H. Freeman.

Merton, R. 1972. "Insiders and Outsiders: A Chapter in the Sociology of Knowledge." *American Journal of Sociology* 78:9-47.

Sayre, A. 1975. *Rosalind Franklin and DNA.* New York: Norton.

Smith, D. E. 1987. *The Everyday World as Problematic.* Toronto: University of Toronto Press.

Sprague, J., and M. K. Zimmerman. 1989. "Quality and Quantity: Reconstructing Feminist Methodology." *The American Sociologist* 20:71-86.

Stacey, J. 1988. "Can There Be a Feminist Ethnography?" *Women's Studies International Forum* 11:21-7.

11. WHEN GENDER IS NOT ENOUGH: WOMEN INTERVIEWING WOMEN

CATHERINE KOHLER RIESSMAN

Narrative analysis is an approach to qualitative interviews (Mishler 1986) that can be applied to women's life stories. As a universal human form for reconstructing and interpreting the past, narratives link our experience of the world and our efforts to describe that experience, or make meaning of it. In the words of White (1981, p. 1), it is through narratives that we "translate knowing into telling." Narrating personal experience can be done in many ways, but the listener may not "hear" what is important to the narrator. The structures of children's stories vary with their cultural background, so that White classroom teachers have difficulty "hearing" narratives of Black children (Michaels 1981; Michaels and Cazden 1986). In the research interview, too, it is likely that "lack of shared cultural norms for telling a story, making a point, giving an explanation and so forth can create barriers to understanding" (Michaels 1985, p. 51). For women interviewing women about their lives, such barriers to understanding are particularly consequential, for they reproduce within the scientific enterprise class and cultural divisions among women that feminists have tried so hard to diminish.

This chapter shows how two women interviewees—one Anglo and one Hispanic—used different narrative genres to make meaning of the same event—marital separation. The Anglo woman organized her narrative temporally; the Puerto Rican woman organized hers episodically. Although both were highly competent narrators, only the Anglo woman was fully understood by the White, middle-class interviewer. She was able to collaborate with this narrator and help her tell her story. In the case of the working-class, Hispanic woman, gender apparently was not enough to create the shared understandings necessary for a successful interview. The lack of shared norms about how a narrative should be organized, coupled with unfamiliar cultural themes in the content of the narrative itself, created barriers to understanding between the Anglo interviewer and the Puerto Rican narrator. As a result, the interview fell short. There was also an added tension in this interview between the interviewer's allegiance to "scientific" interviewing practice—with its norms of distance and objectivity—and her allegiance to women's

217

culture—with its norms of empathy and subjectivity. These multiple strains led to a breakdown in the discourse.

The two interviews were part of a study of the experience of separation and divorce. In all, 104 women and men who had been separated for up to three years were interviewed, using a structured interview schedule. The interviews, conducted in the respondents' homes, were taped and transcribed. The interviewer asked each interviewee "to state in your own words the main causes of your separation." This question and subsequent probes provided the "scaffolding" (Cazden 1983) for the telling of the marital history. Two-thirds of the cases were located through probate court records of the divorced in two counties of a northeastern state; one-third came from interviewee and informant referrals. Comparisons between court cases and referred respondents indicated few differences.

The middle-class woman's response was typical of the form of temporal organization that most interviewees used, working-class and middle-class alike. The working-class Puerto Rican woman's narrative was selected for analysis because it was different, and its meaning was not grasped during the interview. Although other Hispanics also used the episodic form, we cannot generalize as to its typicality because of the small number of Hispanics in our sample, nor can we separate the effects of social class and ethnicity in shaping narrative style. Despite uncertainty about which subpopulations the two interviews represent, there is evidence that these two styles of narrating are used by contrasting groups in other settings (Michaels 1981), and thus illustrate alternative forms for storytelling more generally.

AN UNPROBLEMATIC INTERVIEW

Susan was a 36-year-old, college-educated, White divorced woman who was living with her three children (ages 10, 8, and 5). She had been living apart from her husband for almost three years. Unemployed and looking for a job, she received regular support payments from her ex-husband and still lived in the house, in a middle-class neighborhood, that her mother had helped them buy. Nevertheless, she was experiencing considerable financial strain, for her income was barely half what it was when she was married and the costs of raising her growing children have increased. Typical of many women in her situation, divorce was a financial catastrophe (Weitzman 1985); yet by the usual sociological indicators of years of education and type of neighborhood, Susan would be considered middle-class.

Susan's narrative about the history of her marriage was deeply gendered. In fact, it was an archetypal account of the oppression traditional marriage brings to women, with the accompanying feelings of powerlessness, passivity, and victimization that many women report. Susan told us that she married her husband because she got pregnant; in fact, she mentioned this fact three times, perhaps to excuse her responsibility for the marriage and therefore its failure (Scott and Lyman 1968). She described the gender-based division of labor that characterized the marriage and the burden she felt caring for three children with little help from her husband, who occupied himself with his job. She described how they did not talk about their problems, and how she "buried" her needs. Their emotional estrangement led to sexual disengagement, with separate beds and then separate bedrooms. Finally, the anger "surfaced," and they realized the marriage was over. It was a familiar story, one that the feminist interviewer understood very well.

Not only was the content of Susan's narrative familiar; so, too, was the form in which it was told. The narrator had a strong sense of place and she guided the listener through the various settings, locating the changes in the sleeping arrangements within the context of the family moves; they lived in Providence in 1974 (where they changed from a double to single beds); they moved to her mother's house in 1975, then into their own house the following year (where her husband slept on the third floor), and, finally, to the residence in which the interview takes place (where he had lived in an attic apartment).

The narrative was also organized by time; it began with the decision to marry, recounted the birth of the children, progressed through the years of the marriage, and ended with the separation. This temporal ordering of events into a narrative is a classic form in which individuals remember and recapitulate past experience (Labov 1982; Mandler and Johnson 1977). Although by no means the only one, such narrative sequencing is generally available as a storytelling form in our culture. In Susan's use of time as the organizing principle for her narrative, nothing was out of order (see Table 11.1). She was very clear about the order in which things happened, and she guided the listener through the five-year period recapitulated in the narrative, relating the decline in intimacy to changes in the marital residence and associated sleeping arrangements over time. Through the use of time and place as organizing devices, Susan brought order to her memories of her marriage as she brought order to the interview.

Yet there was an incongruity in the narrative; the events described first (notably having children) and the events described later (not sleeping together and not having sex) were contemporaneous. Thus the

TABLE 11.1 Sequences in Susan's Narrative

I was 25 when I was married
I had the children from day one
The years went by
We stopped talking early on in our marriage
We continued to have children
We had more children / that took up a lot of time
There was no sex
We slept in separate bedrooms / that started out really early in our marriage
When we lived in Providence / right after Nancy was born / she was born in 1974
So then I suggested single beds . . . which is what we did
And then the *following* year in 1975
Then when we moved here / first thing we did was to redo the attic
And then he moved up there as soon as that was done

events as narrated may not be as "real" or "objective" as the form suggests (Mishler 1986, appendix). The interviewer responded not to the incongruities but to the centrality of time in Susan's narrative, and had no difficulty following the sequence of events. Both interviewer and respondent, as middle-class White women, shared the cultural norm that events should be recounted temporally in storytelling (Michaels 1981). The interviewer did not interrupt the flow of the discourse, either to clarify what happened when or to suggest another organizing framework. She collaborated by letting the narrative unfold. By remaining silent at key points, she allowed the narrator "to control the pace and developing content" of the interview (Paget 1983, p. 77)

The interviewer was not passive. Her nonlexical expressions communicated understanding and encouraged the narrator to say more, and she asked for clarification at several points, building upon what the narrator said immediately before and further prompting another temporally ordered sequence. Her probes and encouragement made possible the recounting of this marital history. The smooth interaction provided evidence that the interviewer intuitively understood the genre—a temporally ordered narrative—in which the interviewee was retelling her experience.

Besides using time to order and thereby structure her narrative, Susan employed time in still another way. Although stories typically are told in the simple past tense (Labov 1982), Susan often used the habitual past in constructing her narrative (Gee 1985) saying, for example,

"He'd come home and then I would say." She conveyed the feeling of blurred time by this dexterous use of verb tense, adeptly conveying the repetitious nature of her husband's unavailability. Near the end of her narrative, Susan returned to her perception of blurred time during the marriage, again making artistic use of verb tense as well as repetition to communicate the experience of "just existing" through time. She also changed pronouns from the personal "we," "I," and "he" that she used earlier in the narrative to the general "you" and then back to "we" at the end. These shifts, and especially the use of the impersonal "you" to describe a distinctly personal perception, communicated her alienation at the time of the marriage from her self as she knew it at the time of the interview. The use of the impersonal voice also expressed her sense of passivity or inability to bring about any change over the many years of her marriage and, perhaps, her growing identification with women in similar situations.

The interviewer heard the narrator's experience of blurred time and, further, participated in the construction of Susan's explanation for the marital separation. For example, after Susan's coda to the first section of her narrative ("We really have a bad marriage"), the interviewer commented: "and you gradually just realized that." Later, she checked out her sense of the *gradual* unfolding of awareness about how bad the marriage was with her question, "So it just gradually dawned on both of you that you should get separated or?" Through her repetition of the word "gradually" she helped Susan develop her theme.

Susan's narrative was a deeply woman-centered account of the costs of a gender-based division of labor in marriage, and the interviewer heard it as such. About midway through Susan's narrative, there was an open display of the bond that was developing between interviewer and interviewee as women when Susan said "You know men snore," and they both laughed. This was a moment of solidarity between women. Elsewhere, the interviewer's attentive listening and nonlexical cues indicated that she appreciated how oppressive marriage was for Susan. She did not interrupt or in other ways indicate that she was having difficulty with the interpretive framework that Susan was using.

In fact, Susan graphically described her growing awareness of what Friedan (1963) has termed the "problem with no name." She grew resentful that she "carried 99 percent of the brunt of everything that had to be done (in the home);" she expected that marriage would involve more than a relationship between "roommates;" and, finally, she became conscious of the fact that she was "just existing," implicitly contrasting this mode of being with her ideal. She alternately invoked images of life, on the one hand, and deadness, on the other, to contrast her expectations about what a marriage should be with the reality of her experience. She twice used the phrase "give and take" to describe her expectations about marriage. Not only did she expect help with child care, she also expected emotional reciprocity. Living fully, for her, involved talking about emotions and problems. Instead, she found herself married to a man who "didn't give a lot" and whose "idea of having an argument was not to discuss it at all." Instead of life—as defined by emotional sharing and reciprocity—Susan experienced a deadness in her marriage; and by invoking images of death in repeated use of the image of burial, Susan visually depicted the idea that her true self was submerged in the marriage. Finally, it "surfaced" in the anger that was the proximate cause of the separation.

In sum at the time of the interview, Susan told the life history of her marriage using linguistic forms that, at the same time as they communicated the uniqueness of her situation, also are "unproblematic" in a more general sense for middle-class listeners. Both the organization and the content of the narrative resonated with the woman interviewer. The interviewer seemed to comprehend the relationship between the structural features of traditional marriage, as described by the narrator, and their psychological effects (buried anger, feelings of powerlessness, and demoralization).

Susan's interview lasted more than three hours. Its impact on the interviewer was conveyed in her written comments after it was over. She commented that financial distress was a major theme, even though the interviewee "had more money than many people we interviewed," suggesting that as a social scientist, the interviewer understood Susan's relative deprivation. The interviewer described a particular interaction during the interview:

> When she looked over her list of names[1] she said, "Oh, my God, they are all women." She was *not* pleased with that discovery, even though she had earlier commented that she gets along with women better. After discovering her displeasure (or as if to emphasize it) she said "Will you be my therapist?" A joke, but meant to express serious anxiety.

As this excerpt reveals, gender was a haunting presence in this interview, constituting both a spoken and unspoken bond between the interviewer and the interviewee, enabling certain things not only to be said and understood but also to be joked about. As a consequence, the interviewer was able to collaborate with Susan and help her tell her life story.

A PROBLEMATIC INTERVIEW

Marta was a 24-year-old, dark-skinned, Puerto Rican woman who lived with her two children (ages 6 and 3) in a small apartment on a lively but shabby street. Separated from her husband for two years, she was unemployed and lived on public assistance, supplemented by child support payments from her ex-husband. Attending a community col-lege, Marta anticipated that her financial situation would improve in the near future, after she got her degree and a job. She hoped to be a parole officer some day. By the usual sociological indicators, Marta would be considered working-class.

Marta's interview lasted more than four hours. It had several lengthy interruptions, as described in the interviewer's notes:

> After about one hour, some friends came over to M's house and she had to stop. I went to a corner store for lunch and called back (as she had suggested I do). She said that she now had an emergency on her hands and I would have to come back another day. During second try, we had to stop in the middle to go pick up her two children from a day-care center that was located about five minutes away by car. She had no car. So I drove. . . . While I was at her house people constantly came over and called. Very peopled life.

As in the interview with Susan, a woman-to-woman bond started to develop as the interviewer stepped outside the traditional professional role of interviewer and entered Marta's world. She clearly liked and admired Marta for her richly peopled life, and her final post-interview comment was that Marta was "enormously outgoing and warm and friendly."

Yet gender empathy was not enough in this interview; the interviewer had trouble following Marta's narrative about the history of her mar-riage. It is important to note that the difficulty in understanding what Marta was saying was not linguistic (at least in a narrow sense), for she spoke English well. Nor was the problem one of inhibition, for the interviewer's probes resulted in a very lengthy narrative (a much longer one than Susan's, in fact). But the point of the narrative was not im-mediately clear.

Marta's narrative was not organized temporally. Unlike Susan, she did not start at the beginning and recount the events of the marriage in chronological order. Time as well as place changed repeatedly through-out the narrative, starting with Marta's opening statement. The opening foreshadowed the issue of conflict over gender roles—a theme both Susan and Marta shared, but with Marta the interviewer was confused and tried to regain control by steering the narrator back to the interview question—the causes of separation.

Over and over, the interviewer demonstrated confusion about time and tried to get Marta to construct a chronically ordered narrative. As a White, middle-class woman, the interviewer was accustomed to hearing narratives in a particular format—events encoded in a series of temporally ordered narrative clauses (Labov 1982; Michaels 1981), such as Susan used. Through repeated use of the phrase "and then," the interviewer tried to control the interview, which had gotten away from her. She asked Marta to order the seemingly jumbled events into a form that *she* could understand. When Marta obliged, the interviewer expressed relief: "OK, gotcha (laugh). I didn't have the order of it." The chronology of the events may have been clearer but their meaning for the narrator, and how, cumulatively, they led to the demise of the marriage was not. To understand the causes of Marta's separation, time could not be used as an organizing principle.

Marta used an episodic frame to structure her account of marital separation. Unlike Susan, who told a linear and temporally ordered narrative, Marta's account displayed the complex development of a theme through a series of related episodes. Each incident restated the theme in a different way. In this genre, time, place, and characters shift across the major episode boundaries, with an important overall theme developed by seemingly distinct episodes. The connections between the individual episodes must be inferred by the listener. This narrative structure is not unique to Marta; it has been observed, in a less developed form, in the stories minority children tell in classroom situations (Michaels 1981, 1985; Michaels and Cazden, 1986).

A structural analysis of the narrative showed that Marta's narrative was about cultural conflict. Each episode provided an instance of such conflict, which was discovered only after repeated listening to the tape and repeated readings of the transcript. Only a close analysis of the narrative's form revealed its meaning. The points at which the interviewer became confused were particularly instructive. These examples of breakdown in the discourse illuminated "the interactional work that usually goes unnoticed in smooth exchanges" (Michaels 1985, p. 37).

Marta introduced the theme of her narrative quite early when she said: "He had more growing up to do than I did. I was too advanced for him in a lot of ways." While she told the interviewer that she and her husband were different on the dimension of "growing" and "advancement," the precise meaning of these phrases did not become clear until later in the narrative. Like an abstract (Labov 1982), the two lines hinted and summarized but did not fully explicate. The interviewer did not hear that a major theme had been introduced with the phrases "growing" and "advancement," and thus her probe focused on a statement about "irresponsibility" that Marta had made earlier. This interruption did not stop the narrator, who went on to develop her theme in the first of five related episodes.

The first episode—superficially about going out and staying home—approached the theme of cultural conflict in the marriage in an oblique way. Marta said that she and her husband had different ideas about how to spend their leisure time together. She wanted to "go out" to a restaurant or movie and "be sociable," whereas he wanted either to go out with his friends alone or to stay at home with the immediate family. At one level, Marta was decrying the gender-segregated leisure patterns characteristic of working-class marriages (Halle, 1984; Rubin 1976). This episode took on additional meanings, because the marital partners were not only working-class but also migrants from Puerto Rico. In this context, "going out" versus "staying home" may be a metaphor for something broader—acculturation, perhaps. She wanted to participate in the public world, whereas he wanted her to remain in the private. As Marta summed up the point of this episode, "I guess it was outgoing versus not outgoing." This statement can be read in several ways. The interviewer's probe suggested that she read it as a personality characterization of Marta's husband (he wasn't an outgoing person and therefore didn't like to go to restaurants, "because there'd be people there"). Marta rejected this interpretation and proceeded to develop what she meant by "outgoing" in a second episode.

The theme of cultural difference was given its second rendering in the topic of doing things "as a family" in episode 2. The issue was not merely going out or staying home, as the first episode suggested, but the kinds of things that count as shared leisure. Marta's husband was not entirely a homebody, as she portrayed him in the first episode. He was active in a weekend softball game. Although she said she "enjoyed watching the games" and admits that "we all had a great time," this type of outing was not what Marta defined as doing "things as a family." She concluded this episode with a return to the topic of "going out."

Upon closer inspection, "his" and "her" leisure activities, as portrayed in Marta's account, were not only gender-and-class-based but also culturally based. Softball games are a major arena for male socializing in Puerto Rico, and this tradition has continued with migration, even in urban neighborhoods in the United States. Although women and children are encouraged to watch and to socialize with their friends at these events, playing the game is a distinctly male activity. It continues the socializing patterns of the island, as going out with male friends and being with family do. In contrast, going out to restaurants and to movies is a more Americanized leisure pursuit.

The narrator developed the theme of differences in degree of acculturation in the third episode of her narrative, also on the topic of socializing. For Marta, "going out" also meant doing things without her husband, such as dining out with friends and relatives. She said that "he didn't like that very much" and, in fact, felt "threatened by it." Especially in working-class Puerto Rican families, married women are expected to remain in the home when they are not at their jobs (Nash and Icken Safa 1980). Certainly, socializing in public places without the company of the husband is not approved behavior for married women.

The scene of conflict shifted in the fourth episode of the narrative. After a long pause, Marta introduced the topic of employment. She intimated that it was not the fact that she was employed that bothered her husband. Historically, a large percentage of Puerto Rican women have worked to supplement the family income (Garcia-Preto 1982). Rather, it was the type of job that Marta had and her psychological investment in it that threatened him. She worked in the fire department, with men. As she stated, "I guess the friendship of *those strange men* didn't appeal to him very much." Her employment might have been acceptable if it had been women's work. Instead, she had entered the male world of power and authority. Marta aspired to a career in corrections, and, earlier in the narrative, she stressed how she liked to work and contrasted this with her husband's lack of commitment to his job.

Marta was completing college, surpassing her husband in education as well. Her ambition had led her to "go out" into the world to better her situation. This may be why her husband "felt threatened" and why he may have placed such an emphasis on staying home. Achievement-oriented and acculturated, Marta had stepped outside the traditional role for women in Puerto Rican culture. Her husband, her narrative said, resisted Americanization and clung to island ways, including some of the negative aspects of machismo (De La Cancela 1981). His marginality may also have been due to harsh socioeconomic conditions (Bonilla and Campos 1981).

As a woman, the interviewer heard the struggle over gender roles in Marta's marriage, for she suggested in a probe question that Marta's husband wanted her to quit her job at the fire department. In the coda to this fourth episode in the narrative, Marta explicitly stated the conflict: her husband's allegiance to traditional beliefs about women's proper role in Puerto Rican culture and her growing involvement in the new American culture of women's self-actualization. Speaking in the voice of her husband she said,

> Yes, definitely yes.
> Just quit in general and just stay home
> take care of the children
> take care of my house
> and him
> and never mind what my, my wants, desires were.

Although the interviewer was sensitive to the issue of gender roles, she did not appreciate the particular conflicts that gender roles create for a Puerto Rican woman, their significance to Marta, or the relationship between gender roles and culture conflict. She understood each episode, but did not grasp the theme that tied them together, because the "point" of the narrative had to be inferred. In a summarizing statement after the fourth episode, she made no reference to the related themes of culture conflict and gender roles. The voice of science spoke as she enumerated the "causes" of Marta's separation: "So the major things you see as causing it [the separation] are, one, his irresponsibility and, two, his going, not wanting to do things with the family." She did not understand the major causes at all. The lack of shared experience between the middle-class interviewer and the working-class Puerto Rican interviewee created barriers to understanding. In this case, gender congruity was not enough to create shared meanings.

The lack of rhythmicity between narrator and interviewer about meaning was evident at numerous points. Marta rephrased what she was saying over and over in order to try to make the interviewer understand. She used "pop sociology" (in phrases such as "antisociable" and "communication"). She said over and over again, in different ways, what the point of her narrative was. It might be argued that her use of an episodic structure was both a cause and a consequence of the lack of rhythmicity between the women. Marta needed to use so many episodes with the same underlying theme of acculturation because this theme was not heard. Paradoxically, her use of an episodic structure contributed further to misunderstanding.

The misunderstanding was nowhere more evident than in the fifth episode of the narrative, in which Marta most explicitly articulated the theme of culture conflict. Marta introduced this last episode by harking back to the topic of family, to her the family of origin and not the conjugal family. She introduced the episode with an abstract of the content that will follow—"his family and my family are two different people"—suggesting that the families were from two different cultures. She began to specify the ways in which they were different, saying his family was "island-type oriented" and hers was "city oriented."

The interviewer was totally lost; she interrupted and hesitated. She did not see the relevance of this material on the two families to the question she had asked about the causes of the separation, even though she had had no difficulty when Susan brought her husband's Irish mother into her account. With Marta, the relevance of the differences between the two Puerto Rican families was not understood, even though she provided background knowledge (Agar 1980), telling the interviewer that her family and her husband's family were different on a variety of dimensions and presenting a series of contrasts that depicted the two families as polar opposites (see Table 11.2). The descriptors she used suggest that a core element differentiating the families was cultural. In her family, the children were American-born and thus spent their formative years in the United States before they returned to Puerto Rico, placing her family further along on the continuum of acculturation than his family, who migrated when the children were grown (Mizio 1974). Pace of living and family values follow from these differences. Marta's earlier comments about her husband's orientation to "staying home" and her desire to "go out" took on added meaning in light of these family differences.

Contradictions lay at the core of this episode, as well as at the core of Marta's account in general. Both the form and the content of the discourse reveal the complexities and paradoxes in Marta's perceptions of the irreconcilable cultural differences between the two families. Marta described her family as having "a more easygoing fast type living." She described his family as "very old-fashioned," but she disparaged his mother's sexual freedom. She described her father as "very passive" and yet "the strength" of the family. Nonetheless, the marriage failed, she suggested, because of a clash in cultures—a clash that resonated within her, as well as between her and her ex-husband, and between the families.

The cultural opposition between the two families was manifested in their contrasting attitudes toward women's work outside the home. Marta's parents, like many urban, middle-class Puerto Ricans, had greater sympathy for female autonomy whereas her ex-husband's parents, like the rural agricultural class from the island, had more traditional views. For this latter group, the roles of husband and wife are clearly defined, with the husband having the authority to control his wife and children (Garcia-Preto 1982). In her narrative, Marta communicated the opposition of the two views about women's autonomy by

TABLE 11.2 Cultural Conflict in Marta's Narrative

His Family	Her Family
Island-oriented	City-oriented
Children born in Puerto Rico	Children born in U.S.
Slow	Fast
Old-fashioned	Modern
Immoral	—
Dead marriage	Active marriage
Loud and intoxicated	Loud but cooperative
Accusatory and rejecting	Accepting
No feeling of togetherness	Always stuck together
Light-skinned	Dark-skinned

adopting the voice of each set of parents. Through role playing, she conveyed to the listener the contrasting families' prescriptions about how she, as a married woman, should lead her life:

"Well, why can't she stay home more often."
"She should take more care of the house."
"Children come first
so does husband those are first priorities."
[Interviewer: "ahh"]
My mother says yes or my father
"Yes children have to be taken care of
and yes a home has to be looked after
but the wife also has things that she needs to do for herself
we're only human beings."

The meaning of Marta's comment in the first episode of her narrative became clear. By progressive standards, she *was* more "advanced" than her husband, and his family as well. He (and they) had "more growing up to do."

As an emancipated woman herself, the interviewer heard the significance of Marta's struggle for independence, but she missed the importance of kin and culture in the marital history. Her nonlexical expression ("ahh") indicated that she seemed to share Marta's assessment about the oppressive nature of traditional attitudes about women's proper place, but throughout the fifth episode, her probe questions relentlessly returned to the marital dyad. From the middle-class White interviewer's perspective, marriage is first and foremost a relationship between two people. Marta's husband's parents were relevant only insofar as they "put pressure" on Marta to give up her aspirations. This incomplete perspective was insensitive to class and cultural differences. In Puerto

Rican culture, marriage is not a dyadic relationship but much more explicitly a union of two families (Fitzpatrick 1981). From Marta's perspective, the marriage failed because the two families' values, and subsequent pressures, could not be reconciled. As a consequence, she answered the question about the causes of the separation by telling the *family* history, within which the *marital* history was embedded. The interviewer, in her struggle to make sense of what she was hearing, missed this crucial point.

Both the lack of cultural understanding and the lack of temporal form contributed to the interviewer's inability to follow the narrative. In an interchange about a girl from Puerto Rico that Marta's husband's family had picked out for him, Marta moved back in time to the period of her courtship. She changed place as well, for the events and conversations she reported took place in Puerto Rico. The interviewer's confusion about when and where these events happened was repeated and blatant. The interviewer had assumed that the girl from Puerto Rico was directly implicated in the breakup of the marriage, but Marta was retelling the story of what happened when she was 16 years old and courting—events that happened eight years previously. In Marta's symbolic framework, these events were central to the causes of the separation.

The heart of the final episode was contained in an emotional retelling about the girl her husband was supposed to have married—

> This was the girl that that that that
> caused a lot of heartaches [pause] and a lot of [pause]
> bitterness I guess on my part.

The narrator's pauses, repetitions, and choice of language all flagged the significance of this passage. As another woman, the interviewer heard these signs of affect and momentarily abandoned her focus on the marital dyad and the recent past to inquire about this relationship, which predated the marriage. Marta responded by telling of the continuing psychological presence of this other woman. Her thoughts returned again to her husband's family and she said poignantly:

> I never knew what it was they saw in her. [Interviewer: "mhm"]
> Not that I was Miss Perfect
> I do have my faults but
> I don't know [pause]

Marta told the interviewer that, in preferring the girl from Puerto Rico to her, her husband's family had rejected her. Given the significance of family in Puerto Rican culture, this may well have been the death blow to the marriage. For at the same time as Marta disparaged the lack of acculturation of her husband's family, she also wanted to be accepted by them. Divorce from the family was the price Marta paid for being "too advanced." She talked of the pain of things that could not be changed—her skin color, his family's rejection of her—at the same time as she celebrated her change and growth.

Again we see contradictions at the core of the narrative. In a variety of ways, Marta suggested that an intracultural tension existed not only in the two families, but within herself as well. For example, she stressed over and over the similarities between the families ("both of our parents came from the same place" and "we're both being Spanish"). At the same time, she emphasized the differences in traditions and values. Her hurt about the girl from Puerto Rico suggested she wanted to be accepted by her husband's family, and yet she ridiculed their backwardness. The birth of two children outside of marriage when she was quite young belied Marta's identification with the new American woman. Consensual unions are common among *less* acculturated Puerto Ricans (Fitzpatrick 1981); yet Marta implied her family was *more* acculturated than his. Finally, Marta displayed ambivalent feelings about the patriarchal Puerto Rican family. Marta blamed her husband for not being responsible and not providing for his family, but she later deprecated his "male-chauvinistic-type attitude" toward her college aspirations. Marta no longer saw machismo as a desirable characteristic, as traditional Puerto Rican culture does; instead, she explicitly stated her ambivalence by criticizing it.

At many levels, the clash of cultures within Puerto Rican culture was the theme of Marta's narrative. The complex development of this theme was achieved by a narrator who constructed her "point" by using a series of interconnected episodes, each of which bore on the essential conflict. The genre Marta used to tell her story—an episodically structured narrative—was exquisitely appropriate to the theme she tried to convey. It was both dramatic and persuasive precisely because she presented this scene and that scene, this instance and that instance, present time and past time, thereby underscoring the deep nature of the conflict. Although narrative analysts have tended to treat time as critical (thereby displaying the preoccupation in Western culture with forward sequencing), Marta's narrative vividly shows how other deep structures besides time organize experience. Further, the episodic form of her discourse was reflective of Marta's life, which, rather than being linear and progressive as Susan's was, had been a mosaic of seemingly disjointed events: birth and youth in the United States, adolescence on the island, return migration to the mainland for early adulthood. Typical of many Puerto Ricans, this back-and-forth migration was associated with a pattern of dismantling and reconstructing of familial and community ties (Garcia-Preto 1982). Just as the trajectory of Marta's life had been different, so too was the style of her discourse.

Sadly, the clash in cultures was reproduced in the interview process itself. In this interview gender congruity was not enough to overcome ethnic incongruity. The bond between the woman interviewer and woman interviewee was not sufficient to create the shared meanings that could transcend the divisions between them. As a consequence of their differences, the narrator and the interviewer did not develop a shared discourse. Confusion and misunderstanding ensued. The interviewer's misunderstanding appears to have come from both the form of the narrative (its episodic rather than temporal ordering) and its content (marriage as a relationship between families rather than between husband and wife). As Marta's husband failed to collaborate with her to create a shared life due to cultural disjunctures between them, so too did Marta and the interviewer fail to collaborate in the development of an account due to a different set of cultural disjunctures.

THE RESEARCH INTERVIEW
AS A COLLABORATIVE PROCESS

A number of methodological issues confront feminist scholars doing life-history interviews. At the most basic level, the analytic process requires qualitative open-ended interviews. Yet, as our analysis has shown, social-science interviewing practices—even from the qualitative tradition—may cut off narrative flow. At the next level, we need access to detailed transcriptions to do the analytic work. Speech that has been "cleaned up" to be more readable loses important information. For example, our analysis of the rhythmicity in the interview with Susan, and the absence of it in the interview with Marta, was made possible by close attention to features of language that might well have been deleted from a traditional transcript. Relatedly, the analysis of life history interviews requires attention to narrative form. As we have suggested, Susan and Marta both conveyed the meanings that events had for them through the use of particular narrative genres. Yet traditional qualitative analysis would have fragmented their long answers, not respecting the ways in which each organized her account of marital failure. Lastly, life histories can contribute to sociological analysis of gender only if the data include contrasting cases that explicate the diversity of women's experiences (Riessman 1990) and the variety of narrative forms used by different cultures.

Oakley (1981, p. 58) reminds us that giving the subjective situation of women greater visibility in sociology requires rethinking many assumptions that are taken for granted about the proper roles of interviewer and respondent:

> The mythology of "hygienic" research with its accompanying mystification of the researcher and the researched as objective instruments of data production [must] be replaced by the recognition that personal involvement is more than dangerous bias—it is the condition under which people come to know each other and to admit others into their lives.

However, gender and personal involvement may not be enough for full "knowing." Oakley (1981), quite correctly, identifies the sources of bias contained in interviewing procedures that objectify both the subject of study and the interviewer by "controlling" the conditions of their interaction. In the interview with Marta, the woman interviewer brought the culture of science into the interview—for example, by creating a numbered listing of the causes of separation out of Marta's narrative—thereby misinterpreting the meaning of the events that the narrator was trying to convey. The interviewer and the narrator struggled over who would control the topic and what constituted an adequate answer to the items on the schedule. The interviewer tried to impose White middle-class standards about how a narrative should be organized on Marta's episodically structured account, which produced not coherence but confusion.

Interviewing as a scientific method of data collection and analysis is a social practice, "a gutsy, human enterprise, not the work of robots programmed to collect pure information" (Gould 1981, p. 21). The development of a life history can be a collaborative process among the women who interview women and the women who analyze and interpret the interview material. In Susan's case, the interviewer was exquisitely sensitive to the subtle cues provided by the narrator, thereby helping Susan develop a coherent account of her marital failure. The interviewer was not passive, did not merely listen to the material and record it, but helped produce the unfolding account (Bell 1985; Fisher and Groce 1986; Paget 1983). This collaborative process was aided by gender, class, and cultural congruity, which produced the unspoken but shared assumptive world of the two women. They implicitly agreed about how a narrative should be organized and about the content that was relevant to an account of marital separation. In Marta's case, despite gender congruity, the joint construction of an account of marital failure was hindered by the lack of shared cultural and class assumptions. The interviewer held on to the White middle-class model of temporal organization and thus could not make sense of the episodic form that Marta used—the dramatic unfolding of a series of topics that were stitched together by theme rather than by time. The narrator did not understand the interviewer's implicit expectations about discourse form, and the interviewer did not understand the narrator's allusion to meaningful themes of kin and cultural conflict. As a result, they were unable to collaborate.

Both Susan's and Marta's discourse styles were equally effective, but they made different interpretive demands on the listener (Collins 1985). In both cases, "expansion" (Labov and Fanshel 1977) was needed to make sense of the discourse and the analysis of the structure of each narrative illuminated meanings embedded in the texts. Through analytic work, the point that tied Marta's narrative together was recovered, even though it had been missed by the interviewer. This second chance to collaborate with a narrator by unearthing the meanings of her apparently disjointed replies is not available if collaboration on the first level of interviewing has failed entirely. Although the interviewer had trouble interviewing Marta, it was not a total failure; Marta's voice was not totally dominated by the White middle-class cultural voice of science.

This chapter raises a number of issues about interviewer-interpreter-interviewee congruity. As Merton (1972) suggests, there are costs and benefits to being an "insider" or "outsider" to an experience by virtue of one's group membership. Perfect congruity is rarely possible in interviewing and begs the question of which of the many social characteristics at issue are the most important to a particular situation (Satow and Lorber 1976). Marta's interview might have been smoother if it had been conducted by a Puerto Rican man, but the gender nuances might have been missed. The ideal interviewer might have been a Puerto Rican woman; but more generally, good life history interviewing requires attending to the voice of the lifeworld (Mishler 1984), and a corresponding muting of the voice of science. If we are to help our interviewees recall and report experiences in their own voices, it is necessary to listen with a minimum of interruptions and to take cues from those we study. In the analysis of their narratives, we can attend to their forms and meanings, letting our subjects' voices speak for themselves. Perfect congruence between interviewer, interviewee, and interpreter is probably not possible, not even always desirable. As social scientists, we do not relive experiences but interpret and generalize from them. However, if a sensitive collaboration has not occurred in the interview and the analysis, we may have "heard" nothing.

NOTE

1. Interviewees were asked to name the people they knew who had helped them with a series of tasks, and a list of these network members was made so that specific questions could be asked about each person.

REFERENCES

Agar, M. 1980. "Stories, Background Knowledge and Themes: Problems in the Analysis of Life History Narrative." *American Ethnologist* 7:233-9.

Bell, S. E. 1985. "Narrative of Health and Illness: DES Daughters Tell Stories." Paper presented at Annual Meeting, Sociologists for Women in Society, Washington, DC.

Bonilla, F., and R. Campos. 1981. "A Wealth of Poor: Puerto Ricans in the New Economic Order." *Daedalus* 110:133-76.

Cazden, C. 1983. "Peakaboo as an Instruction Model: Discourse Development at School and at Home." Pp. 33-58 in *The Sociogenesis of Language and Human Conduct: A Multi-Disciplinary Book of Readings,* edited by B. Bain. New York: Plenum.

Collins, J. 1985. "Some Problems and Purposes in Narrative Analysis in Educational Research." *Journal of Education* 167:57-70.

De La Cancela, V. 1981. "Towards a Critical Psychological Analysis of Machismo: Puerto Ricans and Mental Health." *Dissertation Abstracts International* 42:368-B.

Fisher, S., and S. Groce. 1986. "Accounting Practices: Informational Processing in Medical Interviews." Paper presented at Eleventh World Congress of Sociology, New Delhi, India.

Fitzpatrick, J. P. 1981. "The Puerto Rican Family." Pp. 189-241 in *Ethnic Families in America: Patterns and Variations,* 2nd ed., edited by C. H. Mindel and R. W. Habenstein. New York: Elsevier.

Friedan, B. 1963. *The Feminine Mystique.* New York: Dell.

Garcia-Preto, N. 1982. "Puerto Rican Families." Pp. 164-86 in *Ethnicity and Family Therapy,* edited by M. McGoldrick, J. K. Pearce, and J. Giordano. New York: Guilford.

Gee, J. P. 1985. "The Narrativization of Experience in the Oral Style." *Journal of Education* 167:9-35.

Gould, S. J. 1981. *The Mismeasure of Man.* New York: Norton.

Halle, D. 1984. *America's Working Man: Work, Home, and Politics Among Blue-Collar Property Owners.* Chicago: University of Chicago Press.

Labov, W., 1982. "Speech Actions and Reactions in Personal Narrative." Pp. 219-47 in *Analyzing Discourse: Text and Talk,* edited by D. Tannen. Washington, DC: Georgetown University Press.

——— and D. Fanshel. 1977. *Therapeutic Discourse: Psychotherapy as Conversation.* New York: Academic Press.

Mandler, J. M., and N. Johnson. 1977. "Remembrance of Things Parsed: Story Structure and Recall." *Cognitive Psychology* 9:111-51.

Merton, R. 1972. "Insiders and Outsiders: A Chapter in the Sociology of Knowledge." *American Journal of Sociology* 78:9-47.

Michaels, S. 1981. " 'Sharing Time:' Children's Narrative Styles and Differential Access to Literacy." *Language and Society* 10:423-42.

———. 1985. "Hearing the Connections in Children's Oral and Written Discourse." *Journal of Education* 167:36-56.

——— and Courtney Cazden. 1986. "Teacher-Child Collaboration as Oral Preparation for Literacy." Pp. 132-54 in *Acquisition of Literacy: Ethnographic Perspectives,* edited by B. B. Schieffelin. Norwood, NJ: Ablex.

Mishler, E. 1984. *The Discourse of Medicine: Dialectics of Medical Interviews.* Norwood, NJ: Ablex.

———. 1986. *Research Interviewing: Context and Narrative.* Cambridge, MA: Harvard University Press.

Mizio, E. 1974. "The Impact of External Systems on the Puerto Rican Family." *Social Casework* 55:76-83.

Nash, J., and H. Icken Safa. 1980. *Sex and Class in Latin America.* New York: Bergin.

Oakley, A. 1981. "Interviewing Women: A Contradiction in Terms." Pp. 30-61 in *Doing Feminist Research,* edited by H. Roberts. Boston: Routledge and Kegan Paul.

Paget, M. A. 1983. "Experience and Knowledge." *Human Studies* 6:67-90.

Riessman, C. Kohler. 1990. *Divorce Talk: Women and Men Make Sense of Personal Relationships.* New Brunswick, NJ: Rutgers University Press.

Rubin, L. 1976. *Worlds of Pain: Life in the Working Class Family.* New York: Basic Books.

Satow, R. L., and J. Lorber, 1976. "Cultural Congruity and the Use of Paraprofessionals in Community Mental Health Work." *Sociological Symposium* 23:17-26.

Scott, M. B., and S. M. Lyman. 1968. "Accounts." *American Sociological Review* 46:46-62.

Weitzman, L. 1985. *The Divorce Revolution.* New York: Free Press.

White, H. 1981. "The Value of Narrativity in the Representation of Reality." Pp. 1-23 in *On Narrative,* edited by W.J.T. Mitchell. Chicago: University of Chicago Press.

12. RACE AND CLASS BIAS IN QUALITATIVE RESEARCH ON WOMEN

LYNN WEBER CANNON
ELIZABETH HIGGINBOTHAM
MARIANNE L. A. LEUNG

Feminist research has relied heavily on qualitative methodologies (Cook and Fonow 1986; Grant, Ward, and Rong 1987; Roberts 1981; Stacey and Thorne 1985; Ward and Grant 1985). In-depth qualitative studies can reveal much about social processes that women experience, but like all research methods, they have limitations. Prominent among them are the relatively small and homogeneous samples that constitute the subjects of each study. Although in-depth analysis of small homogeneous samples is a key to discovering the unique quality of subjects' lives, if this approach is used repeatedly on the same population, it can block discovery of the diversity of human experience. Although qualitative research on women has accumulated useful data in many substantive areas, too often the emergent body of knowledge excludes women of color and working-class women (Zinn, Cannon, Higginbotham, and Dill 1986).

Correcting this imbalance in feminist scholarship requires theoretical conceptualizations that include all dimensions of inequality, more complex research designs, and strategies that confront the obstacles to the incorporation of diverse groups of women. This chapter discusses the obstacles to integrating race and class into qualitative research on women and offers some solutions to the problem. It reports the sampling strategy for an in-depth study of Black and White professional, managerial, and administrative women, and the obstacles to achieving a sample balanced by the race and class background of the subjects and the gender composition of their occupations.

We found that White women working in male-dominated occupations who were raised in middle-class families volunteered to be research subjects more often than any other group. We suggest that this difference is due to the higher concentration of White women of middle-class origins in the population of middle-class women and to fewer obstacles to their participation in research projects. In order to get Black women to participate, we had to use more labor-intensive recruitment strategies, such as verbal contact, usually face-to-face, with Black women researchers or other Black women working with the research team. Interviews also took more time to complete because of interruptions and canceled appointments. When Black women felt assured that the research was worthwhile, they were eager to participate.

This chapter discusses the sample selection for a study designed to control race and class background. The subjects were women employed full-time as professionals, managers, and administrators; the methodology used in-depth interviews. We report here the problems we faced in subject recruitment and the strategies we used to produce a heterogeneous sample. Our study suggests that researchers who are committed to incorporating subjects of different races and classes in their qualitative research designs must be prepared to allow more time and money for subject recruitment and data collection.

THE STUDY

The study explored the relationship of race, class, and gender inequality to the general well-being and mental health of full-time employed professional, managerial, and administrative women in the United States. Data were collected with face-to-face, focused, life-history interviews, lasting 2 to 3 hours each.

We wanted a sample of 200 Black and White professionals, managers, and administrators from the Memphis, Tennessee, metropolitan area. As is the case with many studies of women, there was no way to randomly sample the specific population of concern. We employed a quota sample structured by three dimensions of inequality: race and class background of the respondent and the gender composition of her occupation. We dichotomized the three dimensions, creating an eight-cell, $2 \times 2 \times 2$ design. Each cell contained 25 cases, a sample size large enough to allow statistical estimates of the relationships of the three major independent variables with other variables in the study.

Study Parameters

We restricted the study to women born between 1945 and 1960 who were 25 to 40 years old at the time of the interview, because their formal education took place at a time when greater funds and opportunities were available for working-class and Black women to attend college. Seeking to examine institutional supports for upward mobility through college attendance (e.g., the role of high school counselors and teachers), we restricted the study to full-time employed college graduates who had gone to college immediately or within two years of finishing high school. Because we wanted to compare Black and White women raised in middle-class and working-class families, we excluded nurses (a popular occupation for mobile working-class women but rarely the choice of women from middle-class families) and physicians (few working-class women can secure funds needed to cover years of medical education). Because many White teachers but few Black teachers in the area are employed in the private sector, we limited the sample of primary and secondary school teachers to those employed in the public schools.

Our interest in investigating how class background manifests itself in the lives of middle-class women required that our sample include women in the full range of middle-class positions (e.g., professionals, managers, and administrators). The sample included women in each of three primary relations of control over the working class: political (supervision), economic (ownership), and ideological (mental labor), in order to shed light on issues such as the nature of social interactions across class lines (Braverman 1974; Ehrenreich and Ehrenreich 1979; Poulantzas 1974; Vanneman and Cannon 1987). The study also examined how women of different races, from different class backgrounds, and with different support networks manage these across-class contacts.

Since professional networks tend to be homogeneous and insular, we set quotas for the proportions of professionals, managers, and administrators and, within each of those broad categories, for specific occupations. To match regional representation, the design called for 60 percent professionals and 40 percent managers and administrators in the male-dominated occupations and 76 percent professionals and 24 percent managers and administrators in the female-dominated occupations. Within each gender-composition category, we selected particular occupations for inclusion in the sample, based on their regional proportions among professionals, managers, and administrators.

Finally, subjects were selected to minimize confounding race or class background with their occupations. A growing body of evidence indicates that, in addition to gender segregation in the labor force, substantial race segregation occurs as well (National Committee on Pay Equity 1987). Given the structural relations among race, class, and occupation, we could easily draw a sample of upwardly mobile working-class or Black women who are concentrated in the specific occupations that are more open to them (e.g., public school teaching, social work). To avoid the confounding of race, class background, and occupation, we selected subjects so that each race and class-background category contained women from the same or closely related occupations. For example, in the category of professionals in male-dominated fields, the sample included equal numbers of Black and White lawyers raised in working-class and middle-class families. Subjects were also classified into three age groupings defined by birth cohort (1956-1960, 1951-1955, and 1945-1950) to prevent over-representation of any age group in a race, class background, or specific occupational category.

Every few weeks, volunteers who met all study parameters were sorted according to all of the stratifying variables (race, class, gender composition of occupation, professional versus managers and administrators, specific occupation, and age category). We then randomly selected subjects to interview from each pool.

RECRUITMENT OF SUBJECTS

Less Labor-Intensive Outreach Strategies

The first subject recruitment strategies we employed were less labor-intensive. These strategies, quite common in sociological and psychological research, consisted mainly of letters to organizations and individuals known to fit the study criteria, and announcements in the local media (radio programs, daily newspaper, a business daily magazine, and so on) describing the study and asking for volunteers.

All 46 women's organizations that were listed in the public library's most recent list and were likely to include members eligible for the study received letters. This included both professional organizations such as the American Society of Certified Public Accountants and social organizations such as the National Council of Negro Women. The letters asked that organizations inform their members of the study and offered to send study-team members to speak to their groups if they so desired. Individuals interested in participating in the study received a personal letter containing a general description of the study and describing the criteria for inclusion in it (i.e., age 25-40; direct route to college degree; full-time employed professional, manager, or administrator). Regarding the three major independent variables in the study, the letter indicated our interest in studying the life histories of Black and White women in male- and female-dominated occupations. The letter did not mention social class.

Volunteers completed a one-page information form and returned it to the authors' university. Since the women knew the eligibility criteria, the sampling frame included almost all of the volunteers.

Less labor-intensive strategies reached more White than Black subjects. As Table 12.1 reveals, we recruited 22.9 percent of the Whites but only 3.7 percent of the Blacks through the media (see columns 3 and 6). Letters to occupational groups garnered 31.2 percent of the Whites and 13.4 percent of the Blacks. In all, these strategies reached 74.1 percent of the White but only 38.8 percent of the Black women volunteers.

More Labor-Intensive Outreach Strategies

After tracking the characteristics of the women who responded to letters and media solicitations, we started using more labor-intensive strategies to recruit other categories of women. Those strategies included personal presentations to women's organizations' meetings, snowball techniques of calling individuals to recommend others for the study, and identifying special newsletters to receive advertisements.

Most Black women (61.2 percent) were recruited through labor-intensive strategies such as presentations at meetings and, most often, through word-of-mouth snowball techniques. We recruited over half (56 percent) of the Black volunteers through direct contact by project staff or by other Black women professionals who either participated in the study themselves and recommended other names to their interviewer or worked with the project staff from the beginning of the study to recruit volunteers.

CLASS BACKGROUND AND OUTREACH STRATEGIES

Despite a strong race effect, class background did not influence the success of the recruitment strategies (see columns 1, 2, 4, and 5 in Table 12.1). Within each race, every recruitment strategy was about equally likely to reach subjects from working- and middle-class backgrounds. The one exception is the 11.8 percent greater likelihood of reaching White middle-class as opposed to White working-class volunteers through occupational mailing lists. Such a difference may have resulted from greater concentrations of women of middle-class origins in the particular occupations for which we had mailing lists.

RACE AND CLASS BACKGROUND OF THE VOLUNTEERS

After nine months of subject recruitment, 400 women employed as professionals, managers, and administrators had volunteered to participate in the study. Of the total, 134 or 33.5 percent were Black, and 266

TABLE 12.1 Success of Subject Recruitment by Race and Class Origins

	Black			White		
Type of Strategy	Working Class 49% (N = 84)	Middle Class 51% (N = 50)	Total Black 100% (N = 134)	Working Class 32.3% (N = 86)	Middle Class 67.7% (N = 180)	Total White 100% (N = 266)
Less labor intensive						
mass media	6.0 (5)	—	3.7 (5)	27.9 (24)	20.6 (37)	22.9 (61)
occupational mailing lists	14.2 (12)	12.0 (6)	13.4 (18)	23.2 (20)	35.0 (63)	31.2 (83)
other mailings	20.2 (17)	24.0 (12)	21.7 (29)	18.6 (16)	20.6 (37)	20.0 (53)
subtotal	40.4	36.0	38.8	69.7	76.1	74.1
More labor intensive						
organizational presentations	6.0 (5)	4.0 (2)	5.2 (7)	4.7 (4)	2.2 (4)	3.0 (8)
snowball technique	53.6 (45)	60.0 (30)	56.0 (75)	25.6 (22)	21.6 (39)	22.9 (61)
subtotal	59.6 (50)	64.0 (32)	61.2 (82)	30.3 (26)	23.8 (43)	25.9 (69)
Total	100 (84)	100 (50)	100 (134)	100 (86)	100 (180)	100 (266)

NOTE: For each item, the top row of figures represents percentages; the numbers in parentheses indicate the number of subjects.

or 66.5 percent were White. According to the 1980 census, Black women constituted 25.3 percent of the women employed as professionals, managers, or administrators in the Memphis Standard Metropolitan Statistical Area (U.S. Bureau of the Census 1983). Since Black women's concentration in the middle class had not greatly increased during the period from 1980 to 1985 (Higginbotham 1987), we felt that Black women had volunteered at a rate consistent with—and perhaps slightly higher than—their representation in the population under study. However, we used different recruitment strategies to achieve these roughly equivalent rates of volunteering among Black and White women. Had we not employed different strategies, our sample would have been disproportionately White.

There were 170 volunteers with working-class origins, and 230 with middle-class origins. The class origins of these professional and managerial women differed significantly for Blacks and Whites. Of the 400 volunteers, 180 (45.0 percent) were Whites raised middle class, 86 (21.5 percent) were Whites raised working class, 84 (21.0 percent) were Blacks raised working class, and 50 (12.5 percent) were Blacks raised middle class.

Although our data do not permit a thorough examination of the issue, two factors seem likely to have produced a pool of volunteers that was heavily weighted to White women who had come from and stayed in the middle class, and among Black women, to the upwardly mobile. These factors are the race and class background of the population of middle-class women employed full-time and the structural and social psychological factors restricting Black women's participation in this kind of research.

POPULATION PARAMETERS

Our sample was not random; so we cannot infer directly from these data that two-thirds of the Black middle-class women were upwardly mobile whereas two-thirds of White middle-class women were born into the middle class. However, these proportions are plausible, because the extent of intraclass mobility from the working class to the professional-managerial class in the United States has never been high (Coleman and Rainwater 1978; Ryan and Sackrey 1984; Vanneman and Cannon 1987).

At first glance, a sample with one-third of its Whites upwardly mobile might seem to over-represent that group. But the post-World War II era (especially between the late 1950s and the early 1970s) brought the greatest increase in the size of the professional-managerial class (Vanneman and Cannon 1987). In addition, the economic boom of the 1960s and early 1970s, coupled with the breakdown of racial barriers, nearly doubled the size of the Black middle-class population, a larger increase than for Whites (Cannon 1984). Consequently, after World War II and for the first time in American history, the Black class structure began to approximate the White class structure (Vanneman and Cannon 1987; Wilson 1978).

It was the "baby-boom" generation educated in the 1960s and 1970s, who benefited most from post-World War II changes and who are the subjects of our study. They reached college age just as the civil rights movement brought down legal segregation, and a strong economy provided the financial support for college attendance among large numbers of Black and working-class youth. Thus we feel confident that the proportions of upwardly mobile volunteers in our sample approximate their prevalence in the population.

Obstacles to Participation

Some social-psychological and structural factors militated against Black women's participation. These factors were skepticism about the purpose of the research, worries about protection of anonymity, and structural obstacles such as less free time. Dominant-group women have less reason than minority-group women to suspect that they or members of their group will be exploited in research (Zinn 1979). As a result, White women in this study were more than twice as likely to respond to letters or media solicitations, but personal contact was usually required to recruit Black subjects. The contact enabled Black women to gain the assurances they needed that neither they nor others would be exploited by the research process or its products.

We expected that the Black women might also be apprehensive about participating, because the request came from researchers at a predominantly White educational institution. Anticipating many of these concerns, we devised research strategies to minimize their impact. For example, we made explicit in every communication about the study that the co-principal investigators for the study were a Black and a White woman, that the research team was bi-racial, and that we sought both Black and White subjects. We also sent Black members of the research team to speak to exclusively Black Groups, White members to speak to exclusively White groups, and a bi-racial team to speak to every group that had both Black and White women. Only Black interviewers interviewed Black subjects, and White interviewers interviewed White subjects.

Despite the above precautions, more Black than White women required additional assurance, especially about guarantees of anonymity. Many Black middle-class subjects were highly visible in the community as, for example, the only or one of a few bank vice presidents, newscasters, university administrators, library branch directors, or judges. White women in similar positions were more numerous, if not in a single firm, at least throughout the city. The Black women were more likely to ask for specific details, for example, about how we would refer to them in any future reports, before they felt comfortable about the protection of their anonymity.

In addition, it became clear that these Black middle-class women had less free time than the White middle-class women to devote to activities like participation in social science research. Even though there were no racial differences in marital status in the final sample, 65 percent of the Black women had children, and 65 percent of the White women had no children. It was more difficult to schedule and complete interviews with Black volunteers. They had less free time to devote to the project, were often unable to complete the interview in one sitting, and were more likely to cancel scheduled interviews because of unforeseen circumstances. We did not interpret these actions as reflecting resistance to the project or the interview because these women continued to express an interest in participation, and almost all did in fact complete the interview.

Female-Dominated Occupations

Although we cannot be sure of the population distribution across class origins of the middle-class women, census data do indicate the gender-composition of the female middle-class labor force. In the Memphis SMSA, 55 percent of the women professionals, managers, and administrators worked in female-dominated occupations. The volunteers for our study, however, came mainly from male-dominated occupations—57 percent of the Black ($N = 76$) and 56 percent ($N = 148$) of the White women volunteers.

Many women in female-dominated occupations also appeared to have less control over their time and less free time. Scheduling and completing interviews with women teachers, for example, was more difficult than with lawyers or administrators who could block out time during the work day while secretaries held their calls. Thus in the cases of both Black women and women in female-dominated occupations, greater persistence was required to recruit subjects, to schedule, and to complete interviews. These structural realities meant that the White interviewers completed their interviews sooner than the Black interviewers. White interviewers were then able to facilitate the work of Black project team members by assisting with transcriptions, coding, and other activities.

BIASED SAMPLES—BIASED RESULTS

Although we have only begun to analyze the data from the study, we have already identified several areas in which we would have made false inferences had we not attended to the race and class background of the middle-class women. For example, we investigated the level of social supports that women received in making the transition from high school to college (Cannon, Higginbotham, and Leung 1987; Newsome 1986). The working-class women received far less financial support and information from family. Since the typical Black woman volunteer for our study was raised in a working-class family, while the typical White volunteer was raised in a middle-class family, had we not attended to the class background of the women as well as their race, we would have concluded that these middle-class Black women had received far less family support than White women. Such a conclusion could easily have fueled a "cultural deficit" interpretation. Had we not interviewed Black women raised in middle-class families and White women from the working-class, we would have neglected a small but theoretically significant segment of professional and managerial women. Failing to recognize their experiences could greatly distort our conclusions about how they had reached their current occupations and class positions.

CONCLUSIONS

Such qualitative research frequently involves face-to-face contact between researcher and subject, open-ended rather than closed-ended questions, unstructured rather than structured interview schedules, samples are typically small. To generate theory, it is much more useful if the small samples under study are relatively homogeneous, because extreme diversity makes the task of identifying common patterns almost impossible. Unfortunately, as a result, much of the newly emerging scholarship on women excludes women of color and working-class women of all races. For example, in her review of research on women's occupational experiences, Harkess (1985) reports that the most commonly studied group of women workers is still white-collar workers and that, even among them, women working in male-dominated spheres receive the most attention, despite the fact that the majority of women still work in female-dominated occupations (Dill, Cannon, and Vanneman 1987; Reskin 1984).

Feminist research in sociology and psychology is replete with caveats like that reported in a study that sampled White undergraduate students at a private university to identify "generational differences in women's attitudes toward the female role in society." The authors, Slevin and Wingrove (1983) state, "Selection of subjects this way avoided the complexities of analysis which would have been introduced by racial and regional differences" (p. 611). Chodorow's (1978) study, *The Reproduction of Mothering*, drew criticism for "trying to explain the perpetuation of a certain kind of mothering—middle class, psychologically oriented, and achievement-oriented (husbands and sons toward careers, mothers and daughters toward perfect children)—in short, the hothouse tending of two or three offspring in an isolated nuclear family" (Lorber 1981, p. 485).

For some researchers, issues of race or class never surface until the research is completed. Hertz (1986) stated in her book, *More Equal Than Others: Women and Men in Dual-Career Marriages,* "Although this was not a deliberate sampling strategy, all respondents were Caucasian" (p. 217). However, the exclusion of other groups frequently takes place despite feminist researchers' awareness of the importance of the many dimensions of inequality.

In some cases, feminist researchers make politically motivated decisions to exclude particular groups from research. In her powerful study, *Father-Daughter Incest,* Herman (1981) took account of dominant-culture views of minority families and the potential for misuse of results in her decision to exclude minority women:

All of the informants [40 women] were white. We made the decision to restrict the interviewing to white women in order to avoid even the possibility that the information gathered might be used to fuel idle speculation about racial differences. (p. 68)

While such deliberate exclusion might be protective, the pervasiveness of exclusionary practices produces a cumulative impact on the empirical generalizations that constitute the elements of feminist theory. As a result, the prevailing literature, which seems to identify particular "social realities," merely represents White and middle-class experiences. The social realities of other groups, such as minorities and the working classes, become relegated to side issues in the field (Zinn et al. 1986).

REFERENCES

Braverman, H. 1974. *Labor and Monopoly Capital.* New York: Monthly Review Press.
Cannon, L. Weber. 1984. "Trends in Class Identification Among Blacks from 1952 to 1978." *Social Science Quarterly* 65:112-26.
———, E. Higginbotham, and M.L.A. Leung. 1987. "Race and Class Bias in Research on Women: A Methodological Note." Working Paper 5. Center for Research on Women, Memphis State University, Memphis, TN.
Chodorow, N. 1978. *The Reproduction of Mothering.* Berkeley: University of California Press.
Coleman, R. P., and L. Rainwater. 1978. *Social Standing in America: New Dimensions of Class.* New York: Basic Books.
Cook, J. A., and M. M. Fonow. 1986. "Knowledge and Women's Interests: Issues of Feminist Epistemology and Methodology in Feminist Sociological Research." *Sociological Inquiry* 56:2-29.

Dill, B. Thornton, L. Weber Cannon, and R. Vanneman. 1987. "Race and Gender in Occupational Segregation." Pp. 13-70 in *Pay Equity: An Issue of Race, Ethnicity, and Sex*. Washington, DC: National Committee on Pay Equity.

Ehrenreich, B., and J. Ehrenreich. 1979. "The Professional-Managerial Class." Pp. 5-45 in *Between Labor and Capital*, edited by P. Walker. Boston: South End Press.

Grant, L., K. B. Ward, and X. L. Rong. 1987. "Is There an Association Between Gender and Methods in Sociological Research?" *American Sociological Review* 52:856-62.

Harkess, S. 1985. "Women's Occupational Experience in the 1970's: Sociology and Economics." *Signs: Journal of Women in Culture and Society* 10:495-516.

Herman, J. 1981. *Father-Daughter Incest*. Cambridge, MA: Harvard University Press.

Hertz, R. 1986. *More Equal Than Others: Women and Men in Dual-Career Marriages*. Berkeley: University of California Press.

Higginbotham, E. 1987. "Employment for Professional Black Women in the Twentieth Century." Pp. 73-91 in *Ingredients for Women's Employment Policy*, edited by C. Bose and G. Spitze. Albany: SUNY Press.

Lorber, J. 1981. "On *The Reproduction of Mothering*: A Debate." *Signs: Journal of Women in Culture and Society* 6:482-6.

National Committee on Pay Equity. 1987. *Pay Equity: An Issue of Race, Ethnicity and Sex*. Washington, DC: National Committee on Pay Equity.

Newsome, Y. 1986. "Class Obstacles to Higher Education: An Examination of the High School Experiences of Black Professional Women." Master's thesis, Memphis State University, Memphis, TN.

Poulantzas, N. 1974. *Classes in Contemporary Capitalism*. London: New Left Books.

Reskin, B. F. 1984. "Sex Segregation in the Workplace." Pp. 1-12 in *Gender at Work: Perspectives on Occupational Segregation and Comparable Worth*. Washington, DC: Women's Research and Education Institute of the Congregational Caucus for Women's Issues.

Roberts, H. 1981. *Doing Feminist Research*. Boston: Routledge & Kegan Paul.

Ryan, J., and C. Sackrey. 1984. *Strangers in Paradise: Academics from the Working Class*. Boston: South End Press.

Slevin, K. F., and C. R. Wingrove. 1983. "Similarities and Differences Among Three Generations of Women in Attitudes Toward the Female Role in Contemporary Society." *Sex Roles* 9:609-24.

Stacey, J., and B. Thorne. 1985. "The Missing Feminist Revolution in Sociology." *Social Problems* 32:301-16.

U.S. Bureau of the Census. 1983. "Detailed Population Characteristics: Tennessee." *U.S. Census of the Population, 1980*. Washington, DC: Government Printing Office.

Vanneman, R., and L. Weber Cannon. 1987. *The American Perception of Class*. Philadelphia: Temple University Press.

Ward, K. B., and L. Grant. 1985. "The Feminist Critique and a Decade of Published Research in Sociology Journals." *Sociological Quarterly* 26:139-57.

Wilson, W. J. 1978. *The Declining Significance of Race*. Chicago: University of Chicago Press.

Zinn, M. Baca. 1979. "Field Research in Minority Communities: Ethical, Methodological, and Political Observations by an Insider." *Social Problems* 27:209-19.

———, L. W. Cannon, E. Higginbotham, and B. Dill. 1986. "The Cost of Exclusionary Practices in Women's Studies." *Signs: Journal of Women and Culture in Society* 11:290-303.

V.

Racial Ethnic Identity and Feminist Politics

Feminism is a social and political movement whose aim is to change existing gender relations and structured gender inequality. However, there are a variety of theoretical perspectives or frameworks, and therefore differing political strategies, aimed at accomplishing this goal. In effect, there are different "feminisms" based on different assumptions and interpretations of why gender inequality exists, what mechanisms maintain it, and how it can be corrected (Connell 1987; Donovan 1987; Eisenstein 1983; Jagger and Rothenberg 1984). Certain ideological assumptions that underlie what are commonly called liberal, radical, Marxist, socialist, and cultural feminist perspectives or frameworks dictate goals and strategies for personal and political change.

It is important to note that none of these categories is absolute and that political strategies and goals can, and do, overlap as feminists attempt to create coalitions to achieve certain goals, for example, maintaining legal and safe access to abortion for all women. There is also, according to Jagger and Rothenberg (1984, p. xv), broad agreement on ending sexual harassment, rape, and the physical and sexual abuse of women and children. Sexual and procreative freedom is a goal also widely agreed upon, as is women's opportunity to participate fully in the work force and in political life. However:

> Beyond these basic agreements . . . sharp differences between feminists emerge . . . grounded partly on women's differences in experience and information, partly on differences in their values, and partly on differences in how they conceptualize and interpret the information available to them. . . . [C]onversely, the way in which we conceptualize reality affects our actual experience of it. . . . [D]ifferences in experience, values, and modes of understanding are often bound together in an integrated and systematic theory of society. (Jagger and Rothenberg 1984, p. xv)

Given these differences, how can we know who and what "woman" is, and who can presume to speak for women? Denise Riley gives voice to the quest for women's identity by asking "Am I that name?" (1988). Since the categories "woman" and "women" are socially constructed, they reflect the complex interconnections of class, race, ethnicity, and gender, and create differences that can become barriers to solidarity among women.

Bell Hooks (1989) tries to address the differences and commonalities by discussing the dangers inherent in feminism's method of consciousness-raising and its slogan: "The personal is the political." In this culture, at this time, personal too often translates into the private, the narcissistic. Hooks goes on to say that

> to take woman to the self as starting point for politicization, woman who, in white-supremacist, capitalist patriarchy, is particularly made, socially constructed, to think only me—my body—I constitute a universe—all that truly matters. To take her—this woman—to the self as starting point is necessarily risky. (p. 105)

Bell Hooks believes emphasis on the self is risky because feminists can lose sight of the political. If the political is synonymous with the personal, one can remain private and introspective, with no need to reach out or connect, "no way to become the radical feminist subject."

The core of any political movement for change is solidarity. Change is not made alone, by individuals; it is made collectively. The women's movement has always believed this premise but has had difficulty putting it into practice. Originally, and still to a great extent, the women's movement in the United States remains middle class and White. In addition to Hooks (1981, 1984), other women of color have argued that this narrowness of perspective has been a major obstacle in creating coalitions, and yet they continue to strive to integrate and demand inclusion in a struggle that is ultimately a shared one (Cole 1986; Davis 1981, 1989; Giddings 1984; Joseph and Lewis 1981; Omolade 1985).

The three chapters in this section continue to raise the question of differences and commonalities among women and the problems involved in creating an inclusive women's movement that genuinely takes into account differences of race, ethnicity, class, and sexual preference.

Esther Ngan-Ling Chow writes from the perspective of Asian American women. In Chapter 13, "The Development of Feminist Consciousness Among Asian American Women," she outlines some of the barriers to their participation in the larger women's movement. Like Baca Zinn did in her chapter on family, Ngan-Ling Chow treats racial ethnic identity as structural rather than cultural. She illuminates the areas where bias and discrimination as well as preoccupation with economic survival prevent Asian American women from joining White women in the struggle for gender equality. Asian American women do not deny their gender oppression, but pressures resulting from their subordinate position in their families and ethnic communities impede the move toward solidarity with other women. These same cross pressures, however, can ultimately develop a transcendent feminist consciousness.

Alma M. Garcia takes up the same theme from within the Chicana community of women in Chapter 14, "The Development of Chicana Feminist Discourse, 1970-1980." She notes, as does Ngan-Ling Chow, that women of color are beginning to organize as they become aware of their oppression and as they find the wherewithal to fight it. Both Garcia and Ngan-Ling Chow show that some of this consciousness-raising came about through struggling with men of color in protesting racism, discrimination, and segregation. Just as women in the peace and the Civil Rights movements discovered that men made the speeches and got the glory, while they made the coffee, did the typing, and handled other behind-the-scenes domestic chores (Piercy 1970), Asian American women and Chicanas wanted to participate more fully in their respective racial ethnic groups' struggles for liberation and felt blocked by men's sexism.

Garcia states that African American, Asian American, and Chicana women must examine the relationship between their own racial ethnic struggles for liberation and their involvement with the feminist struggle to end sexist oppression. None of these groups of women sees the relationship as an either-or question but as a matter of spreading out scarce resources of energy or "gynergy" (Daly 1987, p. 77). When faced with resistance from White women in the form of tokenism in leadership positions or condescension based on stereotypes and ethnocentrism, women of color are apt to return to putting their energies into their own communal struggles.

As with the mainstream feminist movement, Asian American, Chicana, and African American women also face harassment and charges of lesbianism that stem from men's fears that the struggle against sexism will defuse issues of cultural nationalism (see also Lorde 1984). All of these cross-pressures makes coalition-building very difficult for women of color.

Lynn Chancer in Chapter 15, "New Bedford, Massachusetts, March 6, 1983-March 22, 1984: The 'Before and After' of a Group Rape," shows how the divisions among women paradoxically can deepen in the face of common experiences, in this case, the fearful possibility and actuality of rape. Faced with the pervasiveness of violence against them by men, some women retreat into a denial of that possibility and distance themselves from the victims of rape and abuse (Caputi 1989).

Chancer also sheds light on the part the media plays in creating and maintaining differences among women and among men and women in the same ethnic community. In New Bedford, the media created an atmosphere of "us versus them" between the Portuguese immigrant community of New Bedford and the "outsiders," the media representatives themselves. This defensive position then led to blaming the victim: "If she hadn't let herself be raped, none of these people would be here judging our community." Feminists who defended the rape survivor were included with the outsiders and faced the same hostility, which took the form of accusations of breaking up the family and tearing down traditional moral values.

The conflict enlarged from cultural differences exacerbated by language barriers into differences about sexual practices and behavior, as well as conflict over traditional and changing gender roles, such as single working parent versus full-time homemaker. These re-translated into Portuguese values versus dominant White Anglo-American values. For the women, the conflict became an issue of loyalty to an ethnic community, and their men, or allegiance with feminist women.

For ethnic women and women of color, such conflicts have diminished the goals of the women's movement. These splits have deepened between women who feel that their first priority is to redress the racial and class discrimination against them and their men and women who feel oppressed as women not only by the larger society but also by men of their own race and class. It is within this context that Bell Hooks (1989) voices her concern about maintaining the political struggle. She does not want to do away with the personal: "the naming of the self as a site for politicization" (p. 106). But she does want to re-emphasize that identity politics cannot be an end in itself. Rather, "the personal is the political" should be a

> dialectic . . . the link between efforts to socially construct self, identity in an oppositional framework, one that resists domination, and allows for the greatest degree of well-being. . . . Politicization necessarily combines this process (the naming of one's experience) with critical understanding of the concrete material reality that lays the groundwork for that personal experience . . . It enables feminist thinkers to talk about identity in relation to culture, history, politics, whatever and to challenge the notion of identity as static and unchanging. To explore identity in relation to strategies of politicization, feminist thinkers must be willing to see the female self anew, to examine how we are gendered critically and analytically from various standpoints. (1989, pp. 107, 108, 110)

Once feminist politics can empower women within their own communities, in their diverse struggles, and also link them up in a world-wide movement, feminism will be an unbeatable force.

REFERENCES

Caputi, J. 1989. "The Sexual Politics of Murder." *Gender & Society* 3:437-56.

Cole, J. B. (ed.). 1986. *All American Women: Lines That Divide, Ties That Bind.* New York: Free Press.

Connell, R. W. 1987. *Gender and Power.* Stanford, CA: Stanford University Press.

Daly, M. 1987. *Websters' First New Intergalactic Wickedary of the English Language.* Boston: Beacon Press.

Davis, A. Y. 1981. *Women, Race and Class.* New York: Random House.

———. 1989. *Women, Culture and Politics.* New York: Vintage.

Donovan, J. 1987. *Feminist Theory: The Intellectual Traditions of American Feminism.* New York: Ungar.

Eisenstein, H. 1983. *Contemporary Feminist Thought.* Boston: G. K. Hall.

Giddings, P. 1984. *When and Where I Enter . . . The Impact of Black Women on Race and Sex in America.* New York: William Morrow.

Hooks, B. 1981. *Ain't I a Woman: Black Women and Feminism.* Boston: South End Press.

———. 1984. *Feminist Theory: From Margin to Center.* Boston: South End Press.

———. 1989. *Talking Back: Thinking Feminist, Thinking Black.* Boston: South End Press.

Jagger, A. M., and P. S. Rothenberg. 1984. *Feminist Frameworks.* New York: McGraw-Hill.

Joseph, G. I., and J. Lewis. 1981. *Common Differences: Conflicts in Black & White Feminist Perspectives.* Boston: South End Press.

Lorde, A. 1984. *Sister Outsider.* Trumansberg, NY: Crossing Press.

Omolade, B. 1985. "Black Women and Feminism." Pp. 247-57 in *The Future of Difference,* edited by H. Eisenstein and A. Jardine. New Brunswick, NJ: Rutgers University Press.

Piercy, M. 1970. "The Grand Coolie Damn." Pp. 473-92 in *Sisterhood Is Powerful,* edited by R. Morgan. New York: Vintage Books.

Riley, D. 1988. *"Am I That Name?" Feminism and the Category of "Women" in History.* Minneapolis: University of Minnesota Press.

13. THE DEVELOPMENT
OF FEMINIST CONSCIOUSNESS
AMONG ASIAN AMERICAN WOMEN

ESTHER NGAN-LING CHOW

Like other women of color, Asian American women as a group have neither been included in the predominantly White middle-class feminist movement, nor collectively begun to identify with it (Chia 1983; Chow 1989; Dill 1983; Loo and Ong 1982; Yamada 1981). Although some Asian American women have participated in social movements within their communities or in the larger society, building ties with White feminists and other women of color is a recent phenomenon for Asian American women. Since Asian American women are a relatively small group in the United States, their invisibility and contribution to the feminist movement in the larger society may seem insignificant.[1] Furthermore, ethnic diversity among Asian American women serves as a barrier to organizing and makes it difficult for these women to identify themselves collectively as a group. Because approximately half of Asian American women are foreign-born, their lack of familiarity with the women's movement in the United States and their preoccupation with economic survival limit their feminist involvement. The use of demographic factors such as size, ethnic diversity, and nativity, without an examination of structural conditions, such as gender, race, class, and culture, will not permit an adequate understanding of the extent of feminist activism of Asian women in the United States.

What are the social conditions that have hindered Asian American women from developing a feminist consciousness, a prerequisite for political activism in the feminist movement? From a historical and structural perspective, this chapter argues that the feminist consciousness of Asian American women has been limited by their location in society and social experiences. A broader perspective is needed to understand the development of feminist consciousness among Asian American women who are subject to cross-group pressures.

The intent of this chapter is primarily conceptual, describing how gender, race, class, and culture intersect in the lives of Asian American

255

women and how their experiences as women have affected the development of feminist consciousness. The ideas are a synthesis of legal documents, archival materials, and census statistics; participant observation in the civil rights movement, feminist movement, Asian American groups, and Asian American organizations since the mid-1960s; interviews and conversations with Asian American feminists and leaders; and letters, oral histories, ethnic newspapers, organizational newsletters, films, and other creative writings by and about Asian American women.

GENDER CONSCIOUSNESS:
PRECURSOR OF FEMINIST CONSCIOUSNESS

Gender consciousness is an awareness of one's self as having certain gender characteristics and an identification with others who occupy a similar position in the sex-gender structure. In the case of women, an awareness of femaleness and an identification with other women can lead to an understanding of gendered power relations and the institutional pressures and socialization processes that create and maintain these power relations (Weitz 1982). Ultimately, gender consciousness can bring about the development of feminist consciousness and the formation of group solidarity necessary for collective action in the struggle for gender equality (Christiansen-Ruffman 1982; Green 1979; Houston 1982).

Being female, awareness of gender roles, and identification with other women are the major ingredients in building gender consciousness. However, it is necessary to understand the social contexts in which the gender consciousness of Asian American women has developed. Domination by men is a commonly shared oppression for Asian American women. These women have been socialized to accept their devaluation, restricted roles for women, psychological reinforcement of gender stereotypes, and a subordinate position within Asian communities as well as in the society at large (Chow 1985). Within Asian communities, the Asian family (especially the immigrant one) is characterized by a hierarchy of authority based on sex, age, and generation, with young women at the lowest level, subordinate to father-husband-brother-son. The Asian family is also characterized by well-defined family roles, with father as breadwinner and decision-maker and mother as a compliant wife and homemaker. Although they are well protected by the family because of their filial piety and obedience, women are socially alienated from their Asian sisters. Such alienation may limit the development of gender and feminist consciousness and render Asian women politically powerless in achieving effective communication and organization, and in building bonds with other women of color and White feminists.

In studying the majority of women activists who participated in various movements for oppressed groups, Blumberg (1982) found that participation in these movements affected the development of gender consciousness among women, which later, because of sexism in the movements, was transformed into a related but distinctive state of awareness—a feminist consciousness. For Asian American women, cross-group allegiances can hinder the development of feminist consciousness or expand it into a more universal view. Women who consider racism and classism to be so pervasive that they cannot embrace feminism at the same level may subordinate women's rights to other social concerns, thus limiting the development of feminist consciousness. Women who are aware of multiple oppressions and who advocate taking collective action to supersede racial, gender, and class differences may develop a feminist consciousness that transcends gender, racial, class, and cultural boundaries.

AWAKENING FEMINIST CONSCIOUSNESS

In the wake of the civil rights movement in the early 1960s and the feminist movement in the mid-1960s, Asian American women, following the leads of Black and Hispanic women, began to organize (Chow 1989; Ling and Mazumdar 1983; Lott and Pian 1979; G. Wong 1980). Initially, some of the better educated Asian American women formed women's groups to meet personal and family needs and to provide services to their respective organizations and ethnic communities. These groups, few in number and with little institutionalized leadership, were traditional and informal in nature, and usually supported philanthropic concerns (G. Wong 1980). Although there had been a few sporadic efforts to organize Asian American women around specific issues and concerns that did not pertain to women (e.g., the unavailability or high cost of basic food, Angel Island, the World War II internment of Japanese Americans), these attempts generally lacked continuity and support, and the organization of Asian American women was limited as a political force. Nevertheless, these activities, as stepping stones for future political activism, allowed Asian American women to cultivate their gender consciousness, to acquire leadership skills, and to increase their political visibility.

In the late 1960s and early 1970s, many Asian American women activists preferred to join forces with Asian American men in the struggle against racism and classism (Fong 1978; G. Wong 1980; Woo 1971). Like Black and Hispanic women (Cade 1970; Dill 1983; Fallis 1974; Hepburn et al. 1977; Hooks 1984; Terrelonge 1984), some Asian American women felt that the feminist movement was not attacking racial and class problems of central concern to them. They wanted to work with groups that advocated improved conditions for people of their own racial and ethnic background or people of color, rather than groups oriented toward women's issues (Fong 1978; G. Wong 1980; Woo 1971), even though they may have been aware of their roles and interests and even oppression as women.

As Asian American women became active in their communities, they encountered sexism. Even though many Asian American women realized that they usually occupied subservient positions in the male-dominated organizations within Asian communities, their ethnic pride and loyalty frequently kept them from public revolt (Woo 1971). More recently, some Asian American women have recognized that these organizations have not been particularly responsive to their needs and concerns as women. They also protested that their intense involvement did not and will not result in equal participation as long as the traditional dominance by men and the gendered division of labor remain (G. Wong 1980). Their protests have sensitized some men and have resulted in changes of attitudes and treatment of women, but other Asians, both women and men, perceived them as moving toward separatism.

Asian American women are criticized for the possible consequences of their protests: weakening of the male ego, dilution of effort and resources in Asian American communities, destruction of working relationships between Asian men and women, setbacks for the Asian American cause, cooptation into the larger society, and eventual loss of ethnic identity for Asian Americans as a whole. In short, affiliation with the feminist movement is perceived as a threat to solidarity within their own community. All of these forces have restricted the development of feminist consciousness among Asian American women and their active participation in the feminist movement. (For the similar experience of Black women, see Hooks 1984.)

Other barriers to political activism are the sexist stereotypes and discriminatory treatment Asian American women encounter outside their own communities. The legacy of the Chinese prostitute and the slave girl from the late nineteenth century still lingers. American involvement in Asian wars continues to perpetuate the image of Asian women as cheap whores and exotic sexpots (e.g., images such as "Suzie Wong" for Chinese women, the "geisha girl" in the Japanese teahouse, the bar girls in Vietnam). The "picture bride" image of Asian women is still very much alive, as U.S. soldiers and business men brought back Asian wives from China, Japan, Korea, and Vietnam with the expectation that they would make perfect wives and homemakers. In the last few years, a systematic importation of Asian "mail-order brides" through advertisements in newspapers and magazines has continued to exploit them as commodities, a practice that has been intensively protested by many Asian American communities. Mistreatment, desertion, divorce, and physical abuse of Asian wives or war brides have been major concerns for Asian American women (Kim 1977). The National Committee Concerned with Asian Wives of U.S. Servicemen was specifically organized to deal with these problems.

The result of these cross-pressures is an internal dilemma of choice between racial and gender identity at the personal level and between liberation for Asian Americans (in the broader sense for all racial and ethnic minority groups) and for women at the societal level. Lee (1971) reported interviews with two Asian American feminists who reflected the mixed feelings of many Asian American women. One woman, Sunni, said:

> We are *Asian* women. Our identity is *Asian,* and this country recognizes us as such. We cannot afford the luxury of fighting our Asian counterparts. We ought to struggle for Asian liberation first, and I'm afraid that the "feminist" virtues will not be effective weapons. There is no sense in having only women's liberation while we continue to suffer oppression as Asians. (p. 119)

Another woman, Aurora, took the opposite view:

> History has told us that women's liberation does not automatically come with political revolutions; Asian liberation will not necessarily bring Asian women's liberation. . . . We ought to devote our energies to feminism because a feminist revolution may well be the only revolution that can bring peace among people. (p. 119)

When Asian American women began to recognize injustice and became aware of their own strengths as women, some developed a feminist consciousness, giving top priority to the fight against sexism and for women's rights. Others sought to establish women's caucuses within existing Asian American organizations (e.g., the Organization of Chinese American Women), while still others attempted to organize separately outside of the male-dominated Asian American organizations (e.g., the Organization of Pan American Women and the National Network of Asian and Pacific Women).

Asian American women began to organize formally around women's issues in the early 1970s. Yet many of these groups were short-lived because of lack of funding, grass-roots support, membership, credible leadership, or strong networking. Those that endured included women's courses and study groups sponsored by Asian American studies programs on college and university campuses, multilingual and multicultural service programs in women's health or mental health centers (e.g., the Asian Pacific Health Project in Los Angeles and the Asian Pacific Outreach Center in Long Beach, the Pacific Asian Shelter for Battered Women in Los Angeles), and writers' groups (Pacific Asian American Women Writers West).

A few regional feminist organizations have been formally established and are in the process of expanding their influence and building up their networks from the grass-roots level to the national one. These organizations include the National Organization of Pan Asian Women, the National Network of Asian and Pacific women, Asian American Women United, the Philipino Women's League, the Filipino American Women Network, the Vietnamese Women Association, and the Cambodian Women for Progress, Inc.[2] These feminist organizations aim to advance the causes of women and racial and ethnic minorities, to build a strong Asian sisterhood, to maximize the social participation of Asian American women in the larger society, and to effect changes through collective efforts in education, employment, legislation, and information. The active participants in these feminist organizations are mostly middle-class Asian women, college students, professionals, political activists, and a few working-class women (G. Wong 1980).

RACIAL CROSS-PRESSURES

For Asian American women, joining the White feminist movement is a double-edged sword because they experience oppression not only as women in a society dominated by men but also as minorities facing a variety of forms of racism that are not well understood by White feminists (Chia 1983; Chow 1982; Fujitomi and Wong 1976; Kumagai 1978; Loo and Ong 1982). The structural racism of American institutions, which limits access to resources, opportunities, prestige, privileges, and power, affects all the racial and ethnic minority groups of which Asian American women are a part (Chow 1989; Dill 1983; Hepburn et al. 1977; LaRue 1976; Loo and Ong 1982; Palmer 1983; Wong and Yamada 1979).

Historically, legal restrictions, as one form of racism, have been used to exploit cheap labor, to control demographic growth, and to discourage family formation by Asians in the United States. These restrictions also hindered the development of gender consciousness and political power among Asian American women. Since the mid-1850s, the legal and political receptivity to Asian American men and women has been low (Elway 1979; Pian 1980). U.S. immigration policies generally have emphasized imported cheap labor and discouraged the formation of family unity. Some laws specifically targeted Asian American women. As early as the 1850s, the first anti-prostitution law was passed in San Francisco, barring traffic of Chinese women and slave girls. The Naturalization Act of 1870 and the Chinese Exclusion Act of 1882 forbade the entry of wives of Chinese laborers. In 1921, a special act directed against Chinese women kept them from marrying American citizens. The Exclusion Act of 1924 did not allow alien-born wives to enter the United States, but did allow their children to come; this act separated many families until the passage of the Magnuson Act in 1943. The Cable Act of 1932 stipulated that American-born Chinese women marrying foreign-born Asians would lose their U.S. citizenship, although they could regain it later through naturalization. The passage of anti-miscegenation laws (e.g., the California Anti-Miscegenation Law in 1906), which were ruled unconstitutional by the U.S. Supreme Court in 1967, barred marriage between Whites and "Mongolians" and laborers of Asian origins, making it impossible for Asians to find mates in this country. As a result, bachelor communities consisting mainly of single Asian men became characteristic of many Asian groups, especially the Chinese (Glenn 1983).

In spite of political pressures, repressive immigration laws, and restrictive and discouraging economic hardships, a few Asian women did come to the United States. Chinese women came in the 1850s, followed by Japanese women in the late 1890s and Filipino and Korean women in the early part of the twentieth century. These women were "picture brides," merchant wives, domestics, laborers, and prostitutes. In the popular literature, they were generally portrayed as degraded creatures, cheap commodities, and sex objects who took jobs from Whites, spread disease and vice, and corrupted the young. Descriptions of their sexist, racist, and economically deprived living conditions reveal a personal and private resistance marked by passive acceptance, suppression of feelings, silent protest, withdrawal, self-sacrifice, and hard work (Aquino 1979; Gee 1971; Jung 1971; Louie 1971; J. Wong 1978; Yung 1986).

The repressive immigration laws were repealed after World War II, and the number of Asian families immigrating to the United States increased. By 1980, the sex ratio of this racial and ethnic group was balanced for the first time in U.S. history. Women now constitute half of the Asian American population (U.S. Bureau of the Census 1981). Although many of the repressive laws that conspired to bar the socio-political participation of Asian American men and women have changed, the long-term effects of culture, socioeconomic, and political exploitation and oppression are still deeply felt, and there are new forms of discrimination and deprivation. The passage of the Immigration Reform and Control Act of 1986, setting restricted immigration quotas for family members of Asian Americans and Hispanic Americans, recalls earlier repressive legislation. As long as legal circumstances restrict the immigration of the mothers, daughters, and sisters of the Asian American women in the United States, the full development of their gender and feminist consciousness will be hampered.

The long history of racism in the United States has left its mark on feminism. Some Asian American women feel repelled by the racial composition, insensitivity, and lack of receptivity of some White women in the feminist movement (Fong 1978; Yamada 1981). They argue that White feminists do not fully understand or include issues and problems that Asian American women confront. White feminists are not aware of or sympathetic to the differences in the concerns and priorities of Asian American women. Without understanding the history and culture of Asian American women, some White feminists have been impatient with the low level of consciousness among women of color and the slow progress toward feminism of Asian American women.

Although some degree of acceptance of Asian American women and of women of color by certain segments of the White feminist movement has occurred, many problems remain (Bogg 1971; Dill 1983; Hepburn et al. 1977; Hooks 1984; Lee 1971). Ideological acceptance does not necessarily lead to full structural receptivity. Conscious and rigorous efforts to recruit Asian American women and other women of color openly, to treat them as core groups in the movement, and to incorporate them in the organizational policy and decision-making levels have not been made by White feminist organizations. Marynick Palmer (1983) points out that ethnocentrism is a major reason that feminist organizations treat race and class as secondary and are not fully accepting women of color. Hooks (1984) is critical of a feminist movement based on the White women who live at the center and whose perspectives rarely include knowledge and awareness of the lives of women and men who live at the margin. Thornton Dill (1983, p. 131) states, "Political expediency drove white feminists to accept principles that were directly opposed to the survival and well-being of blacks in order to seek to achieve more limited advances for women." The same is true for Asian American women.

Inconsistencies between attitudes and behavior of White women are highly evident in the "token" membership of minority women in some feminist organizations, which indicates simply a superficial invitation to join. For women of color, the frustrations of not being included in the "White women's system" run parallel to the experiences of White women who try to break into the "old boy's network." Consequently, Asian American women feel more comfortable making allies with other women of color (e.g., the National Institute for Women of Color) than with their White counterparts. Although there are interethnic problems among Asian American women and between them and other women of color, social bonding and group allegiance are much more readily established, and common issues are more easily shared on the basis of race and ethnicity. A separate movement for women of color may be a viable alternative for the personal development of Asian American women and other women of color and for their struggle for liberation and social equality.

ECONOMIC CONDITIONS AND CLASS CLEAVAGES

Economic exploitation and class cleavages also account for the limited development of feminist consciousness and political activism among Asian American women. American capitalism demands cheap labor and the economic subordination of certain groups, resulting in a dual or split labor market. Certain minorities, primarily Blacks, Mexican Americans, and Asian Americans, are treated as internal colonized groups and are exploited culturally, politically, and economically (Almquist 1984; Blauner 1972; Bonacich 1972).

Asian American women have lived in racially segregated internal colonies such as Chinatown, Little Tokyo, and Little Saigon. They have experienced social isolation, ghettoization, poverty, and limited opportunities for personal growth and emancipation. Limited resources and lack of access to information, transportation, and social services have made them rely on their families for support and protection. They must also work to maintain their families financially. The labor force participation of Asian American women is much higher than that of White and Black women (U.S. Bureau of the Census 1983), but many of them have worked in the secondary labor market sector, which is character-ized by long working hours, low pay, and low prestige. Although their educational levels are relatively high, 70 percent are concentrated in clerical, service, and blue-collar work, and are facing tremendous underemployment (U.S. Bureau of the Census 1983; U.S. Commission on Civil Rights 1978).

Cultural values that emphasize hard work and that place a stigma on idleness prevent Asian American women from not working and going on welfare. Asian American households generally have a greater num-ber of multiple breadwinners per family than the general U.S. popula-tion. The financial burdens on many Asian American women pressure them to continue struggling for economic survival for the good of their families, sacrificing their own interests, and suppressing their feelings and frustrations even in the face of gender and racial discrimination. They have little time to examine the implications of their economic sit-uations; they do not fully understand the dynamics of class position; and they are not likely to challenge the existing power structure.

How economic and class conditions hinder feminist consciousness and political activism is evident for Chinese working-class women living in Chinatowns in many cities. Subject to the impact of internal colonization, their work world is an ethnic labor market that offers few good jobs, low pay, long hours, limited job advancement, and relative isolation from the larger society. The film *Sewing Women* (Dong 1982) vividly describes the ways in which a working-class Chinese woman attempts to balance her family, work, and community responsibilities. Unionization of garment factory workers in Chinatown is only the beginning of a long process of political struggle for these women.[3]

In a study of Chinatown women, Loo and Ong (1982) identify the major reasons for the lack of integration of these working-class women into the feminist movement. First, Chinatown women do not relate comfortably to people outside their ethnic subgroup, which produces social distancing and alienation. Second, Chinatown women face varied problems, so no political movement that addresses only one of these will claim their allegiance. Third, although the women's movement aims to improve conditions for all women, the specific concerns of Chinatown's women are often not those of the women's movement. For instance, health, language, and cultural adjustment are major issues for low-income immigrant women. These are not the foci of the women's movement. Fourth, Loo and Ong demonstrate that the psychological profile of Chinatown women is not that of political activists. Chinatown women lack a sense of personal efficacy or control over outcomes in their lives, do not have a systematic understanding of the structural and cultural elements of a society that produces sexism, and tend to blame themselves for social problems. And finally, Chinatown women perceive themselves as having more in common with Chinatown men than with White middle-class women.

Although class cleavages exist among Asian American women, political allegiance is easily achieved because of racial bonding. Initially, highly educated and professional, middle-class Asian American women organized politically and involved themselves in the feminist movement, in some cases organizing Asian American women's groups (G. Wong 1980). Although some of these groups may tend to advance middle-class interests, such as career mobility, there have also been efforts to incorporate the needs of working-class Asian American women. Because race and ethnicity cut across classes and provide a base for political identification, economic barriers are much easier to overcome among Asian American women than between them and White women. Nevertheless, there is still a great need to address issues concerning working-class Asian American women and to mobilize them to join feminist efforts.

CULTURAL FACTORS AND BARRIERS

Asiatic and U.S. cultures alike tend to relegate women to subordinate status and to work in a gendered division of labor. Although Asiatic values emphasizing education, achievement, and diligence no doubt have accounted for the high aspirations and achievements of some Asian American women, certain Asiatic values, especially when they are in conflict with American ideas, have discouraged Asian women from actively participating in the feminist movement (Chow 1982, 1985). Adherence to Asiatic values of obedience, familial interest, fatalism, and self-control may foster submissiveness, passivity, pessimism, timidness, inhibition, and adaptiveness, rather than rebelliousness or political activism. Acceptance of the American values of independence, individualism, mastery of one's environment through change, and self-expression may generate self-interest, aggressiveness, initiative, and expressive spontaneity that tend to encourage political activism; but these values are, to a large extent, incompatible with the upbringing of Asian American women.

Although cultural barriers seem to pose a greater internal problem for Asian American women, lack of knowledge and understanding of the cultural and language problems faced by Asian American women widens the gap between them and White women (Moschkovich 1981).

Further effort to enhance cultural awareness and understanding is needed in order for women of all kinds to develop a transcendent consciousness, a more inclusive experience of sisterhood.

CONCLUSION

Paradoxically, Asian American women (like other women of color) have much to gain from the White feminist movement; yet they have had a low level of participation in feminist organizations. Since feminist consciousness is a result as well as a source of feminist involvement, Asian American women have remained politically invisible and powerless. The development of feminist consciousness for Asian American women cannot be judged or understood through the experience of White women. Conversely, White women's understanding and definition of feminist consciousness needs to be more thoroughly rooted in the experiences of women of color. The same cross-pressures that hinder the political development of women of color could be a transcending political perspective that adds gender to their other consciousness and thus broadens political activism.

NOTES

1. According to the 1980 Census, there are 3.5 million Asian Americans in this country, constituting 1.5 percent of the total U.S. population. Women constitute 51 percent of the total Asian American population in the United States.

2. *Philipino* and *Filipino* are acceptable terms used to describe people from the Philippines and can be used interchangeably. The U.S. Bureau of Census has used the term Filipino since 1900. Now Filipino is a commonly used term for the group and it also can be found in *Webster's Dictionary.*

3. Personal discussion with the union representative in Local 23-25 of the ILGWU in New York Chinatown.

REFERENCES

Almquist, E. M. 1984. "Race and Ethnicity in the Lives of Minority Women." Pp. 23-453 in *Women: A Feminist Perspective,* 3rd ed., edited by Jo Freeman. Palo Alto, CA: Mayfield.

Aquino, B. A. 1979. "The History of Philipino Women in Hawaii." *Bridge* 7:17-21.

Blauner, R. 1972. *Racial Oppression in America.* New York: Harper & Row.

Blumberg, R. L. 1982. "Women as Allies of Other Oppressed Groups: Some Hypothesized Links Between Social Activism, Female Consciousness, and Feminism." Paper presented at the Tenth World Congress of the International Sociological Association, August 16-22, Mexico City.

Bogg, G. L. 1971. "The Future: Politics as End and as Means." Pp. 112-5 in *Asian Women,* edited by Editorial Staff. Berkeley, CA: University of California Press.

Bonacich, E. 1972. "A Theory of Ethnic Antagonism: The Split Labor Market." *American Sociological Review* 37:547-59.

Cade, T. 1970. *The Black Woman.* New York: Mentor.

Chia, A. Yun. 1983. "Toward a Holistic Paradigm for Asian American Women's Studies: A Synthesis of Feminist Scholarship and Women of Color's Feminist Politics." Paper presented at the Fifth Annual Conference of the National Women's Studies Association, Columbus, OH.

Chow, E. Ngan-Ling. 1982. *Acculturation of Asian American Professional Women.* Washington, DC: National Institute of Mental Health, Department of Health and Human Services.

———. 1985. "Acculturation Experience of Asian American Women." Pp. 238-51 in *Beyond Sex Roles,* 2nd ed, edited by A. G. Sargent. St. Paul, MN: West.

———. 1989. "The Feminist Movement: Where Are All the Asian American Women?" Pp. 362-77 in *Making Waves: An Anthropology of Writings By and About Asian American Women,* edited by Asian Women United of California. Boston: Beacon Press.

Christiansen-Ruffman, L. 1982. "Women's Political Culture and Feminist Political Culture." Paper presented at the Tenth World Congress of the International Sociological Association, Mexico City.

Dill, B. Thornton. 1983. "Race, Class, and Gender: Prospects for an All-Inclusive Sisterhood." *Feminist Studies* 9:131-50.

Dong, A. 1982. *Sewing Women.* San Francisco: Deep Focus.

Elway, R. Fujiki. 1979. "Strategies for Political Participation of Asian/Pacific Women." Pp. 133-9 in *Civil Rights Issues of Asian and Pacific Americans: Myths and Realities.* Washington, DC: Commission on Civil Rights.

Fallis, G. Valdes. 1974. "The Liberated Chicana—A Struggle Against Tradition." *Women: A Journal of Liberation* 3:20.

Fong, K. M. 1978. "Feminism Is Fine, But What's It Done for Asian America?" *Bridge* 6:21-2.

Fujitomi, I., and D. Wong. 1976. "The New Asian American Women." Pp. 236-48 in *Female Psychology: The Emerging Self,* edited by S. Cox. Chicago, IL: Science Research Association.

Gee, E. 1971. "Issei: The First Women." Pp. 8-15 in *Asian Women,* edited by Editorial Staff. Berkeley, CA: University of California Press.

Glenn, E. Nakano. 1983. "Split Household, Small Producer and Dual Wage Earner: An Analysis of Chinese-American Family Strategies." *Journal of Marriage and Family* 45:35-46.

Green, P. 1979. "The Feminist Consciousness." *Sociological Quarterly* 20:359-74.

Hepburn, R. A., V. Gonzalez, and C. Preciado de Burciaga. 1977. "The Chicana as Feminist." Pp. 266-73 in *Beyond Sex Roles,* edited by A. Sargent. St. Paul, MN: West.

Hooks, B. 1984. *Feminist Theory: From Margin to Center.* Boston: South End Press.

Houston, L. N. 1982. "Black Consciousness Among Female Undergraduates at a Predominantly White College: 1973 and 1979." *Journal of Social Psychology* 118:289-90.

Jung, B. 1971. "Chinese Immigrant Women." Pp. 18-20 in *Asian Women,* edited by Editorial Staff. Berkeley, CA: University of California Press.

Kim, B. 1977. "Asian Wives of U.S. Servicemen: Women in Shadows." *Amerasia Journal* 4:91-115.

Kumagai, G. L. 1978. "The Asian Women in America." *Bridge* 6:16-20.

LaRue, L. 1976. "The Black Movement and Women's Liberation." Pp. 216-25 in *Female Psychology: The Emerging Self,* edited by S. Cox. Chicago, IL: Science Research Associates.

Lee, G. M. 1971. "One in Sisterhood." Pp. 119-21 in *Asian Women,* edited by Editorial Staff. Berkeley, CA: University of California Press.

Ling, S., and S. Mazumdar. 1983. "Editorial: Asian American Feminism." *Cross-Currents* 6:3-5.

Loo, C., and P. Ong. 1982. "Slaying Demons With a Sewing Needle: Feminist Issues for Chinatown Women." *Berkeley Journal of Sociology* 27:77-88.

Lott, J., and C. Pian. 1979. *Beyond Stereotypes and Statistics: Emergence of Asian and Pacific American Women.* Washington, DC: Organization of Pan Asian American Women.

Louie, G. 1971. "Forgotten Women." Pp. 20-3 in *Asian Women,* edited by Editorial Staff. Berkeley, CA: University of California Press.

Moschkovich, J. 1981. "—But I Know You, American Women." Pp. 79-84 in *This Bridge Called My Back: Writings by Radical Women of Color,* edited by C. Moraga and G. Anzaldua. Watertown, MA: Persephone.

Palmer, P. Marynick. 1983. "White Women/Black Women: The Dualism of Female Identity and Experience in the United States." *Feminist Studies* 9:152-70.

Pian, C. 1980. "Immigration of Asian Women and the Status of Recent Asian Women Immigrants." Pp. 181-210 in *The Conference on the Educational and Occupational Needs of Asian Pacific American Women.* Washington, DC: National Institute of Education.

Terrelonge, P. 1984. "Feminist Consciousness and Black Women." Pp. 557-67 in *Women: A Feminist Perspective,* 3rd ed, edited by J. Freeman. Palo Alto, CA: Mayfield.

U.S. Bureau of the Census. 1981. *1980 Census of Population: Supplementary Reports.* Washington, DC: U.S. Department of Commerce.

———. 1983. *1980 Census of Population: Detailed Population Characteristics.* Washington, DC: Department of Commerce.

U.S. Commission on Civil Rights, 1978. *Social Indicators of Equality for Minorities and Women.* Washington, DC: Commission on Civil Rights.

Weitz, R. 1982. "Feminist Consciousness Raising, Self-Concept, and Depression." *Sex Roles* 8:231-41.

Wong, G. Q. 1980. "Impediments to Asian-Pacific-American Women Organizing." Pp. 89-103 in *The Conference on the Educational and Occupational Needs of Asian Pacific American Women.* Washington, DC: National Institute of Education.

Wong, J. Mende. 1978. "Prostitution: San Francisco Chinatown, Mid and Late Nineteenth Century." *Bridge* 6:23-8.

Wong, N., M. Woo, and M. Yamada. 1979. *3 Asian American Writers Speak Out on Feminism.* San Francisco, CA: SF Radical Women.

Woo, M. 1971. "Women + Man = Political Unity." Pp. 115-6 in *Asian Women,* edited by Editorial Staff. Berkeley, CA: University of California Press.

Yamada, M. 1981. "Asian Pacific American Women and Feminism." Pp. 71-5 in *This Bridge Called My Back: Writings by Radical Women of Color,* edited by C. Moraga and G. Anzaldua. Watertown, MA: Persephone.

Yung, J. 1986. *Chinese Women of America: A Pictorial History.* Seattle: University of Washington Press.

14. THE DEVELOPMENT OF CHICANA FEMINIST DISCOURSE, 1970-1980

ALMA M. GARCIA

Between 1970 and 1980, a Chicana feminist movement that addressed the specific issues that affected Chicanas as women of color developed in the United States. The growth of the Chicana feminist movement can be traced in the speeches, essays, letters, and articles published in Chicano and Chicana newspapers, journals, newsletters, and other printed materials.[1]

During the 1960s, American society witnessed the development of the Chicano movement, a social movement characterized by a politics of protest (Barrera 1974; Muñoz 1974; Navarro 1974). The Chicano movement focused on a wide range of issues: social justice, equality, educational reforms, and political and economic self-determination for Chicano communities in the United States. Various struggles evolved within this movement: the United Farmworkers unionization efforts (Dunne 1967; Kushner 1975; Matthiesen 1969; Nelson 1966); the New Mexico Land Grant movement (Nabokov 1969); the Colorado-based Crusade for Justice (Castro 1974; Meier and Rivera 1972); the Chicano student movement (Garcia and de la Garza 1977); and the Raza Unida Party (Shockley 1974).

Chicanas participated actively in each of these struggles. By the end of the 1960s, Chicanas began to assess the rewards and limits of their participation. The 1970s witnessed the development of Chicana feminists whose activities, organizations, and writings can be analyzed in terms of a feminist movement by women of color in American society. Chicana feminists outlined a cluster of ideas that crystallized into an emergent Chicana feminist debate. In the same way that Chicano men were reinterpreting the historical and contemporary experience of Chicanos in the United States, Chicanas began to investigate the forces shaping their own experiences as women of color.

The Chicana feminist movement emerged primarily as a result of the dynamics within the Chicano movement. In the 1960s and 1970s, the American political scene witnessed far-reaching social protest movements whose political courses often paralleled and at times exerted influence over each other (Freeman 1983; Piven and Cloward 1979). The development of feminist movements has been explained by the participation of women in larger social movements. Macias (1982), for example, links the early development of the Mexican feminist movement to the participation of women in the Mexican Revolution. Similarly, Freeman's (1984) analysis of the White feminist movement points out that many White feminists who were active in the early years of its development had previously been involved in the new left and civil rights movements. It was in these movements that White feminists experienced the constraints of domination by men. Black feminists have similarly traced the development of a Black feminist movement during the 1960s and 1970s to their experiences with sexism in the larger Black movement (Davis 1981; Dill 1983; Hooks 1981, 1984; Joseph and Lewis 1981; White 1984). In this way, then, the origins of Chicana feminism parallel those of other feminist movements.

ORIGINS OF CHICANA FEMINISM

Rowbotham (1974) argues that women may develop a feminist consciousness as a result of their experiences with sexism in revolutionary struggles or mass social movements. To the extent that such movements are male dominated, women are likely to develop a feminist consciousness. Chicana feminists began the search for a "room of their own" by assessing their participation within the Chicano movement. Their feminist consciousness emerged from a struggle for equality with Chicano men and from a reassessment of the role of the family as a means of resistance to oppressive societal conditions.

Historically, as well as during the 1960s and 1970s, the Chicano family represented a source of cultural and political resistance to the various types of discrimination experienced in American society (Zinn 1975a). At the cultural level, the Chicano movement emphasized the need to safeguard the value of family loyalty. At the political level, the Chicano movement used the family as a strategic organizational tool for protest activities.

Dramatic changes in the structure of Chicano families occurred as they participated in the Chicano movement. Specifically, women began to question their traditional female roles (Zinn 1975a). Thus, a Chicana feminist movement originated from the nationalist Chicano struggle. Rowbotham (1974, p. 206) refers to such a feminist movement as "a colony within a colony." But as the Chicano movement developed during the 1970s, Chicana feminists began to draw their own political agenda and raised a series of questions to assess their role within the

Chicano movement. They entered into a dialogue with each other that explicitly reflected their struggles to secure a room of their own within the Chicano movement.

DEFINING FEMINISM FOR WOMEN OF COLOR

A central question of feminist discourse is the definition of feminism. The lack of consensus reflects different political ideologies and divergent social-class bases. In the United States, Chicana feminists shared the task of defining their ideology and movement with White, Black, and Asian American feminists. Like Black and Asian American feminists, Chicana feminists struggled to gain social equality and end sexist and racist oppression. Like them, Chicana feminists recognized that the nature of social inequality for women of color was multidimensional (see Chapter 13; Cheng 1984; Hooks 1981). Like Black and Asian American feminists, Chicana feminists struggled to gain equal status in the nationalist movements dominated by men and also in American society. To them, feminism represented a movement to end sexist oppression within a broader social protest movement. Again, like Black and Asian American feminists, Chicana feminists fought for social equality in the 1970s. They understood that their movement needed to go beyond women's rights and include the men of their group, who also faced racial subordination (Hooks 1981). Chicanas believed that feminism involved more than an analysis of gender because, as women of color, they were affected by both race and class in their everyday lives. Thus, Chicana feminism, as a social movement to improve the position of Chicanas in American society, represented a struggle that was both nationalist and feminist.

Chicana, Black, and Asian American feminists were all confronted with the issue of engaging in a feminist struggle to end sexist oppression within a broader nationalist struggle to end racist oppression. All experienced male domination in their own communities as well as in the larger society. In Chapter 13, Ngan-Ling Chow identifies gender stereotypes of Asian American women and the patriarchal family structure as major sources of women's oppression. Cultural, political, and economic constraints have, according to Ngan-Ling Chow, limited the full development of a feminist consciousness and movement among Asian American women. The cross-pressures resulting from the demands of a nationalist and a feminist struggle led some Asian American women to organize feminist organizations that, however, continued to address broader issues affecting the Asian American community.

Black women were also faced with addressing feminist issues within a nationalist movement. According to Thornton Dill (1983), Black women played a major historical role in Black resistance movements and, in addition, brought a feminist component to these movements (see also Davis 1981). Black women have struggled with Black men in nationalist movements but have also recognized and fought against the sexism in such political movements in the Black community (Hooks 1984). Although they wrote and spoke as Black feminists, they did not organize separately from Black men.

Among the major ideological questions facing all three groups of feminists were the relationship between feminism and the ideology of cultural nationalism or racial pride, feminism and feminist-baiting within the larger movements, and the relationship between their feminist movements and the White feminist movement.

CHICANA FEMINISM AND CULTURAL NATIONALISM

Throughout the 1970s and now, in the 1980s, Chicana feminists have been forced to respond to the criticism that cultural nationalism and feminism are irreconcilable. In the first issue of the newspaper, *Hijas de Cuauhtemoc,* Nieto Gomez (1971) stated that a major issue facing Chicanas active in the Chicano movement was the need to organize to improve their status as women within the larger social movement. Flores (1971b, p. i), another leading Chicana feminist, stated:

> [Chicanas] can no longer remain in a subservient role or as auxiliary forces in the [Chicano] movement. They must be included in the front line of communication, leadership and organizational responsibility. . . . The issue of equality, freedom and self-determination of the Chicana—like the right of self-determination, equality, and liberation of the Mexican [Chicano] community—is not negotiable. Anyone opposing the right of women to organize into their own form of organization has no place in the leadership of the movement.

Supporting this position, Rincon (1971) argued that a Chicana feminist movement that sought equality and justice for Chicanas would strengthen the Chicano movement. Yet in the process, Chicana feminists challenged traditional gender roles because they limited their participation and acceptance within the Chicano movement.

Throughout the 1970s, Chicana feminists viewed the struggle against sexism within the Chicano movement and the struggle against racism in the larger society as integral parts of Chicana feminism. As Nieto Gomez (1976, p. 10) said:

> Chicana feminism is in various stages of development. However, in general, Chicana feminism is the recognition that women are oppressed as a group and are exploited as part of *la Raza* people. It is a direction to be responsible to identify and act upon the issues and needs of Chicana women. Chicana feminists are involved in understanding the nature of women's oppression.

Cultural nationalism represented a major ideological component of the Chicano movement. Its emphasis on Chicano cultural pride and cultural survival within an Anglo-dominated society gave significant political direction to the Chicano movement. One source of ideological diagreement between Chicana feminism and this cultural nationalist ideology was cultural survival. Many Chicana feminists believed that a focus on cultural survival did not acknowledge the need to alter relations between men and women within Chicano communities. For example, Chicana feminists criticized the notion of the "ideal Chicana," which glorified Chicanas as strong, long-suffering women who had endured and kept Chicano culture and the family intact. To Chicana feminists, this concept represented an obstacle to the redefinition of gender roles. Nieto (1975, p. 4) stated:

> Some Chicanas are praised as they emulate the sanctified example set by [the Virgin] Mary. The woman *par excellence* is mother and wife. She is to love and support her husband and to nurture and teach her children. Thus, may she gain fulfillment as a woman. For a Chicana bent upon fulfillment of her personhood, this restricted perspective of her role as a woman is not only inadequate but crippling.

Chicana feminists were also skeptical about the cultural nationalist interpretation of machismo. Such an interpretation viewed machismo as an ideological tool used by the dominant Anglo-society to justify the inequalities experienced by Chicanos. According to this interpretation, the relationship between Chicanos and the larger society was that of an internal colony dominated and exploited by the capitalist economy (Almaguer 1974; Barrera 1979). Machismo, like other cultural traits, was blamed by Anglos for blocking Chicanos from succeeding in American society. In reality, the economic structure and colony-like exploitation were to blame.

Some Chicana feminists agreed with this analysis of machismo, claiming that a mutually reinforcing relationship existed between internal colonialism and the development of the myth of machismo. According to Sosa Riddell (1974, p. 21), machismo was a myth "propagated by subjugators and colonizers, which created damaging stereotypes of Mexican/Chicano males." As a type of social control imposed by the dominant society on Chicanos, the myth of machismo distorted gender relations within Chicano communities, creating stereotypes of Chicanas as passive and docile women. At this level in the feminist discourse, machismo was seen as an Anglo myth that kept both Chicano and Chicanas in a subordinate status. As Nieto (1975, p. 4) concluded:

> Although the term "machismo" is correctly denounced by all because it stereotypes the Latin man . . . it does a great disservice to both men and women. Chicano and Chicana alike must be free to seek their own individual fulfillment.

While some Chicana feminists criticized the myth of machismo used by the dominant society to legitimate racial inequality, others moved beyond this level of analysis to distinguish between the machismo that oppressed both men and women and the sexism in Chicano communities in general, and in the Chicano movement in particular, that oppressed Chicana women (Chavez 1971; Cotera 1977; Del Castillo 1974; Marquez and Ramirez 1977; Riddell 1974; Zinn 1975b). According to Vidal (1971, p. 8), the origins of a Chicana feminist consciousness were prompted by the sexist attitudes and behavior of Chicano men, which constituted a "serious obstacle to women anxious to play a role in the struggle for Chicana liberation."

Furthermore, many Chicana feminists disagreed with the cultural nationalist view that machismo could be a positive value within a Chicano cultural value system. They challenged the view that machismo was a source of masculine pride for Chicanos and therefore a defense mechanism against the dominant society's racism. Although Chicana feminists recognized that Chicanos faced discrimination from the dominant society, they adamantly disagreed with those who believed that machismo was a form of cultural resistance to such discrimination. Chicana feminists called for changes in the ideologies responsible for distorting relations between women and men. One such change was to modify the cultural nationalist position that viewed machismo as a source of cultural pride.

Chicana feminists called for a focus on the universal aspects of sexism that shape gender relations in both Anglo and Chicano culture.

Although they acknowledged the economic exploitation of all Chicanos, Chicana feminists outlined the double exploitation experienced by Chicanas. Sosa Riddell (1974, p. 159) concluded: "It was when Chicanas began to seek work outside of the family groups that sexism became a key factor of oppression along with racism." Flores (1971a, p. 4) summarized some of the consequences of sexism:

> It is not surprising that more and more Chicanas are forced to go to work in order to supplement the family income. The children are farmed out to a relative to baby-sit with them, and since these women are employed in the lower income jobs, the extra pressure placed on them can become unbearable.

Thus, while the Chicano movement was addressing the issue of racial oppression facing all Chicanos, Chicana feminist argued that it lacked an analysis of sexism. Similarly, Black and Asian American women stressed the interconnectedness of race and gender oppression. Hooks (1984, p. 52) analyzes racism and sexism in terms of their "intersecting, complementary nature." She also emphasizes that one struggle should not take priority over the other. White (1984) criticizes Black men whose nationalism limited discussions of Black women's experiences with sexist oppression. The writings of other Black feminists criticized a Black cultural nationalist ideology that overlooked the consequences of sexist oppression (Beale 1975; Cade 1970; Davis 1971; Joseph and Lewis 1981). Many Asian American women were also critical of the Asian American movement whose focus on racism ignored the impact of sexism on the daily lives of women. The participation of Asian American women in various community struggles increased their encounters with sexism (see Chapter 13). As a result, some Asian American women developed a feminist consciousness and organized as women around feminist issues.

CHICANA FEMINISM AND FEMINIST-BAITING

The systematic analysis by Chicana feminists of the impact of racism and sexism on Chicanas in American society and, above all, within the Chicano movement was often misunderstood as a threat to the political unity of the Chicano movement. As Cotera (1977, p. 9), a leading voice of Chicana feminism, pointed out:

> The aggregate cultural values we [Chicanas] share can also work to our benefit if we choose to scrutinize our cultural traditions, isolate the positive

attributes and interpret them for the benefit of women. It's unreal that *Hispanas* have been browbeaten for so long about our so-called conservative (meaning reactionary) culture. It's also unreal that we have let men interpret culture only as those practices and attitudes that determine who does the dishes around the house. We as women also have the right to interpret and define the philosophical and religious traditions beneficial to us within our culture, and which we have inherited as our tradition. To do this, we must become both conversant with our history and philosophical evolution, and analytical about the institutional and behavioral manifestations of the same.

Such Chicana feminists were attacked for developing a "divisive ideology"—a feminist ideology that was frequently viewed as a threat to the Chicano movement as a whole. As Chicana feminists examined their roles as women activists within the Chicano movement, an ideological split developed. One group active in the Chicano movement saw themselves as "loyalists" who believed that the Chicano movement did not have to deal with sexual inequities since Chicano men as well as Chicano women experienced racial oppression. According to Nieto Gomez (1973, p. 35), who was not a loyalist, their view was that if men oppress women, it is not the men's fault but rather the system's.

Even if such a problem existed, and they did not believe that it did, the loyalists maintained that such a matter would best be resolved internally within the Chicano movement. They denounced the formation of a separate Chicano feminist movement on the grounds that it was a politically dangerous strategy, perhaps Anglo-inspired. Such a movement would undermine the unity of the Chicano movement by raising an issue that was not seen as a central one. Loyalists viewed racism as the most important issue within the Chicano movement. Nieto Gomez (1973, p. 35) quotes one such loyalist:

> I am concerned with the direction that the Chicanas are taking in the movement. The words such as liberation, sexism, male chauvinism, etc., were prevalent. The terms mentioned above plus the theme of individualism is a concept of the Anglo society; terms prevalent in the Anglo women's movement. The *familia* has always been our strength in our culture. But it seems evident . . . that you [Chicana feminists] are not concerned with the *familia*, but are influenced by the Anglo woman's movement.

Chicana feminists were also accused of undermining the values associated with Chicano culture. Loyalists saw the Chicana feminist movement as an "anti-family, anti-cultural, anti-man and therefore an anti-Chicano movement" (Gomez 1973, p. 35). Feminism was, above all, believed to be an individualistic search for identity that detracted from the U.S. movement's "real" issues, such as racism. Nieto Gomez (1973, p. 35) quotes a loyalist as stating:

> And since when does a Chicana need identity? If you are a real Chicana then no one regardless of the degrees needs to tell you about it. The only ones who need identity are the *vendidas,* the *falsas,* and the opportunists.

The ideological conflicts between Chicana feminists and loyalists persisted throughout the 1970s. Disagreements between these two groups became exacerbated during various Chicana conferences. At times, such confrontations served to increase Chicana feminist activity that challenged the loyalists' attacks, yet these attacks also served to suppress feminist activities.

Chicana feminist lesbians experienced even stronger attacks from those who viewed feminism as a divisive ideology. In a political climate that already viewed feminist ideology with suspicion, lesbianism as a sexual lifestyle and political ideology came under even more attack. Clearly, a cultural nationalist ideology that perpetuated stereotypical images of Chicanas as "good wives and good mothers" found it difficult to accept a Chicana feminist lesbian movement.

Moraga's writings during the 1970s reflect the struggles of Chicana feminist lesbians who, together with other Chicana feminists, were finding the sexism evident within the Chicano movement intolerable. Just as Chicana feminists analyzed their life circumstances as members of an ethnic minority and as women, Chicana feminist lesbians addressed themselves to the oppression they experienced as lesbians. As Moraga (1981, p. 28) stated:

> My lesbianism is the avenue through which I have learned the most about silence and oppression. . . . In this country, lesbianism is a poverty—as is being brown, as is being a woman, as is being just plain poor. The danger lies in ranking the oppressions. The danger lies in failing to acknowledge the specificity of the oppression.

Chicana, Black, and Asian American feminists experienced similar cross-pressures of feminist and lesbian-baiting attacks. As they organized around feminist struggles, these women of color encountered criticism from both male and female cultural nationalists, who often viewed feminism as little more than an "anti-male" ideology. Lesbianism was identified as an extreme derivation of feminism. A direct connection that viewed feminism and lesbianism as synonymous was frequently made. Feminists were labeled lesbians, and lesbians feminists. Attacks against feminists—Chicanas, Blacks, and Asian Americans—derived from the existence of homophobia within each of these communities. As lesbian women of color published their writings, attacks against them increased (Moraga 1983).

Responses to such attacks varied within and between the feminist movements of women of color. Some groups tried one strategy and later adopted another. Some lesbians pursued a separatist strategy within their own racial and ethnic communities (Moraga and Anzaldua 1981; White 1984). Others attempted to form lesbian coalitions across racial and ethnic lines. Both strategies represented a response to the marginalization of lesbians produced by recurrent waves of homophobic sentiments in Chicano, Black, and Asian American communities (Moraga and Anzaldua 1981). A third response consisted of working within the broader nationalist movements in these communities and the feminist movements within them in order to challenge their heterosexual biases and resultant homophobia. As early as 1974, the "Black Feminist Statement" written by a Boston-based feminist group—the Cohambee River Collective—stated (1981, p. 213): "We struggle together with Black men against racism, while we also struggle with Black men against sexism." Similarly, Moraga (1981) challenged the white feminist movement to examine its racist tendencies; the Chicano movement, its sexist tendencies; and both, their homophobic tendencies. In this way, Moraga (1981) argued that such movements to end oppression would begin to respect diversity within their own ranks.

Chicana feminists as well as Chicana feminist lesbians continued to be labeled *vendidas* or "sellouts." Chicana loyalists continued to view Chicana feminism as associated, not only with melting into White society but, more seriously, with dividing the Chicano movement. Similarly, many Chicano males were convinced that Chicana feminism was a divisive ideology incompatible with Chicano cultural nationalism. Nieto Gomez (1976, p. 10) said that "[with] respect to [the] Chicana feminist, their credibility is reduced when they are associated with [feminism] and White women." She added that, as a result, Chicana feminists often faced harassment and ostracism within the Chicano movement. Similarly, Cotera (1973, p. 30) stated that Chicanas "are suspected of assimilating into the feminist ideology of an alien [White] culture that actively seeks our cultural domination."

Chicana feminists responded quickly and often vehemently to such charges. Flores (1971a, p. 1) answered these antifeminist attacks in an editorial in which she argued that birth control, abortion, and sex education were not merely White issues. In response to the accusation that feminists were responsible for the "betrayal of [Chicano] culture and heritage," Flores said, "Our culture hell"—a phrase that became a dramatic slogan of the Chicana feminist movement.

Throughout the 1970s, Chicana feminists' defense against those claiming that a feminist movement was divisive for the Chicano movement was to reassess their roles within the Chicano movement and to call for an end to domination by men. Their challenges of traditional gender roles represented a means to achieve equality (Longeaux y Vasquez 1969a, 1969b). In order to increase the participation of and opportunities for women in the Chicano movement, feminists agreed that both Chicanos and Chicanas had to address the issue of gender inequality (Chapa 1973; Chavez 1971; Cotera 1977; Del Castillo 1974; Moreno 1979). Furthermore, Chicana feminists argued that the resistance that they encountered reflected the existence of sexism on the part of Chicano males and the antifeminist attitudes of the Chicana loyalists. Nieto Gomez (1973, p. 31), reviewing the experiences of Chicana feminists in the Chicano movement, concluded that Chicanas "involved in discussing and applying the women's question have been ostracized, isolated and ignored." She argued that "in organizations where cultural nationalism is extremely strong, Chicana feminists experience intense harassment and ostracism" (1973, p. 38).

Black and Asian American women also faced severe criticism as they pursued feminist issues in their own communities. Indeed, as their participation in collective efforts to end racial oppression increased, so did their confrontations with sexism (Hooks 1984; White 1984). Ngan-Ling Chow (Chapter 13) describes the various sources of such criticism directed at Asian American women:

> Asian American women are criticized for the possible consequences of their protests: weakening the male ego, dilution of effort and resources in Asian American communities, destruction of working relationships between Asian men and women, setbacks for the Asian American cause, co-optation into the larger society, and eventual loss of ethnic identity for Asian Americans as a whole. In short, affiliation with the feminist movement is perceived as a threat to solidarity within their own community.

Similar criticism was experienced by Black feminists (Hooks 1984; White 1984).

CHICANA FEMINISTS AND WHITE FEMINISTS

It is difficult to determine the extent to which Chicana feminists sympathized with the White feminist movement. A 1976 study at the

University of San Diego that examined the attitudes of Chicanas regarding the White feminist movement found that the majority of Chicanas surveyed believed that the movement had affected their lives. In addition, they identified with such key issues as the right to legal abortions on demand and access to low-cost birth control. Nevertheless, the survey found that "even though the majority of Chicanas . . . could relate to certain issues of the women's movement, for the most part they saw it as being an elitist movement comprised of white middle-class women who [saw] the oppressor as the males of this country" (Orozco 1976, p. 12).

Nevertheless, some Chicana feminists considered the possibility of forming coalitions with White feminists as their attempts to work within the Chicano movement were suppressed. Since White feminists were themselves struggling against sexism, building coalitions with them was seen as an alternative strategy for Chicana feminists (Rincon 1971). Almost immediately however, Chicana feminists recognized the problems involved in adopting this political strategy. As Longeaux y Vasquez (1971, p. 11) acknowledged, "Some of our own Chicanas may be attracted to the white woman's liberation movement, but we really don't feel comfortable there. We want to be a Chicana *primero* [first]." For other Chicanas, the demands of White women were "irrelevant to the Chicana movement" (Hernandez 1971, p. 9).

Several issues made such coalition building difficult. First, Chicana feminists criticized what they considered to be a cornerstone of White feminist thought, an emphasis on gender oppression to explain the life circumstances of women. Chicana feminists believed that the White feminist movement overlooked the effects of racial oppression experienced by Chicanas and other women of color. Thus, Del Castillo (1974, p. 8) maintained that the Chicana feminist movement was "different primarily because we are [racially] oppressed people." In addition, Chicana feminists criticized White feminists who believed that a general women's movement would be able to overcome racial differences among women. Chicanas interpreted this as a failure by the White feminist movement to deal with the issue of racism. Without the incorporation of an analysis of racial oppression to explain the experiences of Chicanas as well as of other women of color, Chicana feminists believed that a coalition with White feminists would be highly unlikely (Chapa 1973; Cotera 1977; Gomez 1973; Longeaux y Vasquez 1971). As Longeaux y Vasquez (1971, p. 11) concluded: "We must have a clearer vision of our plight and certainly we cannot blame our men for the oppression of the women."

In the 1970s, Chicana feminists reconciled their demands for an end to sexism within the Chicano movement and their rejection of the saliency of gender oppression by separating the two issues. They clearly identified the struggle against sexism in the Chicano movement as a major issue, arguing that sexism prevented their full participation (Fallis 1974; Gomez 1976). They also argued that sexist behavior and ideology on the part of both Chicano men and Anglos represented the key to understanding women's oppression. However, they remained critical of an analysis of women's experiences that focused exclusively on gender oppression.

Chicana feminists adopted an analysis that began with race as a critical variable in interpreting the experiences of Chicano communities in the United States. They expanded this analysis by identifying gender as a variable interconnected with race in analyzing the specific daily life circumstances of Chicanas as women in Chicano communities. Chicana feminists did not view women's struggles as secondary to the nationalist movement but argued instead for an analysis of race and gender as multiple sources of oppression (Cotera 1977). Thus, Chicana feminism went beyond the limits of an exclusively racial theory of oppression that tended to overlook gender and also beyond the limits of a theory of oppression based exclusively on gender that tended to overlook race.

A second factor preventing an alliance between Chicana feminists and White feminists was the middle-class orientation of White feminists. While some Chicana feminists recognized the legitimacy of the demands made by White feminists and even admitted sharing some of these demands, they argued that "it is not our business as Chicanas to identify with the white women's liberation movement as a home base for working for our people" (Longeaux y Vasquez 1971, p. 11).

Throughout the 1970s, Chicana feminists viewed the White feminist movement as a middle-class movement (Chapa 1973; Cotera 1980; Longeaux y Vasquez 1970; Martinez 1972; Nieto 1974; Orozco 1976). In contrast, Chicana feminists analyzed the Chicano movement in general as a working-class movement. They repeatedly made reference to such differences, and many Chicana feminists began their writings with a section that disassociated themselves from the "women's liberation movement." Chicana feminists as activists in the broader Chicano movement identified as major struggles the farm-workers movement, welfare rights, undocumented workers, and prison rights. Such issues were seen as far removed from the demands of the White feminist movement, and Chicana feminists could not get White feminist organizations to deal with them (Cotera 1980).

Similar concerns regarding the White feminist movement were raised by Black and Asian American feminists. Black feminists have documented the historical and contemporary schisms between Black and White feminists, emphasizing the socioeconomic and political differences (Davis 1971, 1983; Dill 1983; LaRue 1970). More specifically, Black feminists have been critical of the White feminists who advocate a female solidarity that cuts across racial, ethnic, and social class lines. As Thornton Dill (1983, p. 131) states:

> The cry "Sisterhood is powerful!" has engaged only a few segments of the female population in the United States. Black, Hispanic, Native American, and Asian American women of all classes, as well as many working-class women, have not readily identified themselves as sisters of the white middle-class women who have been in the forefront of the movement.

Like Black feminists, Asian American feminists have also had strong reservations regarding the White feminist movement. For many Asian Americans, white feminism has focused primarily on gender as an analytical category and has thus lacked a systematic analysis of race and class (see Chapter 13; Fong 1978; Wong 1980; Woo 1971).

White feminist organizations were also accused of being exclusionary, patronizing, or racist in their dealings with Chicanas and other women of color. Cotera (1980, p. 227) states:

> Minority women could fill volumes with examples of put-down, put-ons, and out-and-out racism shown to them by the leadership in the [White feminist] movement. There are three major problem areas in the minority-majority relationship in the movement: (1) paternalism or materialism, (2) extremely limited opportunities for minority women . . . , (3) outright discrimination against minority women in the movement.

Although Chicana feminists continued to be critical of building coalitions with White feminists toward the end of the 1970s, they acknowledged the diversity of ideologies within the White feminist movement. Chicana feminists sympathetic to radical socialist feminism because of its anti-capitalist framework wrote of working-class oppression that cut across racial and ethnic lines. Their later writings discussed the possibility of joining with White working-class women, but strategies for forming such political coalitions were not made explicit (Cotera 1977; Marquez and Ramirez 1977).

Instead, Del Castillo and other Chicana feminists favored coalitions between Chicanas and other women of color while keeping their respective organizations autonomous. Such coalitions would recognize the inherent racial oppression of capitalism rather than universal gender oppression. When Longeaux y Vasquez (1971) stated that she was "Chicana *primero*," she was stressing the saliency of race over gender in explaining the oppression experienced by Chicanas. The word *Chicana*, however, simultaneously expresses a woman's race and gender. Not until later—in the 1980s—would Chicana feminist ideology call for an analysis that stressed the interrelationship of race, class, and gender in explaining the conditions of Chicanas in American society (Cordova et al. 1986; Zinn 1982), just as Black and Asian American feminists have done.

Chicana feminists continued to stress the importance of developing autonomous feminist organizations that would address the struggles of Chicanas as members of an ethnic minority and as women. Rather than attempt to overcome the obstacles to building a coalition between Chicana feminists and White feminists, Chicanas called for autonomous feminist organizations for all women of color (Cotera 1977; Gonzalez 1980; Nieto 1975). Chicana feminists believed that sisterhood was indeed powerful but only to the extent that racial and class differences were understood and, above all, respected. As Nieto (1974, p. 4) concludes:

> The Chicana must demand that dignity and respect within the women's rights movement which allows her to practice feminism within the context of her own culture. . . . Her approaches to feminism must be drawn from her own world.

CHICANA FEMINISM: AN EVOLVING FUTURE

Chicana feminists, like Black, Asian American, and Native American feminists, experience specific life conditions that are distinct from those of White feminists. Such socioeconomic and cultural differences in Chicano communities directly shaped the development of Chicana feminism and the relationship between Chicana feminists and feminists of other racial and ethnic groups, including White feminists. Future dialogue among all feminists will require a mutual understanding of the existing differences as well as the similarities. Like other women of color, Chicana feminists must address issues that specifically affect them as women of color. In addition, Chicana feminists must address those issues that have particular impact on Chicano communities, such as poverty, limited opportunities for higher education, high school dropouts, health care, bilingual education, immigration reform, prison reform, welfare, and, most recently, United States policies in Central America.

The decade of the 1980s has witnessed a rephrasing of the critical question concerning the nature of the oppression experienced by Chicanas and other women of color. Chicana feminists, like Black feminists, are asking what are the consequences of the intersection of race, class, and gender in the daily lives of women in American society, emphasizing the simultaneity of these critical variables for women of color (Garcia 1986; Hooks 1984). In their labor-force participation, wages, education, and poverty levels, Chicanas have made few gains in comparison to White men and women and Chicano men (Segura 1986). To analyze these problems, Chicana feminists have investigated the structures of racism, capitalism, and patriarchy, especially as they are experienced by the majority of Chicanas (Ruiz 1987; Segura 1986; Zavella 1987). Clearly, such issues will need to be explicitly addressed, analytically and politically, by an evolving Chicana feminist movement.

NOTE

1. For bibliographies on Chicanas see Balderama (1981); Candelaria (1980); Loeb (1980); Portillo, Rios, and Rodriguez (1976); and Baca Zinn (1982, 1984).

REFERENCES

Almaguer, T. 1974. "Historical Notes on Chicano Oppression." *Aztlan* 5:27-56.

Balderama, S. 1981. "A Comprehensive Bibliography on La Chicana." Unpublished paper, University of California, Berkeley.

Barrera, M. 1974. "The Study of Politics and the Chicano." *Aztlan* 5:9-26.

———. 1979. *Race and Class in the Southwest.* South Bend, IN: University of Notre Dame Press.

Beale, F. 1975. "Slave of a Slave No More: Black Women in Struggle." *Black Scholar* 6:2-10.

Cade, T. 1970. *The Black Woman: An Anthology.* New York: Signet.

Candelaria, C. 1980. "Six Reference Works on Mexican American Women: A Review Essay." *Frontiers* 5:75-80.

Castro, T. 1974. *Chicano Power.* New York: Saturday Review Press.

Chapa, E. 1973. "Report from the National Women's Political Caucus." *Magazin* 1:37-9.

Chavez, H. 1971. "The Chicanas." *Regeneraçion* 1:14.

Cheng, L. 1984. "Asian American Women and Feminism." *Sojourner* 10:11-2.

Cohambee River Collective. 1981. "A Black Feminist Statement." Pp. 210-8 in *This Bridge Called My Back: Writings by Radical Women of Color,* edited by C. Moraga and G. Anzaldua. Watertown, MA: Persephone.

Cordova, T., et al. 1986. *Chicana Voices: Intersections of Class, Race, and Gender.* Austin, TX: Center for Mexican American Studies.

Cotera, M. 1973. "La Mujer Mexicana: Mexicano Feminism." *Magazin* 1:30-2.

———. 1977. *The Chicana Feminist.* Austin, TX: Austin Information Systems Development.

———. 1980. "Feminism: The Chicana and Anglo Versions: An Historical Analysis." Pp. 217-34 in *Twice a Minority: Mexican American Women,* edited by M. Melville. St. Louis, MO: C. V. Mosby.

Davis, A. 1971. "Reflections on Black Women's Role in the Community of Slaves." *Black Scholar* 3:3-13.

———. 1981. *Women, Race and Class.* New York: Random House.

Del Castillo, A. 1974. "La Vision Chicana." *La Gente:* 8.

Dill, B. Thornton. 1983. "Race, Class, and Gender: Prospects for an All-Inclusive Sisterhood." *Feminist Studies* 9:131-50.

Dunne, J. 1967. *Delano: The Story of the California Grape Strike.* New York: Strauss.

Fallis, G. Valdes. 1974. "The Liberated Chicana—A Struggle Against Tradition." *Women: A Journal of Liberation* 3:20.

Flores, F. 1971a. "Conference of Mexican Women: Un Remolino. *Regeneraçion* 1(1):1-4.

———. 1971b. "El Mundo Femenil Mexicana." *Regeneraçion* 1(10):i.

Fong, K. M. 1978. "Feminism Is Fine, But What's It Done for Asia America?" *Bridge* 6:21-2.

Freeman, J. 1983. "On the Origins of Social Movements." Pp. 8-30 in *Social Movements of the Sixties and Seventies,* edited by J. Freeman. New York: Longman.

———. 1984. "The Women's Liberation Movement: Its Origins, Structure, Activities, and Ideas." Pp. 543-56 in *Women: A Feminist Perspective,* edited by J. Freeman. Palo Alto, CA: Mayfield.

Garcia, A. M. 1986. "Studying Chicanas: Bringing Women into the Frame of Chicano Studies." Pp. 19-29 in *Chicana Voices: Intersections of Class, Race, and Gender,* edited by T. Cordova et al. Austin, TX: Center for Mexican American Studies.

Garcia, F. C., and R. O. de la Garza. 1977. *The Chicano Political Experience.* North Scituate, MA: Duxbury.

Gomez, A. Nieto. 1971. "Chicanas Identify." *Hijas de Cuauhtemoc* (April):9.

———. 1973. "La Femenista." *Encuentro Femenil* 1:34-47.

———. 1976. "Sexism in the Movement." *La Gente* 6(4):10.

Gonzalez, S. 1980. "Toward a Feminist Pedagogy for Chicana Self-Actualization." *Frontiers* 5:48-51.

Hernandez, C. 1971. "Carmen Speaks Out." *Papel Chicano* 1(June 12):8-9.

Hooks, B. 1981. *Ain't I a Woman: Black Women and Feminism.* Boston: South End Press.

———. 1984. *Feminist Theory: From Margin to Center.* Boston: South End Press.

Joseph, G., and J. Lewis. 1981. *Common Differences: Conflicts in Black and White Feminist Perspectives.* Garden City, NY: Doubleday.

Kushner, S. 1975. *Long Road to Delano.* New York: International.

LaRue, L. 1970. "The Black Movement and Women's Liberation." *Black Scholar* 1:36-42.

Loeb, C. 1980. "La Chicana: A Bibliographic Survey." *Frontiers* 5:59-74.

Longeaux y Vasquez, E. 1969a. "The Woman of La Raza." *El Grito del Norte* 2(July):8-9.

———. 1969b. "La Chicana: Let's Build a New Life." *El Grito del Norte* 2(November):11.

———. 1970. "The Mexican-American Woman." Pp. 379-84 in *Sisterhood Is Powerful,* edited by R. Morgan. New York: Vintage.

———. 1971. "Soy Chicana Primero." *El Grito del Norte* 4(April 26):11.

Macias, A. 1982. *Against All Odds.* Westport, CT: Greenwood.

Marquez, E., and M. Ramirez. 1977. "Women's Task Is to Gain Liberation." Pp. 188-9 in *Essays on La Mujer,* edited by R. Sanchez and R. Martinez Cruz. Los Angeles: UCLA Chicano Studies Center.

Martinez, E. 1972. "The Chicana." *Ideal* 44:1-3.

Matthiesen, P. 1969. *Sal Si Puedes: Cesar Chavez and the New American Revolution.* New York: Random House.

Meier, M., and F. Rivera. 1972. *The Chicanos.* New York: Hill & Wang.

Moraga, C. 1981. "La Guera." Pp. 27-34 in *This Bridge Called My Back: Writings by Radical Women of Color,* edited by C. Moraga and G. Anzaldua. Watertown, MA: Persephone.

———. 1983. *Loving in the War Years.* Boston: South End Press.

Moraga, C., and G. Anzaldua. (eds.). 1981. *This Bridge Called My Back: Writings by Radical Women of Color.* Watertown, MA: Persephone.

Moreno, D. 1979. "The Image of the Chicana and the La Raza Woman." *Caracol* 2:14-5

Muñoz, C., Jr., 1974. "The Politics of Protest and Liberation: A Case Study of Repression and Cooptation." *Aztlan* 5:119-41.

Nabokov, P. 1969. *Tijerina and the Courthouse Raid.* Albuquerque: University of New Mexico Press.

Navarro, A. 1974. "The Evolution of Chicano Politics." *Aztlan* 5:57-84.

Nelson, E. 1966. *Huelga: The First 100 Days.* Delano, CA: Farm Workers Press.

Nieto, C. 1974. "The Chicana and the Women's Rights Movement." *La Luz* 3(September):10-11, 32.

———. 1975. "Consuelo Nieto on the Women's Movement." *Interracial Books for Children Bulletin* 5:4.

Orozco, Y. 1976. "La Chicana and 'Women's Liberation.' " *Voz Fronteriza* (January 5):6, 12.

Piven, F. Fox, and R. A. Cloward. 1979. *Poor People's Movements: Why They Succeed, How They Fail.* New York: Vintage.

Portillo, C., G. Rios, and M. Rodriguez. 1976. *Bibliography on Writings on La Mujer.* Berkeley: University of California Chicano Studies Library.

Riddell, A. Sosa. 1974. "Chicanas en el Movimiento." *Aztlan* 5:155-65.

Rincon, B. 1971. "La Chicana: Her Role in the Past and Her Search for a New Role in the Future." *Regeneraçion* 1(10):15-7.

Rowbotham, S. 1974. *Women, Resistance and Revolution: A History of Women and Revolution in the Modern World.* New York: Vintage.

Ruiz, V. L. 1987. *Cannery Women, Cannery Lives: Mexican Women, Unionization, and the California Food Processing Industry, 1930-1950.* Albuquerque: University of New Mexico Press.

Segura, D. 1986. "Chicanas and Triple Oppression in the Labor Force." Pp. 47-65 in *Chicana Voices: Intersections of Class, Race and Gender,* edited by T. Cordova et al. Austin, TX: Center for Mexican American Studies.

Shockley, J. 1974. *Chicano Revolt in a Texas Town.* South Bend, IN: University of Notre Dame Press.

Vidal, M. 1971. "New Voice of La Raza: Chicanas Speak Out." *International Socialist Review* 32:31-3.

White, F. 1984. "Listening to the Voices of Black Feminism." *Radical America* 18:7-25.

Wong, G. Q. 1980. "Impediments to Asian-Pacific-American Women Organizing." Pp. 89-103 in *The Conference on the Educational and Occupational Needs of Asian Pacific Women.* Washington, DC: National Institute of Education.

Woo, M. 1971. "Women + Man = Political Unity." Pp. 115-6 in *Asian Women,* edited by Editorial Staff. Berkeley: University of California Press.

Zavella, P. 1987. *Women's Work and Chicano Families: Cannery Workers of the Santa Clara Valley.* Ithaca, NY: Cornell University Press.

Zinn, M. Baca. 1975a. "Political Familism: Toward Sex Role Equality in Chicano Families." *Aztlan* 6:13-27.

————. 1975b. "Chicanas: Power and Control in the Domestic Sphere." *De Colores* 2/3:19-31.

————. 1982. "Mexican-American Women in the Social Sciences." *Signs: Journal of Women in Culture and Society* 8:259-72.

————. 1984. "Mexican Heritage Women: A Bibliographic Essay." *Sage Race Relations Abstracts* 9:1-12.

15. NEW BEDFORD, MASSACHUSETTS, MARCH 6, 1983—MARCH 22, 1984: THE "BEFORE AND AFTER" OF A GROUP RAPE

LYNN S. CHANCER

On March 6, 1983, a young woman went into Big Dan's in New Bedford, Massachusetts, about 9:00 p.m. for some cigarettes and a drink. She emerged several hours later, screaming and half-naked, reporting that she had been gang raped on a pool table in the middle of the still-open bar while a group of male spectators watched and cheered the others on. No one called the police.

On March 14, 1983, a crowd estimated at between 2,500 (*New York Times* 1983b) and 4,000 (New Bedford *Standard Times* 1984c) marched outside New Bedford's city hall in a candle-lit protest organized by a coalition of 12 women's groups throughout the Northeast. One placard they carried read, "Rape Is Not a Spectator Sport."

On March 22, 1984, one year later, a crowd gathered around the same spot for another silent vigil. This larger group of 6,000 to 8,000 men and women lit candles, not to protest the rape, but to protest the conviction of four of the six men who had been tried as rapists. This crowd asserted that the defendants, all of whom were Portuguese, had been victimized by ethnic prejudice. They held up signs urging, "Remember—Justice Crucified, March 17, 1984," and extended a hero's embrace to the two acquitted men who had been in the bar the night the rape occurred (New Bedford *Standard Times* 1984l).

Initially, New Bedford's sympathies seemed to be aligned behind the young woman: Outrage, horror, and sadness were expressed in the area around Big Dan's as reports of the rape circulated (*New York Times* 1983c). Yet, within the space of a year, many Portuguese residents came to feel that the social and economic prejudice they had experienced as immigrants found symbolic expression in the treatment of the "Portuguese rapists." Their anger turned against the raped woman, their sense of identification toward the defendants (*New York Times* 1984b).

This chapter focuses on two issues: (1) how and why did large numbers of people within New Bedford's Portuguese community come to place their allegiance with, or shift it onto, the rapists rather than the rape victim, and (2) in particular, how and why did many Portuguese women participate and take leading roles in the pro-defendants' movement, a stance that at first glance seems to contravene their interests as women?

RAPE THEORIES AND VICTIM BLAMING

Two theories of why rape occurs are particularly applicable to the New Bedford case because they illuminate the relationship between sexual and ethnic or class factors and the conflict that can develop between them. A classic representative of the first theory, Brownmiller's *Against Our Will: Men, Women and Rape* (1975) explains rape in terms of power exercised by men over women through sexual coercion. This power is rooted, for Brownmiller, in biology, that is, differences of physical strength. The second position assumes that the crime stems from social conflicts other than the sexual one immediately implied in the act of rape. This argument is exemplified by radical criminologists Schwendinger and Schwendinger, who contend in *Rape and Inequality* (1983) that rape is a historically specific phenomenon linked to women's relative degradation as capitalism arose. According to the Schwendingers, capitalism perpetuates not only women's oppression but ethnic and racial oppression as well, producing a culture of violence of which rape is symptomatic.

The two theories, therefore, are at odds. Brownmiller accords priority to sexual politics as an explanation of rape, whereas the Schwendingers stress ethnic, racial, and class inequities. The Schwendingers are explicit in their criticism of Brownmiller, accusing her of insufficient evidence and a tendency to universalize rape and to treat all men as a "class" of possible rapists. *Rape and Inequality* suggests that rape will wither away with capitalism's demise and the concomitant lessening of ethnic and racial prejudices upon which it feeds. Brownmiller's feminist thesis suggests that sexual relationships based in a patriarchal system of power cannot be reduced to a function of class or ethnic powerlessness. The Schwendingers, however, contend that sexual oppression alone cannot explain why a particular act of rape takes place in a given social context.

Also relevant to the New Bedford rape is attribution theory, which studies the circumstances under which victims will or will not be held responsible for crimes committed against them (Acock and Ireland 1983; Alexander 1980; Burt 1980; Williams and Holmes 1981). Insofar as it is concerned with actors' own interpretations of situations, attribution theory is tied to the social interactionist tradition (Quinney 1974).

Some attribution researchers have been sympathetic to victims, while others have blamed victims. Feminists conducting attribution research have used Lemert's (1951) concepts of primary and secondary deviation to explain the "second assault" to which women are frequently subjected by their communities after they have been raped (Williams and Holmes 1981). At the other extreme is the work of Amir, who sought to dispel the notion that rape victims play no part in their own victimization. Amir (1971) studied 646 rapes in Philadelphia and concluded that 122 (or 19 percent) were situations in which the victim "actually, or so it was deemed, agreed to sexual relations but retracted before the actual act or did not react strongly enough when the suggestion was made by the offenders" (p. 266). In his view, "victim participation" can be derived from "risky situations marred with sexuality, especially when she uses what could be interpreted as indecency in language and gestures, or constitutes what could be taken as an invitation to sexual relations" (p. 266). Amir's criteria for judging which rapes were seemingly victim-precipitated are police records and his own interpretation of supposedly provocative behavior.

The empirical findings of feminist attribution theorists about factors that increase the likelihood that people will blame rape victims are similar to the five criteria Amir (1971) used to establish which of his 646 forcible rapes he judged to be victim-precipitated. According to both Amir and feminist attribution researchers, rape victims tend to be held more responsible for their own victimization under the following circumstances: first, when they have had some prior acquaintance with their attacker, as opposed to when rape is "stranger to stranger" (Alexander 1980; Weis and Borges, 1983; Williams and Holmes 1981); second, when there is evidence of a previous bad reputation or nontraditional behavior on the part of the victim (Alexander 1980; Burt 1980; Williams and Holmes 1981); third, when a pickup took place in a bar (Williams and Holmes 1981); fourth, when alcohol was present in the situation; Amir notes that 23.8 percent of what he classified as victim-precipitated rapes took place in a bar, compared with 7.2 percent of rapes he did not consider victim-precipitated; fifth, when the rape took place in close proximity to the victim's residence (Williams and Holmes 1981). For Amir, 35 percent of his victim-precipitated cases involved drinking, as opposed to 20 percent of those he considered non-victim-precipitated. Amir also found that 86 percent of the rapes he called victim-precipitated took place close to home, compared with 67 percent of those categorized non-victim-precipitated.

Attribution researchers have also observed that victim blaming is more likely in communities with traditional sexual attitudes. Both Acock and Ireland (1983) and Burt (1980) related attitudes toward rape to general sexual beliefs. Williams and Holmes (1981) examined the way in which rape and ethnicity affect reaction to rape victims and whether a second assault is more likely to occur among some groups than others. Following 61 women treated for rape in San Antonio, Texas, who were either "White Anglo," Black, or Mexican American, Williams and Holmes found that Mexican American women had greater difficulty than Blacks or White Anglos in recovering from postrape trauma because of their community's relatively more rigid notions of gender roles. The raped woman, they discovered, was likely to be blamed not only by Mexican American men but also by other Mexican American women, whom Williams and Holmes concluded to be even harsher in their judgments of the victim. Their most important finding is that a rape victim is more likely to suffer secondary recriminations when the community or subculture of which she is a part holds traditional attitudes toward sexuality and male-female roles.

In her study of 313, mostly women, nurses in a major urban hospital, Alexander (1980) found a tendency for victims to be judged more harshly when the observer felt similarly vulnerable to possible rape. According to Alexander, the view of the rape victim as partly responsible stems from a "real world" thesis that defines justice as the rewarding of good behavior and the punishment of bad. To the extent that rape calls the maintenance of this conception into question, the observer tries to neutralize the threat by believing the victim could have controlled the situation. The more a nurse herself engaged in rule-following behavior, the more likely she was to believe the rape victim was partly responsible and to exonerate her assailant to some degree.

In the next section, I will examine whether the rape in New Bedford confirmed or denied these theories of victim-blaming. My account is based on mainstream news reports.[1] Mainstream news reporting has been accused of highlighting events rather than analysis (Gitlin 1980). In their reports of the New Bedford case, the media focused on the support of the Portuguese community for the defendants and said nothing about those (including women) who may not have felt sympathetic toward them. However, it is the phenomenon of these Portuguese men and women who were supportive of the rapists, no matter how large or small the group, that needs to be explained. There is little doubt that a substantial portion of New Bedford's Portuguese population participated in demonstrations supporting the defendants after they were convicted of rape. It is to this subgroup—and not to the entire Portuguese population of New Bedford—that I will be referring when I use the term *the community* or *the Portuguese community.*

HOW AN ETHNIC COMMUNITY CAME TO CONFUSE THE RAPISTS WITH THE RAPED

The Town

Herman Melville referred to New Bedford in *Moby Dick* as "the dearest place to live in all New England." First settled by the Portuguese in 1652, New Bedford was a thriving center of both whaling and textile manufacture in the eighteenth century. It was a well-known fishing port in the nineteenth century, but by the twentieth, whaling had died out entirely, and the textile industry had deteriorated. John Bullard, leader of a project to restore New Bedford's waterfront, dated the onset of economic depression in the town to 1928, when a textile strike occurred. Because of the eroding manufacturing base, the city never returned to a state of prosperity and has had one of the highest unemployment rates in Massachusetts (*New York Times* 1984i).

Irish and English families immigrated to New Bedford in the nineteenth century and still constitute a substantial segment of the population. The change in immigration laws in 1965, which earlier had imposed a quota against the Portuguese, was rapidly followed by so large an influx of Portuguese immigrants that their numbers swelled to nearly 60 percent of the population of New Bedford. The Portuguese, therefore, including four of the defendants central to this account, were relatively new both to New Bedford and the United States. New Bedford and neighboring Fall River were able to support several Portuguese-language newspapers and radio stations that were especially important in fostering a sense of community.

New Bedford's economy still depends on the fishing industry and local textile mills. A New Bedford family frequently has two wage earners, the wife working in a mill and the husband working on a boat fleet harvesting scallops (*New York Times* 1983b; New Bedford *Standard Times* 1984k). Many new businesses, such as furniture outlets, variety stores, and car dealerships, have been opened by Portuguese immigrants, who have also made contributions to the renovation of the downtown area through the opening of pubs, shops, and restaurants. The Portuguese also take credit for purchasing more efficient boats, which boosted the fishing industry. Despite their numerical dominance in the town, the only Portuguese official in 1983 was District Attorney Ronald Pina. Northern Europeans dominated other positions of power.

The Rape

On March 6, a 21-year-old woman of Portuguese descent (New Bedford *Standard Times* 1984q) living in a Portuguese neighborhood put her two small daughters to bed and went to Big Dan's, a local bar, to buy a pack of cigarettes. The brief description of the rape that follows is based on information from the trial, as reported in the *New York Times* (1983a, b; 1984b, c, d, f, g) and the New Bedford *Standard Times* (1984a). The jury heard many, sometimes conflicting, stories in the course of coming to the guilty verdict.

The young woman initially said she "lost count" of how many times she was raped, but later acknowledged that there were about 9 or 10 men present in the bar that night, which was corroborated by others. There was some question of the extent to which she interacted with two of the defendants, whom she knew in a casual way from living in the same area, but it was generally agreed that she had a drink at the bar while Daniel Silva, Victor Raposo, and several other men played pool in the middle of the room. At some point late in the evening, according to her testimony and that of bartender Carlos Machado, she had a verbal exchange with Silva, after which Silva and another defendant carried her across the room toward the pool table. The woman, all reports concur, screamed and sobbed. Two of the men then pulled off her pants while another two held her down. Silva raped her, and Raposo and John Cordeiro forced her to engage in oral sex. The *New York Times* reported that Jose Veira's role was "confined" mainly to tickling Mr. Silva with a straw. A few others who were in the room cheered, Machado testified, while a third pair of defendants (the unrelated Jose Medeiros and Virgilio Medeiros), stopped the bartender from calling the authorities and shouted "do it, do it." The rape went on for over two hours. After midnight, the woman ran out of the bar, was picked up by a passerby, and proceeded to call the police.

The story of the rape—with, as first reported, its extraordinary and horrifying imagery of a bar packed with cheering men as a woman was raped "countless times" on a pool table—rapidly spread through New Bedford and made its way into local and then national news. The community's initial reaction appeared universally to be one of shock and outrage. In the area around Big Dan's, one man spoke about what he would do to anyone who ever tried something similar with *his* daughter. Another, who identified himself as Portuguese, thought every man who cheered ought to be fined $1,000 and the money given to a program that would help rape victims. The rape sparked a heightened awareness of sexual violence toward women in New Bedford, and a

$68,000 grant from the city permitted a 24-hour, decently staffed Rape Crisis Project to open (*New York Times* 1983b). In the immediate aftermath of the rape, a coalition of women's groups marched through the streets of New Bedford.

Nevertheless, as we shall see, this initially sympathetic response within the Portuguese community toward the raped woman was short-lived and slowly was replaced by increasing hostility. The findings of the attribution theorists about commonly held attitudes toward rape are supported by the assignment of some degree of responsibility to the raped woman. The New Bedford case is a classic example of what attribution researchers have called a victim perceived as "illegitimate" (Holmstrom and Burgess 1978) and what Amir called "victim-precipitated" rape.

Returning to five of Amir's criteria for victim precipitation, which feminist attribution theorists also find to be associated frequently with victim-blaming, the young woman in the New Bedford case was casually acquainted with several of the men who attacked her; she lived in the neighborhood; she was attacked in a bar where, of course, alcohol was present; and, according to the mores of the traditional Portuguese community, she was engaging in nontraditional behavior by leaving her children and going to a drinking place alone at night. However, while these victim characteristics might create a tendency toward the attribution of blame, they do not explain the extreme hostility to which the young woman was subjected more and more in the year following the rape as she brought the rapists to trial. This extremity differentiates the New Bedford case from those studied in the literature on rape. Nor can the characteristics of the victim explain why the rapists came to be defended. Even if victims are blamed for provoking the rape, the rapists are usually believed guilty and punishable. Fundamental to the difference between the New Bedford and other rape cases was the combination of ethnic and sexual prejudice, which then came to be magnified by the media.

The Media Reports and Community Response

Subtle by-products of the rape started to nag at the minds of people within the Portuguese community as the case gained notoriety. Radio broadcasters and news media kept referring to the "Portuguese rapists." *Hustler* magazine, combining sexism with an ethnic slur, printed a post-card of a nude woman waving from a pool table that was captioned, "Greetings from New Bedford, Massachusetts, the Portuguese Gang-Rape Capital of America" (*Hustler* 1983b, p. 21). Ronald Pina, the New

Bedford district attorney prosecuting the case, criticized the terminology, saying, "When was the last time you ever heard of an Irish rapist?" (New Bedford *Standard Times* 1984d). A local radio station received calls demanding that all Portuguese be shipped back to Europe, and two of the defendants actually did face possible deportation. The station aired the opinions of those who thought the rapists should be castrated or given the death penalty (*The New York Times* 1984a).

Members of the Portuguese community reacted defensively. In a brief period of time, a potential for identification between the defendants and the community was forged because of their common vulnerability to these recurrences of anti-Portuguese discrimination in New Bedford. In time, defense of the Portuguese rapists became inseparable from defense of the Portuguese community.

The anti-Portuguese slurs that appeared after the rape led to the formation of two defense committees, the Committee for Justice and the Portuguese American Defense League. Spokespersons and founders of the Committee for Justice included two women, Emily Sedgwick and Alda Melo, while the Portuguese American Defense League was started by, among others, Raymond and Katherine Castro, publishers of the Portuguese newspaper *O Jornal* (*New York Times* 1984d, i; New Bedford *Standard Times* 1984k). Both groups sought to ensure the defendants a fair trial and voiced their objections to anti-Portuguese statements. One of the Committee for Justice's first acts was raising about $20,000 in bail, which helped to procure the release of four of the defendants.[2]

Despite the committees, sympathy for and identification with the defendants did not yet extend beyond a vocal fraction of the Portuguese population of New Bedford and Fall River. As time elapsed, however, these feelings became more general and more entrenched. In addition to the surfacing of ethnic prejudice, the economic price of the bad publicity exacerbated hostilities. Big Dan's closed down and was replaced by a discount bakery. At a bar across the street, the owner complained that he had had to sacrifice thousands of dollars in business from customers too frightened to come to his establishment. Similar fears about financial losses and hurt job prospects due to bad publicity were echoed by other residents, contrasting painfully with the pride the Portuguese community took in its recent economic achievements.

Empathy for the defendants grew, too, in a perverse dialectical relationship with the main architect of bad publicity—the media. Journalists and cable television crews prepared to descend on New Bedford for the trial—the first criminal case in American history to be nationally televised (*New York Times* 1984e, i). At the M & C restaurant, near Big

Dan's, a sign was posted urging, "Please—no reporters in for interviews" (*New York Times* 1984d; New Bedford *Standard Times* 1984h).

Community Reaction to the Trial

The barrage of exposure peaked with the opening of the trial on February 24, 1984. From that point on, virtually every newspaper on the East Coast carried developments in the case on an almost daily basis. The trial was covered on network news stations as well as on the local cable program that broadcast it live. During the four weeks of the trial, most publications printed details of each witness's lengthy testimony. The victim was on the stand for fifteen hours. Myriad stories centered around the packed-to-capacity courtroom or the various groups monitoring the proceedings for fairness. Women's groups attended the trial to ensure against sexist treatment of the rape victim, while representatives from the Committee for Justice watched for signs of anti-Portuguese bias (*New York Times* 1984h, i).

Photos showed four of the defendants wearing headphones to hear the trial translated from English to Portuguese. Other articles concentrated on the Portuguese neighborhood in which the rape had occurred. New Bedford residents were reminded again and again of anti-Portuguese discrimination.

The bars and restaurants of the town were crowded with people gathered to watch "the spectacle" of their neighbors on TV (*New York Times* 1984i). One person in the area around Big Dan's remarked disgustedly, "It stinks," as he watched the trial; another walked away from the screen complaining that the trial cost too much in tax dollars (New Bedford *Standard Times* 1984e). One letter to the editor of the *Standard Times* begged the press to cease their coverage, stating that it reflected badly on New Bedford (New Bedford *Standard Times* 1984b); another bemoaned the paper devoting so much space to "garbage" like the rape case (New Bedford *Standard Times* 1984f).

By the time the trial drew to a close, collective hurt and defensiveness turned into anger at the press, and then at the rape victim without whom the problem would never have arisen. The Portuguese community began to feel that it, not the woman, had been raped, and as if the woman, not the Portuguese, were the rapist. One of the defense lawyers, Judith Lindahl, stated in court that the girl had been "willing," that she had encouraged the men's advances (New Bedford *Standard Times* 1984g). She argued that even if they had raped the young woman, rape was a common crime in America, so why had the Portuguese men been singled out as the focus of a nationally publicized trial?

The closeness of much of New Bedford's Portuguese community also fostered minimization of the rape and defense of the rapists. Many people had been neighbors for years. It was difficult for them to believe that six boys they had known from childhood had committed a serious crime. One resident, Mrs. Carreiro, said that she might have felt differently about the rape if it had happened in California. As it was, she knew the men and was convinced that they must have been provoked (New Bedford *Standard Times* 1984e, g). Carol Maciel and Victor Raposo had been dating since she was 14, and she continued to stand by him. Danny Silva's heart condition evoked sympathy. As one man put it, "Hey, what hurts me is that Danny Silva was in here last night and he said, 'I don't know when I'm going to see you again' " (New Bedford *Standard Times* 1984h, o). Collective indignation emerged, suggesting that in close-knit communities, it may be the attributer's rather than the victim's past acquaintance with the rapists that contributes to the shifting of responsibility.

On March 17, 1984, two of the defendants, Daniel Silva and Jose Vieira, were found guilty. Outside the courtroom after the verdict, several of the defendants' supporters shouted and cursed; others cried. A few threatened news reporters with violence, and Vieira's father swung with a cane at a free-lance television camerawoman (New Bedford *Standard Times* 1984h). As Silva and Vieira were led to a van, a waiting crowd cheered, and someone yelled, "Why wasn't she home with her kids?" Another shouted, "Why don't they bring the girl out in handcuffs? Get her, too!" (New Bedford *Standard Times* 1984h).

Responses in local Portuguese neighborhoods included, "I hope the Portuguese get together and do a number on this city." The decision was called a "bum deal." One man suggested that "Portuguese Power" buttons, which hadn't sold several years earlier, should now be marketed. Outrage even reverberated beyond New Bedford's borders, in Portugal itself. The story of Silva and Vieira's convictions received front-page coverage in the *Diario de Noticas,* a state-funded but independent daily; it was mentioned in most other major Lisbon papers as well. A follow-up editorial in *Diario de Noticas* reiterated charges of anti-Portuguese prejudice in the "hardworking Portuguese colony of Massachusetts," stating that "in a country where indecent assaults occur every 20 minutes . . . would there have been such a wave of indignation if the people involved had not belonged to an ethnic minority?" (as reported in the New Bedford *Standard Times* 1984k).

Decisions on the other four defendants were not handed down until five days later. In the time between the two decisions, District Attorney Pina and several jurors received threats against their lives and were given increased police protection. The sister and nephew of the rape victim felt they had no choice to but to leave New Bedford permanentl (New Bedford *Standard Times* 1984h, k). On a local radio station, caller referred to the rape victim by name, calling her "dead meat" (Nev Bedford *Standard Times* 1984 h, i). The New Bedford case had come full circle. Portuguese residents, originally the objects of publicly broadcast calls of hate, were now placing similar calls themselves.

On March 23, 1984, the *Standard Times* reported: "Split Verdict: Guilty, 2 Freed." Two of the remaining defendants, Victor Raposo and John Cordeiro, had been convicted the previous day of aggravated rape, while the jury had concluded that the evidence against Jose Medeiros and Virgilio Medeiros was insufficient to merit punishment. As Raposo walked to the sheriff's van, he shouted. "You call this justice? This ain't no justice. We're Portuguese. That's why we're found guilty" (New Bedford *Standard Times* 1984i, e). Virgilio Medeiros ran from the courthouse into a throng of cheering supporters. When asked if a rape had occurred in Big Dan's a year earlier, he said, "No . . . never . . . no" (New Bedford *Standard Times* 1984l).

The Committee for Justice and the Portuguese American Defense League organized a candle-lit protest. The victim was no longer the raped woman; the victims were the defendants and the Portuguese community. The police estimated the crowd in attendance to be about 6,000; Antonio Cabral, President of Portuguese Americans United, believed it was closer to 8,000 (New Bedford *Standard Times* 1984l). At the rally, Medeiros was hoisted into the air by marchers, some of whom carried "Justice Crucified" signs. The defendants were said to have been convicted on flimsy evidence; there were comments about the jury taking only five hours to reach a verdict on Silva and Vieira. Many women attended the March 22 vigil. A poster carried by a group of women read, "Boston Women Say Railroading Portuguese Men Won't Fight Rape." The *Standard Times* wrote of "grandmothers and babes in arms," and noted that women who rarely went to demonstrations were present to show pride in their Portuguese heritage. Delores Medeiros (not necessarily related to either Virgilio or Jose, since Medeiros is a common Portuguese name) spoke of the unfairness of the convictions, and Carol Maciel, Raposo's fiancée, walked at the front of the crowd so that Victor could see her. "An injustice was done," she said (New Bedford *Standard Times* 1984m).

On Friday afternoon, March 23, a larger crowd gathered outside the Fall River Superior Courthouse. The police and *Standard Times* reporter Arthur Hirsch put attendance at about 10,000 to 15,000—the Portuguese defense groups claimed a larger number. The procession was led by Jose Medeiros and Virgilio Medeiros who received, according to Hirsch, "a hero's welcome" (New Bedford *Standard Times* 1984m). Once again, women were well-represented, and some bitterly and coldly criticized the young woman who had been raped. Catherine Gabe, interviewing women marchers, quoted Virginia Faria of New Bedford expounding a variation of the "just world" theme: "I am Portuguese and proud of it. I'm also a woman, but you don't see me getting raped. If you throw a dog a bone, he's gonna take it—if you walk around naked, men are just going to go for you" (New Bedford *Standard Times* 1984m). Another woman commented, "Rape is a crime but not when a girl walks in and puts her arms around Victor, and starts kissing him." Another woman, Alda Machado of Fall River, said, "They did nothing to her. Her rights are to be home with her two kids and to be a good mother. A Portuguese woman should be with her kids and that's it" (New Bedford *Standard Times* 1984m). Ann Botelho said, "She should get punished, too. If they raped her, she was the aggravator. I'm sorry to say it but I think it was her." Two hundred of Botelho's co-workers had been allowed to walk off their jobs at Rondo Sportswear in Fall River to attend the rally. "The only ones who stayed," said Botelho, "were just the ones on that girl's side and that wasn't many."

On Monday, March 26, 1984, the four convicted rapists were sent to prison. That morning, Chief Court Officer Peter Cordeiro said that Judge William Young had received petitions signed by 16,000 people asking for leniency for the men (New Bedford *Standard Times* 1984h). The sentences, from 9 to 12 years each, with probation available to two of the defendants in 4 years, were considered harsh by supporters. After serving their sentences, Vieira and Raposo would face possible, albeit unlikely, deportation (New Bedford *Standard Times* 1984n, p). About 600 people watched as the men were taken away.

As her sister and nephew had done before her, the young woman who had been raped in Big Dan's moved to Miami from New Bedford shortly after the second set of verdicts. Her lawyer noted that her testimony had resulted not in four but in five verdicts. She, too, had been convicted—her sentence, exile.

The Role of the Media

The Portuguese heritage of the rape victim was seldom, or only casually, mentioned in media accounts of the New Bedford rape. The media's omission resulted from playing up events without analysis of their context (Altheide 1976; Epstein 1975; Gitlin 1980). In this case, newspaper and television reports first featured feminist demonstrations and ignored the ethnic issue that was eventually used against the victim. Later, the media reported on the demonstrations by the Portuguese community without reference to the victim's Portuguese heritage, mirroring the community's own disinterest. Had the victim's ethnic background been part of the media's story, the community would have been hard-pressed to focus on ethnic discrimination to defend the rapists, and Portuguese women might not have had to choose between identification with the victim as a woman and identification with the rapists as Portuguese.

The media also played a role in arousing people's sensitivities simply by their saturation of the case. People in the community often responded defensively as much to media reports as to actual events. The media spotlight contributed both to the sexual and ethnic conflict, and to the creation of still another motivation for blaming the victim; it was much easier to attack her than the amorphous "media." Yet, although the media played a significant part in inflaming negative feelings toward the rape victim, antagonism would probably have emerged in any event because of the symbolic sexual threat the young woman posed to the community's traditional values.

SEXUALITY AND ETHNICITY

Men and women in the community became angry at the young woman not only because of the consequences of her rape, which included anti-Portuguese feeling and unwelcome media coverage, but also because of the rape itself. They were incensed at the young woman for having "let herself" be raped—for having been in a bar, a sexual object of "temptation" to the male customers that night, and for drinking and smoking in men's territory instead of remaining properly at home with her children. The Portuguese community's defense of the Portuguese rapists rather than the Portuguese rape victim is partly explicable in terms of this sexual and gender ideology.

For any young woman to have gone into a bar one night and emerge several hours later to walk home safely by herself may have implied that it was appropriate for a woman to leave her children at home for a few hours to go and have a drink, that being a single woman in a bar was no more unusual than being a single man in a bar, and that there was nothing objectionable about casual flirting. In short, such a scenario presumes the existence of sexual freedom and equality for women, and a cultural community that accepts such independence.

Although sexual freedom was theoretically possible within the Portuguese community, since most women who enter bars in Portuguese neighborhoods are not raped, it was hardly encouraged. Portuguese families in New Bedford are typically organized along traditional lines with conventionally asymmetric roles for men and women. Although both women and men are commonly wage earners, women work to bolster the family's income and still bear primary responsibility for child care and housework. Although sexual mores may be changing in younger people, women are still generally expected to confine sexual activity to the legitimate channels of marriage (Rosen 1985).

A *Standard Times* letter to the editor depicted the New Bedford rape as the product of a clash between cultures. The author, offering an example of Thorsten Sellin's cultural conflict theory of deviance, stated that "had the men stayed in the Azores, a woman would most probably not have gone amongst them in a bar," and the rape would never have occurred. It is dangerous, the man continued, to isolate oneself from the reality of "living in another and very different land" (Letter to the Editor, New Bedford *Standard Times* 1984j). The young woman who walked into Big Dan's that night was not "Portuguese" insofar as she was deviating from the approved values of the community. Since she was not a "good" woman who followed legitimized rules but a "whore," the Portuguese community symbolically excommunicated her by acting as though her common heritage with them did not exist. She was seen as deserving of punishment for having transgressed sexual standards. The New Bedford case, therefore, confirms Williams and Holmes's expectation that a second assault upon rape victims will be particularly harsh if the community of which they are a part insists upon traditional notions of sexuality and gender roles (Williams and Holmes 1981).

However, while Williams and Holmes found victim blaming to be most severe in the traditional Mexican American community, it nevertheless characterized the Black and White Anglo communities as well. Similarly, while the Portuguese community was traditional, its notions about rape are not at odds with American culture—in this sense, the community was quite correct in wondering why it was being singled out. To deny the generality of sexist ideology surrounding rape, as if it were confined to the Portuguese, is indeed, ironically enough, to discriminate on the basis of ethnicity. In fact, a few months prior to the New Bedford rape, *Hustler* magazine ran an article in which a waitress in a bar was gang-raped on a pool table and exploded in multiple orgasms (*Hustler* 1983a). Whether or not the men in New Bedford actually read the article, it is clear that the same violent culture produced both events.

But this does not explain the community's defense of the rapists, because protesting ethnic discrimination and applauding the defendants were separable issues. That the two were conflated can only be explained with reference to gender rather than *ethnic* prejudice—here, the sexist treatment that uniquely surrounds the criminal prosecution of rape. Had the New Bedford case involved a murder, for example, the brutal slaying of a man in a bar by six Portuguese men, it might have been much more difficult for the community to neutralize the defendants' crime by focusing on anti-Portuguese discrimination. People might not have believed that the victim provoked his or her own murder, robbery, or mugging. Only with assaults associated with sex does a widespread blame-the-victim mentality facilitate defense of the perpetrators in societies dominated by men. In the case of Robert Chambers, charged with slaying 18-year-old Jennifer Levin in Central Park following "violent sex," Levin's diary was subpoenaed by Chambers' attorney, Jack Litman, in order to demonstrate that she had previously been sexually active (*New York Times,* 1987). Litman also defended Richard Herrin, the Yale graduate who murdered his college girlfriend, Bonnie Garland, and employed the similar strategy of showing "provocative" behavior, that is, the old arguments of "victim precipitation."

Transgression of sexual values was a critical factor in the angry responses evoked by the New Bedford rape; however, responses were different for men and women. For traditional Portuguese men, the young woman, by living some vague approximation of sexual liberation, represented a threat to their remaining stronghold of power, the family. Feelings of devastation or inferiority stemming from ethnic prejudice, as the Schwendingers (1983) and Williams and Holmes (1981) point out, amount to one form of powerlessness; greater freedom for women could conceivably create another. Community antagonism toward the rape victim and support of the rapists symbolizes a kind of social control similar to dominant men punishing transgressing women by deliberate rape (Brownmiller 1975).

Alignment with the rapists also cast the women of the community into the role of social control agents, despite the fact that, for them, the rape was simultaneously an act committed by a member of a subordinate group that has experienced prejudice—the Portuguese—and an act committed against a member of an even more subordinate group— women. Women who were active in the pro-defendants movement might have responded to the ethnic but not the sexual subordination of the two groups to which they simultaneously belonged. Anti-Portuguese prejudice was commonly recognized and accepted by the community as a whole, but sexual oppression was not. For the women as well as the men in the community, ethnic loyalty was legitimate and built into the fabric of daily understanding. Feminist loyalties, based on a sense of sexual oppression, were not.

Many of the women may have had marriages and relationships they found satisfying and apparently equal, if separate, divisions of labor; some women shared in running the civic and economic affairs of the community. For these women, the rape victim also posed a symbolic threat, since she called into question a particular life-style—the roles adopted and the rules followed by the average woman in her daily life. For those women who may have perceived themselves as oppressed, the rape victim's symbolic import was to call that very life-style into question without offering any practical alternative.

Women could at least feel secure in their Portuguese community, where they had homes and jobs. For Carol Maciel, Victor Raposo's girlfriend, to support the rape victim would have meant recognizing that a man she had known since she was 14 could conceivably turn against *her*. For Mrs. Carreiro, acquainted with "these boys" and maybe with other men who had been in the bar, to start thinking of her male neighbors as adversaries might imply that there really were no rewards for adhering to the "good woman" role of wife and mother. If their roles were demeaned, or the rules supporting them loosened, women who had followed them would feel obsolete, as if they, too, had been demeaned and the significance of their existence called into question. Their belief in a "just world" was at stake. Finally, to defend the rape victim would have pitted them against the men in the community, on whose love and economic and social support the women depended.

Given the anxiety the rape victim may have provoked, both literally and figuratively, the anger of the Portuguese women may have been even greater than that felt by the men. Whereas both had parallel sources of anger—ethnic prejudice and aspersions cast upon a way of life in which each had vested interests—only the women could have reacted on the basis of a third motivation. Unlike the men, the women had to repress any sense that they, too, might be in danger of being raped by men whom they knew; that they, too, might potentially, or maybe even had been, victimized by other forms of sexual violence such as battering; that they, too, were constrained in their assertions of independence; or simply that they might have silent, gnawing discontents about some part of their own lives as mothers, daughters, and wives. The women would have had to repress any such doubts or face the uncomfortable realities that might have been exposed had they identified with the raped woman. If the rape victim had not represented something the women in the community sensed they had to fight, their response against her might not have been so vehement. By virtue of this reaction formation, it may not have been enough for the Portuguese women to remain neutral. They had to prove that they were at least as much as, if not more, anti-rape victim than the men, by aligning themselves with their dominant group. Thus they not only participated in, but were in the forefront of, the pro-defendant movement.[3]

CONCLUSION

The events in New Bedford suggest a need for feminist community organizations to be consciously oriented toward a multiple- rather than a one-issue vision. The crisis center formed in the immediate aftermath of the rape served a crucial function but could not assuage broader fears about feminism exacerbated by the catalyzing incident. Had a prior feminist presence reached deeply into the everyday life of the community, the reaction to the rape might have been more sympathetic toward the victim. A community feminist center and outreach program formed before the crisis event might have been able to defuse the anti-feminist, pro-ethnic demonstrations. Women who were trusted in the Portuguese community, and who had some familiarity with the feminist perspective on rape, might have been able to prevent a second assault upon the raped woman. They also might have been able to rally the community in such a way that it would have been possible for ethnic prejudice to be protested without in any way condoning the act of rape.

That instead a sizable number of New Bedford's Portuguese population came, in the short space of a year, to support the perpetrators rather than the victim of a gang rape suggests that subordinate groups that have suffered from an invidious legacy of prejudice may tend to deny wrongdoings committed by their members. This tendency is produced by a structural dilemma in which discriminated-against groups rightly perceive themselves to be caught. If a subordinate group admits that one of its members has done something both it and the dominant culture agrees to be wrong and criminal, there is a fear that negative stereotypes will be reinforced. To the Portuguese community of New Bedford, to proclaim the culpability of the rapists was to indict the entire group and prove that prejudices about immigrants were justified. Thus, returning to the theoretical position taken by the Schwendingers with regard to rape, New Bedford does exemplify the way in which ethnic (or, by extension, racial) oppression can exacerbate, not so much rape itself, but hostile community reaction to it. This analysis suggests that a community's reaction might not be as extreme if a past history of ethnic tension, and media magnification of that tension, did not exist.

The attribution theory literature suggests that victim-blaming would have occurred in any event, even if to a lesser degree, because of commonly held sexist attitudes toward the circumstances under which the rape occurred. The New Bedford case is a particularly poignant rebuttal to the Schwendingers' theory of rape as a function of capitalism, racism, or ethnicity. Their position cannot theoretically explain why the community responded to the Portuguese heritage of the rapists but *not* the Portuguese heritage of the rape victim. In New Bedford, ethnicity can be canceled out on both sides of the equation, leaving little doubt that sexual politics played a fundamental role in the unfolding of the case as well as in the community's response. One is left to surmise that Brownmiller's theory of rape as exercise of sexual power is, at the very least, a necessary if not sufficient explanation of the New Bedford case.

Given the complexities of the ethnic and sexual resentments her rape had generated, the woman who was raped in New Bedford deserves great admiration for having had the courage to prosecute her assailants. In doing so, she shifted responsibility and blame back to the rapists, where they properly belong.

CODA

After having researched and written this article, I was greatly saddened to read in the *New York Times*, December 18, 1986, that Cheryl Araujo, 25, died in a car accident south of Miami, Florida. Ms. Araujo was the "young woman" who was raped in New Bedford.

NOTES

1. The account of developments in New Bedford between 1983 and 1984 is based upon all *New York Times* articles written on the case in 1983 and 1984, all New Bedford *Standard Times* pieces in February, March, and April of 1984, articles in *Time* and *Newsweek,* and a well-researched article by Rosen (1985).

2. The exact amount of bail raised and the number of defendants released were inconsistently reported by the *New York Times* (1983a, b).

3. This psychological analysis may also explain why the Mexican American women studied by Williams and Holmes (1981) were sometimes even more blaming of the rape victim than Mexican American men.

REFERENCES

Acock, A. C., and N. K. Ireland. 1983. "Attribution of Blame in Rape Cases: The Impact of Norm Violation, Gender, and Sex Role Attitudes." *Sex Roles* 9:179-93.

Alexander, C. 1980. "The Responsible Victim: Nurses' Perceptions of Victims of Rape." *Journal of Health and Social Behavior* 21:22-33.

Altheide, D. L. 1976. *Creating Reality: How TV News Distorts Events.* Beverly Hills, CA: Sage.

Amir, M. 1971. *Patterns in Forcible Rape.* Chicago: University of Chicago Press.

Brownmiller, S. 1975. *Against Our Will: Men, Women and Rape.* New York: Simon & Schuster.

Burt, M. R. 1980. "Cultural Myths and Supports for Rape." *Journal of Personality and Social Psychology* 38:217-30.

Epstein, E. J. 1975. *Between Fact and Fiction: The Problem of Journalism.* New York: Vintage.

Gitlin, T. 1980. *The Whole World Is Watching: Mass Media in the Making and Unmaking of the New Left.* Berkeley: University of California.

Holmstrom, L. L., and A. W. Burgess. 1978. *The Victim of Rape: Institutional Reactions.* New York: Wiley-Interscience.

Hustler, 1983a. "Dirty Pool." (January).

———. 1983b. Photograph. (August).

Lemert, E. M. 1951. *Social Pathology.* New York: McGraw-Hill.

New Bedford *Standard Times.* 1984a. "Bartender Tells His Story." (March 1).

———. 1984b. "In Their Own Words." (March 4).

———. 1984c. "Rape Trials Rigged Against Woman." (March 5).

———. 1984d. "I've Seen Devils, Bartender Admits." (March 6).

———. 1984e. "Woman Was Outraged." (March 7).

———. 1984f. "Defendant Threatened Bartender." (March 9).

———. 1984g. "Defendant: She Was Willing." (March 15).

———. 1984h. "Verdict: 2 Guilty of Rape." (March 18).

———. 1984i. "Jury Security Tightened." (March 19).

———. 1984j. "Portuguese Plan Marches." (March 20).

———. 1984k. "Candlelight Vigil to Dramatize Immigrants Inner Struggles." (March 22).

———. 1984l. "Split Verdict; 2 Guilty, 2 Innocent." (March 23).

———. 1984m. "10,000 Fill the Streets, Press Blasted for Publicity." (March 24).

———. 1984n. "Four Sent to Prison." (March 26).

———. 1984o. "Crowd Hurls Death Threats at DA." (March 27).

———. 1984p. "Harassment Forced Victim to Move." (March 29).

———. 1984q. "Court Officers Recall Trial." (April 1).

New York Times. 1983a. "Woman's Rape in a Bar Enrages New Bedford." (March 11).

———. 1983b. "Barroom Rape Shames Town of Proud Heritage." (March 17).

———. 1983c. "Six Plead Not Guilty in Rape at Barroom." (March 18).

———. 1983d. "2 Accused in Barroom Rape Released on Bail." (March 19).

———. 1984a. "Trial of Six Starts Today in Pool Table Rape in Massachusetts." (February 6).

———. 1984b. "Court in New Bedford Rape Hears Woman's Testimony." (February 25).

———. 1984c. "Reports to Police Questioned in New Bedford Rape Trials." (February 28).

———. 1984d. "Bartender Testifying in Rape Case Says He Sensed Trouble at Tavern." (March 3).

———. 1984e. "Rape Trial Keeps Massachusetts Area on an Emotional Edge." (March 4).

———. 1984f. "Witness Continues to Verify Account of Barroom Rape." (March 6).

———. 1984g. "Barroom Rape Trial Hears of Failed Call." (March 8).

———. 1984h. "Rape Trial Is Monitored by a Woman's Coalition." (March 9).

———. 1984i. "Portuguese Immigrants Fear Rape Case May Set Back Gains." (March 17).

———. 1986. "Victim in Noted Rape Case in Automobile Accident." (December 18).

———. 1987. "Judge Rules Out Using Victim's Diary in Trial." (January 29).

Quinney, R. 1974. *Critique of Legal Order: Crime Control in Capitalist Society.* Boston: Little, Brown.

Rosen, E. 1985. "The New Bedford Rape Trial." *Dissent* 32:207-11.

Schwendinger, J. R., and H. Schwendinger. 1983. *Rape and Inequality.* Beverly Hills, CA: Sage.

Weis, K., and S. Borges. 1973. "Victimology and Rape: The Case of the Legitimate Victim." *Issues in Criminology* 8:71-115.

Williams, J. E., and Karen A. Holmes. 1981. *The Second Assault: Rape and Public Attitudes.* Westport, CT: Greenwood.

VI.

Deconstructing Gender

What would it take to make women and men truly equal? Women's work in social reproduction (bearing, caring for, and socializing children) is indispensable in all societies, yet women's status varies, depending on the extent to which having and raising children is valued and caring for small children also allows women to participate in economic production. In general, the more women contribute to economic production, the higher their social status. The other aspect of production that affects the status of women is whether they have control over the distribution of surplus they produce.

Given these principles, the question of gender equality and its attainment differs enormously from society to society, with economic production a major structural variable in determining the status of women. In societies where women are major economic producers and also control the sale of the surplus, as in sub-Saharan Africa, they have a high status. But if Eurocentric ideas that men should be the main breadwinners are adopted, there is a danger that women's position in these societies will erode.

In the patriarchal societies in the Middle East and Asia, upper-class women are virtually forbidden from engaging in economic activities, and poor women's work is at a subsistence level. Their work is needed to feed a family, but does not improve their social status because land and other means of production are held by a small group—upper-class men. For such societies, revolution may erode the basis for upper-class men's domination and improve the material status of the poor, both women and men. However, patriarchal ideas about women's proper place may still prevail (Stacey 1983).

In societies undergoing industrial development where upper-class men continue to own the means of production, such as in Central or South America, the availability of paid employment may enable women to contribute to the family economy, but they are likely to be paid less than men, and their relative position will still be one of inequality (Benería and Roldán 1987). Migration may improve women's immediate status within the family, but as material well-being improves,

women are again relegated to a secondary position in claims ove
economic resources (Glenn 1986).

In postindustrial societies in Europe or the North American continen
where women seem to have achieved the greatest equality, continue
racial and gender discrimination stratify men and women, with wome
of color in the most disadvantageous economic position (Hooks 1984
Gender equality in these societies is closely tied to racial equality an
a more egalitarian economic structure.

The second major variable that constructs gender inequality is men'
and women's differential involvement in procreation. In human soc
eties, control over sexuality, fertility, and child care is not dictated b
biology, but by cultural values and political power (O'Brien 1981; Paig
and Paige 1981; Rothman 1989). Where women have a central posi
tion in a society, they are valued as mothers, and when their daughter
psychologically identify with them, they develop strong personalitie
(Chodorow 1974). In Western industrialized societies, where men ar
dominant and women's main role is mothering, daughters grow u
needing relationships to be psychologically whole, while sons develo
independent, assertive egos (Chodorow 1978).

Although gendered personality structure may make it difficult fo
individuals to break out of prescribed roles, to a great extent, the worl
and family structure of a society prescribes those roles in the first place
Because men are supposed to be the breadwinners, work organization
pay them higher wages and discourage mothers from working. It i
therefore not surprising that even in dual-career marriages, when chil
dren come, men increase their work time to make more money, an
women cut down their work time to engage in child care (Hertz 1986)
Women's lesser earning capacity means that they contribute less to th
family income, and thus their status becomes that of "junior partner."
Their work in child care, emotional sustenance, and housework, since
it is not paid, becomes virtually invisible and thus does not give them
equal status.

Achieving gender equality for women who seem to have all the
advantages means restructuring both work organizations and family life
to make it easier to divide economic and family responsibilities more
equally between spouses. However, single parents and working-class
women and men also need the opportunity for career advancement and
family life. The practical solutions, shared child care and shared economic resources, were offered by the Israeli kibbutz movement. Yet, as
Judith Buber Agassi shows in Chapter 16, "Theories of Gender Equality: Lessons from the Israeli Kibbutz," the practice fell short of the
theory because gender equality was not a priority. In the major ways

that such equality could have been achieved—encouragement of women to engage in the most valued productive work and in important political decisions, and allocation of men to child-care work—the kibbutz movement failed.

In any society, religion helps to construct and also legitimate the social positions of women and men (Sanday 1981). The Catholic Church, the dominant religion in many countries, venerates women, but constructs their roles on a biological basis. Sexuality and procreation are defined physiologically, except for the Virgin Mary, the only woman to transcend the body. This definition of womanhood then justifies their exclusion from the priesthood and from ecclesiastic power. Susan A. Farrell, in Chapter 17, " 'It's Our Church, Too!' Women's Position in the Catholic Church Today," discusses the ways Catholic feminist ethicists are redefining women's roles and challenging the power of the male Church leaders in an attempt to gain religious gender equality.

Ideally, to achieve true gender equality, there would have to be social structural changes in psychological development, sexual dominance, economic and cultural production, and parenting (Chafetz 1990). That would necessitate what Hartsock (1983, pp. 231-51) calls a "feminist historical materialism," envisioning changes in parenting, in sexual scripting, and in the division of labor in the marketplace and the family. But before such a revolution can even be imagined, gender as a social construct needs to be dismantled—if not in practice, at least in theory. In Chapter 18, "Dismantling Noah's Ark," Judith Lorber asks for a thought experiment—to imagine a social order without gender as a major building block. In such a society, women and men would be sorted into jobs randomly or on the basis of choices that had not been patterned by gender expectations. Pay scales would be based on what everyone needs to live a decent life. Kinship would be redefined and care of children would be shared among all adult kin. Each woman would decide whether and how many children she would have. Every adult's and every child's sexuality would celebrate people doing a variety of things and thinking a variety of thoughts. Political power would be a prerogative of all responsible people.

The rest of the thought experiment is up to you—to imagine how gender could be deconstructed and what it would be like to live in a world where you did not constantly "do gender."

REFERENCES

Benería, L., and M. Roldán. 1987. *The Crossroads of Class and Gender: Industrial Homework, Subcontracting, and Household Dynamics in Mexico City.* Chicago: University of Chicago Press.

Chafetz, J. Saltzman. 1990. *Gender Equity.* Newbury Park, CA: Sage.

Chodorow, N. 1974. "Family Structure and Feminine Personality." Pp. 43-66 in *Woman, Culture and Society,* edited by M. Z. Rosaldo and L. Lamphere. Stanford, CA: Stanford University Press.

———. 1978. *The Reproduction of Mothering.* Berkeley: University of California Press.

Glenn, E. Nakano. 1986. *Issei, Nisei, War Bride.* Philadelphia: Temple University Press.

Hartsock, N.C.M. 1983. *Money, Sex, and Power: Toward a Feminist Historical Materialism.* New York: Longman.

Hertz, R. 1986. *More Equal Than Others: Women and Men in Dual-Career Marriages.* Berkeley: University of California Press.

Hooks, B. 1984. *Feminist Theory: From Margin to Center.* Boston: South End Press.

O'Brien, M. 1981. *The Politics of Reproduction.* New York: Routledge and Kegan Paul.

Paige, K. Ericksen, and J. M. Paige. 1981. *The Politics of Reproductive Ritual.* Berkeley: University of California Press.

Rothman, B. Katz. 1989. *Recreating Motherhood.* New York: Norton.

Sanday, P. Reeves. 1981. *Female Power and Male Dominance: On the Origins of Sexual Inequality.* Cambridge: Cambridge University Press.

Stacey, J. 1983. *Patriarchy and Socialist Revolution in China.* Berkeley: California University Press.

16. THEORIES OF GENDER EQUALITY: LESSONS FROM THE ISRAELI KIBBUTZ

JUDITH BUBER AGASSI

The Israeli kibbutz has been viewed as a valid test case for a wide array of social science theories because it differs from nearly all modern industrial societies in its communal arrangements of ownership, division of labor, organization of work, consumption, infant and child care, and education. Although the number of people living in Israel in kibbutzim is relatively small—about 100,000—it appears to be more visible than nearly all other forms of small alternative societies, usually known as communes. Israeli kibbutzim have maintained their basic structures of shared work, both domestic and productive, shared child care, and pooled economic resources for three generations.

Although the kibbutz has been considered a test case for clusters of theories ranging from Freudian infant psychology to the sociology of work organizations, perhaps the most prominent are theories of gender roles and gender stratification. One collection of essays (Palgi et al. 1983) on the kibbutz as a test case for theories of gender equality offers an integration of different views. What is still needed is the systematic presentation and evaluation of the full array of theories of gender stratification for which the kibbutz experience has been claimed to stand as a test case—or for which, by any stretch of the imagination, this could be claimed. This evaluation needs to make clear which theory is testable by recourse to evidence provided by the kibbutz experience and which cannot be so tested, as well as which of the testable theories are supported and which are refuted. (Some theories, though testable by kibbutz evidence, are better tested by other and weightier evidence.)

This chapter offers such an evaluation. I shall list the theories in question; in each case, I shall examine whether the kibbutz can be used as a valid test case, and indicate in passing when better and weightier test cases exist. When the kibbutz can serve as a valid test case, I shall assess whether the kibbutz historical experience and current social order support or refute the theory in question. Finally, I shall suggest improvements of explanatory theories of gender stratification and of the theoretical foundations for strategies in the struggle for gender equality.

THEORIES OF GENDER INEQUALITY

The theories are grouped according to their main themes: production and property relations; family structure and household; social roles, especially organizational work roles; and sexuality. Theories belonging to the first group are mainly economic; the theories in the second and third groups are economic, sociological, anthropological, psychological, and even biological. In the fourth and last group, the most conspicuous theories are psychoanalytic.

Production and Property Relations

Many theories concerning the status of women have originated within socialist thought, which blames the existing material inequality in society for most or all of its ills. Socialists assume the feasibility of the elimination or great reduction of this material inequality and with it the elimination of almost all social inequalities as well as status hierarchies. In line with this assumption, socialists generally expect that the smaller the differentials in standards of living or property in a society, the smaller also the status differentials between men and women.

Marxism locates the origins of all inequality more specifically in the private ownership of the means of production by one class and contends that the elimination of all inequalities will be effected by the expropriation of the privately owned means of production by the revolutionary proletariat and by their subsequent administration by society for the benefit of all. According to Engels ([1884] 1972), the cause of women's inferior status is class society and the forms of family organization it produces; once class society is abolished, and the state withers away, the patriarchal family will also disappear. Engels blamed capitalism for the current separation of the place of reproductive work, that is, the family home, from the place of productive work, that is, the factory, which has made women's participation in social production more difficult and limited. According to Engels, capitalists want to keep women reproducing the labor force without pay, while serving as a cheap reserve army of labor. His program for full equality for women was their full participation in social production. Engels did not assume that the socialist revolution and the elimination of the capitalists as a class would automatically overcome all the obstacles to women's equality.

He added two assumptions concerning household and marriage; they belong to the second group of theories as classified here.

Several modern materialist theories that stress the central importance of women's place in production for their status in society have been developed by Brown (1970, 1975), Sanday (1973), and Lesser Blumberg (1984). Brown's earlier version (1970), based on an analysis of the anthropological literature, explains the greatly varying degree of women's contribution to subsistence production as depending on the degree of compatibility of child minding with the kind and conditions of subsistence production in each society. Her later explicit theory of gender equality is based on the analysis of the exceptionally high status of women in Iroquois society. She found that this status cannot be "attributed to the size of the women's contribution to Iroquois subsistence. The powerful position of Iroquois women was the result of their control of the economic organization of their tribe" (1975, p. 251). Sanday (1973) uses samples from Murdock's "Ethnographic Atlas" (1967) to test the theory that women's high participation in subsistence production results in high social status. She refutes it by pointing to the existence of societies whose women, although they contribute over half of their society's subsistence, nevertheless have extremely low status. Consequently, she reformulates her theory to say that participation in subsistence production is a necessary but not sufficient condition for women's high status. Lesser Blumberg's theory is sociological and is relevant to industrial as well as simple societies. She claims that it is only the production of surplus resources, and access to and control over these resources, that translates into power or valued status—for men and women alike.

Family Structure and Household

Engels's first additional assumption was that the private family household condemns women to household work and child care and thus to inequality. Women can become equal, then, only through the dissolution of the private family household by the socialization of domestic services and child-raising. Engels's second assumption deals with women's unequal status and financial dependence within marriage: According to Engels, only propertyless proletarian marriage can be based on "individual sex-love," that is, on genuine free choice, and only in such a marriage can women be equal.

Modern sociological feminist theory has continued the severe criticism of the conventional family household for burdening women with all or most of the unpaid domestic and child-care work and of conventional marriage for causing women's economic dependence and limiting their autonomy. As a precondition for gender equality, they call for extensive changes in both the marriage contract and the household division of labor. Several theories are based on the assumption of the feasibility of gender-egalitarian family households and egalitarian, long-term, heterosexual partnerships in the future. These, it is predicted, will come about as a result of one or more of the following factors: the decline of women's economic dependence on men, the increase in women's control over reproduction, the improvement and greater availability of nondomestic child-care services, the reduction and greater flexibility of occupational working time, and men's gradual realization that a gender-egalitarian dual role of occupational and of family work is in their own long-term interest (Agassi 1989; Bernard 1975; Lewis and Sussman 1986; Mason and Lu 1988; Pleck and Sawyer 1974; Rapoport and Rapoport 1971; Whicker and Kronenfeld 1986).

In examining the nuclear family household as a capitalist and patriarchal institution that prevents all but a minority of women, who employ other women to perform services at relatively low pay, from having a career, Hunt and Hunt (1982) argue that to expect men in nuclear family households to undertake half of the household and child-care work is unrealistic. They reject as stultifying to children's development their supervision for much of the day in child-care centers or in schools. The best alternative, according to Hunt and Hunt, is a household with more than two adults, in which children systematically participate in domestic work.

Additional theoretical questions that have to be considered are the significance of women's status in marriage or in the household for their status in the community and the society at large, and vice versa. Lesser Blumberg argued in 1984 that the economic independence of women may be sufficient for their acquisition of equal power (i.e., equal status) in marriage and in the household without, however, being sufficient for women's equal status in the community or larger society.

Social Roles, Especially Occupational Roles

Modern liberal feminist theories of gender equality are based on the assumption that in order for women to achieve equal status, all stereotyped social roles for men and women have to be abolished. Conventional women's work roles assign to them the major responsibility for unpaid domestic and especially child-care work, and thus handicap them in their occupational roles. Despite the legal rights of women to equality in employment, men use women's actual or presumed domestic handicaps to perpetuate de facto discrimination by forcing women into a small number of occupational roles that are segregated according to labor-market types and working-time schedules and that have lower pay and prestige than comparable men's occupations. Employed women's inferior income is used as a justification for the perpetuation of their unequal burden of domestic and child-care work and their inferior power within the family. Their segregated and inferior occupational roles also hinder their acquisition of economic and political power. It is in the short-term interest of men of all strata to use the unpaid domestic services of women and to prevent women from competing with them for the better jobs (Agassi 1977; Bergmann 1974, 1986; Epstein 1981; Kanter 1977a, 1977b, 1982; Lorber 1984; Mednick et al. 1975; Reskin 1988; Reskin and Hartman 1986).

This theory of gender inequality is usually applied to industrialized societies alone; a generalized version of it has been applied by some anthropologists to preliterate societies. These anthropologists assert that the more work activities are carried out by both women and men indiscriminately, the higher the status of women; the more rigid the segregation of women and men during work activities, the lower the status of women. The idea behind this theory is quite general; there are no separate but equal functions or roles (Bacdayan 1977; Rosaldo and Lamphere 1974; Sacks 1974). Thus, even if women perform central roles in food production, as long as they are excluded from roles that provide access to means of exchange, they are devoid of prestige and political power. Similarly, as long as women are barred from significant political or ritual roles, there is no genuine gender equality.

The liberal feminists' theory includes the claim that the abolition of gender segregation of occupational roles is necessary for the achievement of women's equality. It follows that for the acquisition of gender equality, all domestic consumption work and all child-care work—as well as the responsibility for its performance—must also be freed of gender stereotyping and must be divided equally between partners and between parents. These theories are thus linked to the theories of family structure and household.

A different modern anthropological non-materialist theory of gender roles is suggested by Schlegel (1977), who claims it is of no importance whether work activities are gender-segregated as long as the creation myths and ritual system of the society evaluate and celebrate women's activities as highly as men's. According to Schlegel, neither segregation of work roles nor participation in production determines the status of women and men, but only the spiritual evaluation of their activities. Reeves Sanday's later work (1981) downplays her earlier emphasis on production and presents a theory of women's status rather similar to Schlegel's. She claims that for gender equality, what is needed is a high mythical and cultural evaluation of birth, as well as women's participation in sacred roles. Unlike Schlegel, Sanday does not dismiss the significance of gendered role segregation for women's status; she claims that "[symbolic] sex role plans determine the sexual division of labor" (p. 6) and "whether or not men and women mingle or are largely separated in everyday affairs plays a crucial role in the rise of male dominance" (p. 7).

All of the gender stratification theories mentioned so far agree that gender equality is both desirable and feasible. We come now to two gender-role theories that claim that gender equality is unfeasible and that attempts to achieve it are therefore unwise.

The first theory argues that gender roles are biologically given and thus unchangeable. According to this theory, during the millennia of the infancy of the human species, males and females had radically different experiences; these have implanted in each individual a "biogrammar" that makes male humans better disposed to pursue action and adventure within male groups, much like their presumed activities during the hunting stage of humanity, whereas it makes female humans better disposed to pursue the domestic and maternal activities. Hence, all attempts to equalize gender roles will be in vain, because they will be opposed to biogrammar differences (Tiger 1969; Tiger and Shepher 1975).

Variants of the biogrammar theory can be found in Trivers (1972) and Wilson (1975); they claim that most higher vertebrates, humans included, exhibit an asymmetry of parental investment between male and female. This unequal investment, they say, is the foundation of the sexual division of labor, since the female, by investing generously in offspring, has to forgo investment in alternative tasks (see also Shepher and Tiger 1983).

The second theory that shares the thesis of the inevitability of gender inequality is that of pre-cultural motivational disposition (Spiro 1979). According to this theory, there is a gender difference in the degree of the need for initial parenting. The alleged cause is possibly the human biogrammar, possibly human anatomy (women's "inner space" predisposes them to domestic maternal interests), or possibly the difference in the psychological development of male and female infants. The Freudian version is that penis envy drives girls inevitably toward mothering; castration fear drives boys inevitably away from primary child care.

A variant of this theory, less traditionally psychoanalytical yet still somewhat Freudian, is Chodorow's (1978). According to Chodorow, gender equality is both desirable and feasible, but its attainment depends on fundamental changes in human behavior: As long as only mothers—or substitute mothers—care for babies during the first stages of infancy, women will develop a personality different from that of men, and that personality will shape their attitudes and behavior in work and family roles. In Chodorow's view, gender equality could be achieved, but only if babies of both sexes would be nurtured, from birth onward, equally by women and men. This theory can therefore also be classified as a theory of family structure.

Sexuality

One radical feminist theory of gender inequality condemns marriage, and any other form of long-term heterosexual liaison, as detrimental to women's equality, not because of economic dependence or double work burden, but because of the inevitability of the resulting emotional dependence of women on men (Atkinson 1970a, 1970b; Firestone 1971).

Another radical feminist theory of gender inequality is that of obligatory heterosexuality (Rich 1980; Rubin 1975), which derives from Lévi-Strauss and from Freud as interpreted by Lacan. The basic form of male dominance, according to Lévi-Strauss, is men's use of women as objects of exchange. Women are raised, according to Lacan's reading of Freud, to internalize their inferior status by being pushed from birth to see heterosexuality as obligatory. Denied the choice of any form of sexuality except passive heterosexuality, Lacan claims that women accept marriage and the responsibility for mothering as the only option open to them. This theory allows for the feasibility of gender equality; as a necessary—yet perhaps not sufficient—condition, it postulates, as does Chodorow's theory, equal nurturing for infants from birth by men and women.

MacKinnon (1987) presented the radical feminist view that the basis of all gender inequality is the sexual violation of women, namely, violence against women in the forms of rape, wife battering, sexual abuse of children, sexual harassment, non-voluntary prostitution, and pornography. According to MacKinnon, the concentration on legal and occupational equality cannot touch this core oppression and so will necessarily fail to achieve gender equality. According to a socialist variant of this theory, the root cause of men's violence against women lies in the frustrations and injuries generated in men by class society (Schwendinger and Schwendinger 1983).

THE KIBBUTZ AS A THEORETICAL TEST CASE

Are men and women equal in the kibbutz social order? If they are, which theories of gender equality are thereby corroborated and which are refuted? If they are not equal, which theories are thereby corroborated and which are refuted? First, criteria to determine equal status are needed. As components of status, I propose (1) access to resources; (2) autonomy, that is, the freedom to make life choices and the freedom of movement; and (3) power, that is, participation in the making of decisions concerning the members of the social group through membership and active participation in the decision-making institutions, and the holding of positions of power—economic, political, and ideological (Agassi 1979).

Are Kibbutz Women and Men Equal?

Access to Resources. Kibbutz women receive the same basic resources as kibbutz men in meals, foodstuffs, clothing, housing, and pocket money. They also receive the same health services and have the same rights to maintenance in old age. Kibbutz members, women and men, usually receive no wages or salaries, so that there is no differential caused by women's lesser income. Salaries and pensions paid to those members who work outside the kibbutz are handed over to the kibbutz. Nevertheless, because of the polarization of work roles, men as a group have considerably easier access to certain material resources, such as the use of a car, an office, or an apartment in town and travel abroad for activities on behalf of the kibbutz movement, for studies and occupational training, and even for longer periods of employment—for example, as agricultural advisers to Third World countries. Non-material resources should be included here as well. The most important of these are the intrinsic rewards from occupational work; and of these, kibbutz women have considerably fewer than kibbutz men.

Autonomy. Kibbutz society limits occupational choice mainly because of the economic constraints of its organization. Each kibbutz has a limited set of occupational slots to be filled by its members. Within the given constraints, however, men have considerably wider occupational choice than women do. There is another important aspect to the autonomy of life choices: A kibbutz member may contemplate leaving the kibbutz. Here, men kibbutz members obviously enjoy an advantage because men's occupational qualifications—civil and military—are much more suitable for outside paid work than women's.

Freedom of movement is an important part of autonomy, which may be hard to distinguish from access to a car or even from having a driver's license, both of which are significantly scarcer among kibbutz women than men. But there is also the important question of the relative constraints on movement and on time due to the obligations of private household services and of private child care. Although the gap between kibbutz women and men may be smaller here than elsewhere, it still exists and reduces women's autonomy significantly more than men's.

Power. In the kibbutz, some positions of power, such as heading the branches of the economy, are not formal jobs; and some, such as the central positions of secretary, treasurer, and economic manager, are formal jobs. Since the industrialization of most kibbutzim, there are factory managers, laboratory managers, and other positions in regional industrial enterprises of all sorts. Kibbutz members also serve in the financial, economic, cultural, and administrative positions of the kibbutz federations; in the trade union federation and its large business sector; and finally, in Israeli political parties, parliament, and—occasionally—government offices and agencies. Few kibbutz women work in any agricultural or industrial branch of the kibbutz long enough to acquire the expertise and seniority needed to become its head or to become a member of the appropriate economic or financial committees and to become in due course committee chairperson. Women do serve on educational and social committees and sometimes also become their heads. Yet it is from the position of head of an agricultural branch or industrial enterprise, and especially that of chairperson of the economic committee, that the candidates for the central positions of power in the kibbutz movement are chosen. Some women serve as secretaries of kibbutzim, very few as treasurers; women as economic directors are still a rarity.

Experience in the internal positions of power is the stepping stone to external positions of power. There has been one woman national secretary of a kibbutz federation. The kibbutz federations usually send one token woman at a time into national politics. Although holding of these positions gives access to decision-making—and to many of the material and non-material rewards mentioned above—much of the kibbutz local and federation policy is discussed in the general assembly of each kibbutz, which meets once a month. The overwhelming majority of the items on the agenda are economic and thus outside the expertise of most women members. Women attend these meetings less frequently than men, and they largely refrain from participation in debates.

There is no full agreement on the evaluation of women's status in the kibbutz. All agree that women have a somewhat lower status than men but disagree as to the locus of this inferiority of status. All agree that women participate less than men in political debates and hold fewer positions of power, but some belittle the difference in autonomy and deny the very existence of any difference in access to resources. Nor is there full agreement as to how gender-segregated the kibbutz division of labor is. Those who consider gender inequality inevitable as well as those who demand its abolition agree that it is extensive; others consider it minimal and unimportant (Palgi and Rosner 1983).

DOES THE KIBBUTZ CORROBORATE OR REFUTE THEORIES OF GENDER INEQUALITY?

Production and Property Relations

Kibbutzim are modern communities where differences in the standard of living and in the property of members are very small. Kibbutzim should therefore, according to socialist theory, have egalitarian gender relations. Since they do not, the theory that blames property differentials for gender inequality is refuted.

In the kibbutz, the means of production are common property, but it is doubtful whether the kibbutz can serve as a proper test case for Marx's theory (Marx and Engels [1848] 1972). His theory envisaged the expropriation of the means of production on a large societal—preferably even an international—scale, whereas the collective kibbutz settlements function within a national society that is capitalist. The socialist countries are better test cases. They show that the nationalization of the means of production does not produce equality between women and men (Heitlinger 1979; Michal 1975; Molyneux 1984; Scott 1979).

Engels ([1884] 1972) tied the disappearance of the family as it was known to him, and of the subjugation of women in general, to the end of class society. Since the kibbutz introduced some far-reaching changes in the functions of the family, broke up the household, and, especially in the early days, tended to disregard conventional religious rituals of marriage, the erroneous impression was created that the institution of the family had been abolished there. The disappointing discovery of the absence of full equality for women in the present-day kibbutz was then, following Engels's theory, blamed on the gradual reestablishment and strengthening of the family in the kibbutz. Yet the assumptions that in the early kibbutzim there was no family and no gender inequality are false. The kibbutz, therefore, cannot serve as a test case for the theory that blames class society and the family structure that it produces for the subjugation of women (for research on changing functions of the family and the status of women in the kibbutz, see Safir 1983a; Shilo 1981; Talmon-Garber 1956).

As to the theory that women's equality hinges on their full participation in production, kibbutz experience does not accord with it. Kibbutz homes and workplaces, for most members, are as near each other as in any pre-industrial society. Most child care and service work takes place, not in the family dwelling, but in the collective public sector, where nearly all of it is performed by women. In the kibbutz, the generally endorsed principle is that all adult women work a full workday in the public sector. If we deem production to be any employment outside the private family household, then kibbutz women fully participate, and therefore, according to the theory that blames women's lack of full participation in production for their inequality, they should be equal to men. Since they are not, that theory is refuted.

Marx and Engels ([1848] 1972) considered work in the public sector of industrial society to be production; in present-day highly industrialized societies, more people work in services than in production. The content of much of the service work done in the labor market is indeed often very similar to that done in the private household; namely, it is "reproductive" work, to use Engels's terminology. We might, therefore, reformulate Engels's theory of participation in production to say that women will have achieved equality when they participate as much as men in the production of objects and goods, not of services. In this version, Engels's theory would not be refuted by the kibbutz experience but would be left open, since women do mainly service work.

Brown, in her 1970 theory, considered women's rate of participation in "subsistence production" important for their status. This theory was clearly limited to simple, non-industrialized societies in which all, or most, of the most needed goods are produced within the local community. The kibbutz nowadays is as far removed from such a state of material self-sufficiency as any village in a complex and industrialized society. Kibbutz kitchen managers even buy most of the needed foodstuffs. Therefore the kibbutz cannot serve as a test case. Neither can it be used to test Brown's 1975 theory that the high status of Iroquois women is due to their control of the economic organization of their tribe, because kibbutz women do not control the economic organization of their industrialized small communities to any higher degree than do women in other modern societies.

In industrialized society, or in capitalism, according to Engels ([1884] 1972), women's unpaid work in the home is regarded as of especially low prestige and even becomes invisible, because at the present cash nexus stage of economic development, the worth of a person is judged by the worth of his or her paid work, and the worth of market work is the wage or salary it brings. This contrast between paid and unpaid work does not exist in the kibbutz. No member or resident there exchanges labor power for cash. It follows, then, that women's reproductive work should not be devalued in the kibbutz. But work in the communal service branches, which is performed overwhelmingly by women, has for decades been regarded there as of lesser value, as "not productive," and is of lower prestige than work done primarily by men in agriculture, industry, and administration, which is highly valued.

What does the kibbutz experience have to offer regarding women as an exploitable reserve army of labor? With collective ownership of the means of production and collective consumption patterns, kibbutz women's participation in public-sector work nearly equals that of men. What about permanence? In principle, kibbutz members should be ready to fill any work position for which they are qualified. There are no formal employment contracts within the kibbutz, and, except for some elective positions, there are no fixed and limited periods of tenure. Yet a comparison of women's and men's work histories reveals that women switch much more frequently than men among different jobs, workplaces, and branches. Women, much more than men, are drafted to perform seasonal rush jobs in agriculture. So, even in the kibbutz, women seem to be a reserve army of labor.

Sanday (1973) suggested several factors that might be responsible for the fact that in some societies women, though contributing much to production have, or had, very low status—their not producing "strategic" goods, not producing goods for exchange, or not having control over their own products—but she did not develop these suggestions into a new theory that could be tested.

According to Lesser Blumberg (1984), even where women participate equally in production or contribute more than men to the satisfaction of the needs of society, they nevertheless have less power than men as long as men control the scarce and desired resources that serve as vehicles for exchange: such control is the way to power. Lesser Blumberg uses the kibbutz as a test case for her theory. According to her observations, although kibbutz women and men may be equal in the home, women definitely possess less political power than men. She explains this inequality as the result of the gradual process of women's exclusion from the production and control of surplus value—namely, from the production of lucrative agricultural and industrial goods for the market—and the increasing concentration of women in use-value production—namely, the internal service branches.

Lesser Blumberg (1976, 1984) thus claims the kibbutz experience as corroboration for two parts of her general theory of gender status, namely, that equality of power (or status) of women within marriage and the home will (or may) result from their equality of economic power with their spouses and that women's equal production and control of surplus value is the necessary pre-condition for their equal power (or status) on any higher level of social organization.

According to my observation and understanding, most kibbutz women do not possess equal power in marriage, so I do not see the kibbutz as corroborating the first part of Lesser Blumberg's theory. (This will be explained in some detail in the next section.) I do agree with her claim that the kibbutz experience serves as a test case for the central part of her theory—that production and control of surplus value are needed for social power and status—and that it strongly corroborates it. However, her contention that kibbutz women were originally more involved in production than they are now is questionable.

FAMILY STRUCTURE AND HOUSEHOLD

Engels ([1884] 1972) criticized the private family household for condemning women to household and child-care work; he proposed, instead, that such work be done communally. Here, the kibbutz serves as a unique test case. For several decades, the small kibbutz family dwelling had no cooking or laundry facilities, and in most kibbutzim they had no beds for infants and children. No private food-processing and very little food-serving work was performed in the family dwelling. The child-care work performed in the late afternoon and on days off (usually Saturdays) was mainly supervision of play, putting young children to bed in the children's house, and common play and leisure activities, not the staple cleaning, clothing, and feeding of children and the usual training work that accompanies these activities. Today, some food—especially cakes—may be prepared, and entire meals may be served and consumed at home; kibbutz dwellings have become larger, and in many kibbutzim, children have bedrooms in their parents' homes. But in the largest kibbutz federation, the Kibbutz Artzi, communal sleeping arrangements for children, from birth to the end of high school, remain the rule. Thus, in the kibbutz, the socialization of housework and child-care work has gone farthest over a considerable length of time. Yet women are not equal in the kibbutz. If we accept the kibbutz as a valid test case here, we must conclude that the socialization of family work does not suffice to make women equal.

As to Engels's claim that the "monogamic" marriage was detrimental to women's equality among all but propertyless partners, in the kibbutz, choice of partners and marriage does not involve any property considerations, since kibbutz members are collective property holders. However, the norm of monogamic marriage, namely, of heterosexual liaison of one man and one woman, intended to be of some permanence, is accepted in the kibbutz. If we interpret Engels to mean that women's financial dependence on men in monogamic marriage is the root cause of gender inequality in society, as well as within the relationship, then the kibbutz experience, where marriage does not involve women's economic dependence on their partners, would support the theory at the private level only if kibbutz women indeed had equal power in marriage. At the public level, the kibbutz experience clearly refutes Engels: economic independence of wives does not translate into equal status in the larger society.

The claim that economic or financial independence raises the status or power of women in marriage has been widely endorsed by feminists. Status or power in marriage includes access to family resources; management of the family budget; making major decisions concerning the couple and children, such as choice of residence, employment, schooling, leisure activities, and so on; equal division of, and responsibility for, housework and child care; control over sexual and procreative behavior; and ability to initiate divorce. Kibbutz women are not financially dependent on their partners. Is their relative status in marriage equal to that of their partners, or is it at least considerably higher than that of women of a comparable socioeconomic, educational, and ethnic stratum outside the kibbutz? In the majority of cases, kibbutz husbands and wives are not equal, and the status of kibbutz wives is not considerably higher than similar Israeli wives' status.

Several of these components of status in marriage have not been empirically studied. Access to everyday resources supplied by the collective is certainly equal; it is popularly claimed and empirically supported that women have considerable influence on the use of the couple's "personal budget" (Selier 1973). I have mentioned above the unequal access to some resources that pertain to autonomy, especially in the sense of freedom of movement. Because of occupational differentiation men have, on the average, more contact with, and spend more time in, the world outside the kibbutz and thus are less controlled by the very powerful communal public opinion (Spiro 1956). The result is an inequality of power in marriage, certainly an inequality in control over sexual behavior.

Since the collective has a major influence on many decisions, the economic independence of wives may be irrelevant. Decisions about job choice, further training or study by partners, and educational or occupational decisions concerning the future of their children may be greatly affected by the current gender-role attitudes in the collective, which may be very traditional. Because of gendered occupational differentiation, there also is a marked imbalance in the effect of major decisions concerning one partner on the other. Changes that advance the occupational career of the male partner much more frequently affect the female partner's career negatively than the other way around.

In addition to control over the couple's personal budget, only one other component of power in marriage, the division of private housework and private child-care work between kibbutz spouses, has been empirically studied (Palgi and Rosner 1983, p. 265) and is claimed to be equal. Palgi and Rosner base their claim of equality in kibbutz marriage on three rather limited studies of the division of private family work. On the basis of these reports, they contend that kibbutz men, especially kibbutz fathers, perform many private family work activities or participate in a relatively high proportion of them when compared with men outside the kibbutz. Their own research, the Kibbutz Artzi study, used answers given by women members of their federation to questions concerning their evaluation of the degree of gender equality in kibbutz families compared with Israeli families outside (not with families of an equal socioeconomic and educational stratum). Seventy-five percent of the women evaluated kibbutz families as more egalitarian. Since there was no time-budget study, we cannot compare the average time spouses spend on private household and child-care work. Nor was it reported which partner is usually held responsible for which chore. Both items of information would be needed for the resolution of the question of the gender division of private family work in the kibbutz. Information on the same two items from comparable Israeli non-kibbutz families would be needed to resolve the problem of whether kibbutz women are more equal in status and power within marriage than economically dependent wives.

I assume that a perfectly egalitarian division of residual private family work is precluded by the different time and space schedules of men's and women's public work in the kibbutz. Women, on the average, work a somewhat shorter workday than men, and their workplaces are nearer to home and children's houses; consequently, in the afternoons, women, not men, pick up supplies and laundry and, most important, small children. Many more fathers than mothers are absent from home during part of the week, and at times, even for weeks, they work outside the kibbutz settlement or study or serve in the military reserves. (This last item is of course due to the unequal role division in Israeli society: mothers are exempt from reserve duty.) In addition, kibbutz norms put squarely on the mother the responsibility for the physical and emotional well-being of babies and small children, and also consider baking and serving food to family and guests women's work and obligation. In short, as long as public work roles remain gender-segregated, and gender-role stereotypes are not resolutely broken, a fully egalitarian division of private family work cannot be achieved—even when there is no financial dependence of wives on husbands.

Is the kibbutz a good test case of the advantages to women of multi-adult households and communal housework, child care, and education? It may well be that the existence in the kibbutz of separate, private family dwellings, with residual consumption and child care, runs counter to the image of communal households. Many kibbutzim may be considered too large, and their social structure too formalized, for genuine communal living. Nevertheless, since the kibbutz does not permit the private employment of one woman by another for the performance of household or child-care work, and does much of this work communally, it conforms to a feminist egalitarian communal image. It also integrates a considerable amount of housework and collective infant-care work into the daily schedules of grade-school and teenage children. As a group of adults who take a common responsibility for the maintenance, care, and education of all their children, as well as the common maintenance and care of their old, the kibbutz appears to fulfill the central functions of a multi-adult communal household. But most of the adults who do this care-work are women. As a test case, then, the kibbutz indicates that a small society that functions according to communalistic principles can nevertheless also practice a division of labor in which nearly the entire collective child-care and personal service work is performed by women. It is not necessarily easier in a multi-adult, communal household than it is in a nuclear family household to achieve a gender-egalitarian division of family work (as studies of other communes have also indicated; see, for example, Abrams et al. 1976, Wagner 1982).

Social Roles, Especially Occupational Work Roles

For occupational as well as for family roles, kibbutz experience corroborates the core thesis of the gendered-work-role theory, according to which the equalization of social roles is the key to gender equality. Even in this rather egalitarian society, as long as occupational roles are segregated by gender, women's roles tend to offer them less access to important material and non-material resources, grant them less autonomy, prevent their equality of power in marriage, and, above all, prevent their equal participation in economic and political power—as most of the roles having these advantages are filled by men.

Kibbutz experience teaches two important specific lessons concerning occupational segregation. First, the vicious circle of the unequal, gendered division of routine personal service and child-care work and the unequal, gendered division of productive and professional work may operate without the intervening factor of unequal, gendered wage scales. Second, even in a society in which there is no unpaid and paid work, as long as the routine personal service and child-care work, performed either within a private family household or in a communal kitchen or children's house, is allocated to women only, it depresses women's status.

Thus, kibbutz experience supports the mainstream feminist demand for the radical desegregation of gendered social roles as necessary for the elimination of women's social inferiority. It also supports the hypothesis (recently sharply reformulated by Reskin 1988) of the existence of short-term interests common to men of all social strata in keeping the status quo of women performing less-liked activities and of preventing women from equally competing with men for more valued and intrinsically more satisfying activities and roles, which, not incidentally, also offer access to scarce privileges and greater influence on major social decisions.

If women's nurturant work were equally evaluated and celebrated in the kibbutz, then the kibbutz could serve as a test case for Schlegel's (1977) and Sanday's (1973) theory that this is the key to gender equality. In the kibbutz, just as in most other societies, women's activities are not equally valued, nor is there full gender equality; hence the kibbutz is not in conflict with that theory, nor is it a special test case for it. Nevertheless, the kibbutz experience may be of interest for testing a special interpretation of that theory.

Cultural feminists advocate that, as a major strategy, women's maternal and nurturing activities be celebrated in order to gain from society evaluation and support for these activities, which should be equal—at the very least—to that granted to men's technical, acquisitive, and competitive activities. This variant, then, is a theory of the feasibility of a special kind of value change in modern society. It has found non-feminist adherents among some writers who denied the negative effect of work-role segregation on the status of women in the kibbutz, because, they said, women's work activities are, objectively, of equal value to kibbutz society. Since the kibbutz is not an acquisitive, capitalist society, income and profit do not count most in the kibbutz; the quality of the life of its members, and above all the birth and well-being of its children, are supposedly of the highest value. For decades, these kibbutz ideologues demanded that women's collective service and child-care activities be celebrated and their "image" be improved. These demands met with no response from either women or men and, finally, these ideologues came to realize—under pressure—that the gendered occupational polarization would have to be reduced;. The failure in this small manageable community to upgrade women's objectively poorer work roles by declaring them equal, the failure even there to effect attitude changes by an appeal to officially held values, should serve as a caution to cultural feminists.

The defenders of the biogrammar theory of gender inequality, Tiger and Shepher (1975), take the kibbutz experience as the best corroborating test case possible. It is to their credit that they were the first to publish observations concerning the great extent of gendered occupational segregation and inequality of political participation in the kibbutz. They argue that kibbutz society had originally been based on egalitarian ideology and planned as an egalitarian social order, with men and women equally economically active and equally free of private domestic work and traditional private child care. Progressively, they observe, social and political equality between the women and men in the kibbutz constantly diminished, and the allocation of work reverted to the traditionally gender-polarized division of labor. This reversion, they say, was a victory of nature over nurture; it was demanded by women, who preferred work in the service branches and who pushed for the constant expansion of private domestic and maternal activities. (This description of kibbutz history as a process of radical change concerning women's roles and women's status does not agree with historical research, but unfortunately has been widely accepted.)

In actuality, the kibbutz is a bad test case for the biological theories of gender inequality. The social structure of the kibbutz was never egalitarian as to gender roles, since men never fully participated in domestic and child-care work (Agassi 1979). The principle that all members were active outside the private household and that none was paid was considered a sufficient expression of egalitarianism. It was the kibbutz social structure, not kibbutz women, that pushed toward the traditional polarization of work roles. The desire to increase the size of the kibbutz population is held by men as well as women, and the birthrate is significantly higher compared with the same Israeli socioeconomic stratum. In principle, kibbutz children receive high-level care all day, and, in many kibbutzim, day and night. Since child care is not deemed a position suitable for men to hold on a permanent basis in the kibbutz, as elsewhere in Israeli society, and since the kibbutz movement has long opposed the hiring of outside labor for child care, the inescapable consequence is that most kibbutz women must spend a large portion of their working life in child care, that is, in so-called maternal activities. They did not prefer these roles; for many years, they have expressed dissatisfaction with their limited occupational roles. The only way the demand to switch from collective to familial sleeping arrangements for children could have been effected was by a majority vote in the kibbutz general meetings, where men are usually both more active and more heavily represented. To the extent that women actively supported the broadening of private consumption and child care, their frustration with their communal work roles may well have been an important cause.

The other two biological theories, that of unequal parental investment (Shepher and Tiger 1983; Trivers 1972; Wilson 1975) and that of pre-cultural motivational disposition (Spiro 1979) resemble the first one as far as the possibility of the kibbutz serving as test case. Shepher and Tiger used the parental investment theory to explain the agreement of kibbutz women to communal child-care arrangements in the early days of the kibbutz movement as in accord with objective maximal maternal investment under the harsh economic and security conditions that prevailed then. Later on, kibbutz teenage girls were required to work in the children's homes; only recently has that been true of the teenage boys of one federation (Hertz and Baker 1983). Thus, girls were socialized into and trained for child-care work (Safir 1983b); their later acceptance of this role did not emerge from a greater biological disposition for maternal investment.

In sum, kibbutz experience does not corroborate biological theories of gender inequality, nor does it refute them. Only the success or failure of an attempt to establish a stable practice of equal sharing by men and women of parenting, service work, and production of valued goods would constitute a test case of the theories of the unchangeable, or precultural, or biological differences between the genders in their tendencies and capacities.

Because kibbutz babies are reared from birth in communal children's houses, it has been claimed that there is no special bond between mother and infant in the kibbutz, which therefore can serve as a test case for the theory of gendered personality development (Chodorow 1978). The kibbutz, however, is not at all revolutionary in its methods of infant nurturing. Kibbutz mothers are encouraged to breast-feed, and during the first six months, the mother tends her baby at regular intervals, whereas kibbutz fathers have no more body contact with their infants during the first stage of development than do fathers generally in modern Western society. During the mother's absence from the children's house, the infant is attended to and nurtured by other women. Thus, the kibbutz is not a test case for Chodorow's contention that the only way to achieve the equality of social roles and of social status of women and men is by putting infants into the care of both male and female caretakers from the very start.

SEXUALITY

The kibbutz cannot be used as a test case for the radical feminist rejection of all long-term heterosexual liaisons as detrimental to women's equality, since kibbutz ideologues have considered marriage and the family as basic to the success and the stability of the kibbutz. Singles are considered a problem to themselves and to the kibbutz, and considerable social pressure is used to ensure relatively early marriage. Kibbutz norms concerning premarital and extramarital sex, contraception, and abortion (except for the religious kibbutzim) do not differ from those of the rest of the secular population in Israel. Since kibbutz norms deny the very existence of male or female homosexual relations or liaisons within the kibbutz population, the kibbutz cannot serve as a test case for the theory that presents obligatory heterosexuality as a major instrument for the subjugation of women.

Does the kibbutz serve as a test case for MacKinnon's (1987) theory of gender inequality as sexual oppression? As long as MacKinnon does not clearly designate any one social factor as responsible for sexual oppression, this cannot be determined. In the case of the socialist variant of this theory, which assumes the major cause of men's sexually violent behavior to be class society, if we assume the kibbutz not to be a class society, it could serve as a test case. We would then have to ask whether forms of sexual violence against women, such as rape, incest, wife battering, sexual harassment, involuntary prostitution, or pornography, are absent or less prevalent in the kibbutz than in Israeli society. I do not know of any empirical study on this subject. Were such a study undertaken, should it—in order to test the theory—include the possible resort of kibbutz men to sexual harassment, prostitutes, or pornography outside the confines of the kibbutz? The official ideology of the entire kibbutz movement is certainly radically opposed to all these forms of behavior, and the occurrence of deviant behavior would be denied vehemently by kibbutz members. There have been no public reports, and in the absence of any research, we will have to let the matter rest.

THE FUTURE CONTRIBUTION OF THE KIBBUTZ TO GENDER EQUALITY

Can the kibbutz make specific contributions in the search for institutional forms that permit and encourage genuinely equal status for women? In modern industrialized societies, it has become evident that in order to break the vicious circle of women's inferior status in the family and in the labor market, the traditional patterns of work, especially time patterns, have to be altered. The kibbutz is the collective employer of most of its members. It has shown innovative initiative in the past; for example, for its older members, it shortened and made work time flexible; in order to equalize the sharing of disliked work, such as serving in the dining hall and night-watching, it has had a long-standing arrangement of work rotation. It also has a tradition of mid-career changes, extended study leaves, and combinations of manual and cerebral work (Cherns 1980). The kibbutz could just as well work out a system in which all of its women and men, or all of its parents, performed all non-professional communal child-care work on a rotational basis in conjunction with their occupational work. It could also recruit both women and men for professional work in the communal education of infants and young children. Thus, women, equally with men, would be free to pursue all the available technical and professional work roles, achieving more satisfaction in work, and, in due course, also gaining equal status with men in the kibbutz.

A first step in this direction was taken by the Kibbutz Artzi Federation in 1980 (Palgi et al. 1983, p. 303). A resolution adopted then declared that both men and women bear the responsibility for children's education; it was decided to aim at filling 20 percent of the professional jobs of educating young children with men, and to recruit suitable men and women for the non-professional jobs in child care to serve for a specified number of years. Most important, high-school boys were to participate in the care of pre-schoolers, which had until then been done by girls only.

This first step would not have been taken had women not organized published (Silver 1984), raised consciousness, formulated goals, and started to work out strategies. The women's movement came late to the kibbutz, not until the end of the seventies. Until then, the word *feminis* was a swear word. The perennial arguments against feminism were the following: there is no room for a separate women's organization in the kibbutz; quotas are alien to the kibbutz; we have already achieved gender equality. So, perhaps an additional important theory is corroborated by kibbutz experience: there is no chance for gender equality in a modern society without some autonomous women's organization fighting for it.

REFERENCES

Abrams, P., et al. 1976. *Communes, Sociology and Society.* Cambridge: Cambridge University Press.

Agassi, J. Buber. 1977. "The Unequal Occupational Distribution of Women in Israel." *Signs: Journal of Women in Culture and Society* 2:88-94.

———. 1979. "Kibbutz and Sex Roles." *Crossroads: International Dynamics and Social Change* 4:145-73.

———. 1989. "The Design of Working Time and the Status of Women." Pp. 251-7 in *The Redesign of Working Time,* edited by J. Buber Agassi and S. Heycock. Berlin: Edition Sigma.

Atkinson, Ti-Grace. 1970a. "The Institution of Sexual Intercourse." Pp. 42-7 in *Notes from the Second Year: Radical Feminism,* edited by Shulamit Firestone and Anne Koedt. New York: Radical Feminism.

———. 1970b. "Radical Feminism." Pp. 37-41 in *Notes from the Second Year: Radical Feminism,* edited by S. Firestone and A. Koedt. New York: Radical Feminism.

Bacdayan, A. S. 1977. "Mechanistic Cooperation and Sexual Equality Among the Western Bantoc." Pp. 270-91 in *Sexual Stratification: A Cross-Cultural View,* edited by Alice Schlegel. New York: Columbia University Press.

Bergmann, B. R. 1974. "Occupational Segregation, Wages and Profits Where Employers Discriminate by Race and Sex." *Eastern Economic Journal* 1:103-10.

———. 1986. *The Economic Emergence of Women.* New York: Basic Books.

Bernard, J. 1975. *Women, Wives, Mothers: Values and Options.* Hawthorne, NY: Aldine de Gruyter.

Blumberg, R. Lesser. 1976. "Kibbutz Women: From the Fields of Revolution to the Laundries of Discontent." Pp. 319-444 in *Women of the World: A Comparative Study,* edited by L. B. Iglitzin and R. Ross. Santa Barbara, CA: ABC-Clio.

———. 1984. "A General Theory of Gender Stratification." Pp. 23-101 in *Sociological Theory: 1984,* edited by R. Collins. San Francisco: Jossey-Bass.

Brown, J. K. 1970. "A Note on the Division of Labor by Sex." *American Anthropologist* 72:1073-8.

———. 1975. "Iroquois Women: An Ethnographic Note." Pp. 235-51 in *Toward an Anthropology of Women,* edited by R. R. Reiter. New York: Monthly Review Press.

Cherns, A. (ed.). 1980. *Quality of Working Life and the Kibbutz Experience.* Norwood, PA: Norwood Editions.

Chodorow, N. 1978. *The Reproduction of Mothering.* Berkeley, CA: University of California Press.

Engels, F. [1884] 1972. *The Origin of the Family, Private Property, and the State.* New York: Pathfinder Press.

Epstein, C. Fuchs. 1981. *Women in Law.* New York: Basic Books.

Firestone, S. 1971. *The Dialectic of Sex: The Case for Feminist Revolution.* New York: Bantam.

Heitlinger, A. 1979. *Women and State Socialism: Sex Inequality in the Soviet Union and Czechoslovakia.* London: Macmillan.

Hertz, R., and W. Baker. 1983. "Women and Men's Work in the Israeli Kibbutz: Gender and Allocation of Labor." Pp. 154-73 in *Sexual Equality: The Israeli Kibbutz Tests the Theories,* edited by M. Palgi, J. Blasi, M. Rosner, and M. Safir. Norwood, PA: Norwood Editions.

Hunt, J. G., and L. L. Hunt. 1982. "Dilemmas and Contradictions of Status: The Case of the Dual Career Family." Pp. 181-91 in *Women and Work: Problems and Perspectives,* edited by R. Kahn-Hut, A Kaplan Daniels, and R. Colvard. New York: Oxford University Press.

Kanter, R. Moss. 1977a. *Men and Women of the Corporation.* New York: Basic Books.

————. 1977b. "Women in Organizations: Sex Roles, Group Dynamics, and Change Strategies." Pp. 371-86 in *Beyond Sex Roles,* edited by A. G. Sargent. St. Paul, MN: West.

————. 1982. "The Impact of Hierarchical Structures on the Work Behavior of Women and Men." Pp. 234-47 in *Women and Work: Problems and Perspectives,* edited by R. Kahn-Hut, A. Kaplan Daniels, and R. Colvard. New York: Oxford University Press.

Lewis, R. A., and M. B. Sussman (eds.). 1986. *Men's Changing Roles in the Family.* New York: Haworth.

Lorber, J. 1984. *Women Physicians: Careers, Status and Power.* New York: Tavistock.

MacKinnon, C. A. 1987. *Feminism Unmodified: Discourses on Life and Law.* Cambridge, MA: Harvard University Press.

Marx, K., and F. Engels. [1848] 1972. "The Communist Manifesto." In *The Marx-Engels Reader,* edited by R. Tucker. New York: Norton.

Mason, K. Oppenheim, and Yu-Hsia Lu. 1988. "Attitudes Toward Women's Familial Roles: Changes in the U.S., 1977-1985." *Gender & Society* 2:39-57.

Mednick, M. Shuch, S. Tandny, and L. W. Huffman. (eds.). 1975. *Women and Achievement: Social and Motivational Analyses.* New York: John Wiley.

Michal, J. M. 1975. "An Alternative Approach to Measuring Income Inequality in Eastern Europe." Pp. 256-75 in *Economic Development in the Soviet Union and Eastern Europe.* Vol. 1, edited by Z. M. Fallenbuchl. New York: Praeger.

Molyneux, M. 1984. "Women in Socialist Societies: Problems of Theory and Practice." Pp. 55-90 in *Of Marriage and the Market,* edited by K. Young, C. Wolkowitz, and R. McCullough. London: Routledge & Kegan Paul.

Murdock, G. P. 1967. "Ethnographic Atlas: A Summary." *Ethnology* 6(2):109-236.

Palgi, M., and M. Rosner. 1983. "Equality Between the Sexes in the Kibbutz: Regressions or Changed Meaning." Pp. 25-96 in *Sexual Equality: The Israeli Kibbutz Tests the Theories,* edited by M. Palgi, J. Blasi, M. Rosner, and M. Safir. Norwood, PA: Norwood Editions.

Palgi, M., J. Blasi, M. Rosner, and M. Safir. (eds.). 1983. *Sexual Equality: The Israel Kibbutz Tests the Theories.* Norwood, PA: Norwood Editions.

Pleck, J., and J. Sawyer. 1974. *Men and Masculinity.* Englewood Cliffs, NJ: Prentice-Hall.

Rapoport, R., and R. Rapoport. 1971. *Dual Career Families.* Hammondsworth: Penguin.

Reskin, B. F., 1988. "Bringing the Men Back In: Sex Differentiation and the Devaluation of Women's Work." *Gender & Society* 2:58-75.

—— and H. Hartman (eds.). 1986. *Women's Work: Sex Segregation on the Job.* Washington, DC: National Academy Press.

Rich, A. A. 1980. "Compulsory Heterosexuality and Lesbian Existence." *Signs: Journal of Women in Culture and Society* 5:631-60.

Rosaldo, M. Z., and L. Lamphere (eds.). 1974. *Women, Culture and Society.* Stanford, CA: Stanford University Press.

Rubin, G. 1975. "The Traffic in Women: Notes on the Political Economy of Sex." Pp. 157-210 in *Toward an Anthropology of Women,* edited by R. R. Reiter. New York: Monthly Review Press.

Sacks, K. 1974. "Engels Revisited: Women, the Organization of Production and Private Property." Pp. 207-22 in *Women, Culture and Society,* edited by M. Z. Rosaldo and L. Lamphere. Stanford, CA: Stanford University Press.

Safir, M. P. 1983a. "The Kibbutz—An Experiment in Social and Sexual Equality? An Historical Perspective." Pp. 100-29 in *Sexual Equality: The Israeli Kibbutz Tests the Theories,* edited by M. Palgi, J. Blasi, M. Rosner, and M. Safir. Norwood, PA: Norwood Editions.

——. 1983b. "Sex Role Socialization: Education in the Kibbutz." Pp. 216-20 in *Sexual Equality: The Israeli Kibbutz Tests the Theories,* edited by M. Palgi, J. Blasi, M. Rosner, and M. Safir. Norwood, PA: Norwood Editions.

Sanday, P. Reeves. 1973. "Toward a Theory of the Status of Women." *American Anthropologist* 75:1682-700.

——. 1981. *Female Power and Male Domination.* Cambridge: Cambridge University Press.

Schlegel, A. (ed.). 1977. *Sexual Stratification: A Cross-Cultural View.* New York: Columbia University Press.

Schwendinger, J. R., and H. Schwendinger. 1983. *Rape and Inequality.* Beverly Hills, CA: Sage.

Scott, H. 1979. "Women in Eastern Europe." Pp. 177-98 in *Sex Roles and Social Policy: A Complete Social Science Equation,* edited by J. Lipman-Blumen and J. Bernard. Beverly Hills, CA: Sage.

Selier, F. 1973. "Some Functional and Structural Aspects of Family Life in Communal Society: The Financial Sector of the Kibbutz Family." Unpublished paper.

Shepher, J., and L. Tiger. 1983. "Kibbutz and Parental Investment." Pp. 45-56 in *Sexual Equality: The Israeli Kibbutz Tests the Theories,* edited by M. Palgi, J. Blasi, M. Rosner, and M. Safir. Norwood, PA: Norwood Editions.

Shilo, M. 1981. "The Women's Farm in Kineret, 1911-1917: A Solution to the Problem of Working Women in the Second Aliya." Pp. 246-83 in *The Jerusalem Cathedra,* edited by L. I. Levine. Detroit, MI: Wayne State University.

Silver, V. 1984. *Male and Female Created He Them; The Problem of Sexual Equality in the Kibbutz.* Yad Tabenkin. (In Hebrew.)

Spiro, M. 1956. *Kibbutz: Venture in Utopia.* Cambridge, MA: Harvard University Press.

——. 1979. *Gender and Culture: Kibbutz Women Revisited.* Durham, NC: Duke University Press.

Talmon-Garber, Y. 1956. "The Family in Collective Settlements." Pp. 116-26 in *Transactions of the Third World Congress of Sociology.* Vol. 4. London: International Sociological Association.

Tiger, L. 1969. *Men in Groups.* New York: Random House.

———— and J. Shepher. 1975. *Women in the Kibbutz.* New York: Harcourt, Brace, Jovanovich.

Trivers, R. L. 1972. "Parental Investment and Sexual Selection." Pp. 136-79 in *Sexual Selection and the Descent of Man (1871-1971),* edited by B. G. Campbell. Chicago: Aldine.

Wagner, J. G. (ed.). 1982. *Sex Roles in Contemporary American Communes.* Bloomington: Indiana University Press.

Whicker, M. L., and J. Jacobs Kronenfeld. 1986. *Sex Role Changes: Technology, Politics, and Policy.* New York: Praeger.

Wilson, E. O. 1975. *Sociobiology: A New Synthesis.* Cambridge, MA: Harvard-Belknap.

17. "IT'S OUR CHURCH, TOO!" WOMEN'S POSITION IN THE CATHOLIC CHURCH TODAY

SUSAN A. FARRELL

How do women go about living in an institution that many find patriarchal, clericalist, bureaucratic, and oppressive? This chapter examines some of the issues facing women in the contemporary Roman Catholic Church. The women discussed in this chapter do not want to, and have no intention of, leaving the church. Contrary to prior reform movements these women are asserting that they are the church, too, and have invested much of their lives in living out what to them is the gospel message. Living and working in great tension between what the institution is, and what they envision it could and should be, Catholic feminists are searching for alternative models of church while maintaining their identity as Roman Catholics. These women, theologians, ethicists, sisters, and laywomen, have taken to heart and are trying to bring to fulfillment the message of the church itself, declared in the "Pastoral Constitution on the Church in the Modern World" *(Gaudium at Spes)*:

> Where they have not yet won it, women claim for themselves an equity with men before the law and in fact. . . . With respect to the fundamental rights of the person, every type of discrimination, whether social or cultural, whether based on sex, race, color, social condition, language, or religion, is to be overcome and eradicated as contrary to God's intent. For in truth it must still be regretted that fundamental personal rights are not yet being universally honored. Such is the case of a woman who is denied the right and freedom to choose a husband, to embrace a state of life, or to acquire an education or cultural benefits equal to those recognized for men. (Abbott 1966, pp. 207, 227-28)

The task that these women see for themselves is radical reform from within the church, without being coopted or so marginalized that they have no impact on the institution.

WOMEN'S POSITION IN THE CATHOLIC CHURCH TODAY

According to Wallace (1988), Roman Catholic women are creating a new social reality which "represents a shift from their passive and subservient roles vis-á-vis the clergy to a more active participation in the life of the Church" (p. 25). Influenced by the secular women's movement in which many are active, Roman Catholic women want and are demanding more participation at higher levels of the organizational church. More and more women, both lay and religious, are filling administrative positions, jobs that only ordained clergymen used to do. Although these opportunities for women in some measure come from the current shortage of priests, women have also been encouraged by the Second Vatican Council's call in the early 1960s for greater involvement of the laity in the day-to-day life of the church (Abbott 1966).

However, women's continued advancement and increased participation at higher organizational levels is blocked by church practice and discipline that does not allow the ordination of women to the priesthood. All top-level positions of authority and decision-making in the Roman Catholic Church are held by ordained celibate men, which also effectively removes married men from these positions. In essence, as the *Declaration on the Question of the Admission of Women to the Ministerial Priesthood* (Sacred Congregation for the Doctrine of the Faith 1976) states and as has been repeated by Pope John Paul II, women cannot be ordained because they cannot act *in persona Christi* (in the person of Christ) because they are not biological men (1988, pp. 89-90). Thus, the hierarchical structure of the church and its division of labor is based very clearly on a biologized concept of sex and gender.

The organizational structure of Roman Catholicism reveals what Acker (see Chapter 8) states is often hidden in modern bureaucratic organizations, a negative view of sexuality that is linked to misogyny and heterosexism. According to Acker, organizations are "gendered processes in which both gender and sexuality have been obscured through a gender-neutral, asexual discourse" (p. 163). The ideology underlying the Roman Catholic organizational structure that denies ordination to women and also represses men's sexuality becomes the example par excellence of Acker's point that "gender is a constitutive element in organizational logic" (p. 168). Obscuring sexuality also hides human procreation and "helps to reproduce the underlying gender relations" (p. 172).

FEMINIST SCHOLARS' CHALLENGE

Feminist scholars in Christianity and Roman Catholicism have illustrated the origins and results of the patriarchal religious ideology upon which the hierarchy of Roman Catholicism is constructed. According to Schüssler Fiorenza (1984):

> Much feminist theological writing accepts a twofold pre-supposition: that the root of women's oppression is dualistic thought or patriarchalism as a mind set or projection, and that monotheistic religions of Judaism and Christianity constitute the bedrock of Western patriarchalism. This hierarchical pattern of Western society, culture, and religion is characterized by the split between subject-object, superior-inferior, spirituality-carnality, life-death, mind-body, men-women. . . . They have fashioned an absolute transcendent God in the image of men and declared women "the other" who cannot image or represent God. (pp. 296-7)

Schüssler Fiorenza is summarizing the work done by many Jewish, Christian, and post-Christian feminist theologians and philosophers who have uncovered the patriarchal roots of Judeo-Christianity and the Judeo-Christian roots of patriarchy.[1] In this androcentric ethical discourse, as it has been institutionalized in Christianity and the Roman Catholic church, women have not been acknowledged as full moral agents by men. This view is based on a patriarchal interpretation of the creation stories in Genesis.

Post-Christian feminist Mary Daly insists that since genesis stories were written by men and their conception of God is irrevocably androcentric, they cannot be useable for and by women (1973, 1978, 1984). Based on this conclusion, Daly herself left the Roman Catholic Church believing the Judeo-Christian tradition to be intrinsically patriarchal and beyond redemption. Other Christian and Roman Catholic feminists, however, are trying to reclaim the past, arguing that religious mythology has been subverted by men to serve their interests. It is a feminist project to deconstruct and then reconstruct a past to make it into a useable present and to transform it for a liberated future for women in the church (Fiorenza 1983, pp. 28-32).

Trible (1978) gives an intriguing alternate interpretation of Genesis. According to Trible, the creation stories are hierarchically told, going from the simplest to the most complex creatures. Woman, being the last created, is the pinnacle of creation. She also makes note of wrongly translated names and genders. "Adam" actually means "humankind," not "man." The full quote is "Let us make humankind in our image, after our likeness; and let *them* have dominion (Genesis 1:26) (her emphasis,

1978, p. 18). Jewish midrash (a collection of interpretations of and commentaries on Biblical texts, especially those written during the first ten centuries C.E.) offers a variety of creation stories that provide feminists with an alternative to the patriarchally accused and condemned Eve. Called Lilith stories, Plaskow (1974) retells one version that has Adam complaining to God that Lilith, his first wife, does not obey him, she is an "uppity woman" (p. 341). He wants another more tractable woman. God complies. He gives Adam Eve and Lilith leaves the garden. She roams outside the garden wall, calling to Eve. When Eve climbs the garden wall and meets her, Lilith recounts her story: "They taught each other many things, and told each other stories, and laughed together, and cried, over and over, till the bond of sisterhood grew between them. . . . And God and Adam were expectant and afraid the day Eve and Lilith returned to the garden, bursting with possibilities, ready to rebuild it together" (pp. 342-3).

These scholars are transforming theological discourse using a well-honed feminist method: the experience of oppression discovered through the sharing of life stories. Welch (1985) describes this method as being simultaneously a way of doing research and an act of resistance:

> This politicization gives women the courage to persist in resistance, recognizing that their difficulties have not only an individual basis but a social and political basis as well. (pp. 41-2)

Using Daly's vision of a community of sisterhood as a locus of "creative resistance," Welch says that this experience of sisterhood is

> an experience of resistance and liberation, an affirmation of an identity that is different from that imposed by the dominant patriarchal social structures. The experience of resistance is itself a denial of the necessity of patriarchy; it is a moment of freedom, the power to embody momentarily an alternative identity. This affirmation serves as the ground for political resistance to social structures. (1985, pp. 41-2)

Linking this experience of oppression with a critique of mainstream religion offered by liberation theology, Welch goes on to describe the task of the feminist theologian in the church:

> The philosopher or theologian of resistance then brings the skills of his or her training in analysis and synthesis to bear on the power relations manifest in oppression . . . an analysis of the concrete mechanisms of exclusion and domination. . . . In theology, commitment and reflection have

led to . . . works that describe specific histories of oppression, criticize the role of the church and theology in that oppression, and offer alternative interpretations of the gospel and *eccelsia* [church]. (1985, pp. 42-3)

It is this understanding of their role as resisters, subversives, and, ultimately, transformers of a patriarchal church that sustains feminists who choose to remain in the institution.

FEMINIST ETHICISTS

One group that has maintained this embattled position of working from within are Roman Catholic feminist ethicists. Choosing to focus on sexual ethics, they highlight the sense of struggle and conflict between official church discourse and feminist discourse. Even in the larger society, sexuality is a "contested zone" (Weeks [1985] 1989, p. 4), but it is especially so in Roman Catholicism. Feminist ethicists are engaging in a struggle for meaning in a discourse that men have dominated for centuries.

The first task of Christian feminist theologians and ethicists was the critique of ethics and moral theology that revealed its androcentric and patriarchal bias (see especially Andolsen, Gudorf, and Pellauer 1985; Daly 1978; Fiorenza 1983; Harrison 1985; Heyward 1989; Ruether 1975, 1983). Using Foucault's (1979) insight that sexuality is also a locus of power, Christian feminist ethicists have linked the institutional church's sexual repressiveness and misogyny with the question of women's ordination.[2] The Roman Catholic Church has also made sexual issues, particularly abortion, a litmus test for orthodoxy and evidence of loyalty to Rome. Outstanding male theologians such as Charles Curran, Matthew Fox, Hans Küng, and Edward Schillebeeckx have been censured, had teaching licenses revoked, and been silenced (a Vatican discipline that prohibits the person in question from speaking or writing about a particular subject, usually because the theologian has disagreed with, or is challenging, the official Vatican position). These sanctions have usually been invoked over areas of disagreement concerning either sexual ethics or perceived support for increased participation by women in the ministry, especially ordination.

Understanding the nature of the church as a complex social organization can help contextualize the ethical discourse and why it is perceived as a threat to the hierarchy. The Roman Catholic Church fits Weber's (1978) model of a hierocracy:

A "hierocratic organization" is an organization which enforces its order through psychic coercion by distributing or denying religious benefits. . . . A compulsory hierocratic organization will be called "church" insofar as its administrative staff claims a monopoly of the legitimate use of hierocratic coercion. (p. 54)

In the Roman Catholic Church, religious benefits, for example, grace, mainly come through the sacraments. Except for baptism, only ordained priests can administer the sacraments. Technically, in matrimony, the couple administers the sacrament to each other, but a priest must be present to witness it and bless the couple, which is really the distribution of a special grace. Despite some relaxation of administration because of the shortage of priests, an ordained minister is preferred for administering the sacraments. Because all women and most men are excluded, a small minority of Roman Catholic men do indeed possess a monopoly over the dispensation of the sacraments and the graces that accompany them and, ultimately, the salvation that all Catholics desire.

Using their own judgment, priests can also deny the sacraments. For example, in California, a Catholic woman running for public office was denied communion because of her pro-choice stand on abortion. A few years ago, a young woman was denied confirmation because her mother worked in a women's health clinic where abortions were performed. Excommunication is the ultimate sanction that can be brought to bear against Roman Catholics who disobey. There is only one case where excommunication is automatic. According to the new code of canon law, "A person who procures a successful abortion incurs an automatic excommunication" (Canon 1398, Canon Law Society 1983).

Clearly, punishment is more likely to be meted out for "sins" related to sexual than other practices because no other act incurs automatic excommunication. Women, and men who support them, are also more likely to be targets of sanctions and reprimands. The signers of the *New York Times* (October 7, 1984) advertisement advocating discussion and a "diversity of opinions regarding abortion" in the Roman Catholic community, especially members of religious orders directly under Vatican authority, were special targets of a campaign of harassment. Those priests, sisters, and brothers of religious communities who did not formally retract, or whose religious communities did not do so for them, "were penalized by segments of the institutional church" (*Declaration of Solidarity*, 1986, p. 21).

Laypersons not associated with an official Roman Catholic institution were not so hard-pressed, because it was difficult for the hierarchy either to locate them or to sanction them. A number of laywomen I interviewed felt that their "lowly status" has a positive side in that it allows them to teach or function as ethical practitioners in a way not readily observable by the institutional church. They therefore believe they have a more subversive role. Women who have no official standing in the institutional church, in contrast to nuns and sisters, are outside many of the watchdog agencies of the Vatican, such as the Sacred Congregation for Religious Communities. Although their lives may be irrelevant to the church except for their so-called biological function of procreation, their usefulness as teachers, pastoral assistants, counselors, and the myriad voluntary positions they fill makes them necessary to the functioning of the church. From these positions, they can quietly subvert the dominant discourse with little fear of incurring sanctions.

Canon law is like the U.S. Constitution; it is the core of the laws and regulations that govern the life of the institutional church. However, because the ruling body of the church is the Curia, which is made up only of celibate clergymen, women and laymen have no input into creating, changing, or maintaining these laws. The monopoly is not simply one of an elite class based on economics or education. It is also clearly based on gender and sexual practices. Laws relating to sexual behavior are rooted largely in the "naturalness" of heterosexuality. Heterosexual intercourse is regulated by limiting its practice to the confines of the social institution of marriage and mainly for the purposes of procreation and regulation of concupiscence (strong sexual desire). Women, and men associated with women in sexual relationships, i.e., heterosexual marriage (which for the institutional church is the only acceptable sexual relationship), are barred from ordination and therefore from the ruling class of the institution.

The roots linking authority and power with sexist and heterosexist ideology go back to struggles with Gnosticism and Manicheism in the early history of Christianity, the influence of stoicism on the early church fathers, especially Augustine, and the consolidation of church power in the Holy Roman Empire (Katchadourian 1989). According to Heyward (1989)

> The Council of Elvira (Spain), at which for the first time an explicitly antisexual code was made law for western christians, was held in 309 C.E. . . . [T]he christian church still operates on the basis of this same antisexual

dualism, which is in effect, an antifemale dualism. From the second century on, the church had portrayed sex as something pertaining to women and as evil, "the devil's gateway." This attitude, for the first time, is canonized at the dawn of the era in which the church's social, political, and economic power is inaugurated. (pp. 42, 44)

Based on the image of Eve as seductive temptress, Christian theologians have associated women with sexuality and viewed both with deep suspicion and fear. Throughout the history of Christianity and Roman Catholicism, theologians, moralists, and ethicists have inveighed against women as corrupt, weak, lustful, evil "daughters of Eve" and to be avoided at all costs. Debates raged over whether women were fully human, possessed of rational souls, or capable of redemption. In Augustine's view, women were unfortunately needed for procreation, which seemed to be the only reason for their existence (Prusak 1977, p. 8). Thomas Aquinas concurred, and Roman Catholic theology and ethics has had to try to redeem women by concentrating on their biological function (Daly [1968] 1975, 1973, 1978; Osiek 1977; Tavard 1977; Quistlund 1977). Using Mary, Jesus' mother, as a counterpoint, the church fathers and scholastics resolved women into dualistic images: virgin-mother or whore—the latter a negative image, the former an improbable achievement.

Feminist ethicists seeking to transform the discourse are up against an ideological authoritarianism wherein sexual ethics are based in biological determinism and constructed on a belief in "natural law." In addition, as illustrated in anti-choice rhetoric, the discourse is deontological: it is more concerned with duties, the minimal threshold for conformity, absolute values, and universalization of standards, laws, and guidelines than with consequences of actions, extenuating circumstances, and social contexts. According to its major proponent, Immanual Kant, *deontological ethics* consists of the will to do one's duty for duty's sake, which . . . is the essence of human morality (Lake 1986, p. 480 and footnote 6, p. 480). A concrete example of deontological behavior is conformity to moral rules, for example, the Ten Commandments. According to Lake, "In a deontological ethical system, it is by definition right to obey the rules and wrong to disobey them" (p. 482). Rules and laws are stripped of their historical and social context and universalized. It is an abstract and absolute ethic which does not ask about consequences (Weber 1946, p. 120). There are no people, no contextualized lived experience, nothing that takes into account the "average deficiencies of people" (p. 121).

FEMINIST ETHICAL DISCOURSE

Since issues of sexuality have become the testing sites of sin and error, feminist ethical discourse presents a major challenge to traditional religious institutions, especially the Catholic Church. In an ironic way, women have been and continue to be the "objects" of both sides of this discourse. For traditional male theologians, it is women's sexuality that must be controlled, restrained, constrained, regulated, and harnessed for procreative reasons. Men's sexuality gets out of hand only because of women: Either they tempt men or they fail to satisfy them and thus are responsible when men lose control (Weeks [1986] 1989, p. 32, 38-9). Encyclicals, Vatican declarations, and official instructions concerning sexuality have been directed primarily toward women's sexual behavior and their responsibilities in marriage and child-rearing. Frequently addressed to bishops, theologians, pastors, and other official churchmen, they exhort them to keep "the faithful" faithful. In matters of sexuality, the burden of conformity is on women, who fail as wives and mothers when they do not conform to the church's teachings.

John Paul II's recent (1988) encyclical, *On the Dignity and Vocation of Women,* is a prime example of patriarchal institutional discourse that bases the official church's understanding of women and sexuality on a socially constructed belief in biologically determined gender roles, especially surrounding parenthood:

> Scientific analysis fully confirms that the very physical constitution of women is naturally disposed to motherhood—conception, pregnancy and giving birth—which is a consequence of the marriage union with the man. At the same time this corresponds to the psychophysical structure of women. . . . Motherhood as a *human* fact and phenomenon is fully explained on the basis of the truth about the person. Motherhood *is linked to the personal structure of the woman and to the personal dimension of the gift:* "I have brought a man into being with the help of the Lord" (Genesis 4:1). (pp. 64-5, his emphasis)

John Paul's underlying belief is that mothers are more important in raising children than fathers are and that there is no connection between men's procreative role in conception and their social role as fathers; only mothers are socially defined by their procreative role:

> Although both of them together are parents of their child, *the woman's motherhood constitutes a special "part" in this shared parenthood,* the most demanding part. Parenthood—even though it belongs to both—is realized much more fully in the woman, especially in the prenatal period.

It is the woman who "pays" directly for this shared generation, which literally absorbs the energies of her body and soul. It is therefore necessary that *the man* be fully aware that in their shared parenthood he owes *a special debt to the woman*. No program of "equal rights" between women and men is valid unless it takes this fact fully into account. (1988, p. 65, his emphasis)

Schüssler Fiorenza, in an effort to refute this essentialist notion of women, agrees with feminist social theorists such as Katz Rothman (1989) about the social construction of motherhood. She quotes Judith Plaskow:

nature and motherhood are human constructs and institutions, on the one hand, and . . . women's physicality is a "resource rather than a destiny," and the ground "of all we make ourselves to be" on the other hand. (Fiorenza 1984, pp. 297-8)

The ideology expressed by John Paul II is also the basis for church laws prohibiting contraception, abortion, new reproductive technologies, and homosexuality, as well as "camouflage (for) the issue of power" (Quistlund 1977, p. 265). It is an ideology that, despite reference to "scientific analysis" and "anthropological truths," still remains androcentric. This official discourse refers to "eternal truths" taught by the male *magisterium* to whom they have been revealed. It is not open to discussion nor can a diversity of opinion be tolerated. Challenge would upset the natural order of creation—two complementary "sexes" with God-given roles. Woman-centered theology and ethics would threaten the power structure because questioning the "natural order" also questions man's superior place in the social order, and thereby the ownership of truth and authority by celibate clergymen.

It is precisely this ideology that the discourse of feminist ethicists *does* challenge. In their alternative view of women and men, gender identities and roles and sexual identities and practices are constituted out of the centrality of women's lived experience. Analysis of women's experiences brings to light a crucial component of the social construction of feminist ethics: women's experiences are not homogeneous:

Women's lives are very different. Among differences that seem most significant are the following: Some women are mothers; others are not. Some women come from upper-class backgrounds; others from the middle class; still others from the working class or from poverty. Some are lesbian; some, hetero-sexual. Women are Black, White, Native American, Asian-American, or Latina. Women are Jewish, Catholic, Protestant, adherents to other traditional world religions, followers of the Goddess, or nonreligious. Women have very different work experiences as homemakers, clerical workers, service workers, factory operatives, managers, or professionals. If feminist ethics is to be based on the experience of *all* women, then such differences in experience must be acknowledged and incorporated into feminist theory. (Andolsen, Gudorf, and Pellauer 1985, p. xv)

This statement summarizes the quality of feminist ethics: constant re-creation in the crucible of the diversity of women's experiences. Unlike the institutional church, feminist ethics recognizes women as moral agents who are capable of making their own choices—even if they are not the best ones, even if they make mistakes. It also understands those choices as made in reference to a particular community: family, neighborhood, workplace.

Carol Robb, a feminist ethicist of "resistance," lays out a framework for a feminist ethics that starts with "reflection upon very concrete situations" (1985, p 213). She notes that defining the problem is a political act. Like Gilligan (1982) she believes that women's morality and ethics cannot be tested with prefabricated, androcentric dilemmas, since women reconstruct these dilemmas for themselves and create inventive ways to solve them. Robb goes on to enumerate the guidelines she believes are important for "doing ethics." Ethicists must gather data about the historical situation and context; they must analyze the roots of oppression; they must uncover loyalties—community ties as well as political ones; and finally a theory of values has to be clarified.

A FEMINIST THEORY OF VALUES

The issue of variance has become problematic for feminists. Various models for a value system have been proposed, creating heated debates not only within the feminist community but within the ethical community at large.[3] Robb (1985), for example, asks if "feminists have claim to any values independent of either a theory that biology is determinative, or a commitment to social justice shared with others" (p. 215), e.g., commitments to racial or economic justice.

Ethics generally recognizes three modes: teleological, deontological (discussed earlier), and situation-response. The *teleological mode* identifies "goals toward which people should aspire," acknowledging "*gradations* of right and wrong." Contingencies and consequences may mitigate an act that is formally proscribed by "interjecting subjective interpretations in uncertain circumstances" (Lake 1986, pp. 480-1, 486). Robb (1985) claims that "feminist ethics is done largely in the teleological mode, when the understanding of teleology allows for inclusion of the relational mode" (1985, p. 216). The *situation-response mode* "holds that there are no a priori right or wrong actions. Rather, moral value is determined only as a result of human choice in concrete situations. . . . [S]ituationism is highly individualistic, emphasizing the constitutive role of human choice in ethical determinations." (Lake 1986, p. 486).[4]

Referring to Daly, Robb agrees that feminist ethics is "metaethical." Setting it up as opposed to conventional ethics, Daly states that:

> radical feminist metaethics is of a deeper intuitive type than "ethics." The latter, generally written from one of several (but basically the same) patriarchal perspectives, works out of hidden agendas concealed in the texture of language, buried in mythic reversals which control "logic" most powerfully because unacknowledged. Thus for theologians and philosophers, Eastern and Western, and particularly for ethicists, woman-identified women do not exist. The metaethics of radical feminism seeks to uncover the background of such logic. . . . [I]t is, of course, a new discipline that "deals critically" with nature, structure, and the behavior of ethics and ethicists. (Daly 1978, p. 13)

With Daly, Robb reminds us that feminist ethics is critical and a discourse of resistance, but she maintains that its teleology, or relational mode, must be inclusive, which distinguishes it from simple utilitarianism (1985, p. 217) and situation ethics, both of which emphasize the individual, leaving out the community and social context of the moral agents. Robb emphasizes the importance of inclusive relationality, while "*granting the complexities* of this method" (1985, p. 217, my emphasis), "making the connections" among the family, the community, and the workplace. Inclusive relationality means taking into account the social and cultural differences among women and includes the economic dimension in moral decision-making, especially the way it often constrains women's choices (Harrison 1984, 1985). Gilligan has characterized women's morality as an "ethic of responsibility" (1982); Noddings (1984) calls it an "ethic of caring."

Feminist ethics criticizes the notion of "the moral agent as dispassionate and disengaged . . . for its failure to recognize the social foundation of self" (Robb 1985, p. 217). Building on Gilligan's critique of Kohlberg's moral dilemmas and moral decision-making, Robb and other feminists (Harding, 1986; Parlee, 1979) reject what they see as an androcentric notion of moral agent who stands outside a social context. The construction of an idealized human moral agent has been shown to actually mean "man" in its particular sense and not the so-called inclusive sense which male ethicists, theologians, and philosophers maintain is what they "really mean" (Andolsen, Gudorf, and Pellauer 1985, p. xxii).

The detached moral agent ignores, hides, and makes invisible the inequality between men and women (Robb 1985). Ignoring social context and relations within a family, community, or workplace limits women's moral agency:

> In this sense, the economic dependency of women in the family, the inequality of pay and promotion in the labor force tied to women's role as child-bearer and child-rearer, the possibility of sexual harassment or physical abuse from a stranger or an intimate, and further, in psychological terms, the tendency toward lack of ego differentiation in women's personality formation, are all factors impinging upon women's sense of self which can be autonomous confronting or defining ethical situations. (Robb 1985, p. 218)

Nevertheless, according to Robb, motivation will make us know the right thing and gets us to do it. This willingness to "do the right thing" begins "when women become engaged in collective efforts of self-definition. . . . [they create] an energy which overcomes or at least mitigates against alienation between the will and the right" (Robb 1985, p. 218).

A DISCOURSE OF RESISTANCE

Repeatedly, feminist ethicists return to community and relationships as the grounding for both resistance and revisioning. Roman Catholic feminists understand church to be a community of believers for whom "there are no more distinctions between Jew and Greek, slave and free, male and female" (Galatians 3:28). They see their role within the institutional church as prophetic: calling the church to a more faithful living out of the gospel message which they see as nonhierarchical and inclusive, not exclusive and hierarchically bureaucratic. Schüssler Fiorenza (1979) articulates a feminist model of church based on Jesus' exhortation to his followers "to call no man 'father' . . . nor should you be called 'leader' " (Matthew 23:9-11). Initiated by a lay Catholic organization, "Call to Action," and supported by the Women's Ordination Conference, a recent advertisement, "A Call for Reform in the Catholic Church," linked abuse of authority and power with sexism, clericalism, racism, ethnocentrism, heterosexism, and classism (*Call to Action* 1990). Lernoux (1989) sees various reform movements as aligned with liberation theology as does Welch (1985). Lernoux sees all, as the subtitle of her last book put it, as "the struggle for world Catholicism."

Roman Catholic feminists refuse to leave or be put out of the church. Instead, they are fighting from within, creating resistance and alternative voices. Feminist ethicist Mary Hunt (1990) envisions a coalition of the disenfranchised groups who are attempting to reform the institution. The most active are what she calls "the women-church groups" (p. 3). *Women-church* is a term used to describe a movement rather than a single organization. Comprised of several national organizations like the Women's Ordination Conference, Conference for Catholic Lesbians, Women's Alliance for Theology, Ethics, and Ritual (WATER—Mary Hunt is a codirector), and Catholics for a Free Choice, Women-church is also made up of local feminist base communities which function as alternatives to parish churches.

Women-church is a loose women-centered alliance, a way of saying that "we are religious while not institutionally affiliated" (Hunt 1990, p. 3). Although eclectic enough to include other religious traditions, many remain Christian in their orientation and spirituality. What they have rejected is not the basic Christian message but its present institutional embodiment. According to Hunt, of all the lay-led groups in the coalition, Women-church groups, though far from perfect, "show the greatest promise in terms of new models of leadership. . . . [S]uch women-led groups are accomplishing goals and developing organizations that embody a commitment to women's empowerment." (1990, p. 3-4)

For Mary Hunt and other Roman Catholic feminists, the revisioning of the church is the creation of a new moral community which is inclusive yet diverse. In their attempt to deconstruct the institution and reconstruct a new community, they feel that they are also part of the larger feminist project of human liberation. Schüssler Fiorenza (1983) sees Women-church, or what she calls the *ekklesia of women*, as

> overcoming all the structural-patriarchal dualisms between Jewish and Christian women, lay-women and nun-women, homemakers and career women, between active and contemplative, between Protestant and Roman Catholic women, between married and single women, between physical and spiritual mothers, between heterosexual and lesbian women, between church and the world, the sacral and the secular. However, we will overcome these dualisms only through and in solidarity with all women and in

a catholic sisterhood that transcends all patriarchal ecclesiastical divisions. . . . It must be lived in a prophetic commitment, compassionate solidarity, consistent resistance, affirmative celebration, and in grassroots organizations of *ekklesia of women*. (p. 349)

CONCLUSION

Creating a moral community that is viable for both women and men is an important aspect of feminist ethics. It is also a growing concern for social scientists trying to find moral consensus in an increasingly pluralistic world. Sociologist Alan Wolfe sees the moral order being created in the actual discourse and process of attempting to arrive at a consensus. The ethical and moral community and its norms is created by and within the struggle for shared meanings; it is socially constructed by the challenge of marginalized groups: "for society as a whole moral questions are raised whenever an outcast group seeks entry, no matter what the reasons for its liminal status—social class, gender, sexual preference, geography, or color" (Wolfe 1989, p. 216).

Liminality, uniting at the threshold, is certainly what women have experienced in the Roman Catholic Church as well as in the larger society. Their moral and ethical discourse has taken place at the edge of the dominant ideological discourse. These women perceive themselves as challenging the institutional discourse in order to transform not only the discourse but the institution itself. They are in the midst of creating the "new social reality" (Wallace 1988) so that a new ethical vision can emerge, an ethical vision that will transform the institution of which they are an integral part.

NOTES

1. See Buckley 1978; Christ and Plaskow 1979; Daly [1968], 1975, 1973, 1978, 1984; Fiorenza 1983, 1984; Plaskow and Christ 1989; Ruether 1974, 1975, 1983, 1986; Swidler and Swidler 1977 and the *Journal of Feminist Studies in Religion* are a few examples of the ever-increasing amount of scholarship in this field.

2. See Swidler and Swidler (1977) for an extensive and scholarly commentary by the leading theologians and scholars in the U.S. Roman Catholic Church.

3. See works by Cooey, Farmer, and Ross 1987; Gilligan, 1982; Habermas 1984, 1987; Harrison 1985; Hoagland 1988; Kittay and Meyers 1987; MacIntyre 1984; Noddings 1984; Ruddick 1984; Whitbeck 1984; Wolfe 1989.

4. See Lake (1986) for a discussion of the teleological mode versus the deontological with regard to the abortion debate.

REFERENCES

Abbott, W. M. 1966. *The Documents of Vatican II*. New York: America Press.

Andolsen, B. Hilkert, C. E. Gudorf, and M. D. Pellauer (eds.). 1985. *Women's Conscious-ness, Women's Conscience*. San Francisco: Harper & Row.

Buckley, M. I. 1978. "Jesus, Representative of Humanity: What Is Not Assumed Is Not Redeemed." Mimeo. Theology in the Americas and Women's Ordination Conference.

Call to Action. 1990. "Call for Reform in the Catholic Church." *New York Times* (February 28).

Canon Law Society of America. 1983. *Code of Canon Law*. (Latin-English edition). Washington, DC: author.

"Catholic Statement on Pluralism and Abortion." 1984. *The New York Times* (October 7).

Christ, C., and J. Plaskow. (eds.). 1979. *Womanspirit Rising: A Reader in Feminist Religion*. New York: Harper & Row.

Cooey, P. M., S. A. Farmer, and M. E. Ross. 1987. *Embodied Love: Sensuality and Relationship as Feminist Values*. San Francisco: Harper & Row.

Daly, M. [1968]. 1975. *The Church and the Second Sex*. Boston: Beacon.

———. 1973. *Beyond God the Father*. Boston: Beacon.

———. 1978. *Gyn/Ecology: The Metaethics of Radical Feminism*. Boston: Beacon.

———. 1984. *Pure Lust*. Boston: Beacon.

"Declaration of Solidarity." 1986. *Conscience* VII:21.

Fiorenza, E. Schüssler. 1979. "You Are Not to Be Called Father." *Cross Currents* Fall: 301-23.

———. 1983. *In Memory of Her: A Feminist Theological Reconstruction of Christian Origins*. New York: Crossroad.

———. 1984. "Claiming the Center: A Critical Feminist Theology of Liberation." Pp. 293-317 in *Women's Spirit Bonding*. edited by J. Kalven and M. I. Buckley. New York: Pilgrim Press.

Foucault, M. 1979. *The History of Sexuality,* vol. I. New York: Vintage Books.

Gilligan, C. 1982. *In a Different Voice*. Cambridge, MA: Harvard University Press.

Habermas, J. 1984, 1987. *Theory of Communicative Action* vols. 1 & 2. Boston: Beacon.

Harding, S. 1986. *The Science Question in Feminism*. Ithaca, NY: Cornell University Press.

Harrison, B. 1984. *Our Right to Choose*. Boston: Beacon.

———. 1985. *Making the Connections: Essays in Feminist Social Ethics*. Boston: Beacon.

Heyward, C. 1989. *Touching Our Strength: The Erotic as Power and the Love of God*. New York: Harper & Row.

Hoagland, S. L. 1988. *Lesbian Ethics: Toward New Values*. Palo Alto, CA: Institute for Lesbian Studies.

Hunt, M. 1990. "New Coalitions Replacing Church as Faith-Proprietor." *NCR* (February 2).

John Paul II. 1988. *On the Dignity and Vocation of Women*. Boston: St. Paul Books and Media.

Katchadourian, H. A. 1989. *Fundamentals of Human Sexuality,* 5th ed. Fort Worth: Holt, Rinehart, & Winston.

Kittay, E. Feder, and D. T. Meyers. 1987. *Women and Moral Theory*. Savage, MD: Rowman & Littlefield.

Lake, R. 1986. "The Metaethical Framework of Anti-Abortion Rhetoric." *Signs: Journal of Women in Culture and Society* 11:478-99.

Lernoux, P. 1989. *People of God: The Struggle for World Catholicism*. New York: Viking Press.

MacIntyre, A. 1984. *After Virtue*. Notre Dame, IN: Notre Dame University Press.

Noddings, N. 1984. *Caring: A Feminine Approach to Ethics and Moral Education.* Berkeley, CA: University of California Press.

Osiek, C. 1977. "The Church Fathers and the Ministry of Women." Pp. 78-80 in *Women Priests: A Catholic Commentary on the Vatican Declaration,* edited by L. Swidler and A. Swidler. New York: Paulist Press.

Parlee, M. 1979. "Psychology and Women." *Signs: Journal of Women in Culture and Society* 5:121-33.

Plaskow, J. 1974. "The Coming of Lilith." Pp. 341-3 in *Religion and Sexism: Images of Woman in the Jewish and Christian Traditions* edited by R. Radford Ruether. New York: Simon & Schuster.

Plaskow, J., and C. P. Christ (eds.). 1989. *Weaving the Visions: New Patterns in Feminist Spirituality.* San Francisco: Harper & Row.

Prusak, B. P. 1977. "Use the Other Door; Stand at the End of the Line." Pp. 81-4 in *Women Priests: A Catholic Commentary on the Vatican Declaration,* edited by L. Swidler and A. Swidler. New York: Paulist Press.

Quistlund, S. A. 1977. "In the Image of Christ." Pp. 260-70 in *Women Priests: A Catholic Commentary on the Vatican Declaration,* edited by L. Swidler and A. Swidler. New York: Paulist Press.

Robb, C. 1985. "A Framework for Feminist Ethics." Pp. 211-33 in *Women's Consciousness, Women's Conscience* edited by B. Hilkert Andolsen, C. E. Gudorf, and M. D. Pellauer. San Francisco: Harper & Row.

Rothman, B. Katz. 1989. *Recreating Motherhood.* New York: W. W. Norton.

Ruddick, S. 1984. "Maternal Thinking." Pp. 213-30 in *Mothering: Essays in Feminist Theory* edited by J. Trebilcot. Totowa, NJ: Rowman & Allanheld.

Ruether, R. Radford (ed.). 1974. *Religion and Sexism.* New York: Simon & Schuster.

———. 1975. *New Woman New Earth.* New York: Crossroad.

———. 1983. *Sexism and God-Talk: Toward a Feminist Theology.* Boston: Beacon.

———. 1986 *Woman-Church: Theology & Practice.* San Francisco: Harper & Row.

Sacred Congregation for the Doctrine of the Faith. 1976. *Declaration on the Question of the Admission of Women to the Ministerial Priesthood.* Vatican Translation, *L'osservatore Romano.* Boston: The Daughters of St. Paul.

Swidler, L., and A. Swidler (eds.). 1977. *Women Priests: A Catholic Commentary on the Vatican Declaration.* New York: Paulist Press.

Tavard, G. H. 1977. "The Scholastic Doctrine." Pp. 99-106 in *Women Priests: A Catholic Commentary on the Vatican Declaration,* edited by L. Swidler and A. Swidler. New York: Paulist Press.

Trible, P. 1978. *God and the Rhetoric of Sexuality.* Philadelphia: Fortress Press.

Wallace, R. A. 1988. "Catholic Women and the Creation of a New Social Reality." *Gender & Society* 2:24-38.

Weber, M. 1946. "Politics as a Vocation." Pp. 77-128 in *From Max Weber: Essays in Sociology,* edited by H. H. Gerth and C. Wright Mills. New York: Oxford University Press.

———. 1978. *Economy and Society,* Vol. 1. Edited and translated by G. Roth and C. Wittich. Berkeley, CA: University of California Press.

Weeks, J. [1985] 1989. *Sexuality and Its Discontents.* London: Routledge.

———. [1986] 1989. *Sexuality.* London: Routledge.

Welch, S. D. 1985. *Communities of Resistance and Solidarity.* Maryknoll, NY: Orbis.

Whitbeck, C. 1984. "The Maternal Instinct." Pp. 185-98 in *Mothering: Essays in Feminist Theory,* edited by J. Trebilcot. Totowa, NJ: Rowman & Allanheld.

Wolfe, A. 1989. *Whose Keeper?* Berkeley, CA: University of California Press.

18. DISMANTLING NOAH'S ARK

JUDITH LORBER

> Thou shalt come into the ark, thou, and thy sons, and thy wife, and thy sons' wives with thee. And of every living thing of all flesh, two of every sort shalt thou bring into the ark, to keep them alive with thee; they shall be male and female.[1]

> "Did she have a boy or a girl?" I asked. "Why do you want to know?" said my 13-year-old.[2]

It is a paradox of feminist politics that politically, women must act as a group in order to defuse gender as a discriminative status. In the current climate, and no doubt for a long time to come, if women are to gain anything like equal representation in existing institutions, they must push for their rights *as* women. Another necessary political stance has been the valorization of women's characteristics and special perspectives to counter their devaluation in male-dominated cultures. However, both strategies have limits that caution us to keep in mind that equal rights for women as a group and the celebration of women are effective only as short-term politics. The permeation of existing institutions with gender inequality makes the long-term goal of equal opportunity within them a sham (Eisenstein 1981). Glorifying womanliness consolidates female unity and power, but when pushed to extremes, it comes dangerously close to reviving the cult of true womanhood and the ideology of separate spheres (Jagger 1983; Stacey 1983a). The long-term goal of feminism must be no less than the eradication of gender as an organizing principle of post-industrial society.

Feminist theory and research have shown us that gender is a linchpin of social order, but they have not seriously envisaged a social order without gender. Examination of the social bases of gender demonstrates that gender is essentially a social construction, and that relations between women and men are essentially social relations. What is socially constructed can be reconstructed, and social relations can be rearranged. A modern social order without gender is possible, and I would like to sketch what it might look like. So that it is clear what I mean when I speak of *gender* as a set of oppositional relationships that sustain and are sustained by institutionalized patterns of behavior, I begin by analyzing the concept of gender as a social construct.

THE SOCIAL BASES OF GENDER

Gender supposedly rests on an obvious physiological and biological dichotomy, but it can be argued that the concept of physiological and biological dimorphism emerges from our firmly held belief in two and only two genders. In everyday life and in scientific research, Kessler and McKenna (1978) argue, we first attribute sexual dimorphism, and then look for evidence of it in order to have "good reasons" for the original sorting of people into the categories "female" and "male." From the perspective of dialectical materialism, Jagger (1983, pp. 109-12, 125-32) points out, physiological sex differences are socially produced by differences in diet, exercise, work, and selective breeding, and procreation and sexuality are as socially constructed as they are biologically based (see also Longino and Doell 1983; Naftolin and Butz 1981). Most human beings produce both androgens and estrogens, and these are chemically converted into each other, so that "the endocrine nature of the human species is hermaphroditic" (Briscoe 1978, p. 31). Physiological sex differences may be quantitative, but the boundaries between "woman" and "man" are socially located and differentiated by what Gayle Rubin calls a "sameness taboo . . . dividing the sexes into two mutually exclusive categories, a taboo which exacerbates biological differences between the sexes and thereby *creates* gender" (1975, p. 178, her emphasis).

But what about menstruation, lactation, and pregnancy? Do they not demarcate women from men? They do not. Some women are pregnant some of the time; some do not have a uterus or ovaries. Some women breastfeed some of the time; some men lactate (Jagger 1983, p. 165fn). Nonetheless, in the United States, *all* women, whether or not they need a temporary respite from their usual responsibilities, and medical attention because of complications of menstruation or pregnancy, are considered unfit for certain kinds of work, physically fragile, and in potential need of medical attention. The same "protectiveness" is not extended to men, who are as likely to develop prostate troubles as women are to develop menstrual cramps or complications of pregnancy. Only women's potential for pregnancy is used to determine where they can and cannot work, although recent studies have shown that toxic chemicals and other occupational hazards are equally likely to affect normal sperm production (Wright 1979). Gender makes women's procreative physiology the basis for a separate (and stigmatized) status, not the other way around (Goffman 1963; Schur 1984; Wittig 1981).

Extensive studies on early socialization have demonstrated beyond quarrel the social creation of gender identity and genderized behavior in children (Safilios-Rothschild 1979). Through the example, teaching, rewards, and admonishments of parents, siblings, teachers, and other significant adults, the child learns, first, that there are two genders, second, which gender she or he belongs to (and how to refer to them), and finally, how to be (and not be) a proper member of his or her gender. Gender markings and gender identity are created and maintained for children by parents' choice of names, clothing, adornments, toys and games, and by play, books, and the media. Although prepubescent children vary more significantly by size and by physical, intellectual, and emotional development, gender grouping produces socially dimorphic "boys" and "girls." Children internalize and use these forms of identity in developing their self-concepts and in organizing their own social worlds (Bem 1981). The gender division of parenting deepens the development of feminine and masculine personality structure (Chodorow 1978).

As children develop pubescent physical characteristics, their behavior is further dichotomized and organized around gender-appropriate sexual scripts, which vary from society to society and within societies by class, race, religion, and ethnic group (Gagnon and Simon 1973). Anatomical secondary sex characteristics are of less importance as gender markings than the extensive display signals Birdwhistell (1970, pp. 39-46) calls "tertiary sexual characteristics." These create an elaborate communication code of masculinity as contrasted with femininity, that, Birdwhistell says, is made necessary by the relative unimorphism of human beings.

Although physiological distinctions have seemed to be a natural starting place for the social construction of gender, anthropological studies suggest that the division of duties pertaining to food production and child rearing is more central to gender as a socially organizing principle than dichotomous procreative biology.

Gender probably emerged as part of a more efficient division of labor for food production and distribution, for child care, and for teaching survival skills. Gender assumed importance only with the invention of projectile human hunting and the use of fire for food production, Leibowitz (1983) argues. The necessity of teaching these more elaborate skills encouraged a division of labor that increased food supply (Leibowitz 1983; Marwell 1975). Because of the need for women to be both food producers and nurturers, women's work developed certain characteristics (Brown 1970). It is likely to be relatively repetitive and interruptible so that small children can be watched as women work; it is likely to be done where children can be carried along; and it must be relatively safe, so as not to jeopardize the precious societal resources of mothers and surviving children. Men (and adolescents of both genders) do the work that is dangerous, that requires distant travel, and that needs close attention (Freidl 1975).

The division of labor by the requirements of subsistence technology and the need for the group to reproduce itself fits the work women and men do in gathering and hunting societies, in societies based on hoe cultivation (women's work) and plow agriculture (men's work). It also affects the relative status of women and men. When the subsistence technology is compatible with child minding, women contribute significantly to the economic resources of the societal group, and their status tends to be equal to that of men, as in gathering and hunting and horticultural societies (Blumberg 1978; Leacock 1978). When the subsistence technology is not compatible with the care of small children, women tend to be less valued as producers and their consequent social status is low, as in patriarchal agricultural societies based on plow farming and herding. In these societies, women are valued as secondary producers, but the primary production is controlled by land-owning men.

Interwoven with the gendered division of labor are kinship systems that allocate responsibilities for the socialization and social placement of older children, for the care of the elderly, and for the bonding ties between families through out-marriage on the basis of gender. In non-industrial societies, the resources embedded in food distribution, mate choice, and rights to the services and marriage portions of children are ascribed by gender and proliferated into gender-based systems of property ownership and political dominance (Cucchiari 1981; Rubin 1975). The ideological justifications and supports for these arrangements are found in oral and written histories, myths, and religious symbols and rituals (Sanday 1981). In short, in non-industrial societies, gender organizes the social order through kinship and the division of labor.

The shift to industrial capitalism weakened kinship as an organizing principle of society but ironically built gender into the new economic institutions (Blaxall and Reagan 1976; Matthaei 1982; Pinchbeck [1930] 1969). Working-class women were hired, along with their children, as part of a family unit of wage workers headed by the husband (Acker 1988; Hartmann 1976). Married women who remained in the work force continued to be considered secondary workers, and this designation carried over to all women workers, who were systematically paid less than men, and to occupations dominated by women, which consistently have wage structures below that of comparable male-dominated occupations (Milkman 1980; Treiman and Roos 1983).

In today's capitalist economies, women who alternate between work in the home and work in the marketplace provide the necessary reserve army of labor that can be called on during economic expansion and dismissed during recessions. Married women who do not work in the marketplace are also vital to capitalism, for, without pay, they organize consumption and philanthropy, socialize the next generation of male workers and managers, and prepare their daughters to be housewives, mothers, part-time workers, and occupants of the perpetually gender-segregated work force (Glazer 1984; Ostrander 1984; Safilios-Rothschild 1976; Sokoloff 1980; Zaretsky 1976). Socialist economies, despite an ideological commitment to equality for women and high rates of life-long female labor-force participation, also have dual labor markets divided on gender lines, male-female income differentials, and a concentration of women workers at the lower ends of work hierarchies (Dalsimer and Nisonoff 1984; Lapidus 1976, 1978; Loi 1981; Nazzari 1983; Swafford 1978).

The persistence of gender segregation and stratification in the economies of all industrialized countries has ensured that most women would also be barred from significant political participation because of their limited power-base resources (Bengelsdorf and Hageman 1979; Eisenstein 1981; Hartsock 1983; Lapidus 1978; Nelson 1984; Stacey 1983b). As Virginia Woolf succinctly put it in *Three Guineas* (1938, p. 22), "What real influence can we bring to bear upon law or business, religion or politics—we to whom many doors are still locked, or at best ajar, we who have neither capital nor force behind us?" But even those women to whom doors have been opened—professional women, and women with financial and political capital—have, except for a few well-known, male-oriented prime ministers, been kept from the inner circles of power by covert denigration of their competence and legitimacy as leaders (Amundsen 1977; Epstein 1970; Fennell et al. 1978; Lipman-Blumen 1976; Lorber 1984; Martin and Osmond 1982; Reskin 1978; Wolf and Fligstein 1979).

Given the embeddedness of gender in all social structures that make up modern society, would not the erosion of gender boundaries result in social chaos and individual normlessness? In actuality, the solidity of gender as an organizing principle of society has already been eroded by feminist challenges of its petty absurdities and exploitative functions. But no feminist perspective has kept clearly in focus the revolutionary aim of restructuring social institutions without a division of human beings into the social groups called "men" and "women." Liberal feminists have concentrated on espousing equality between the two groups, but not eliminating them as significant social categories. Radical feminists have emphasized the positive aspects of women's traditional qualities, and so have polarized women and men. Marxist feminists have suggested industrializing domestic work, but have not suggested how to get men to share in it. Socialist feminism has come closest to envisaging "a society in which maleness and femaleness are socially irrelevant, in which men and women, as we know them, will no longer exist" (Jagger 1983, p. 330), but their program has tended to concentrate on promulgating democratically run, communally organized workplaces without specifying how to build in genderlessness. They also have tended to pay less attention to restructuring sexuality, friendship, and parenting so as to eliminate gender as an organizing principle of intimate relationships.

What follows is not an attempt to provide a complete prescription for revolution, nor a utopian description of a society without gender, which Gilman (1979), Piercy (1976), and LeGuin (1969) have done so well. Rather, I want to take forward tendencies and policies already familiar to us to show how, if carried through, they could go a long way toward a genderless restructuring of post-industrial society.

SOCIAL STRUCTURES WITHOUT GENDER

In many societies there have been people who moved from one gender to another temporarily or permanently—transvestites, *berdaches*, manly hearted women, *hijras*, actors, impersonators, and in our time, transsexuals. While they challenge the fixedness of gender boundaries and the sex-gender overlap, they do not challenge gender itself. Indeed, cross-dressing, impersonation, transsexuality, male wives and female husbands, and butch-femme homosexuality in many ways strengthen gender, since without a notion of gender differences there is no rationale for crossing over (Altman 1982; Billings and Urban 1982; Blackwood 1984; Raymond 1979).

No more challenging to gender are unisex styles, which may be as simple as a neutrally colored jump suit, as ubiquitous as the polo shirts, jeans, and sneakers seen across the Western world, or as the stylish androgyny recently described in the *New York Times* as follows:

Seen from the back, a young person, radiating a certain sense of style, may be wearing an oversize man's jacket, tight pegged pants, crushed down boots. Slung over the shoulder is a big, soft pouchy bag. The hair will be worn short with some fluff on top. If there is a bit of pierced earring visible, it is probably a woman. Then again, it could also be a young man. (Donovan 1983, p. 108)

To be more than a passing fashion, non-gendered dressing would have to start early, be consistent, and include dress-up as well as play clothes. The unisex style described above is not consistent—men wear earrings in one ear, women in both. Dress makes personal and social statements. As long as gender categories are socially significant, dress will reflect difference and signal gender identification. We cannot erode gender from the skin out.

Similar problems arise with attempts to teach children about biological dimorphism without a cultural overlay (Bem 1983; Money and Ehrhardt 1972; Morgan and Ayim 1984). The significance of genitalia, procreative capacities, and sexuality arise from the social construction of gender and its evaluations and power relations. There is no way to discuss sex and procreation neutrally, that is, free of social and cultural meanings. If we could, the evidence of diverse sexual persuasions throughout history would long ago have made it clear that sexuality is not neatly dichotomous. An increasingly sophisticated procreative technology of artificial insemination, *in vitro* fertilization, egg and sperm donations, and embryo transplants boggles the mind with combinations and permutations of biological parentage, but the innovations are contained in the conventional structures of heterosexual, two-parent families (Lorber 1987; Rothman 1984, 1989).

However, the separation of sexuality and procreation, and biological and social parenting, if carried through into new family and kinship structures, might help to dislodge gender from its central place in recreational sex, child rearing, and intimate emotional relationships. The components of dimorphic sex would then clearly belong to the biological needs of procreation. As Chodorow says:

We cannot know what children would make of their bodies in a nongender or nonsexually organized social world, what kind of sexual structuration or gender identities would develop. But it is not obvious that there would be major significance to biological sex differences, to gender difference, or to different sexualities. There might be a multiplicity of sexual organizations, identities, practices, perhaps even of genders themselves. Particular bodily attributes would not necessarily be so determining of who we are, what we do, how we are perceived, who are our sexual partners. (1979, p. 66fn)

Non-Gendered Families

In post-industrial society, kinship is no longer socially necessary to allocate reciprocal rights and responsibilities for economic cooperation, child rearing, and care of dependents. Without interlocked networks of blood relations and in-laws, women do not have to be exchanged so that men can gain brothers-in-law, and mothers do not have to be socially suppressed so that men can lay claim to children (Paige and Paige 1981; Rubin 1975). Therefore, we can envisage responsible intimate relations and economic cooperation among adults, and between adults and children, that do not depend on gender.

For adults, each must be treated as a single unit for purposes of income, taxation, and all legal rights and responsibilities. Whatever permanent linkages or household arrangements or personal economic exchanges are made in a person's lifetime will then be a matter of formal or informal contracts among consenting adults. Competent adults must take responsibility for children, the frail elderly, the sick, and the mentally incompetent either through state-financed and publicly administered organizations, or personally, through a kind of kinship system, or through a mixture. In an earlier attempt to think through non-gendered parenting arrangements, I suggested that every adult might take legal responsibility for at least one child, and for the parent-child line to become the kinship line for purposes of legal responsibility and emotional sustenance (Lorber 1975). A basic dependent support allowance from the state and well-financed public caretaking, nursing, medical, and educational services would help significantly in smoothing out the differentials in adult resources in these vertical families. If single parenting is felt to be too hermetically intense, several adults could commit themselves to legal responsibility for several dependents as an identifiable family, as Hooks (1984, pp. 133-46) recommends for single mothers.

Non-Gendered Sexuality

Incest taboos, which have always been designations of whom one can and cannot marry, could apply to sexual relationships within the kin groups to protect the dependent from sexual demands from those responsible for them. Other limits to sexual behavior are likely to emerge from community norms, ethics, values, and social priorities. Like other social relations, non-gendered sexual relationships are likely to involve interpersonal manipulation, if not power and exploitation. But if interpersonal and institutional power is not gendered, then the norms and laws governing intimate personal relationships, including the sexual, cannot be oppressive to women or to men, for these will not be significant social categories.

Non-Gendered Procreation

The common presumption has been that without reinforced heterosexuality and displays of masculinity and femininity, no children would be born. While it is highly unlikely that in a random, polymorphous sorting, no heterosexual coupling would take place, no conceptions would occur, no pregnancies would be sustained, and no children born, societies that value procreation are likely to encourage it. As in the present society, pro-natalist and anti-natalist policies in a non-gendered society can be expected to be political decisions. But these procreation decisions would not be made by the men in power for all women, nor would all women be categorized as potential child bearers and child rearers, nor would mothers alone be expected to bear all the burdens of creating and raising the next generation.

There would be social categories of parenting other than "mother" and "father"—child bearers and child rearers, professional caretakers and educators, sperm and egg donors and gestators, legal kin, and emotional supporters. These would not be based on dichotomous differentiations, attached to central social statuses, or designations of ownership. In short, the social roles of mother and father in a non-gendered society would not be indicative of the connection between "parent" and "child." What would be needed are terms of reference more specific to the variety of relationships between responsible adults and dependent children (Rothman 1989).

Non-Gendered Wage Work

Ideally, all work should be equally valued and all wage workers should receive equal compensation for their labor, which is a radical socialist solution to pay inequities. The liberal solution has been to concentrate on the historical discriminatory practices built into the present wage structure and, using the theory of comparable worth, attempt to create a wage structure based on the characteristics of the work itself and the worth of that work to the employer (Feldberg 1984; Treiman and Hartmann 1981). As applied to gender inequities in wages, comparable worth would place women workers on an equal footing with men workers, and thus eliminate much of the basis for women's economic dependence. Ideologically, it would remove the justification of low wages for women as secondary wage earners, eliminate the concept of a higher male family wage, and thus support the erosion of the family division of labor (Feldberg 1984). Indeed, without a restructuring of the compensation for women's work to bring it up to the level of compensation for comparable men's work, treating everyone as an individual legally would exacerbate women's subordinate status and disadvantage those who are legally dependent on them.

If the trend toward single-parent families is to be encouraged so as to break down the gendered pattern of kinship, then a corollary tactic must be to support the fight for a gender-neutral wage structure. In turn, a gender-neutral wage structure would help dismantle the gendered division of labor within the family because it would make women economically self-sufficient. Without superior wages, men would not be able to claim women's domestic services in exchange for primary economic support. Since the two cornerstones of the gendered division of labor—in the family and in the marketplace—are intertwined in industrial societies, they must be dismantled at the same time.

If all competent adults are to have roughly equal responsibility for those who are dependent, they must be compensated equally in one or more ways: a basic public support allowance, payment for their services, payment for wage work other than caretaking. To ensure that care of dependents does not continue to devolve on one group—women (with the cultural justification that they alone have the appropriate skills and temperament)—all adults should get a support allowance for themselves and their dependents. Professional caretaking must be compensated according to its real skill level (Phillips and Taylor 1980), and wages should be based on the content of the work, not the social status of the workers (Acker 1989; Bose and Spitze 1987).

Gender-Neutral Authority and Political Power

Whether authority and political power are seen to derive from membership in strategically placed inner circles of elites or from ownership and control of the means of production, women have been an excluded class, except through their connection with powerful men. Without at this point arguing for a non-hierarchical state or for more democratic ownership of the means of production, both of which are goals feminists might wish to achieve as feminists or as socialists, I would like to consider the strategies for, and possible effects of, gender-neutral access to positions of authority and political power.

Non-gendered access to capital resources and to positions of significant policy-making and authority are dependent on the erosion of gendered kinship and work. Such a structural and ideological shift would drastically alter social relations. Without gendered kinship, gendered inheritance of capital and businesses should disappear. Without a gendered wage structure, men's monopoly of leadership positions in work hierarchies should also diminish, since the underpinnings of male domination in a gender-segregated and gender-stratified occupational structure would be gone.

The converse view, that significant numbers of women in positions of leadership and in control of economic resources can make a difference in social values and in allocations of those resources, is dependent on the maximalization of gender differences and the assumption that women in power will act in the interests of other women (Lorber 1981). But the same purported gender differences and woman-oriented outlook are, in my view, what blocks women from access to those positions and resources. To the extent that women and men are seen as different, dominant men will not trust even women of their own class, religion, race, and training as colleagues, will not sponsor them for entry into elite inner circles of power, nor allow them control of important areas of the economy. The carefully chosen women who do make it to the top do so because they have demonstrated their loyalty to male values, and so, without jeoparding their positions, they cannot act in the interests of women (Laws 1975). Men will no longer see women as essentially different when gender loses its salience as a social category. For this to happen, significant areas of the social order must first be restructured on a non-gendered basis.

GENDER EQUALITY AND THE EROSION OF GENDER

For categories of people to be equal, a social order must be structured for equality of outcome. Equality is a political goal that can encompass equality of gender, but the history of liberal political philosophy demonstrates that women are usually excluded when ascribed statuses are no longer the basis for full-fledged citizenship (Okin 1979). If gender is removed as a qualification for equal treatment under the law, as the Equal Rights Amendment would have done, women and men would have legal equality, but not necessarily social equality. To achieve social equality, we would need scrupulous equality of women and men in care of dependents, allocation of work, wage structure, control of resources, and societal decisions (Chafetz 1984).

In my mind, gender equality is too limited a goal. Unless women and men are seen as socially interchangeable, gender equality does not challenge the concept of differences that leads to separate spheres in the family and marketplace division of labor, which in turn results in women's lesser access to control of valued resources and positions of power. Scrupulous equality of categories of people considered essentially different needs constant monitoring. I would question the very concept of gender itself, and ask why, if women and men are social equals in all ways, there need to be two encompassing social statuses at all.

NOTES

1. King James Version, Book of Genesis.
2. Conversation between author and child in 1982.

REFERENCES

Acker, J. 1988. "Class, Gender, and the Relations of Distribution." *Signs: Journal of Women and Culture in Society* 13:473-97.

———. 1989. *Doing Comparable Worth: Gender, Class, and Pay Equity.* Philadelphia: Temple University Press.

Altman, D. 1982. *The Homosexualization of America.* Boston: Beacon.

Amundsen, K. 1977. *A New Look at the Silenced Majority.* Englewood Cliffs, NJ: Prentice-Hall.

Bengelsdorf, C., and A. Hageman. 1979. "Emerging from Underdevelopment: Women and Work in Cuba." Pp. 271-95 in *Capitalist Patriarchy and the Case for Socialist Feminism,* edited by Z. R. Eisenstein. New York: Monthly Review Press.

Bem, S. Lipsitz. 1981. "Gender Schema Theory: A Cognitive Account of Sex Typing." *Psychological Review* 88:354-64.

———. 1983. "Gender Schema Theory and Its Implications for Child Development: Raising Gender-Aschematic Children in a Gender-Schematic Society." *Signs: Journal of Women and Culture in Society* 8:598-616.

Billings, D. B., and T. Urban. 1982. "The Socio-Medical Construction of Transsexualism: An Interpretation and Critique." *Social Problems* 29:266-82.

Birdwhistell, R. L. 1970. *Kinesics and Context.* Philadelphia: University of Pennsylvania Press.

Blackwood, E. 1984. "Sexuality and Gender in Certain Native American Tribes." *Signs: Journal of Women and Culture in Society* 10:27-42.

Blaxall, M., and B. B. Reagan (eds.). 1976. *Women and the Workplace: The Implications of Occupational Segregation.* Chicago: University of Chicago Press.

Blumberg, R. Lesser. 1978. *Stratification: Socioeconomic and Sexual Inequality.* Dubuque, IA: William C. Brown.

Bose, C., and G. Spitze (eds.). 1987. *Ingredients of Women's Employment Policy.* Albany: SUNY Press.

Briscoe, A. 1978. "Hormones and Gender." Pp. 31-50 in *Genes and Gender,* edited by E. Tobach and B. Rosoff. New York: Gordian Press.

Brown, J. A. 1970. "A Note on the Division of Labor by Sex." *American Anthropologist* 72:1073-8.

Chafetz, J. Saltzman. 1984. *Sex and Advantage.* Totowa, NJ: Rowman & Allanheld.

Chodorow, N. 1978. *The Reproduction of Mothering.* Berkeley: University of California Press.

——. 1979. "Feminism and Difference: Gender, Relation, and Difference in Psychoanalytic Perspective." *Socialist Review* 9:51-69.

Cucchiari, C. 1981. "The Gender Revolution and Transition from Bisexual Horde to Patrilocal Band: The Origins of Gender Hierarchy." Pp. 29-79 in *Sexual Meanings: The Cultural Construction of Gender and Sexuality,* edited by S. B. Ortner and H. Whitehead. Cambridge: Cambridge University Press.

Dalsimer, M., and L. Nisonoff. 1984. "The New Economic Readjustment Policies: Implications for Chinese Urban Working Women." *Review of Radical Political Economics* 16:17-43.

Donovan, C. A. 1983. "A Question of Self-Expression." *New York Times Magazine* 16(Dec. 18):108.

Eisenstein, Z. R. 1981. *The Radical Future of Liberal Feminism.* New York: Longman.

Epstein, C. Fuchs. 1970. "Encountering the Male Establishment: Sex Status Limitations on Women's Careers in the Professions." *American Journal of Sociology* 75:965-82.

Feldberg, R. 1984. "Comparable Worth: Toward Theory and Practice in the United States." *Signs: Journal of Women and Culture in Society* 10:311-28.

Fennell, M. L., P. R. Barchs, E. G. Cohen, A. M. McMahon, and P. Hildebrand. 1978. "An Alternative Perspective on Sex Differences in Organizational Settings: The Process of Legitimation." *Sex Roles* 4:589-604.

Friedl, E. 1975. *Women and Men.* New York: Holt, Rinehart, & Winston.

Gagnon, J. H., and J. W. Simon. 1973. *Sexual Conduct: The Social Sources of Human Sexuality.* Chicago: Aldine.

Gilman, C. Perkins. 1979. *Herland.* New York: Pantheon.

Glazer, N. Y. 1984. "Servants to Capital: Unpaid Domestic Labor and Paid Work." *Review of Radical Political Economics* 16:61-87.

Goffman, E. 1963. *Stigma.* Englewood Cliffs, NJ: Prentice-Hall.

Hartsock, N. C. M. 1983. *Money, Sex, and Power: Toward a Feminist Historical Materialism.* New York: Longman.

Hartmann, H. 1976. "Capitalism, Patriarchy, and Job Segregation by Sex." Pp. 137-69 in *Women and the Workplace: The Implications of Occupational Segregation,* edited by M. Blaxall and B. B. Reagan. Chicago: University of Chicago Press.

Hooks, B. 1984. *Feminist Theory: From Margin to Center.* Boston: South End Press.

Jagger, A. M. 1983. *Feminist Politics and Human Nature.* Totowa, NJ: Rowman & Allanheld.

Kessler, S. J., and W. McKenna. 1978. *Gender: An Ethnomethodological Approach.* Chicago: Chicago University Press.

Lapidus, G. Warshofsky. 1976. "Occupational Segregation and Public Policy: A Comparative Analysis of American and Soviet Patterns." Pp. 119-36 in *Women and the Workplace: The Implications of Occupational Segregation,* edited by M. Blaxall and B. B. Reagan. Chicago: University of Chicago Press.

——. 1978. *Women in Soviet Society.* Berkeley: University of California Press.

Laws, J. Long. 1975. "The Psychology of Tokenism: An Analysis." *Sex Roles* 1:51-67.

Leacock, E. 1978. "Women's Status in Egalitarian Society: Implications for Social Evolution." *Current Anthropology* 19:247-55.

LeGuin, U. 1969. *The Left Hand of Darkness.* New York: Ace Books.

Leibowitz, L. 1983. "Origins of the Sexual Division of Labor." Pp. 123-47 in *Women's Nature: Rationalizations of Inequality,* edited by M. Lowe and R. Hubbard. New York: Pergamon Press.

Lipman-Blumen, J. 1976. "Toward a Homosocial Theory of Sex Roles: An Explanation of the Sex Segregation of Social Institutions." Pp. 15-31 in *Women and the Workplace:*

The Implications of Occupational Segregation, edited by M. Blaxall and B. B. Reagan. Chicago: University of Chicago Press.

Loi, M. 1981. "Chinese Women and the 'Fourth Rope'." *Feminist Issues* 1:51-85.

Longino, H., and R. Doell. 1983. "Body, Bias, and Behavior: A Comparative Analysis of Reasoning in Two Areas of Biological Science." *Signs: Journal of Women and Culture in Society* 9:206-27.

Lorber, J. 1975. "Beyond Equality of the Sexes: The Question of the Children." *Family Coordinator* 24:465-72.

———. 1981. "Minimalist and Maximalist Feminist Ideologies and Strategies for Change." *Quarterly Journal of Ideology* 5:61-6.

———. 1984. *Women Physicians: Careers, Status, and Power.* New York and London: Tavistock.

———. 1987. "*In Vitro* Fertilization and Gender Politics." *Women & Health* 13:117-33.

Martin, P. Y., and M. Osmond. 1982. "Gender and Exploitation: Resources, Structure, and Rewards in Cross-Sex Social Exchange." *Sociological Focus* 15:403-15.

Marwell, G. 1975. "Why Ascription? Parts of a More or Less Formal Theory of the Functions and Dysfunctions of Sex Roles." *American Sociological Review* 40:445-55.

Matthaei, J., 1982. *An Economic History of Women in America: Women's Work, the Sexual Division of Labor and the Development of Capitalism.* New York: Schocken.

Milkman, R. 1980. "Organizing the Sexual Division of Labor: Historical Perspectives on 'Women's Work' and the American Labor Movement." *Socialist Review* 49:95-150.

Money, J., and A. A. Ehrhardt. 1972. *Man & Woman, Boy & Girl.* Baltimore: Johns Hopkins University Press.

Morgan, K. P., and M. Ayim. 1984. "Comment on Bem's 'Gender Schema Theory and Its Implications for Child Development: Raising Gender-Aschematic Children in a Gender-Schematic Society.' " *Signs: Journal of Women and Culture in Society* 10:209-31.

Naftolin, F., and E. Butz (eds.). 1981. "Sexual Dimorphism." *Science* 211:1263-324.

Nazzari, M. 1983. "The 'Woman Question' in Cuba: An Analysis of Material Constraints on Its Solution." *Signs: Journal of Women and Culture in Society* 10:246-63.

Nelson, B. J. 1984. "Women's Poverty and Women's Citizenship: Some Political Consequences of Economic Marginality." *Signs: Journal of Women and Culture in Society* 10:209-31.

Okin, S. M. 1979. *Women in Western Political Thought.* Princeton: Princeton University Press.

Ostrander, S. A. 1984. *Women of the Upper Class.* Philadelphia: Temple University Press.

Paige, K. E., and J. M. Paige. 1981. *The Politics of Reproductive Ritual.* Berkeley: University of California Press.

Phillips, A., and B. Taylor. 1980. "Sex and Skill: Notes Towards A Feminist Economics." *Feminist Review* 6:79-88.

Piercy, M. 1976. *Woman on the Edge of Time.* New York: Fawcett Crest.

Pinchbeck, I. [1930] 1969. *Women Workers and the Industrial Revolution, 1750-1850.* London: Virago Press.

Raymond, J. G. 1979. *The Transsexual Empire: The Making of the She-Male.* Boston: Beacon.

Reskin, B. F. 1978. "Sex Differentiation and the Social Organization of Science." *Sociological Inquiry* 48:3-37.

Rothman, B. Katz. 1984. "The Meanings of Choice in Reproductive Technology." Pp. 22-33 in *Test-Tube Women,* edited by R. Arditti, R. D. Klein, and S. Minden. London: Pandora Press.

————. 1989. *Recreating Motherhood: Ideology and Technology in a Patriarchal Society.* New York: Norton.

Rubin, G. 1975. "The Traffic in Women: Notes on the 'Political Economy' of Sex." Pp. 157-210 in *Toward an Anthropology of Women,* edited by R. Reiter. New York: Monthly Review Press.

Safilios-Rothschild, C. 1976. "Dual Linkage Between the Occupational and Family Systems: A Macrosociological Analysis." Pp. 51-66 in *Women and the Workplace: The Implications of Occupational Segregation,* edited by M. Blaxall and B. B. Reagan. Chicago: University of Chicago Press.

————. 1979. *Sex Role Socialization and Sex Discrimination: A Synthesis and Critique of the Literature.* Washington, DC: National Institute of Education.

Sanday, P. Reeves. 1981. *Female Power and Male Dominance: On the Origins of Sexual Inequality.* Cambridge: Cambridge University Press.

Schur, E. 1984. *Labeling Women Deviant: Gender, Stigma, and Social Control.* New York: Random House.

Sokoloff, N. J. 1980. *Between Money and Love.* New York: Praeger.

Stacey, J. 1983a. "The New Conservative Feminism." *Feminist Studies* 9:559-83.

————. 1983b. *Patriarchy and Socialist Revolution in China.* Berkeley: California University Press.

Swafford, M. 1978. "Sex Differences in Soviet Earnings." *American Journal of Sociology* 43:657-73.

Treiman, D. J., and H. I. Harmann (eds.). 1981. *Women, Work and Wages.* Washington, DC: National Academy Press.

———— and P. Roos. 1983. "Sex and Earnings in Industrial Society: A Nine-Nation Comparison." *American Journal of Sociology* 89:616-50.

Wittig, M. 1981. "One Is Not Born a Woman." *Feminist Issues* 1:47-54.

Wolf, W. C., and N. D. Fligstein. 1979. "Sex and Authority in the Workplace." *American Sociological Review* 44:235-52.

Woolf, V. 1938. *Three Guineas.* New York: Harcourt, Brace, & World.

Wright, M. J. 1979. "Reproductive Hazards and 'Protective' Discrimination." *Feminist Studies* 5:302-9.

Zaretsky, E. 1976. *Capitalism, the Family, and Personal Life.* New York: Harper & Row.

ABOUT THE AUTHORS

Joan Acker first published on gender and organizations in 1974 ("Differential Recruitment and Control: The Sex Structuring of Organizations," with Donald Van Houten, *Administrative Science Quarterly* 19:152-63). The writing of her book, *Doing Comparable Worth* (Temple University Press, 1989), made her realize again the importance of thinking about the social construction of gender in organizations.

Judith Buber Agassi was born in Germany in 1924, and is now an Israeli citizen. She received an M.A. from Hebrew University and a Ph.D. from the London School of Economics. She has taught sociology and political science at Hong Kong University; the University of Illinois; Simmons College; Jerusalem, Tel-Aviv, and Haifa Universities; Siegen and Frankfurt Universities. She is currently Adjunct Professor in Social Science at York University in Toronto. She is the author of *Women on the Job* (1979), *Comparing the Work Attitudes of Women and Men* (1982), and editor with Stephen Heycock of *The Redesign of Working Time: Promise or Threat?* (1989).

Elizabeth M. Almquist is Regents Professor of Sociology at the University of North Texas. Her research interests include occupational gender inequality in societies and labor markets, women's representation in state and national legislatures, and women's status among minority groups cross-nationally. Her research is designed to test macrostructural theories and to discover the connections among race, class, and gender stratification.

Johanna Brenner is Coordinator of Women's Studies and Associate Professor of Women's Studies and Sociology at Portland State University, Oregon. Her analysis of political discourses and organizing strategies draws on her experience as a shop steward and union activist in a traditionally male blue-collar job and as a reproductive rights organizer.

Lynn Weber Cannon is Professor of Sociology and Director of the Center for Research on Women at Memphis State University. Her book, *The American Perception of Class,* co-authored with Reeve Vannerman, was published by Temple University Press (1987). She is currently co-directing a project with Elizabeth Higginbotham on race, social mobility, and women's mental health that is funded by the National Institute for Mental Health.

Lynn S. Chancer is Visiting Assistant Professor in the Sociology Department at Barnard College, New York City. She is the author of a forthcoming book titled *Sadomasochism in Everyday Life: Psychosocial Dynamics of Power and Powerlessness* (Rutgers, 1991), and has written articles on feminist theory, abortion, and the pornography debates within the feminist movement.

Esther Ngan-Ling Chow is Professor of Sociology at the American University, Washington, D.C. She is a feminist scholar and community activist who has conducted studies on gender and racial identities, work, and family life of Chinese and Asian American women. She has also written on issues concerning women of color.

Karen Dugger is Assistant Professor of Sociology at Bucknell University, where she also serves as Co-Director of the Race/Gender Resource Center. She is currently doing research on the racial basis of antifeminism, and is author of a forthcoming article in *Social Science Quarterly* titled "Race Differences in the Determinants of Support for Abortion." In addition to her work on racial ethnic women in the United States, she is examining the impact of various forms of work—professional, informal sector, employment in factories and in the tourist industry—on the class consciousness, gender identity, gender-role attitudes, and autonomy of women on the Caribbean island of Barbados.

Susan A. Farrell is a graduate student in Sociology and Women's Studies at the City University of New York Graduate School and has her master's in theology from St. John's University, New York City. She was managing editor of *Gender & Society* from 1987-1990. Her dissertation is on women and sexual ethics in the Roman Catholic Church.

Alma M. Garcia is Associate Professor of Sociology and Ethnic Studies at Santa Clara University, California, where she is also Director of the Women's Studies Program. Her teaching fields include the comparative study of women of color in the United States. Her publications include articles on Mexican peasant movements and feminist curricular reforms within Chicano Studies. She is national president of Mujeres Activas en Letras y Cambio Social, a Chicana/Latina feminist organization of women in higher education. Her current research focuses on the development of entrepreneurship among Mexican American women.

Karen V. Hansen teaches feminist theory at Brandeis University. She is the co-editor, with Ilene Philpson, of *Women, Class, and the Feminist Imagination: A Socialist-Feminist Reader* (Temple, 1990). Her chapter is part of a larger work-in-progress on the community life of working people in antebellum New England.

Elizabeth Higginbotham is Associate Professor of Sociology and is on the research faculty of the Center for Research on Women at Memphis State University, Tennessee. She has authored several publications on African American women and is currently completing a book titled *Too Much to Ask: The Costs of Black Female Success*. She is also involved in curriculum integration efforts and a research project on mobility among Black and White women.

Deniz Kandiyoti is Senior Lecturer in the Social Sciences Division of Richmond College, London. She is the author of *Women in Rural Production Systems: Problems and Policies* and editor of *Women, Islam and the State* (forthcoming), as well as numerous articles on women in the Middle East, feminist theory, and gender and development issues.

Marianne L. A. Leung received her master's degree in sociology from Memphis State University, Tennessee. She was a research assistant with the Center for Research on Women from 1985 to 1988. She is currently pursuing a degree in twentieth-century American social history at Memphis State University.

Judith Lorber is Professor of Sociology at Brooklyn College and the City University of New York Graduate School, where she is also Coordinator of the Women's Studies Certificate Program. She is the author of *Women Physicians: Careers, Status and Power,* published in 1984 by Tavistock/Methuen, New York and London, and of numerous journal articles on gender, women physicians, and women and health care. Her current research is on the organization of *in vitro* fertilization clinics and couples' experiences with the new procreative technology. She is the founding editor of *Gender & Society.* Her book, *Paradoxes of Gender: Feminist Social Theories*, will be published by Yale University Press.

Michael A. Messner is Assistant Professor of Sociology in the Program for the Study of Women and Men in Society at the University of Southern California. He has co-edited two books: *Men's Lives* (with Michael S. Kimmel, Macmillan, 1989), and *Sport, Men and the Gender Order: Critical Feminist Perspectives* (with D. F. Sabo, Human Kinetics Press, 1990). His forthcoming book is tentatively titled *Power at Play: Organized Sports and the Construction of Masculinity* (Beacon, 1990).

Barbara F. Reskin, Professor of Sociology at the University of Illinois, has been studying sex segregation since 1981. The stability of sex segregation shown in her two National Research Council books led to her recent research on the factors behind women's entry into customarily male occupations and to her interest in sex differentiation as the mechanism that maintains women's subordination.

Catherine Kohler Riessman, sociologist and social worker, teaches in the School for Social Work and the Department of Sociology at Smith College, Northampton. Her recent book *Divorce Talk: Women and Men Make Sense of Personal Relationships,* (Rutgers University Press) analyzes how divorced people construct gendered visions of what marriage should provide, and yet how they mourn gender divisions and blame their divorces on them.

Candace West is Professor of Sociology at the University of California, Santa Cruz. Her past work includes "When the Doctor Is a 'Lady': Power, Status and Gender in Physician-Patient Encounters," "Gender, Language and Discourse" (with Don H. Zimmerman), and "Conversational Shiftwork: A Study Between Women and Men" (with Angela Garcia). Her most recent article is "Not Just 'Doctors' Orders": Directive-Response Sequences in Patients' Visits to Women and Men Physicians," published in *Discourse & Society,* 1990. She is the author of *Routine Complications* (Indiana University Press, 1984).

Don H. Zimmerman is Professor in the Department of Sociology at the University of California, Santa Barbara. In addition to his work with Candace West on gender, he is currently investigating the structure and organization of telephone calls to service organizations and the integration of vocal and nonvocal activities in the work of emergency service dispatch.

Maxine Baca Zinn is Professor of Sociology and Senior Research Associate in the Julian Samora Research Institute at Michigan State University. Her areas of study include family, race, and gender. As a minority sociologist, her special mission is to abstract the findings from research on race and gender to make the discipline of sociology more inclusive. She is the co-author (with D. Stanley Eitzen) of *Diversity in Families* (Harper and Row, 1990) and *The Reshaping of America* (Prentice Hall, 1990) with Bonnie Thornton Dill. She is co-editing a collection of social science works about women of color (Temple University Press, forthcoming).

NOTES

NOTES

NOTES

NOTES